OFFICE*US* Agenda

Edited by
Eva Franch i Gilabert
Amanda Reeser Lawrence
Ana Miljački
Ashley Schafer

la Biennale di Venezia

14. Mostra
Internazionale
di Architettura

Partecipazioni nazionali

Storefront for Art and Architecture

PRAXIS

Lars Müller Publishers

OFFICE *US* Agenda

Agenda is the official catalog for Office*US*
US Pavilion, 14th International Architecture Exhibition –
la Biennale di Venezia

Editors

Eva Franch i Gilabert, Amanda Reeser Lawrence,
Ana Miljački, Ashley Schafer

Lead Copy Editor

Abby Bussel

Copy Editors

Michelle Callinan, Sarah Hirschman, Margaret Ho,
Alexandra Lee Small, Stephanie Marie Tuerk,
Mariel Villeré

Editorial Assistants

Allie Turner

Scripting for Maps and Charts

Gabriel Kozlowski

Illustration Assistants

Kyle Coburn, Emily Chen, Wassef Dabboussi,
Ryan Gagnedin, Juney Lee, Yiyang Min, David Orndorff,
Hao Wu, Yao Xia, Yu Xin

Special Thanks

Michael Abrahamson, Steven Barlow,
Esther Butterworth, John Gollings, Yana Grinblat,
Patrick Herron, Anita Hoffman, Barbara Jones,
Arianne Kouri, Mati Maldre, Jack Masey, Mark
Meerovich, Malgorzata Myc, Peter Y. Navaretti,
Beverly Payeff-Masey, Nikita Payusov,
Jeffrey Turnbull, Beverly Willis

Publisher

Lars Müller Publishers
Zürich, Switzerland
www.lars-mueller-publishers.com

Printing

Kösel, Altusried-Krugzell, Germany

Design

Pentagram: Natasha Jen,
Jeffrey Waldman; Justin Chen, Oeun Kwon

Typefaces

Arial and Times New Roman are the typefaces of the
Office*US* project. These two typefaces are among the
most mundane and readily available on the market,
and as such are frequently used for efficiency by US
offices. With a few necessary exceptions, all Office*US*
deliverables, including this publication, are designed
with these two generic typefaces.

ISBN 978-3-03778-437-2

This publication has been made possible with
funding from The Graham Foundation

OFFICE*US* Agenda

OfficeUS:
100 Years of Export,
25 Issues

1914 McKim, Mead and White *American Academy* Rome, Italy **Ex-Im** The origin, the place of departure, is often a place of return. In 1893, the Beaux-Arts-trained architect Charles Follen McKim, along with Daniel Burnham and other eminent artists and architects, undertook the establishment of a prize for post-graduate study in Rome — the ur-place of the classical — conscious that his journey was one of return. In 1913, four years after his death, and twenty years after the ideological founding of the American Academy in Rome, McKim, Mead & White completed the Academy's American Renaissance-style building that still today houses American recipients of the Rome Prize, and brings Americans back to a certain kind of home. There are no confusions or hesitations in the semiotic journey back to classical Rome, yet the last hundred years have seen far more complex forms, typologies, and forces shaping the architectures of US architects building abroad. An export was an import, was an export, was an import? Henry Killam Murphy *St. Paul's College* Tokyo, Japan ○ Walter Burley Griffin and Marion Mahony *Master Plan for Canberra Federal Capital* Canberra, Australia ○ Henry Killam Murphy *Yale-in-China Campus* Changsha, China ○ Perkins, Fellows and Hamilton *Nanjing University* Nanjing, China ○ Shepley, Rutan and Coolidge *American College for Girls* Constantinople, Turkey ○ Walter Burley Griffin and Marion Mahony *Leeton Town Centre Plan* Leeton, Australia **1915** Frank Lloyd Wright *Imperial Hotel* Tokyo, Japan ○ Walter Burley Griffin and Marion Mahony *Newman College, University of Melbourne* Melbourne, Australia **1918** Henry Killam Murphy *Ginling College for Women* Nanjing, China ○ Henry Killam Murphy *Tsinghua University Campus* Shanghai, China ○ Walter Burley Griffin and Marion Mahony *Master Plan for Castlecrag Residential Community* Sydney, Australia **1919** George A. Fuller Company *Nippon Oil Company Building* Tokyo, Japan ○ Henry Killam Murphy *Yenching University* Beijing, China **1920** Thomas W. Lamb *Pantages Theatre* Toronto, Canada ○ William E. Parsons *Philippine Normal University* Manila, Philippines **1921** Frank Lloyd Wright *Jiyu Gakuen School* Tokyo, Japan ○ George A. Fuller Company *Marunaochi Building* Tokyo, Japan ○ Coolidge and Shattuck *Rockefeller Foundation Peking Union Medical College* Beijing, China **Trojan Horses** Since its founding in 1913, the Rockefeller Foundation's focus on "promoting the well-being of humanity" has amounted to an impact of $14 billion current dollars worldwide. The first building it supported on the basis of missionary purposes and scientific philanthropy, the Peking University Medical Center (PUMC), established US medical and health standards around the globe. Coolidge & Shattuck modeled the building after the Johns Hopkins University School of Medicine, disguised in Chinese traditional materials and styles. On September 12, 1921, Rockefeller Jr. wrote to Rockefeller Sr. "we are delighted beyond expression at the Peking Union Medical College buildings, which are perfectly adapted to the purposes and a great contribution not only to science but to architecture." What architecture? **1922** The Austin Company *Austin Standard Factory* UK, Canada, Venezuela, Cuba, Mexico, Argentina, Peru **1923** Walter Burley Griffin and Marion Mahony *Leonard House Office Building* Melbourne, Australia ○ William Welles Bosworth *Palace at Versailles Restoration* Versailles, France **1924** American Architectural and Engineering Company *Tokyo Women's Christian College* Tokyo, Japan ○ American Architectural and Engineering Company *Hoshi University Main Building* Tokyo, Japan ○ Schultze and Weaver *Hotel Sevilla-Biltmore* Havana, Cuba ○ Walter Burley Griffin and Marion Mahony *Capital Theatre* Melbourne, Australia **1925** Helmle and Corbett *Bush House* London, UK ○ Walker and Gillette *National City Bank of New York Branch Building* Havana, Cuba **1926** Ayres, York and Sawyer *Old Royal Bank Building* Montréal, Canada ○ American Architectural and Engineering Company *US Embassy* Tokyo, Japan ○ Walter Burley Griffin and Marion Mahony *Incinerators for Reverberatory Incinerator and Engineering Company* Melbourne, Sydney, Geelong, Adelaide, Newcastle and Canberra, Australia **1927** Frank Lloyd Wright *Beach Cottages* Dumyat, Egypt ○ Graham, Anderson, Probst & White *Provincial Capital Building* Negros Occidental, Philippines ○ Shreve, Lamb and Harmon *YMCA Jerusalem* Jerusalem, Israel ○ Warren and Wetmore *Lord Nelson Hotel* Halifax, Canada **1928** Cass Gilbert *US Embassy* Ottawa, Canada ○ Antonin Raymond, Architect *Projects for Rising Sun Petroleum Company*, Japan ○ The Austin Company *Automobile Plant and Industrial City* Nijni Novgorod, Russia **1929** Albert Kahn Associates *Stalingrad Tractor and Tank Factory* Stalingrad, USSR ○ Delano and Aldrich *US Embassy* Paris, France ○ Schultze and Weaver *Casino Nacional* Havana, Cuba **1930** Albert Kahn Associates *Chelyabinsk Tractor and Tank Factory* Chelyabinsk, USSR **Best Practices** Launched in Detroit in 1895, the office of Albert Kahn Associates was influenced by Taylorist models of production. Kahn rose to prominence as the architect of industrial buildings for Ford Motor Company and other Detroit automobile manufacturers. His factory design expertise led to Kahn's appointment by Stalin as the architect of the Soviet Union's industrial landscape, laying the foundation for war-time tank production. Working abroad prepared the office for "coordinating experienced experts" in the expansion of factories producing war material in the United States. Albert Kahn Associates still rates today from offices in Detroit, Michigan; Birmingham, Alabama; and Sao Paolo, Brazil. Kahn's office has been seen as a adigm of efficient practice, a precursor of SOM, HOK, and Gensler. If, as HOK's founding partner George Kassabaum suggested 961, modern times required systematic procedures, then what might be the pertinent procedures and tools for contemporary worked, crowd-sourced, technologically augmented, and socially progressive practices? What makes a contemporary "best ctice"? Delano and Aldrich *US Pavilion* Venice, Italy ○ McKim, Mead and White *Hotel Nacional* Havana, Cuba **1931** n Russell Pope *Elgin Gallery, British Museum* London, UK **1932** Antonin Raymond, Architect *Tokyo Golf Club* Asaka, an ○ Thomas W. Lamb *Metro Cinema* Johannesburg, South Africa **1935** Antonin Raymond, Architect *Golconde* rritory Pondicherry, India ○ Walter Burley Griffin and Marion Mahony *Lucknow University Library* Lucknow, India 38 Thomas W. Lamb *Metro Cinema* Mumbai, India **1939** Harrison and Abramovitz *Avila Hotel* Caracas, Venezuela 40 Wurdeman and Becket *Jai Alai Auditorium* Manila, Philippines **1941** Voorhees, Walker, Foley and Smith *Army Air ps Military Bases* Trinidad **1942** Skidmore, Owings and Merrill *Kadena Airbase* Kadena, Okinawa, Japan **1943** hard J. Neutra *Prototype for Open-Air Schools* Puerto Rico ○ Richard J. Neutra *Prototype for Rural Health Centers* erto Rico ○ Richard J. Neutra *Prototype for District Hospitals* Puerto Rico **1945** Paul Williams *Hotel Nutibara* Medellin, ombia ○ Paul Williams *Hotel Granada* Bogotá, Colombia **1946** Edward Durell Stone and Associates *El Panama Hotel* ama City, Panama ○ **1947** Eggers and Higgins *US Embassy* Ankara, Turkey **1948** Harrison and Abramovitz *US bassy* Rio de Janeiro, Brazil ○ Marcel Breuer and Associates *Club Ariston* Mar de Plata, Argentina ○ Skidmore, Owings Merrill *Creole Petroleum Town Plan* Amuay Bay, Venezuela **1949** Lathrop Douglass *Creole Petroleum Corporation* ices Caracas, Venezuela **Crude Ideals** The work of the largest US practices after the 1930s largely followed the path of first in Venezuela, Colombia, and Indonesia, and then in the Middle Eastern Gulf States after World War II. Governmental dquarters and US embassies, vast military cities, new towns for oil workers, airports, banking towers, commercial centers, luxury hotels signaled the intent of newly wealthy oil states to place themselves on the world stage. While US architects sed the specter of petroleum-fueled development and the speculative finance economy to which it gave rise, the oil-rich nts received some of modernism's most complete and comprehensive ideal forms. The meeting of tabula rasa conditions and money allowed the projection of total worlds and ideal cities, perhaps nowhere more clearly than in Brown Daltas's vast King lid Military City (1974–87). The 1990s boom, brought rapid development to the U.A.E., Qatar, Azerbaijan, and other new eritors of the petroleum ideal. As energy policies move towards nationally self-sustainable models, what will be the scope source of the next architectures of energy? Raymond & Rado *Reader's Digest Offices* Japan **1950** Donald Hatch and sociates *Sucre Building* Caracas, Venezuela ○ Edward Durell Stone and Associates, A. L. Aydelott and Associates spital of Social Security for Employees* Lima, Peru ○ Harrison and Abramovitz *US Embassy* Havana, Cuba ○ Holabird, ot and Burgee *Hotel Tamanaco* Caracas, Venezuela **1951** Skidmore, Owings and Merrill *Standard Oil Vacuum npany Facilities and Housing* Sumatra, Indonesia ○ Town Planning Associates *Ciudad Piar and Puerto Ordaz New ns* Bolivar State, Venezuela **1952** Eero Saarinen and Associates *US Embassy* London, UK ○ Holabird, Root and gee *Hotel del Lago* Maracaibo, Venezuela ○ Holabird, Root and Burgee *Hotel Tequendema* Bogotá, Colombia ○ Marcel uer and Associates *UNESCO Headquarters* Paris, France ○ Skidmore, Owings and Merrill *America House* Frankfurt, rmany ○ Skidmore, Owings and Merrill *US Consulate General* Frankfurt, Germany ○ Skidmore, Owings and Merrill ton Hotel* Istanbul, Turkey **Democratizing Action** The US Consulate in Istanbul, housed in the Palazzo Corpi, was the first government-owned diplomatic building in Europe (from 1882–2003) and the first and only one acquired in a poker game. t by Italian architect Giacomo Leoni, the US presence in Istanbul was housed within an architecture devoid of US principles lifestyles. When SOM designed the Hotel Hilton Istanbul in 1952, it reflected Conrad Hilton's business model, whereby politics would be deployed through notions of design and comfort. Under the guise of democracy and freedom, hotels, as tialized capitalist warfare tools, established a place for business meetings to occur, new products to be consumed, and stern lifestyles to be subtly introduced within the collective imaginary and desire structures of cities around the world. els, but also museums, cinemas, and other spaces of collective forms of leisure have been operating as tools in the spatial semination of capitalism and democracy ever since. What democracy? **1953** Ralph Rapson *US Embassy Staff Housing* is, France ○ Raymond & Rado *US Embassy Residence* Tokyo, Japan ○ Raymond & Rado *US Embassy* Jakarta, onesia **1954** Edward Durell Stone and Associates *Phoenicia Intercontinental Hotel* Beirut, Lebanon **Intercontinental** nfort** Juan Trippe, founder of PanAm (Pan American World Airways) in 1927, launched the InterContinental Hotel chain in 6, immediately following WWII, building hotels at each of the airline's new destinations. The majority of the buildings were ceived as infrastructural frameworks taking the form of standard concrete, modular cell structures—the building blocks modernization. Over 135 InterContinental interiors were designed by in-house architect Neil Prince to include the latest t-in technological and architectural innovations, promising comfort, "good life," and an experience of American lifestyle h a regional flair. Meanwhile, InterContinental's rival, Hilton, built "little Americas" providing similar comforts, such as air ditioning, driven by the motivation to secure democratic outposts in contested territories. While globalization continues to ead US notions of comfort against local ones around the earth, the question is moving into outer space. What's the next tier of comfort? **1954** Edward Durell Stone and Associates *US Embassy* New Delhi, India ○ I. M. Pei & Associates e Memorial Chapel* Taichung, Taiwan ○ Ralph Rapson *US Embassy* Copenhagen, Denmark ○ Ralph Rapson *US bassy* Stockholm, Sweden ○ Raymond & Rado *St. Anselm Church* Tokyo, Japan ○ Josep Lluís Sert *Juan Miro Studio*

Palma de Mallorca, Spain ○ Skidmore, Owings and Merrill *US Consular Housing* Bremen, Germany ○ Town Planning Associates *Quinto Palatino* Havana, Cuba ○ Yamasaki and Associates *US Embassy* Kobe, Japan **1955** Donald Hatch and Associates *Las Mercedes Commercial Center* Caracas, Venezuela ○ Hugh Stubbins and Associates *Congress Hall* Berlin, Germany ○ Hugh Stubbins and Associates *US Embassy* Tangier, Morocco ○ Morris Lapidus Associates *Aruba Caribbean Hotel* Aruba, Aruba ○ Raymond & Rado *Gunma Music Center* Gunma, Japan ○ Richard J. Neutra *US Embas* Karachi, Pakistan ○ Josep Lluís Sert *US Embassy* Baghdad, Iraq ○ Skidmore, Owings and Merrill *US Consulate* Düsseldorf, Germany ○ Skidmore, Owings and Merrill *US Consulate and Consular Housing* Stuttgart, Germany ○ The Architects Collaborative *Interbau Housing Block* Hansaviertel, Berlin **1956** A. L. Aydelott and Associates *US Embassy* Manila, Philippines ○ Carl Koch *US Embassy Staff Housing* Belgrade, Yugoslavia ○ Harry Weese Associates *US Embas* Accra, Ghana ○ John Johansen *US Embassy* Dublin, Ireland ○ Vincent G. Kling *US Embassy Office Building* Quito, Ecuador ○ I. M. Pei & Associates *Place Ville-Marie* Montréal, Canada ○ Philip Johnson *Soreq Nuclear Research Center* Rehovot, Israel ○ Skidmore, Owings and Merrill *Banque Lambert* Brussels, Belgium ○ The Architects Collaborative *US Embassy* Athens, Greece ○ Office of International Trade Fairs *US Exhibition, Jeshyn International Fair* Kabul, Afghanistan Office of International Trade Fairs *US Exhibition, International Trade Fair* Zagreb, Yugoslavia ○ Office of International Trade Fairs *US Exhibition, International Trade Fair* Damascus, Syria **1957** Arthur B. Froehlich and Associates *Hipódromo La Rinconada* Caracas, Venezuela ○ Marcel Breuer and Associates *US Embassy* The Hague, Netherlands ○ Morris Lapidus Associates *Arawak Hotel* Jamaica ○ ROMA Design Group *US Consulate Building* Fukuoka, Japan ○ Rogers, Taliaferro and Lamb *US Embassy* Ciudad Trujillo, Dominican Republic ○ The Architects Collaborative *University of Baghdad* Baghdad, Iraq ○ The Office of Ludwig Mies van der Rohe *Ron Bacardi y Compania Building* Mexico City, Mexico ○ United States Information Agency *George C. Marshall House* Berlin, Germany ○ Wiliam B. Tabler Architects *Hotel Ponce Intercontinental* Ponce, Puerto Rico ○ Office of International Trade Fairs *US Exhibition, International Trade Fair* Casablanca, Morocco ○ Office of International Trade Fairs *US Exhibition, International Trade Fair* Bari, Italy ○ Off of International Trade Fairs *US Exhibition, International Trade Fair* Salonika, Greece **1958** Daniel, Mann, Johnson & Mendenhall *US Military Housing* Guam ○ Edward Larabee Barnes Associates *El Monte Renewal Project* San Juan, Pue Rico ○ Edward Larabee Barnes Associates *US Embassy* Tabriz, Iran ○ Welton Becket *Hilton Hotel* Havana, Cuba

Reprogramming Designed by Welton Becket & Associates, Conrad Hilton's modernist "Little America" in Havana opened in 19 Less than ten months later, Castro adopted the hotel for his temporary headquarters following the ousting of President Fulgen Batista. Conrad Hilton's dream "to show the countries most exposed to Communism the other side of the coin—the fruits of the free world," was retroactively and unexpectedly fulfilled in Havana through the communist appropriation of Hilton's built-in comforts, including air conditioning. In its smooth transition between the two dominant political systems, modern architecture came to symbolize the success of both ideologies. In Havana, the communist takeover of Hilton's luxury and comfort, initially intended for the select few, had a distinct ideological function. Though the story of the Havana Hilton may be different from that of Albert Kahn's Soviet factories, which allowed an immediate translation of capitalist efficiencies into socialist war preparedness, or from TAC's parking garage in the city center of Kuwait whose ground-level market was transformed into the Souk Al-Manakh black market stock exchange (famous for its sudden 1982 crash), in all of these cases architecture more tha survives the ideological transformations taking place within it, on occasion it even aids them. Lathrop Douglass *Oil Compan Offices* Bogotá, Colombia ○ Sert, Jackson and Gourley *Fondation Maeght* Saint Paul-de-Vence, France ○ United States Information Agency *US Pavilion, Expo '58 (Universal and International Exposition)* Brussels, Belgium **The Invisibles** "Unfinished Business," the title for the 1958 World's Fair Exhibition in Brussels, developed by the "American Idealism in Action group, displayed "America's view of the problems it expects to face in the next decade and how we envisage their solution: Education, Integration, Reconstruction of Urban Centers, Maintenance of Individualism." The exhibition addressed the concern that "not dealing with the Negro problem would backfire badly." And the exhibition did, in fact, frankly display the US racial and social problems of the day. However, the exhibit drew sufficient pressure from US conservative politicians and some pres that the US government closed it shortly after it opened. Six years later the Civil Rights Act became law and today, fifty years later, many of the same issues persist and new ones have emerged. However, the NSA's surveillance architecture, gender pay inequity, racial profiling in neighborhood enclaves, labor practices on US construction sites, or any of the many contemporary social issues rarely make printed media headlines. Must protest and democracy come with a business model? Pereira and Luckman *Hilton Hotel* Berlin, Germany ○ Yamasaki and Associates *Civil Air Terminal* Dhahran, Saudi Arabia ○ Office c International Trade Fairs *US Exhibition, International Trade Fair* Poznan, Poland **1959** Eero Saarinen and Associates *US Embassy* Oslo, Norway ○ Welton Becket *Hilton Hotel* Cairo, Egypt ○ Joseph Allen Stein and Associates *India International Centre* New Delhi, India ○ The Architects Collaborative *Master Plan for Britz-Buckow-Rudow* Berlin, Germany United States Information Agency *American National Exhibition* Moscow, USSR **Global Citizenship** Charles and Ray Eame film installation "Glimpses of the USA" depicted a day in the life of a US citizen for the American National Exhibition in Moscov in 1959. The project consisted of 2,200 images of how people play, work, and live displayed across seven screens for thirteen minutes, depicting college campuses, cities, highways, and neighborhoods. Today, while political warfare still remains within national boundaries, cultural warfare is played within a global field. From US (the United States) to us (a collective), what are today's "glimpses"? **1960** Edward Durell Stone and Associates *Radiological Laboratories* Trombay, India ○ Eero Saarin nd Associates *Ellinikon International Airport* Athens, Greece ○ Joseph Allen Stein and Associates *American International School* New Delhi, India ○ Marcel Breuer and Associates *IBM Research Center* La Gaude, France ○ orris Lapidus Associates *Ponce de Leon Hotel* San Juan, Puerto Rico ○ I. M. Pei & Associates *US Embassy* Montevideo, ruguay ○ Richard J. Neutra *BEWO-Bau Development I + II* Morfelden-Walldorf, Quickborn, Germany ○ Skidmore, wings and Merrill *Canadian Industries Ltd. Tower* Montréal, Canada **1961** Marcel Breuer and Associates *Ski Resort* aine, France ○ Morris Lapidus Associates *Americana Hotel* San Juan, Puerto Rico ○ Raymond & Rado *Divine Word minary Chapel* Nagoya, Japan ○ Raymond & Rado *Nanzan University Campus* Nagoya, Japan ○ The Architects ollaborative *University of Tunis School of Law* Tunis, Tunisia ○ Victor A. Lundy *US Embassy* Colombo, Sri Lanka ○ United ates Information Agency *"Plastics USA" Traveling Exhibition* Various cities, USSR ○ United States Information Agency *Transportation USA" Traveling Exhibition* Various cities, USSR **1962** Brown Daltas and Associates *Palace of Princess t'emah* Tehran, Iran ○ Brown Daltas and Associates *Coca-Cola Plant* Meshed, Iran ○ Brown Daltas and Associates *fice Tower and Shopping Center* Tehran, Iran ○ Edward Durell Stone and Associates *Water and Power Development uthority* Lahore, Pakistan ○ Edward Durell Stone and Associates *US Government Office Building* New Delhi, India ○ ouis I. Kahn *Indian Institute of Management* Ahmedabad, India ○ Louis I. Kahn *National Capital of Bangladesh* Dhaka, angladesh

Magical States Few state representatives embody the invisible power of resources, or possess the ability to ount magical spectacles of national progress, the way Venezuelan "modern" statesmen did. Even without fantasies induced abundant oil, which were at the core of what Fernando Coronil called "magical states," the production of a nation-state d national mythology have proven to be both intoxicating and especially productive for architecture. As relatively poor third-orld countries emerged as new nations from their respective decolonization processes, all of their modernization projects mediately achieved the mythological status of nation building. These processes had the momentary capacity to turn US chitecture firms into the magical agents of progress and modernity. Commissions like Louis Kahn's National Assembly Complex Dhaka or Edward Durell-Stone's National Assembly and Presidential Palace in Islamabad are direct representations of these w states' democratic processes. When considered in tandem with the Indian Institute of Management in Ahmedabad and e Pakistan Institute of Nuclear Science and Technology, designed by Kahn and Durell-Stone respectively, this constellation projects points to these architects' long term — magical — involvement in the building of the Indian and Pakistani states.

e Office of Ludwig Mies van der Rohe *Neue Nationalgalerie* Berlin, Germany ○ Wiliam B. Tabler Architects *Dublin tercontinental Hotel* Dublin, Ireland ○ Office of International Trade Fairs *US Exhibition, International Trade Fair* Izmir, rkey ○ United States Information Agency *"Medicine USA" Traveling Exhibition* Various cities, USSR **1963** Welton cket *US Embassy* Warsaw, Poland ○ Perkins + Will *National College of Agriculture* Chapingo, Mexico ○ James Stewart lshek Architect *Teijin Institute for Biomedical Research* Tokyo, Japan ○ The Office of Ludwig Mies van der Rohe ronto-Dominion Centre* Toronto, Canada ○ Office of International Trade Fairs *US Exhibition, International Trade Fair na, Peru ○ United States Information Agency *"Technical Books USA" Traveling Exhibition* Various cities, USSR ○ ited States Information Agency *"Graphic Arts USA" Traveling Exhibition* Various cities, USSR **1964** CRS Inc. *King hd University of Petroleum and Minerals* Dhahran, Saudi Arabia ○ Edward Durell Stone and Associates *Secretariat ilding, Government of Lahore* Lahore, Pakistan ○ James Stewart Polshek Architect *Teijin Applied Textile Science Center aka*, Japan ○ Sert, Jackson and Associates *University of Guelph Long Range Development Plan* Ontario, Canada ○ The fice of Ludwig Mies van der Rohe *Westmount Square* Montréal, Canada **1965** Adrian Wilson Associates *US Embassy ancery* Saigon, Vietnam ○ Edward Durell Stone and Associates *Jeddah International Airport* Jeddah, Saudi Arabia ○ ward Durell Stone and Associates *Pakistan Institute of Nuclear Science and Technology* Islamabad, Pakistan ○ Joseph en Stein and Associates *Ford Foundation Headquarters* New Delhi, India ○ Morris Lapidus Associates *San Juan tercontinental Hotel* San Juan, Puerto Rico ○ Morris Lapidus Associates *El Conquistador Resort* Fajardo, Puerto Rico ○ dison, Madison and Madison Architects and Engineers *US Embassy* Dakar, Senegal ○ Sert, Jackson and Associates pphire Bay Resort* St. Thomas, US Virgin Islands ○ Skidmore, Owings and Merrill *Heinz Corporate Headquarters ingdon*, UK ○ The Architects Collaborative *Kuwait Fund for Arab Economic Development* Kuwait City, Kuwait ○ Victor uen International *Master Plan of Tehran* Tehran, Iran ○ United States Information Agency *"Communications USA" aveling Exhibition* Various cities, USSR ○ United States Information Agency *"Architecture USA" Traveling Exhibition rious cities*, USSR **1966** Edward Durell Stone and Associates *Governmental Complex* Islamabad, Pakistan ○ Kevin che John Dinkeloo and Associates *Cummins Engine Company Component Plant* Darlington, England ○ Paul Rudolph ster Plan for Bangladesh Agricultural University* Mymensingh, Bangladesh **1967** Edward Durell Stone and Associates iversity of Islamabad* Islamabad, Pakistan ○ Smith, Smith, Lundberg and Waehler *International Institute Of Tropical riculture* Ibadan, Nigeria ○ Mitchell/Giurgola Architects *US Embassy* Bogotá, Colombia ○ Sert, Jackson and Associates rmel de la Paix Convent* Mazille, France ○ Sert, Jackson and Associates *Ecole des Beaux-Arts et des Arts Appliquées sançon*, France ○ United States Information Agency *US Pavilion, Expo '67 (Canadian World Exhibition)* Montréal, nada **1968** Welton Becket *Hilton Hotel* Manila, Philippines ○ Lathrop Douglass *Parly II Shopping Center* Paris, France ○ uis I. Kahn *Wolfson Center for Engineering* Tel-Aviv, Israel ○ Johnson/Burgee Architects *Bielefeld Kunsthalle* Bielefeld, rmany ○ Sasaki, Dawson, DeMay Associates *Costa Smeralda Resort Master Plan* Sardinia, Italy ○ Sert, Jackson Associates *Fundació Joan Miró* Barcelona, Spain ○ Skidmore, Owings and Merrill *Boots Pure Drug Company*

Headquarters Nottingham, UK ○ Victor Gruen International *Louvain la Neuve Master Plan* Ottigines, Belgium **1969** Christopher Alexander *PREVI Experimental Housing Project* Lima, Peru ○ Haines, Lundberg and Waehler *Centro Sperimentale Metallurgico* Rome, Italy ○ Victor Gruen International *Cap 3000 Shopping Center* Saint Laurent du Var, France ○ Victor Gruen International *Pacific Centre* Vancouver, Canada ○ William L. Pereira & Associates *Amfac Center* Ontario, Canada **1970** Eduardo Catalano *U.S Embassy Buenos Aires* Buenos Aires, Argentina ○ Louis I. Kahn *Family Planning Center* Khatmandu, Nepal ○ Skidmore, Owings and Merrill *W.D. & H. O. Wills Tobacco Processing Plant and Corporate Headquarters* Bristol, UK ○ The Architects Collaborative *Rosenthal Glass Factory* Amberg, Germany ○ United States Information Agency *US Pavilion, Expo '70 (Japan World Exposition)* Osaka, Japan **1971** A. Epstein and Sons International *Polimex-Cekop Food Plant* Ostrada, Poland ○ Paul Rudolph *Daiei Building* Nagoya, Japan ○ Payette and Associates *The Aga Khan University Hospital, Medical College, and School of Nursing* Nairobi, Kenya **1972** Edward Durell Stone and Associates *Babin Kuk Hotel* Dubrovnik, Yugoslavia ○ Harrison and Abramovitz *Tour Gan* La Défense, France Joseph Allen Stein and Associates *Express Towers* Mumbai, India ○ I. M. Pei & Partners *Raffles City* Singapore, Singapore ○ Victor Gruen International *US Embassy* Tokyo, Japan **1973** I. M. Pei & Partners *Canadian Imperial Bank of Commerce* Toronto, Canada ○ Skidmore, Owings and Merrill *Carlton Centre* Johannesburg, South Africa ○ Smith, Hinchman and Grylls *Royal Saudi Air Force Headquarters Building* Riyadh, Saudi Arabia ○ The Architects Collaborative *Souk al Safat, Souk Al Manakh and Souk Al Wataniya* Kuwait City, Kuwait ○ The Architects Collaborative *National Library* Abu Dhabi, UAE **1974** Brown Daltas and Associates *King Khalid Military City* Saudi Arabia, Saudi Arabia ○ Leo A Daly *Saudi Arabian National Guard (SANG) Headquarters* Riyadh, Saudi Arabia ○ Johnson/Burgee Architects *National Center for the Performing Arts* India, Mumbai ○ Skidmore, Owings and Merrill *Tour FIAT* La Défense, France ○ Skidmore, Owings and Merrill *Hajj Terminal, Jeddah International Airport* Jeddah, Saudi Arabia ○ The Architects Collaborative *Montego Bay Hospital* Montego Bay, Jamaica ○ William L. Pereira & Associates *Imperial Medical Center* Tehran, Iran ○ Yamasaki and Associates *Torre Picasso* Madrid, Spain **1975** CRS Group *Arabian-American Oil Company (ARAMCO) Workers' Housing* Dhahran, Saudi Arabia ○ HOK+4 Consortium (Hellmuth, Obata + Kassabaum; CRS Group; Gollins Melvin Ward Partnership [UK]; Syska & Hennessy, Inc.; Dames & Moore) *King Saud University* Riyadh, Saudi Arabia ○ Perkins + Will *Iranzamin School* Tehran, Iran ○ Johnson/Burgee Architects *Centro Banaven* Caracas, Venezuela ○ The Architects Collaborative *Inter-Continental Hotel* Sharjah, UAE **1976** Benjamin Thompson Associates *Intercontinental Hotel* Abu Dhabi, UAE ○ CRS Group *King Abdul Aziz Military City* Riyadh, Saudi Arabia ○ I. M. Pei & Partners *Oversea-Chinese Banking Corporation Centre* Singapore, Singapore ○ Skidmore, Owings and Merrill *Joint Banking Centre* Kuwait City, Kuwait ○ The Architects Collaborative *Hotel Bernardin* Piran, Yugoslavia **1977** Hellmuth, Obata + Kassabaum *King Khaled Airport* Riyadh, Saudi Arabia ○ Hugh Stubbins and Associates *Technical Institute* Shiraz, Iran ○ Skidmore, Owings and Merrill *Master Plan for Yanbu New Town* Yanbu, Saudi Arabia ○ Skidmore, Owings and Merrill *National Commercial Bank* Jeddah, Saudi Arabia ○ The Architects Collaborative *Jubail Industrial City Master Plan* Jubail, Saudi Arabia **1978** A. Epstein and Sons International *Food Processing Facility for Union Carbide* France ○ Fred Bassetti and Company *US Embassy* Lisbon, Portugal ○ CRS Group *Ministry of Foreign Affairs Housing* Riyadh, Saudi Arabia ○ Joseph Allen Stein and Associates *UNICEF Headquarters* New Delhi, India ○ Mitchell/Giurgola Architects *Australian Parliament House* Canberra, Australia ○ William L. Pereira & Associates *Saddam International Airport* Baghdad, Iraq ○ Yamasaki and Associates *Monetary Agency Head Office* Riyadh, Saudi Arabia **1979** A. Epstein and Sons International *Air Force Base* Ramon, Ovda, Israel ○ A. Epstein and Sons International *Tnuva Milk Processing Facility* Rehovot, Israel ○ Leo A Daly *Al Jubail Petrochemical Company Headquarters* Jubail, Saudi Arabia ○ Richard Meier and Partners Architects *Frankfurt Museum for the Decorative Arts* Frankfurt am Main, Germany ○ Skidmore, Owings and Merrill *Al-Ahli Bank* Kuwait City, Kuwait ○ The Architects Collaborative *Porto Carras Resort* Sithonia, Greece ○ The Architects Collaborative *Khulafa Street Development* Baghdad, Iraq ○ Yamasaki and Associates *Sheraton Miyako Hotel* Tokyo, Japan **1980** CRS Group *Yanbu Industrial City Residential District* Yanbu, Saudi Arabia ○ CRS Group *US Embassy* Riyadh, Saudi Arabia ○ Welton Becket *Moscow World Trade Center* Moscow, USSR ○ Hartman-Cox Architects *US Embassy* Kuala Lumpur, Malaysia ○ Paul Rudolph *Colonnade Condominiums* Singapore, Singapore ○ The Architects Collaborative *Institute of Public Administration* Riyadh, Saudi Arabia ○ Wimberly Allison Tong and Goo *Tanjong Jara Beach Hotel* Terengganu, Malaysia **1981** CRS Group *Ruwais New Town* Ruwais, UAE ○ Daniel, Mann, Johnson & Mendenhall *Gagah Madah Plaza* Jakarta, Indonesia Eisenman Architects *IBA Social Housing* Berlin, Germany ○ Murphy/Jahn *11 Diagonal Street* Johannesburg, South Africa John Portman and Associates *Shanghai Centre* Shanghai, China ○ Mitchell/Giurgola Architects *Aviano School* Aviano, Italy ○ Moore Ruble Yudell *Tegel Harbor Phase I Housing* Berlin, Germany ○ Morris Lapidus Associates *Daniel Tower Hotel* Herzliya, Israel ○ Paul Rudolph *Concourse Complex* Singapore, Singapore ○ The Architects Collaborative *Basrah Sheraton Hotel* Basra, Iraq **1982** Arquitectonica *Banco de Credito Headquarters* Lima, Peru ○ Murphy/Jahn *362 West Street* Durban, South Africa ○ Paul Rudolph *Dharmala Sakti Building* Jakarta, Indonesia ○ Skidmore, Owings and Merrill *United Gulf Bank Building* Manama, Bahrain ○ Venturi Rauch and Scott Brown *Khulafa Street Building* Baghdad, Iraq ○ William L. Pereira & Associates *Doha Sheraton Hotel* Doha, Qatar **1983** Harry Weese Associates *US Embassy Housing* Tokyo, Japan ○ I. M. Pei & Partners *Louvre Renovation* Paris, France ○ Richard Meier and Partners Architects *Siemens Headquarters and Research Facilities* Munich, Germany ○ Skidmore, Owings and Merrill *US Embassy* Moscow, Russia

Smart Concrete In 1946, Soviet school children presented a two-foot wooden replica of the Great Seal of the United States to Ambassador Averell Harriman. He hung the seal in his office. On May 26, 1960, Ambassador Henry Cabot Lodge, Jr. presented the same Great Seal to the United Nations, including the embossed bug that had transmitted six years of conversations to the Soviets. Four years after Lodge's accusation, the US State Department announced the discovery of forty hidden microphones embedded in the walls of the US Embassy in Moscow. As a result of a reciprocal agreement between Washington and Moscow, a new location was granted and the US chose SOM to design the new embassy. During the establishment of the "Conditions of Construction," Russians managed to gain control of the production of the building's structure, all under close US supervision. The groundbreaking ceremony was held in October of 1979. In 1985, a routine x-ray test of a structural pillar uncovered anomalies in the concrete superstructure. Further inspection revealed that almost every pillar had been implanted with rudimentary devices creating a passive electrical grid that allowed the building itself to broadcast the conversations it was supposed to protect. Congress approved the demolition of the upper floors of the "smart" concrete building and the rebuilding of a new isolated steel superstructure. Fifteen hundred containers of raw construction materials were shipped from the US to Moscow with diplomatic security clearance so that they would never leave the sight of US agents. While today's informational space is based in portable devices — closer to the 1946 seal — and security threads traverse hackable firewalls, current advances in nanotechnology and actuated technologies might make walls do more than listen or speak. Yamasaki and Associates *Founders Hall* Misono, Japan **1984** CRS Sirrine, Inc. *El Gezirah Sheraton Hotel* Cairo, Egypt ○ John Portman and Associates *Marina Square* Singapore, Singapore ○ Mitchell/Giurgola Architects *Volvo Headquarters* Göteborg, Sweden ○ Moore Ruble Yudell *Humboldt Bibliothek* Berlin, Germany ○ Paul Rudolph *Bond Centre* Hong Kong, China ○ Skidmore, Owings and Merrill *Northwest Frontier Province Agricultural University* Peshawar, Pakistan ○ The Architects Collaborative *GSIS Headquarters* Manila, Philippines **1985** John Portman and Associates *Regent Hotel* Singapore, Singapore ○ Payette Associates *The Aga Khan University Hospital and Medical School Campus* Karachi, Pakistan ○ I. M. Pei & Partners *Bank of China Tower* Hong Kong, Hong Kong ○ James Stewart Polshek Architect *US Embassy* Muscat, Oman **Anger-Love Management** Following the suicide bombings in Beirut in 1983, security became a critical issue for the Office of Foreign Buildings Operations (FBO). The Inman Report, submitted by the State Department in the aftermath of the bombings, called for the replacement of 126 out of 226 diplomatic posts worldwide. Since the attacks on US embassies continued after the Inman Report was adopted, a number of more stringent security measures were added, culminating with the three scales of the Standard Embassy Plan produced and implemented in over twenty new embassies under the guidance of the new head of Bureau of Overseas Building Operations (OBO), retired General Charles Williams. In response to the criticism of both the US foreign policy and of the new crop of US embassies, the Department of State launched the Design Excellence Program in early 2011, which revived the conversation about openness versus security in embassy design. It is no surprise that the most passionate expressions of both positive and negative sentiment towards the US involve its embassy architecture. Suffering the symptoms of larger political currents these sites and architectures provide a particularly valuable opportunity to set the tone of future international relationships. What if the architect's tools went beyond tall walls and distances to include anticipating historical change? Safdie Architects *Ardmore Habitat Condominiums* Singapore, Singapore ○ Skidmore, Owings and Merrill *Canary Wharf Master Plan* London, UK **1986** Edward Durell Stone and Associates *Museo de Antropología de Xalapa* Veracruz, Mexico ○ Frank O. Gehry and Associates *Fish Dance Restaurant* Kobe, Japan ○ Kohn, Pederson, Fox *Westendstraße 1* Frankfurt, Germany ○ Ralph Lerner Architects *Indira Gandhi National Centre for Arts* New Delhi, India ○ Richard Meier and Partners Architects *City Hall and Library* The Hague, Netherlands ○ Skidmore, Owings and Merrill *University of Blida Teaching Hospital and Housing Communities* Blida, Algeria ○ I. M. Pei & Partners *Credit Suisse First Boston at Canary Wharf* London, UK **1987** Eduardo Catalano *U.S Embassy Pretoria* Pretoria, South Africa ○ Gunnar Birkerts and Associates *US Embassy* Caracas, Venezuela ○ Integrus *US Embassy* Bogotá, Colombia ○ Kohn, Pederson, Fox *Goldman Sachs Headquarters* London, UK ○ Richard Meier and Partners Architects *Museum of Contemporary Art* Barcelona, Spain ○ Robert A. M. Stern Architects *Exxx International Headquarters* Voorschoten, Netherlands ○ Cesar Pelli & Associates *One Canada Square at Canary Wharf* London, UK **Profit Margin** The London Docklands, the fabled site of the Canary Wharf development, which congregates the world's financial power to a degree matched only by New York's World Trade Center, was developed by the Canadian firm Olympia & York, the same entity that developed its Manhattan counterpart. Initially master-planned by SOM and subsequently by Koetter Kim, Canary Wharf includes tenants like Citigroup, Lehman Brothers, HSBC, Barclays, J.P. Morgan Chase, and Merrill Lynch, and boasts the building that was London's tallest for two decades, Cesar Pelli's One Canada Square. Canary Wharf has faced financial instability over the years. Olympia & York bought the plan from a previous developer, only to declare bankruptcy as the London commercial property market collapsed in 1992, and then in a slightly different form (as the Canary Wharf Group) they reacquired it in 1995. In 2007, individual buildings in this part of London, now fully transformed from its derelict dockland site and branded as one of the key financial centers of the world, cost over a billion dollars. The developers are now extending Canary Wharf. Dreaming of financial technology tenants they brought the designer of the Google and Facebook offices, Gensler, to re-envision the interior of the 39th floor of One Canada Square as: "Europe's largest Fin/Tech accelerator." At the 2012 Tech Week, Europe proposed that Level39, as the accelerator space is called, "will offer Tech City startups a chance to disrupt the financial sector." Ultimately, every aspect of this development, including the mildly revolutionary hopes for "disruption," is part of a tax and profit speculation at the scale at which private finance has previously shaped cities only in North America.

1988 Arquitectonica *US Embassy* Lima, Peru ○ Eisenman Architects *Koizumi Sangyo Corporation Headquarters* Tokyo, Japan ○ Frank O. Gehry and Associates *Disney Village at Euro Disney Resort* Marne-la-Vallée, France ○ Michael Graves and Associates *Hotel New York at Euro Disney Resort* Marne-la-Vallée, France ○ Gwathmey Siegel Kaufman Architects *Golf Clubhouse at Euro Disney Resort* Marne-la-Vallée, France ○ Antoine Predock Architect PC *Hotel Santa Fe at Euro Disney Resort* Marne-la-Vallée, France ○ Robert A.M. Stern Architects *Newport Bay Club Hotel at Euro Disney Resort* Marne-la-Vallée, France ○ Robert A.M. Stern Architects *Hotel Cheyenne at Euro Disney Resort* Marne-la-Vallée, France **Little Americas (See 218, 254)** John Hejduk *Kreuzberg Tower and Wing* Berlin, Germany ○ John Hejduk *Tegel Housing* Berlin, Germany ○ Kevin Roche John Dinkeloo and Associates *Bouygues World Headquarters* Paris, France ○ Moore Ruble Yudell *Nishiokamoto Housing* Kobe, Japan ○ Moore Ruble Yudell *Potatisakern Housing and Villas* Malmo, Sweden ○ Perry Dean Rogers Partners *US Embassy* Amman, Jordan ○ Skidmore, Owings and Merrill *Bishopsgate Project* London, UK **1989** Frank O. Gehry and Associates *Vitra Design Museum* Weil Am Rhein, Germany ○ Mack Architect(s) *Nexus II Housing* Fukuoka, Japan ○ Steven Holl Architects *Nexus International Housing* Fukuoka, Japan ○ Michael Graves and Associates *Momochi District Apartment Building* Fukuoka, Japan ○ Tigerman McCurry Architects *Momochi District Apartment Building* Fukuoka, Japan ○ Safdie Architects *Modi'in Master Plan* Modi'in, Israel ○ Santos Prescott and Associates *SDC Corporate Headquarters* Tokyo, Japan ○ SITE *Four Continents Bridge* Hiroshima, Japan **1990** Cambridge Seven Associates *Ring of Fire Aquarium and Tempozan Marketplace* Osaka, Japan ○ Eisenman Architects *Nunotami Corporation Headquarters* Tokyo, Japan ○ Gunnar Birkerts and Associates *Latvian National Library* Riga, Latvia **Code Upgrade** In 1989, as the Berlin wall fell and the USSR began to collapse, Gunnar Birkerts received a call from the Latvian Architect Association. They had awarded him the commission for the Latvian National Library and Archives. Birkerts, who had fled Latvia in 1948, could now return to his homeland to build the first national landmark for the newly independent country. But the project was mired in political turmoil, an antiquated code system, and construction delays. By the time the building got off the ground in 2008, almost twenty years after its commission, Birkerts and Associates had helped to rewrite the national fire code, create handicap accessibility standards, and introduced full-scale building enclosure mock-ups to Latvian construction companies. In fact, Birkerts was the first to demand these measures as part of the construction process for all new public buildings. When the Library opens in September 2014, it will culminate a twenty-five year endeavor to bring Latvian building standards up to par with international code. Kevin Roche John Dinkeloo Associates *Ritz Carlton Millenia Singapore Office Buildings and Hotel* Singapore, Singapore ○ Hugh Stubbins and Associates *Yokohama Landmark Tower* Yokohama, Japan ○ Kohn, Pederson, Fox *JR Central Towers and Nagoya Marriott Hotel* Nagoya, Japan ○ Johnson/Burgee Architects *Puerta Europa Towers* Madrid, Spain ○ Wimberly Allison Tong and Goo *The Palace of the Lost City* Sun City, South Africa **1991** Bernard Tschumi Architects *Le Fresnoy Art Center* Tourcoing. France ○ Murphy/Jahn *Messeturm* Frankfurt, Germany ○ Frank O. Gehry and Associates *Guggenheim Museum* Bilbao, Spain **Culture Capital** The Guggenheim Foundation was, in 2014, seeking a curator in urban studies and digital initiatives to launch an international architectural competition for the design of the new Guggenheim Museum in Helsinki as an addition to the Guggenheim global constellation (New York, Bilbao, Abu Dhabi). According to reporting in the Economist from December 2013, a study by AEA Consulting (a New York firm that specializes in cultural projects), two dozen new cultural centers focused on museums, globally branded or not, are currently due to be built in various countries at an estimated cost of $250 billion. In the meantime, the Helsinki project has already prompted protests by the Finns, who express concerns over the global branding of culture. "Visitors' spending in Bilbao in the first three years after the museum opened raised over €100m in taxes for the regional government, enough to recoup the construction costs and leave something over." As culture, and with it architecture, becomes the new currency for the production of capital, what are the effects on the understanding and production of culture? Venturi, Scott Brown and Associates *Sainsbury Wing* National Gallery, London **1992** Frank O. Gehry and Associates *Olympic Fish* Barcelona, Spain ○ Cesar Pelli & Associates *Petronas Towers* Kuala Lumpur, Malaysia ○ Richard Meier and Partners Architect *Daimler-Benz Research Center* Ulm, Germany ○ SITE *Avenue Number Five* Seville, Spain ○ Smith, Hinchman and Grylls *International Islamic University* Kuala Lumpur, Malaysia ○ Steven Holl Architects *Makuhari Bay New Town* Chiba, Japan ○ Steven Holl Architects *Kiasma Museum of Contemporary Art* Helsinki, Finland ○ Venturi, Scott Brown and Associates *Mielparque Nikko Kirifuri Hotel and Spa* Nikko, Japan **1993** Murphy/Jahn *Sony Center Berlin* Berlin, Germany ○ John Hejduk *Memorial Towers* Santiago de Compostela, Spain ○ Kohn, Pederson, Fox *US Embassy* Nicosia, Cyprus ○ Michael Graves and Associates *Castalia* The Hague, Netherlands ○ Michael Graves and Associates *Taiwan National Museum* Taitung, Taiwan ○ Michael Graves and Associates *Momochi Residential Tower* Fukuoka, Japan ○ Richard Meier and Partners Architects *Stadthaus Ulm* Ulm, Germany ○ Safdie Architects *Mamila District* David's Village, Jerusalem **1994** AECOM *Korea Development Bank Headquarters* Seoul, South Korea ○ Arquitectonica *Orchards Scott Hotel and Residences* Singapore, Singapore ○ Bernard Tschumi Architects *School of Architecture* Marne-la-Vallée, Paris ○ Frank O. Gehry and Associates *Cinémathèque Française* Paris, France ○ John Portman and Associates *Menara Multi-Purpose At Capital Square* Kuala Lumpur, Malaysia ○ Philip Johnson Alan Ritchie Architects *Pontiac Marina Millenia Tower* Singapore, Singapore ○ Kallmann McKinnell & Wood Architects *US Embassy* Bangkok, Thailand ○ Kohn, Pederson, Fox *Rothermere American Institute at Oxford University* Oxford, UK ○ Kohn, Pederson, Fox *Shanghai World Financial Center* Shanghai, China ○ Mack Architect(s) *Suter Housing* Maspraich, Switzerland ○ HOK Sport *Hong Kong Stadium* So Kon Po, Hong Kong ○ Safdie Architects ttawa City Hall Ottawa, Canada ○ Santos Prescott and Associates *Dairi Nishi Housing* Kitakyushu, Japan ○ Santos rescott and Associates *Kadota Housing* Kitakyushu, Japan ○ The Leonard Parker Associates *US Embassy* Santiago, hile **1995** Frank O. Gehry and Associates *Dancing House* Prague, Czech Republic ○ Hellmuth, Obata + Kassabaum kyo Telecom Centre Tokyo, Japan ○ Murphy/Jahn *Suvarnabhumi Airport* Bangkok, Thailand ○ Koetter Kim and ssociates *Scottish Equitable Headquarters* Edinburgh, Scotland ○ Kohn, Pederson, Fox *Rodin Pavilion at Samsung Plaza* eoul, South Korea ○ Leo A Daly *Cheung Kong Center* Hong Kong, Hong Kong ○ Mack Architect(s) *Vienna Housing* agramerstrasse Vienna, Austria ○ Mack Architect(s) *Conegliano Housing* Conegliano, Italy ○ Moore Ruble Yudell *US mbassy* Berlin, Germany ○ Morphosis *Sun Tower* Seoul, South Korea ○ Perkins + Will *International School of Beijing* eijing, China ○ Robert A. M. Stern Architects *The Greenbrier at West Village Golf Resort* Fukushima, Japan ○ Safdie rchitects *Vancouver Library Square* Vancouver, Canada **1996** Cannon Design *Sabanci University* Istanbul, Turkey ○ avis Brody Bond *Valeo Electricity* San Luis Potosi, Mexico ○ Jerde Partnership *Canal City Hakata* Fukuoka, Japan ○ rde Partnership *Beursplein* Rotterdam, The Netherlands ○ Jerde Partnership *Roppongi Hills* Tokyo, Japan ○ Kohn, ederson, Fox *Roppongi Hills* Tokyo, Japan ○ Michael Graves and Associates *Hyatt Regency Hotel* Taba Heights, Egypt ○ oore Ruble Yudell *New Town Master Plan* Grand Cayman, Cayman Islands ○ Morphosis *Hypo Alpe-Adria Center* angenfurt, Austria ○ Cesar Pelli & Associates *Edificio República* Buenos Aires, Argentina **Cargo Cult** **Describing the** herworldly impression of "machine-absolute" buildings like SOM's Chase Manhattan Bank in New York, Peter Smithson ote that they "arouse the strongest cargo-cult feelings in foreigners, and are truly hints of une architecture autre." His term ferred to the shock of Melanesian islanders at the mystical sight of US warplanes during World War II and the cargo that companied them, and to the elaborate cult ceremonies they invented after the war to copy the forms of these planes in mboo and paint, hoping this mimicry would bring the same abundance from the gods. Smithson interpreted the "rash of black wers" in England as intending to signify the national "nearness to the fountain of technological culture." His reading of the ulations of the American tradition of expensive and technologically advanced detail as the wishful ritualistic performance uld, at the end of the twentieth century, apply to large swaths of global architectural production. And thus his concluding marks on American architecture become a caution to the architectural field at large: "American architects almost have it de; if they could only stop worrying about architecture." Rafael Viñoly Architects *Tokyo International Forum* Tokyo, Japan ○ TKL *US Ambassador's Residence* Bayan, Kuwait ○ Skidmore, Owings and Merrill *Jin Mao Tower* Shanghai, China ○ nith, Hinchman and Grylls *Caterpillar Inc. Engine Test Cells* Moscow, Russia **1997** AECOM *Kingdom Centre* Riyadh, udi Arabia ○ Eisenman Architects *Memorial to the Murdered Jews of Europe* Berlin, Germany ○ HKS, Inc. *The Venetian acau Resort Hotel* Macau, Macau ○ I. M. Pei Architect *Miho Museum* Shigaraki, Japan ○ Murphy/Jahn *Bayer adquarters* Leverkusen, Germany ○ Murphy/Jahn *Cologne/Bonn Airport Terminal 2* Cologne/Bonn Airport, Cologne, rmany ○ Jerde Partnership *WestEnd City Centre* Budapest, Hungary ○ Kohn, Pederson, Fox *Dongbu Financial Center* oul, South Korea ○ Kohn, Pederson, Fox *De Hoftoren* The Hague, Netherlands ○ Mack Architect(s) *Breitenleerstrasse* using Vienna, Austria ○ Michael Graves and Associates *Miramar Resort Hotel and El Gouna Golf Club* El Gouna, Egypt Payette Associates *Seoul National University International Vaccine Institute* Seoul, South Korea ○ Perkins + Will erican Hospital Dubai, UAE ○ RoTo Architecture *Warehouse C* Nagasaki, Japan ○ RTKL *Warsaw Trade Tower* Warsaw, land ○ Smith, Hinchman and Grylls *Caterpillar Inc. Engine Test Cells* Shanghai, China ○ Hillier Group *Star City Hotel d Casino* Sydney, Australia **1998** Cambridge Seven Associates *Oceanario de Lisboa* Lisbon, Portugal ○ Cannon Design onggi University Master Plan and Teleconference Center Suwon, South Korea ○ H2L2 *International American School of rsaw* Warsaw, Poland ○ Hellmuth, Obata + Kassabaum *US Embassy* Nairobi, Kenya ○ Hellmuth, Obata + Kassabaum Embassy Dar-es-Salaam, Tanzania ○ Jerde Partnership *Namba Parks* Osaka, Japan ○ Kohn, Pederson, Fox *MidCity ace* London, UK ○ Mack Architect(s) *Judenburg West Master Plan* Judenburg, Austria ○ Perkins + Will *Concordia ernational School Shanghai* Shanghai, China ○ Sasaki Associates *Kuwaity City Waterfront Master Plan,* Kuwait City, wait ○ SITE *Fondazione Pietro Rossini Pavilion* Briosco, Italy ○ Skidmore, Owings and Merrill *Atlantico Pavilion* Lisbon, rtugal ○ Studio Daniel Libeskind *Felix Nussbaum Haus* Osnabrück, Germany ○ Wood + Zapata *Xintiandi* Shanghai, ina ○ Wimberly Allison Tong and Goo *Atlantis and The Cove Atlantis at Paradise Island* Paradise Island, Bahamas **99** Arquitectonica *Cyberport Hotel Office and University* Hong Kong, China ○ Cambridge Seven Associates *The ientific Center of Kuwait* Kuwait City, Kuwait ○ Eisenman Architects *City of Culture* Galicia, Spain ○ Gwathmey Siegel ufman Architects *Nanyang Polytechnic* Singapore, Singapore ○ Murphy/Jahn *Munich Airport Center* Germany, ○ rphy/Jahn *Hegau Tower* Singen, Germany ○ Jerde Partnership *Arcade at Cyberport* Hong Kong ○ Kohn, Pederson, Fox nube House and Nile House in River City Prague, Czech Republic ○ Kohn, Pederson, Fox *Endesa Headquarters* Madrid, ain ○ Kohn, Pederson, Fox *Heron Tower* London, UK ○ Moore Ruble Yudell *Tango Bo01 Housing Exhibition* Malmo, eden ○ HOK Sport *Millenium Stadium* Cardiff, Wales ○ Rafael Viñoly Architects *Samsung Jong-ro Tower* Seoul, South rea ○ Rafael Viñoly Architects *University of San Andres Library* Buenos Aires, Argentina ○ Smith, Hinchman and Grylls neral Motors Renault São Paulo, Brazil ○ Smith, Hinchman and Grylls *Renault do Brazil Ayrton Senna Plant* Curitiba, zil ○ Smith, Hinchman and Grylls *General Motors de Mexico GMM Ramos Arizpe 1600 Project* Ramos Arizpe, Mexico ○ dio Daniel Libeskind *Jewish Museum* Berlin, Germany ○ Venturi, Scott Brown and Associates *Provincial Capital lding* Toulouse, France **2000** AECOM *Samsung Cancer Center* Seoul, South Korea ○ Arquitectonica *Longemont Hotel* *and Office Tower* Shanghai, China ○ Diller + Scofidio *Slither Housing* Gifu, Japan ○ Frank O. Gehry and Associates *DZ Bank Buliding* Berlin, Germany ○ Jerde Partnership *Village Park Sakalidis* Athens, Greece ○ Jerde Partnership *Zlote Tarasy* Warsaw, Poland ○ Kallmann McKinnell & Wood Architects *Organisation for the Prohibition of Chemical Weapons (OPCW) World Headquarters* The Hague, Netherlands ○ Kevin Roche John Dinkeloo and Associates *Ciudad Grupo Santander* Madrid, Spain ○ Machado and Silvetti Associates *American University of Beirut Master Plan* Beirut, Lebanon ○ HOK Sport *ANZ Stadium* Sydney, Australia ○ Hellmuth, Obata + Kassabaum *Barclays World Headquarters at Canary Wharf* London, UK ○ SmithGroupJJR *DaimlerChrysler Corporation Pilot Project Study and New Assembly Plant* Rastah, Germany **2001** Arquitectonica *Mangrove West Coast* Shenzhen, China ○ Bernard Tschumi Architects *Acropolis Museum* Athens, Greece ○ Murphy/Jahn *Highlight Munich Business Towers* Munich, Germany ○ Jerde Partnership *Core Pacific City* Taipei, Taiwan ○ Jerde Partnership *Langham Place* Hong Kong ○ Jerde Partnership *Kanyon* Istanbul, Turkey ○ John Portman and Associates *Academic Center, Indian School Of Business* Hyderabad, India ○ Pei Cobb Freed & Partners *Tour EDF* La Défense, France ○ Perkins + Will *One Wall Centre* Vancouver, Canada ○ Robert A. M. Stern Architects *Diagonal Mar Entertainment and Retail Center* Barcelona, Spain ○ RTKL *Shanghai Museum of Science and Technology* Shanghai, China ○ RTKL *Salamanca Train Station* Salamanca, Spain ○ Studio Daniel Libeskind *Imperial War Museum North* Manchester, UK ○ Wimberly Allison Tong and Goo *Emirates Palace* Dubai, UAE **2002** Diller + Scofidio *Blur Building* Lake Neuchatel, Switzerland ○ Hellmuth, Obata + Kassabaum *Darwin Centre Museum* London, UK ○ John Portman and Associates *Beijing Yintai Centre* Beijing, China ○ Kohn, Pederson, Fox *Kipco Tower* Kuwait City, Kuwait ○ Mitchell/Giurgola Architects *Elementary and Secondary School Complex* Aviano, Italy ○ Morphosis *Giant Interactive Group Corporate Headquarters* Shanghai, China ○ Morphosis *Madrid Housing* Madrid, Spain **Housing Public Good** US architecture offices have never established expertise in developing spaces of collective inhabitation. The lack of public housing projects in the US has translated into an absence of new models that attempt to understand the typological, social, and spatial transformations of the collective aspirations of a particular society over time. The expertise of US architects has been developed within the constraints of a client, a program, and a private property line—unable to respond to the social and political questions that their European counterparts, fueled by public competitions, have historically addressed. Those US architects who have desired to explore housing typologies have ventured into foreign lands to test the social and spatial implications of the oldest of all typologies. In 1969, for example, Christopher Alexander won the international competition for a housing project in Lima, Peru. The jury praised his project for "a freshness of approach, a commitment to the dignity and worth of individual, a recognition and understanding of the complex linkages between the individual, his family, his belongings, his neighbors and the entire community are implicit in each part of this proposal." NBBJ *Telenor Headquarters* Oslo, Norway ○ Perkins + Will *Universidade Agostinho Neto Phase I New Campus* Luanda, Angola ○ Sasaki Associates *Beijing Olympics Master Plan* Beijing, China ○ Cho Slade Architecture *Dalki Theme Park* Heyri, Korea ○ SmithGroupJJR *Normandy American Cemetery New Visitor Center* Normandy, France ○ Sorg Architects *US Embassy Compound* Kabul, Afghanistan **Bullets Without Ideology** On February 4, 2002, in the same year that Sorg Architects received the commission to build the embassy compound in Kabul, the CIA used an unmanned Predator drone in a targeted killing for the first time. The strike was in Paktia province, two hundred kilometers south of Kabul, near the city of Khost. The intended target was Osama bin Laden. In 1956, representatives of the United States traveled to Kabul to display national technologies, goods, and pleasures in the Jeshyn International Fair. The design and construction of the US pavilion for that fair, commissioned by Jack Massey, the USIA exhibitions officer, had to be completed in six months. The Geodesic Dome, with patent number US 2,682,235 filed by Buckminster Fuller and awarded in 1954, was the structure chosen by Massey for the cultural display of transportation systems, TV sets, and agricultural techniques. The same structural system has been used over the years around the world as the stage for multiple fairs, civic buildings, art projects, and even direct military operations. In 1967, US antiwar protesters used the US Pavilion in Montreal, the Biosphere, a class 1 frequency 16 icosahedron of seventy-six meters in diameter, to denounce the bombs being dropped in Vietnam with shirts imprinted with "Stop the Bombs" and "Genocide." From domes to drones, how can architecture design and control the performative and ethical aspects of form? Sorg Architects *US Embassy* Bridgetown, Barbados ○ Steven Holl Architects *Beirut Marina Zaitunay Bay* Beirut, Lebanon ○ Zago Architecture *Fine Venture Office Tower* Seoul, Korea **2003** Acconci Studio *Mur Island* Graz, Austria ○ Bernard Tschumi Architects *Limoges Concert Hall* Limoges, France ○ Bernard Tschumi Architects *Alésia Museum and Archaeological Park* Alésia, France ○ Bohlin Cywinski Jackson *Apple Store Ginza* Tokyo, Japan ○ Davis Brody Bond *Valeo Security Systems* São Paulo, Brazil ○ Duany Plater-Zyberk & Company *Loreto Bay Resort Village* Baja California Sur, Mexico ○ Gensler *Government Communication Headquarters* Cheltenham, UK ○ Gluckman Mayner Architects *Mori Arts Center* Tokyo, Japan ○ Machado and Silvetti Associates *Suliman S. Olayan School of Business, American University of Beirut* Beirut, Lebanon ○ Office dA *Tongxian Gatehouse* Beijing, China ○ Cesar Pelli & Associates *Two International Finance Centre* Hong Kong, ○ Richard Meier and Partners Architects *Jubilee Church* Rome, Italy ○ RTKL *Chinese Museum of Film* Beijing, China ○ RTKL *Naberezhnaya Office Towers* Moscow, Russia ○ Skidmore, Owings and Merrill *China World Trade Center* Beijing, China ○ Pelli Clarke Pelli Architects *25 Bank Street at Canary Wharf* London, UK ○ SmithGroupJJR *Shanghai Traditional Chinese Medical University Shuguang Hospital Replacement* Shanghai, China ○ Steven Holl Architects *Linked Hybrid* Beijing, China ○ Steven Holl Architects *Nanjing Sifang Art Museum* Nanjing, China ○ Tod Williams Billie Tsien Architects *Tata Construction Services*

nyan Park Phase I Mumbai, India ○ Wimberly Allison Tong and Goo *Shangri-La's Barr Al Jissah Resort and Spa*
uscat, Oman ○ Wodiczko + Bonder *Memorial to the Abolition of Slavery* Nantes, France **2004** Arquitectonica *Microsoft*
ropean Headquarters Paris, France ○ Arquitectonica *International Finance Centre* Seoul, South Korea ○ Bohlin
winski Jackson *Apple Store Shinsaibashi* Osaka, Japan ○ Gensler *The Gate Building* Dubai, UAE ○ Gluckman Mayner
chitects *Museuo Picasso Malaga* Malaga, Spain ○ Hashim Sarkis Studios *Balloon Landing Park* Beirut, Lebanon ○ NBBJ
dul Aziz Al-Babtain Cultural Waqf Tower Kuwait City, Kuwait ○ Robert A. M. Stern Architects *Torre Almirante* Rio de
neiro, Brazil ○ Safdie Architects *Ben Gurion International Airport* Tel Aviv, Israel ○ Sasaki Associates *Al Azhar Park*
iro, Egypt ○ Studio Shanghai *Shanghai American School* Shanghai, China ○ Studio Shanghai *Wuhan Tiandi* Wuhan,
ina ○ Studio Shanghai *Chongqing Tiandi* Chongqing, China ○ Studio Shanghai *Cambridge Water Town* Shanghai, China
05 AECOM *Shenzhen Meteorological Tower* Shenzen, China ○ Arquitectonica *City of Dreams* Macau ○ Carlos Zapata
dio *Bitexco Financial Tower* Ho Chi Minh City, Vietnam ○ Gluckman Mayner Architects *Hotel Puerta America* Madrid,
ain ○ Hodgetts + Fung *Yamano Gakuen Complex* Tokyo, Japan ○ Integrus *US Embassy Compound* Conakry, Guinea ○
de Partnership *MegaBox* Hong Kong ○ Kohn, Pederson, Fox *China Huaneng Group Headquarters* Beijing, China ○
hn, Pederson, Fox *Kerry Parkside Towers* Shanghai, China ○ Kohn, Pederson, Fox *Songdo International Business*
strict and Convensia Convention Center Incheon, South Korea ○ Kohn, Pederson, Fox *Hysan Place* Hong Kong ○ NBBJ
lcome Trust Sanger Institute Cambridgeshire, UK ○ NBBJ *The Sail at Marina Bay* Singapore ○ Perkins + Will *Tsinghua*
iversity Academy of Art and Design Beijing, China ○ Perkins + Will *Whitby Public Library and Civic Square* Whitby,
nada ○ RTKL *New Jiang Wan Cultural Center* Shanghai, China ○ Safdie Architects *Yad Vashem Holocaust History*
seum Jerusalem, Israel ○ Sasaki Associates *Mangrove Tree Resort* Hainan Island, China ○ Skidmore, Owings and
rrill *Edificio Portico* Madrid, Spain ○ Skidmore, Owings and Merrill *Zifeng Tower* Nanjing, China ○ Hellmuth, Obata +
ssabaum *5 Churchill Place at Canary Wharf* London, UK ○ Steven Holl Architects *Herning Museum of Contemporary Art*
rning, Denmark ○ Studio Daniel Libeskind *The Wohl Centre* Ramat-Gan, Israel ○ Toshiko Mori Architect *Newspaper*
fe, Jinhua Architecture Park Jinhua, China ○ Wimberly Allison Tong and Goo *Atlantis at The Palm* Dubai, UAE **2006**
quitectonica *Westin Lima Hotel and Convention Center* Lima, Peru ○ Arquitectonica *Agricultural Bank of China +*
nstruction Bank of China Shanghai, China ○ Bernard Tschumi Architects *Cultural Center* Bordeaux Cenon, France ○
nnon Design *Cancer Hospital, Tata Medical Centre* Kolkata, India ○ Duany Plater-Zyberk & Company *Schooner Bay*
eat Abaco, Bahamas ○ Gensler *Changi International Airport Terminal 2* Changi, Singapore ○ I. M. Pei Architect *Suzhou*
seum Suzhou, China ○ Murphy/Jahn *Leatop Plaza* Guangzhou, China ○ LOT-EK *Sanlitun North + South* Beijing,
na ○ Michael Graves and Associates *The Nile Corniche* Cairo, Egypt ○ Michael Maltzan Architecture *BookBar, Jinhua*
hitecture Park Jinhua, China ○ Morphosis *Phare Tower* La Défense, France ○ Payette Associates *The Aga Khan*
iversity Faculty of Arts and Sciences Master Plan Karachi, Pakistan ○ Pei Cobb Freed & Partners *Palazzo Lombardia*
an, Italy ○ Perkins + Will *VanDusen Botanical Garden Visitor Centre* Vancouver, Canada ○ HOK Sport *Emirates Stadium*
don, UK ○ Richard Meier and Partners Architects *Ara Pacis Museum* Rome, Italy ○ Sasaki Associates *798 Arts District*
ion Plan Beijing, China ○ Skidmore, Owings and Merrill *Knowledge and Innovation Community* Shanghai, China ○
dmore, Owings and Merrill *Almaty Financial District—Kazkommertsbank Headquarters* Almaty, Kazakhstan ○
dmore, Owings and Merrill *Burj Khalifa* Dubai, UAE **Superlatives (See 186)** Skidmore, Owings and Merrill *Arcapita Bank*
adquarters Manama, Bahrain ○ Skidmore, Owings and Merrill *Al Hamra Tower* Kuwait City, Kuwait ○ Skidmore, Owings
Merrill *Cayan Tower* Dubai, UAE ○ Skidmore, Owings and Merrill *Pearl River Tower* Guangzhou, China ○ Sorg
hitects *US Embassy* Libreville, Gabon ○ Steven Holl Architects *Vanke Center* Shenzen, China ○ Studio Shanghai
gnan Tiandi Foshan, China ○ studio SUMO *Josai University School of Management* Sakado, Japan **2007** Arquitectonica
VA/Torre Begonias Lima, Peru ○ Asymptote Architecture *Yas Marina Hotel* Abu Dhabi, UAE ○ Hellmuth, Obata +
ssabaum *Dubai Marina* Dubai, UAE ○ Jerde Partnership *Dubai Festival Waterfront Centre* Dubai, UAE ○ Kevin Roche
n Dinkeloo and Associates *Convention Centre Dublin* Dublin, Ireland ○ Perkins + Will *Art House Residential Building*
Paulo, Brazil ○ Perkins + Will *Hazel McCallion Academic Learning Centre, University of Toronto* Mississauga, Canada ○
ston Scott Cohen *Nanjing Performing Arts Center* Nanjing, China ○ Preston Scott Cohen *Tel Aviv Museum* Tel Aviv,
el ○ Preston Scott Cohen *Taiyuan Museum* Taiyuan, China ○ Reiser + Umemoto RUR Architecture PC *O-14 Tower*
bai, UAE ○ Richard Meier and Partners Architects *Arp Museum* Rolandseck, Germany ○ Skidmore, Owings and Merrill
Corporate Headquarters Beijing, China ○ Skidmore, Owings and Merrill *Beijing Finance Street* Beijing, China ○
dmore, Owings and Merrill *Zhengzhou Greenland Plaza* Zhengzhou, China ○ Slade Architecture *Barbie Shanghai*
gship Store Shanghai, China ○ Stan Allen Architect *Salim Publishing House, Paju Book City* Paju, South Korea ○
ven Holl Architects *Capitaland Raffles City* Chengdu, China ○ Studio Daniel Libeskind *Royal Ontario Museum* Toronto,
ada ○ Studio Hillier *Rohm and Haas China* Pudong, China **2008** Adrian Smith + Gordon Gill Architecture *Masdar*
adquarters Abu Dhabi, UAE ○ Arquitectonica *Sun and Sky Towers at The Gate Shams* Dubai, UAE ○ Gehry Partners *Art*
ery of Ontario Toronto, Canada ○ Hashim Sarkis Studios *Housing for the Fishermen of Tyre* Abbasiyeh, Lebanon ○
. Pei Architect *Museum of Islamic Art* Doha, Qatar ○ Kohn, Pederson, Fox *Lotte World Tower* Seoul, South Korea ○
n, Pederson, Fox *Two Kingdom Street* London, UK ○ Kohn, Pederson, Fox *Ventura Corporate Towers* Rio de Janeiro,
zil ○ Kohn, Pederson, Fox *Chongqing International Trade and Commerce Center* Chongqing, China ○ NBBJ *Kintex II*

Expo Center Goyang, South Korea ○ Pei Cobb Freed & Partners *Torre Espacio* Madrid, Spain ○ Pelli Clarke Pelli Architect *Torre de Cristal* Madrid, Spain ○ Perkins + Will *Flatiron Building* Vancouver, Canada ○ RTKL *China Science and Technolog Museum* Beijing, China ○ RTKL *Dream Mall* Kaoshuing, Taiwan ○ Sasaki Associates *American University in Cairo New Campus* Cairo, Egypt ○ Sasaki Associates *LuLu Island Neighborhood 3 Arzanah Master Plan* Abu Dhabi, UAE ○ Skidmore Owings and Merrill *US Embassy* Beijing, China ○ Skidmore, Owings and Merrill *Esentai Tower* Almaty, Kazakhstan ○ Skidmore, Owings and Merrill *NATO Headquarters* Brussels, Belgium ○ Kohn, Pederson, Fox *25 Churchill Place at Cana Wharf* London, UK ○ Studio Daniel Libeskind *Westside Shopping and Leisure Centre* Basel, Switzerland ○ STUDIOS Architecture *Louis Dreyfus Grande Armée* Paris, France ○ Vincent James Associates Architects *Charles Hostler Student Center at American University of Beirut* Beirut, Lebanon ○ Weiss/Manfredi *Taekwondo Park* Muju, South Korea **2009** Diller Scofidio + Renfro *Museum of Image and Sound* Rio de Janeiro, Brazil ○ Gehry Partners *Novartis Pharma A.G. Campus* Basel, Switzerland ○ Goettsch Partners *Xi'an City Gateway* Xi'an, China ○ Hellmuth, Obata + Kassabaum *Abu Dhabi National Oil Company Headquarters* Abu Dhabi, UAE ○ Hellmuth, Obata + Kassabaum *Capital Market Authority Tower* Riyadh, Saudi Arabia ○ Kohn, Pederson, Fox *Guangzhou CTF Finance Centre* Guangzhou, China ○ Leong Leong *Philip Lim Store* Seoul, South Korea ○ MOS *Lali Gurans Orphanage and Learning Centre* Jorpati, Nepal ○ over,under an Utile Inc. *Sowwah Island Vision Plan* Abu Dhabi, UAE ○ Pei Cobb Freed & Partners *First International Bank of Israel* Te Aviv, Israel ○ Pei Cobb Freed & Partners *WaveRock* Hyderabad, India ○ Pei Cobb Freed & Partners *World One* Mumbai, India ○ Perkins + Will *Princess Nora Bint Abdulrahman University* Riyadh, Saudi Arabia ○ Perkins + Will *Laboratório Fleury Itaim* São Paulo, Brazil ○ Perkins + Will *McMaster University Engineering Technology Building* Hamilton, Canada ○ Perkins + Will *Claudette McKay-Lassonde Pavilion, Western University* London, Canada ○ Populous *Soccer City* Johannesburg, South Africa ○ Rafael Viñoly Architects *Carrasco International Airport* Montevideo, Uruguay ○ Rafael Viñoly Architects *Fortabat Collection* Buenos Aires, Argentina ○ RTKL *360 Mall* Kuwait City, Kuwait **Big Box Rules (See 12** RTKL *Dolce Vita Tejo Mall* Lisbon, Portugal ○ Selldorf Architects *Abercrombie and Fitch Flagship Store* Tokyo, Japan ○ Studio Shanghai *Naked Stables* Hangzhou, China **2010** Adrian Smith + Gordon Gill Architecture *Kingdom Tower* Jeddal Saudi Arabia ○ Bohlin Cywinski Jackso *Apple Store Ópera* Paris, France ○ Bohlin Cywinski Jackson *Apple Store Pudong* Shanghai, China **Network Patents** On March 20, 1883, five years before the Exposition Universelle of Paris, world leaders who had noticed that inventors did not attend the International Exhibition of Inventions in Vienna for fear that their work would be exploited, proposed creating an international treaty. Known as the Paris Convention, the treaty paved the way for internatio patent laws and helped to enforce them for the first time. Beginning January 6, 2014, the new Global Patent Prosecution Highway pilot program will operate as a trademark agreement among the established national agencies of its seventeen initial partners, which include Australia, Japan, China, Russia, Spain, and the United States. On January 24, 2013, the US Patent & Trademark Office published Apple's latest registered trademark certificate for Apple's "Distinctive Design & Layout." The text describing the identity architecture of the space says: "The mark consists of the design and layout of a retail store. The store features a clear glass storefront surrounded by a paneled façade consisting of large, rectangular horizontal panels over the to of the glass front, and two narrower panels stacked on either side of the storefront within the store." In a surreal twist, the patent of the space was granted in both black and white and in color, as if the stores were only an image. Now that architectu patents can be globally enforced by national institutions, we will surely see many rich regional takes on the perception of the "Apple Aura" that extend just safely beyond the image and form contained within the 4,277,913 and 4,277,914 patent registration numbers. Goettsch Partners *SIP Hengyu International Center Phase I + II* Suzhou, China ○ Hellmuth, Obata + Kassabaum *US Embassy New Office Annex* Moscow, Russia ○ Integrus *US Embassy Compound* Sarajevo, Bosnia and Herzegovina ○ Kennedy and Violich Architecture *IBA Soft House* Hamburg, Germany ○ KieranTimberlake *US Embassy* London, UK ○ Kohn, Pederson, Fox *Worldmark Development at Indira Ghandi International Airport* Gurgaon, India ○ Kohn, Pederson, Fox *International Commerce Centre* Hong Kong, China ○ L.E.FT *Beirut Exhibition Centre* Beirut, Lebanon ○ LOT-EK *APAP Open School* Anyang, South Korea ○ Pelli Clarke Pelli Architects *Shanghai International Finance Center* Pudong, China ○ Perkins + Will *Xi'an Jiaotong-Liverpool University* Shuzhou, China ○ Perkins + Will *Stronach Regional Cancer Centre* Newmarket, Canada ○ Perkins + Will *The Irving Greenberg Family Cancer Centre* Ottawa, Canada ○ Populous *Aviva Stadium* Dublin, Ireland ○ REX *Vakko Headquarters and Power Media Center* Istanbu Turkey ○ Sasaki Associates *Singapore University of Technology and Design Master Plan* Singapore, Singapore ○ SHoP *Botswana Innovation Hub* Gaborone, Botswana ○ SO-IL *Kukje Art Center* Seoul, South Korea **2011** Hashim Sarkis Studios *Byblos Town Hall* Byblos, Lebanon ○ Höweler + Yoon Architecture *Sky Courts* Chengdu, China ○ Jerde Partnership *Konoha Eco-Mall* Fukuoka, Japan ○ Philip Johnson Alan Ritchie Architects *Millenia Walk* Singapore, Singapore ○ MASS Design Group *Butaro District Hospital* Butaro, Rwanda **Doing Good (See 227)** NBBJ *City of Capitals* Moscow, Russia ○ Pelli Clarke Pelli Architects *Iberdrola Tower* Bilbao, Spain ○ Perkins + Will *University of Calgary Energy Environment Experiential Learning Building* Calgary, Canada ○ RTKL *Metropolis Mall* Moscow, Russia ○ Safdie Architects *Marina Bay Sands Integrated Resort* Singapore, Singapore ○ Safdie Architects *Khalsa Heritage Centre* Ananc Sahib, Punjab ○ Sasaki Associates *LuLu Island Neighborhood 3 Rihan Heights Residential Development, Arzanah Maste Plan* Abu Dhabi, UAE ○ Single Speed Design *White Block Gallery* Heyri, South Korea ○ Skidmore, Owings and Merrill *Tianjin World Financial Center* Tianjin, China ○ Studio Daniel Libeskind *Reflections at Keppel Bay* Keppel Bay, Singapor

dio SUMO *Mizuta Museum Of Art* Sakado, Japan ○ Tod Williams Billie Tsien Architects *Asia Society Hong Kong Center*
ng Kong, China ○ WORKac *New Holland Island* St Petersburg, Russia **2012** Adrian Smith + Gordon Gill Architecture
nfu Ecological City Master Plan Chengdu, China ○ AECOM *London 2012 Olympic Legacy Communities Scheme* London,
○ ATOPIA *Waterbank School, Uasonyiro Primary School* Laikipia, Kenya ○ Cannon Design (Yazdani Studio) *Ordos*
staurant Kaokaoshina, Mongolia ○ FXFOWLE Architects *King Abdullah Financial District* Riyadh, Saudi Arabia ○
hry Partners Biomuseo Panama City, Panama ○ Gensler *Incheon International Airport Terminal 2* Incheon, South
rea ○ Gensler *The Avenues* Kuwait City, Kuwait ○ Gensler *Chennai International Airport* Chennai, India ○ Goettsch
rtners Chengdu Poly Towers Chengdu, China ○ Hellmuth, Obata + Kassabaum *Baku Flame Towers* Baku, Azerbaijan ○
SS Design Group Butaro Doctors' Housing Butaro, Rwanda ○ MOS *Krabbesholm Art/Architecture Design School* Kirke
llinge, Denmark ○ NADAAA *Model Home Gallery* Seoul, South Korea ○ NBBJ *Uralkali Corporation* Berezniki, Russia ○
RA Inside Out Museum Beijing, China ○ Organization For Permanent Modernity *Firestation and Youth Center* Asse,
lgium ○ Goettsch Partners *Sowwah Square* Abu Dhabi, UAE ○ Perkins + Will *Simcoe Muskoka Regional Cancer Centre*
rrie, Canada ○ Populous *Olympic Stadium* London, UK ○ Richard Meier and Partners Architects *OCT Shenzhen*
ubhouse Shenzen, China ○ Sasaki Associates *University of Balamand Library Learning Center* El Khoura, Lebanon ○
saki Associates University of Balamand Souk El Gharb Campus Souk El Gharb, Lebanon ○ WORKac *L'Assemblée*
diuese Libreville, Gabon ○ **2013** ATOPIA *Waterbank Dormitory for Girls, Endana Secondary School* Laikipia, Kenya ○
OPIA Waterbank Canteen and Kitchen, Endana Secondary School Laikipia, Kenya ○ Cannon Design (Yazdani Studio)
k Nicklaus Golf Club of Korea New Songdo City, South Korea ○ Hellmuth, Obata + Kassabaum *Kempegowda*
ernational Airport Bangalore, India ○ LEESER Architecture *Tri-Climatic Biosphere* Abu Dhabi, UAE ○ Louise Braverman,
chitect Village Housing Works Staff Residence Kigutu, Burundi ○ Louise Braverman, Architect *Centro de Artes Nadir*
onso Museum Boticas, Portugal ○ NADAAA *University of Toronto Faculty of Architecture, Landscape, and Design* Toronto,
nada ○ NADAAA *University of Melbourne Faculty of Architecture, Building and Planning* Melbourne, Australia **Around**
Clock (See 37, 52, 144) OBRA *Sahne School* Beijing, China ○ Pelli Clarke Pelli Architects *The Landmark* Abu Dhabi,
E ○ Perkins + Will *Antilia House* Mumbai, India ○ Robert A. M. Stern Architects *One Horizon Center* Gurgaon, India ○
bert A. M. Stern Architects Tour Carpe Diem La Défense, France ○ Sasaki Associates *Thu Thiem New Urban Area*
Chi Minh City, Vietnam ○ SHoP *Konza Techno Pavilion+ City* Nairobi, Kenya ○ Zimmer Gunsul Frasca *US Embassy*
grade, Serbia **2014** AECOM *Al Waab City* Doha, Qatar **Labor LEED Today, ethical imperatives are hovering over**
hitectural practices worldwide. The notion of exploitation, environmental or human, is being addressed from a place that
hitecture has still not been able to translate into any of its classical principles for the generation of form, space, or program
ond simply checking, with better or worse taste, a compliance box. The US Green Building Council (USGBC), the developer
he LEED building rating system, was created in 1993. The aura surrounding LEED Platinum certification has become a
ldwide common object of desire among developers and clients, more powerful than any local code. Buildings around the
ld are being designed to enter the club of the consciously responsible in relationship to energy consumption and sustainable
ctices. In a parallel manner, the growing awareness on the conditions of labor in construction sites worldwide makes us
ect about questions of human sustainability and the design principles necessary to be applied, either through measuring tools
esign strategies, to make the building of architecture an ethically sustainable construct. What are the mechanisms for
ducing the desire for human sustainability? Antoine Predock Architect PC *Education City* Doha, Qatar ○ Antoine
dock Architect PC Canadian Museum for Human Rights Ottawa, Canada ○ ATOPIA *PitchKenya Waterbank Sport/*
ool/Community Building, Endana Secondary School Laikipia, Kenya ○ MASS Design Group *Neonatal Intensive Care*
r Rwinkwavu, Rwanda ○ Populous *Olympic Stadium* Sochi, Russia ○ Robert A. M. Stern Architects *Dalian AVIC*
rnational Square Dalian, China ○ Sasaki Associates *Songzhuang Arts and Agriculture City* Beijing, China ○ Single
ed Design Songpa Micro-Housing Seoul, South Korea ○ STUDIOS Architecture *Jaipur Residential Development*
ur, India ○ Toshiko Mori Architect *Cultural Center* Sinthian, Senegal ○ OFFICEUS *ARCHITECTURE NEW WORLD*
375° N, 12.3358° E **Mission Statement "Quality, Integrity, Excellence" these three nouns are the words below the logo of**
Alabama-based construction company CADDELL. They have been involved in a multiplicity of projects made by US firms
nd the globe and in the United States, including the new Jackson County Adult Detention Center. When one explores further
their "ethics" section one reads: "The reputation of Caddell Construction Co. for integrity and fair dealing is one of our
t valuable and protected assets. Caddell conducts its business in strict compliance with applicable laws and regulations
maintains a strong commitment to perform to the highest professional and ethical standards. Caddell is a principal member
e Construction Industry Ethics & Compliance Initiative and has a full-time Ethics Officer. At Caddell, ethics matter and
pliance counts. Neither is optional." Integrity, sustainability, quality or excellence, are some of the most common terms
d in the mission statements of today's architecture firms. A word is a word is a word is a world?

EVA FRANCH i GILABERT, ANA MILJAČKI, ASHLEY SCHAFER:
CURATORS

Office*US* Agenda

The archive of architectural knowledge has never been vaster or flatter. In a field in which nearly all critical driving narratives have been dissolved, when even the smallest idea is preserved for posterity somewhere in the electronic ether, historical baggage is the first to get lost, and with it ideological positions, ingenuity, hopes, and potential lessons for addressing the challenges of our time. Some of those challenges are enduring: social equity, civil rights, access to information, freedom of expression. Others are newly pressing: survival of the planet, resource scarcity, global poverty. In order to begin reconstituting appropriately contemporary forms of political and social imagination out of the depths of the architectural archive, Office*US* presents a specifically global history of the architectural office while mapping aspirations for its future. It locates the intersection of the operations of US architectural firms in the last century and the global impact of their production. A live, working, global *office* surrounded by a survey of nearly a thousand projects produced by US offices abroad between 1914 and 2014, Office*US* serves simultaneously as an archeology of global architectural firms and a critical challenge to them.

The reconsideration of these projects—unfolding on the premises of the US Pavilion over the course of the Venice Biennale—demands that the knowledge contained in the archive be evaluated in the context of contemporary wisdom on the successes and failures of the projects in question. Revisiting one hundred years of US architecture's global production in conditions that are decidedly different from those in which the projects were initially conceived opens it to engagement and "ownership" by a vast and heterogeneous audience. As much as this archaeology demands historical self-consciousness from contemporary production—highlighting the extent to which our present is the inevitable outcome of the histories examined by Office*US*—the six months of the live reactivation of the archive will project alternative futures out of its material.

US Office

"Organization for Efficient Practice" was the title of an inquiry that *Architectural Record* serialized in the early 1960s.[1] One after another, firms dealing with projects of unprecedented size described the state of architectural affairs. Each of the partners, contributing their initials to acronyms (CRS, HOK, DMJM) destined to survive them, offered their approach to running architecture firms, all of them handling exceedingly complicated commissions. Realizing projects at a significant geographical distance from their office headquarters required

[1]
"Organization for Efficient Practice" inquiry ran as a series between 1960 and 1963 in *Architectural Record*.

teamwork for CRS.[2] Working in the context of "enormous freedoms and possibilities" for the architect required dealing with meaning from within the discipline for HOK.[3] Balancing good design with good business motivated the American "mall-maker," Victor Gruen. Organizational diagrams and checklists accompanied statements about the ability to build an effective staffquickly, which was seen as "second in importance only to getting the contract."[4]

Such operationally complex US architectural firms, whose 1960s concerns could not be more topical today, had already been described in 1947 by a key endorser of architectural modernism, historian Henry-Russell Hitchcock, as the paradigmatic opposite of the firms organized around the figure of a singular architectural genius. Hitchcock had proposed that the model of the firm specializing in delivering industrial and basic institutional architecture had originated even earlier, at the turn of the century, with offices like Albert Kahn's — one of the biggest exporters of factories — only to be perfectly embodied by a firm like SOM years later.[5]

More than a decade after Hitchcock's challenge to critics and historians to find a way to appropriately evaluate the work produced by large architectural offices, the Italian journal *Zodiac* considered the "rise to prominence of American architecture" by highlighting figures like Frank Lloyd Wright, Walter Gropius, Minoru Yamasaki, each propped up by large architectural offices at that point.[6] The cultural and economic logic of the postwar Pax Americana had brought foreign commissions that required some large offices to produce civic and representative buildings (not only the most efficient and industrial ones), challenging the basis for the distinction that Hitchcock had made in 1947. His earlier argument morphed into a related one in the 1961 *America* issue of *Zodiac 8*. While no longer insisting on the distinction between the genius and bureaucracy, he held onto the idea that organizational and architectural proficiency went hand in hand, proposing that the global transfer of US expertise in building skyscrapers was occurring jointly with the transfer of office organization. Just as in the late 1920s, when Kahn's tractor factory production in Russia involved a transfer of Taylorist management together with specific architectural expertise in factory construction, it took foreign companies learning how to run their businesses like "American skyscraper firms" in order to build equivalent architectures.[7] During the last century, this logic of the symbiotic architectural and operational transfer applied to the making of universities, museums, and malls, just as much as it did to airports and incinerators.[8]

Self-consciously recasting Hitchcock, Office*US*'s examination of US architectural offices as historical actors and forms of intelligence, together with their production abroad since 1914, is the first contemporary recasting of a set of historical concerns in a series of many that this project will undertake during its operation in Venice. Set in a new relation, Hitchcock's terms of inquiry highlight two sites at which modernism, in the broad sense, was practiced and "absorbed": the office itself and its operation on foreign grounds. The architectural office has been the site of labor and intrigue, of everyday office grind, dress codes, drawing conventions, layers, playlists, inequalities, overtime, and bonuses, as much as it has represented a business lineage,

(2)
Texas firm Caudill Rowlett Scott (CRS) devised a series of strategies (programming, squatting) for managing clients within the United States at a distance from their office and were able to transfer much of that intelligence to their international work. See, "Organization for Efficient Practice 4: Caudill, Rowlett and Scott, Architects-Planners-Engineers," *Architectural Record*, November 1960, 179–84.

(3)
Gyo Obata's opening of the HOK presentation in *Architectural Record* described the context in which architects operated in the sixties as one without any constraints, in response to which he proposed holding onto the disciplinary interior. This perhaps ironically relates a proto-autonomy thesis to corporate architectural production in ways that are seldom discussed. See, "Organization for Efficient Practice 5: Hellmuth, Obata and Kassabaum, Inc., Architects," *Architectural Record*, February 1961, 137–44.

(4)
In one form or another each of the texts about efficient practice address this topic.

(5)
Henry-Russell Hitchcock, "The Architecture of Bureaucracy and the Architecture of Genius," *Architectural Review* 101, 1947, 3–6.

(6)
See the entire issue of *Zodiac 8: America*, edited by Bruno Alfieri, Milan 1961. At this point Gropius was already seventy-five, so his inclusion in *America* at the expense of a real treatment of TAC, is symptomatic of the period's inability to deal with the real nature of a

a family tree of ideas about architectural practice and about architecture. Efficiency, specialization, and collaboration have contributed to the body politics and the business dimensions of US architectural offices. Focus on these offices' work abroad distinguishes those capable of running operations across national boundaries in the last century: the exceptionally "efficient practices."[9]

The basic trends in US architects' work abroad confirm the general understanding of globalization, with the amount of work in the period from 1914 to the 1990s equaling the production of US-designed architecture abroad in the last two decades. But the commissions that US architects built at the beginning of the twentieth century and throughout the Cold War also challenge and complicate the same understanding of architectural globalization. In various ways, US architectural production on foreign land reveals a diverse cast of agents who enabled the work before any multinational companies—globalization's key perpetrators—existed. Varying as much as their motivations do, these include the US government, local political and philanthropic agencies, and national and international clients and developers.

The offices and the actual sites of their architectural impact abroad are linked through the thousand and one stories that implicate the production of architecture within politics, technology, and economy. Like Scheherazade's *One Thousand and One Nights*, these stories form a continuous chain.[10] Whereas in the legend, the nights of storytelling were a brilliant survival tactic, here the stories are ones of desperation, survival, and the triumph of US architecture over the last century and across all continents. In these stories, architecture always depends.[11] Though with different emphases, architecture is a shared concern of many agents; its story neither precedes the circumstances that make it possible nor ends once immortalized by a famous photographer or historian.

When even Turner, the biggest general builder and construction management company in the United States "is an AECOM company," and it seems that the sheer size and operational complexity of the new architectural entity is instigating new qualitative and organizational paradigms, OfficeUS provides a space to resist and challenge the "inevitable" and the inherited models of architectural production.[12]

OfficeUS

As a critical examination of history and a reflection on contemporary possibilities of collaboration, OfficeUS actively prototypes alternatives to existing forms of architectural production in a global context by creating a worldwide network of individuals that forms part of OfficeUS. Although OfficeUS is free of financial pressure—in direct opposition to every US office featured in the exhibition—it performs as an office in key ways.

Each element of OfficeUS recasts a specific operational and spatial logic of the architectural office. OfficeUS is run by OfficeUS Partners,situated in OfficeUS Headquarters, branded by OfficeUS Identity, supplied by the OfficeUS Repository of OfficeUS Project Binders; it relies on consulting and production assistance from its OfficeUS Outposts, strategically located in offices as well as academic, political, and cultural institutions around

complex office. For more on this see Michael Kubo, "The Anxiety of Anonymity: Bureaucracy and Genius in Late Modern Architecture Industry," in Ila Berman and Edward Mitchell (eds). *101st Proceedings: New Constellations New Ecologies*, ACSA, 2013.

⑦
See, Henry-Russell Hitchcock, "The Rise to World Prominence of American Architecture," *Zodiac 8: America*, 1961.

⑧
These are just some of the broad programmatic categories in the OfficeUS *Repository* and exhibition; projects include TAC's University of Baghdad, Yamasaki's Dhahran International Airport, HOK's King Khalid International Airport, and Marion Mahony and Walter Burley Griffin's incinerators across Australia.

⑨
"The US Building Abroad" *Architectural Forum*, January 1955.

⑩
See Anonymous, *Tales from the Thousand and One Nights*, (London: Penguin Classics, 1973).

⑪
Borrowing the title of Jeremy Till's 2009 *Architecture Depends* helps call out something that all architectural offices, especially those operating over large geographical distances from their construction sites, know and embody organizationally: production of architecture depends on many difficult, contingent, messily political, and sometimes banal factors. See Jeremy Till, *Architecture Depends* (Cambridge, MA: The MIT Press, 2009).

⑫
In December 2013, a sign on one of Turner's

the world; it is visited and challenged by a cast of Office*US* Experts who otherwise present themselves as architects, artists, philosophers, scientists, and entrepreneurs. Office*US* communicates with its Outposts, Experts, and the entire Office*US* Network of kindred spirits via Office*US* Portals. Office*US* is constantly revising its operational critique and manifesto, the Office*US* Manual. Office*US*'s daily operations rely on the twenty-five Office*US* Issues in order to devise the future Office*US* Agenda.

Headquartered in the 1930 Delano & Aldrich-designed US Pavilion in Venice, Office*US* is run by the Office*US* Partners, selected from an international call. Office*US* Partners are emerging architects fewer than fifteen years out of school who hold a particular interest in the production of architectural discourse and knowledge. Their explicit task is to look backward and forward simultaneously, submitting both historical material and office protocols to contemporary critique, pessimism, and optimism. Their engagement of this history allows for contemporary interests and challenges to become manifest from within the archive and to be folded into it for posterity.

The history of US architectural offices operating abroad over the last hundred years is presented through a project library, the Office*US* Repository. The establishment of each office and the completion of each architectural project are treated as events in the Repository and presented in the format of the ubiquitous project binder. Chronologically organized, project and office binders, consisting of texts, images, and drawings, allow for historical patterns, geopolitical movements, and architectural themes to emerge from a comparative and cumulative overview. The binders contain basic descriptions as well as information regarding key details and the historical reception of the projects. Together, Office*US* Binders form a repository of knowledge for future production and discourse in general and the foundation for the work of Office*US* Partners.

The selection of projects included in the Office*US* Repository is driven by the importance of the local, global, and historical narratives that they are imbricated within. The ambition for this collection of material is to provide a mirror, a vast register for comparisons, and a dense visual experience.[13] While the Office*US* Repository presents a battering visual experience at a glance, its depth and the operations of the office ensure that the critical mirroring function of the collection is made specific and urgent.

The twenty-five weeks of Office*US* production are scripted in dialogue with twenty-five Office*US* Issues addressing the most pressing questions that endure historically, or that register contemporary anxieties born of practicing in the global context.[14] Each theme, including Anger/Love Management, International Comfort, and Superlatives, has multiple manifestations within the collection of projects in the Repository. Marking the Repository wall through openings that anticipate the work of the office, and manifesting in the office in the form of a wall calendar, each of the twenty-five Office*US* Issues will seed a week of exploration during the Biennale. Together with the Office*US* Agenda, which highlights some of the key historical narratives emerging in the last century of global architectural production, Office*US* Issues provide tools of engagement not only for Office*US* participants but also for Office*US* visitors.

construction sites in Boston read: "Turner is an AECOM company." AECOM, Architecture Engineering and Construction Company, established in the 1990s, currently comprises more than forty entities (some dating back to the 1900s). It is a Fortune 500 company with clients in over 150 countries and outposts on every continent. *World Architecture 100, Building Design*'s annual survey of the top 100 firms, lists four US architecture firms in its 2013 top ten, with AECOM and Gensler a mere fifty employed architects apart (AECOM: 1,370, Gensler: 1,346); in both cases, fee income is noted at more than $400 million.

(13) This ambition is in conscious conversation with Arthur Drexler's "Transformations" show at MoMA in 1979, "to hit in the head with" visual material. See, Arthur Drexler, "Response: Arthur Drexler on 'Transformations'," *Skyline*, Summer 1979, 6.

(14) Office*US* Issues are: Ex-Im, Trojan Horses, Best Practices, Crude Ideals, Democratizing Action, International Comfort, Reprogramming, The Invisibles, Global Citizenship, Magical States, Profit Margin, Smart Concrete, Little Americas, Anger/ Love Management, Cargo Cult, Housing Public Good, Bullets Without Ideology, Code Upgrade, Culture Capital, Superlatives, Big Box Rules, Network Patents, Mission Good, Around the clock, Labor LEED, Mission Statement. Summer 1979, 6.

Flipping through the pages of dusty 1920s issues of *Architectural Forum*, ogling the midcentury archives of Ezra Stoller and Julius Shulman, or Googling contemporary firms, one notices the period changes in the medium and style of the portraits of US architectural offices, but they all show architects at their drafting tables. The table dominates the self-presentation of architectural offices nearly as much as the presence of male architects. As the minimum amount of infrastructure needed for an office, and the most representative site of its operations, the table is at the center of the Office*US* Head-quarters, designed by New York architecture firm Leong Leong. Providing for individual and collective occupation, the table's continuous surface supports and fuses work, display, and play. Every physical piece of the Office*US* Headquarters similarly recasts and estranges work through play and display.

The Office*US* Binders are marked by the firm's latest logo, enlisting the strength of the office identity designs to provide navigation through the Repository. Learning from this history, the Office*US* Identity designed by Natasha Jen/Pentagram constructs a visual interplay between the historical understandings of the corporate, institutional, and avant-garde forms of communication. Permeating the space of the Headquarters in the US Pavilion, Office*US* Identity also holds together four Office*US* publications produced in partnership with Lars Müller: Office*US* Agenda, Office*US* Atlas, Office*US* Manual, and Office*US* New World.

The Office*US* Portals, both physical and digital, contain the historical and real-time technologies and contents produced by and for Office*US*, allowing the entire Office*US* Network to participate in and contribute to the production of ideas and work. The digital and physical platforms, based in open-source technologies, provide social, technological, and actual spaces of convergence and disruption that allow users and visitors to move through time (1914–2014) and space (Venice–the World).

Just as the word *office* is a homonym for the firm and its business and organizational dimensions and for the space in which it operates, the term *agenda* has the capacity to simultaneously refer to a constellation of programmatic aspirations, to a concrete plan of action, and even the device in which these are recorded. Thinking and operating historically and globally, Office*US* collaboratively constructs an agenda for the contemporary and future production of architecture. In this task it is aided by the expertise in the following pages.

AMANDA REESER LAWRENCE, ASHLEY SCHAFER:

EDITORS

Sections Through Office*US*

Agenda slices through the Office*US* exhibition at the Venice Biennale with a series of section "cuts," flattening information in one dimension in order to reveal otherwise concealed adjacencies and alignments, structures and infrastructures. Reconfiguring what we think we know about the US architectural office and its export and revealing an entirely new dimension of structure, these cuts are intentionally and explicitly partial. Thus, *Agenda* enables multiple interpretations of the thousand projects lining the walls of the US Pavilion, while also standing as an independent document that constructs its own stories. Projective rather than simply descriptive, *Agenda* transforms the normative "catalogue" into a tool that both complements and complexifies the material in the exhibition.

Taking Office*US*—the archive of projects and the twenty-five issues listed in the first pages of this book—as its starting point, this publication articulates and consolidates various accounts (often overlapping) of the professionalization of practice, the international transfer and translation of standards and ideologies, and the dissemination and uptake of US design and design practices globally. *Agenda's* three sections—"Expertise," "Exchange," and "Export"—roughly correspond to these three narratives and serve as conceptual containers through which to interpret the work of US architectural firms abroad. They foreground the cross-national relationships—the motivations and intentions—that gave rise to the firms' commissions as well as their design, production, and reception. By establishing connections across and groupings within the vast expanse of the Repository, *Agenda* extracts intellectual threads and locates conceptual affiliations in counterpoint to the rigorously chronological framework of the exhibition.

"Expertise" focuses on architectural practices whose development of specialized knowledge—formal signatures, technical innovations, operational processes, design atmospheres—brought them export commissions. Yet arguably, it is the professionalization of practice itself that stands as the most significant contribution the United States has made to the discipline in the last century as it has shifted from atelier-based studios to corporate partnerships to conglomerate enterprises. "Expertise" traces these developments from Albert Kahn's hierarchical organization and parsing of the design process into component tasks through the midcentury "org-men" of SOM, CRS, and TAC, mapping the history of the office structure alongside its output. This section also traces the development of office furniture systems as a site of architecture's confrontation with information and management, along with shifting contemporary notions of the office and its move into the "boudoir."

"Exchange" considers the multidirectional movement of architectural ideas, techniques, and materials as a reciprocal, though not necessarily equal, relationship. It examines the cultural dialogue enabled by US architectural actions abroad—at many scales and on nearly every continent of the world: urban plans in South America, solar houses in Africa, "supertall" towers in Asia and the Middle East, factories in Russia, incinerators in Australia, museums across the globe. The movement of architects themselves—both émigrés to the United States and expats living abroad—forms an important part of this story, along with the discursive exchanges that accompany the mutual infection of ideas and ideologies Technologies and typologies, too, establish particular currencies of exchange: a US-designed tower or museum is commissioned to serve as imprimatur of a city or country's entry into the global economy; economic capital (the funding of an architectural firm's work) is exchanged for cultural or political capital.

In contrast to the reciprocity of "Exchange," "Export" implies a unidirectional transfer of US culture, spaces, materials, and lifestyle. While the term "export" as applied to architecture is, in reality, a fiction, or more properly a trope, the transpositional nature of export often produces uneasy or contested conditions. This section considers architectures that remain "of" the United States, even as they occupy foreign territory. Iconic buildings and projects—embassies, expos, hotels, and other "little Americas"—are the most didactic forms of architectural export; while a more subtle yet pervasive export of US ideologies occurs through the introduction (and imposition) of standards of so-called progress to third-world cultures in the form of so-called socially responsible projects.

While an exhibition catalogue typically contains explanatory essays and a list of works on display, *Agenda* instead proposes a more radical framework—a second-order curation. The material oscillates between essays, comparative visual narratives, and information graphics that recast the material of Office*US*. Here, the logic of the sectional "cut" is deployed in the range of methodological formats. Essays engage the question of US export via the archive and through the lens of historical framing. Visual narratives bring together drawings, photographs, and diagrams to elucidate connections within the Repository and tell new stories using graphic rather than textual means. And information graphics (largely timelines and map-based material) condense and organize data collected on the thousand projects to allow both an overall picture (where the projects exist in the world, for example, or how they track against fluctuations in global currencies or current events) as well as selective readings of a particular region or time. The diversity in article types reflects the editorial intention to have both the form and content of *Agenda* reflect and enable these different cuts.

This mix of formats reflects a working methodology bringing together technology, culture, politics, history, and project documentation in response to the theme of the professionalization of US practice and its export. *Agenda* operates as a responsive collection, a feedback loop whose structure and content emerged through a dialogue with the material rather than a predetermined editorial structure. Beginning with a desire to cull coherent and revealing stories out of the Repository, and relate them to the curatorial "Issues," this working method has produced a document which recasts the Office*US* exhibition and reframes a body of work that, obscured by time and distance, has been largely written out of the last century's fairly narrow architectural cannon. *Agenda's* sections reveal the operational history and architectural richness of design for export and reactivate the stories of the "invisibles"—women, early solar designers, global standards and codes, corporate firms, oil economies, third-world political dynamics, and others—who were nevertheless radically formative in shaping the global contemporary built environment.

Office*US*: Firms

Date Established and Selected Projects Abroad.

Offices are listed by current or last known name. Projects are listed by date of commission.

1 SmithGroupJJR
2 The Austin Company
3 Shepley Bulfinch
4 McKim, Mead and White
5 Holabird and Root
6 George A. Fuller Company
7 Graham, Anderson, Probst & White
8 Frank Lloyd Wright
9 Perkins, Fellows and Hamilton
10 Albert Kahn Associates
11 Cass Gilbert
12 Warren and Wetmore
13 Ayres, York and Sawyer
14 William Welles Bosworth
15 Delano and Aldrich
16 John Russell Pope
17 Thomas W. Lamb
18 William E. Parsons
19 Walker and Gillette
20 Walter Burley Griffin and Marion Mahony
21 Henry Killam Murphy
22 Helmle and Corbett
23 Leo A Daly
24 A. Epstein and Sons International
25 Raymond & Rado
26 Schultze and Weaver
27 Harrison and Abramovitz
28 Perry Dean Rogers Partners
29 Paul Williams
30 Shreve, Lamb and Harmon
31 Richard J. Neutra
32 Edward Durell Stone and Associates
33 Ellerbe Becket
34 Louis I. Kahn
35 Perkins + Will
36 Adrian Wilson Associates
37 Skidmore, Owings and Merrill
38 A. L. Aydelott and Associates
39 Marcel Breuer Associates
40 The Eggers Group
41 The Office of Ludwig Mies van der Rohe
42 Arthur B. Froehlich and Associates
43 Carl Koch
44 HKS, Inc.
45 Joseph Allen Stein and Associates
46 Morris Lapidus Associates
47 Philip Johnson Alan Ritchie Architects
48 Ralph Rapson
49 Town Planning Associates
50 Zimmer Gunsul Frasca
51 NBBJ
52 Cannon Design
53 H2L2/NELSON
54 The Architects Collaborative
55 Wimberly Allison Tong and Goo
56 CRSS Inc.
57 Daniel Mann Johnson Mendenhall
58 RTKL
59 Bassetti Architects
60 Harry Weese Associates

61 Lathrop Douglass
62 Donald Hatch and Associates
63 John Johansen
64 Edward Larabee Barnes Associates
65 KlingStubbins
66 ROMA Design Group
67 Eero Saarinen and Associates
68 William L. Pereira & Associates
69 Eduardo Catalano
70 Paul Rudolph
71 Victor Gruen International
72 Davis Brody Bond
73 Integrus
74 John Portman and Associates
75 Sasaki Associates
76 Sert, Jackson and Associates
77 John Hejduk
78 Robert P. Madison International, Inc.
79 Victor A. Lundy
80 Hellmuth, Obata + Kassabaum
81 Pei Cobb Freed & Partners Architects
82 Wiliam B. Tabler Architects
83 Yamasaki and Associates
84 Brown Daltas and Associates
85 Mitchell/Giurgola Associates
86 The Leonard Parker Associates
87 Venturi, Scott Brown and Associates
88 Payette Associates
89 Cambridge Seven Associates
90 Gehry Partners
91 Kallmann McKinnell & Wood Architects
92 Michael Graves and Associates
93 Tigerman McCurry Architects
94 Christopher Alexander
95 Gunnar Birkerts and Associates
96 Polshek Partnership
97 Richard Meier and Partners Architects
98 Eisenman Architects
99 Gwathmey Siegel Kaufman Architects
100 Benjamin Thompson Associates
101 Bohlin Cywinski Jackson
102 Gensler
103 Hartman-Cox Architects
104 Kevin Roche John Dinkeloo and Associates
105 Studio Hillier
106 Antoine Predock Architect PC
107 Goettsch Partners
108 Morphosis
109 SITE
110 Machado and Silvetti Associates
111 Tod Williams Billie Tsien Architects
112 Ralph Lerner Architects
113 Kohn, Pederson, Fox
114 Steven Holl Architects
115 Arquitectonica
116 Gluckman Mayner Architects
117 Jerde Partnership
118 Moore Ruble Yudell
119 Pelli Clarke Pelli Architects
120 Robert A. M. Stern Architects

121 FXFOWLE Architects
122 Koetter Kim and Associates
123 Mack Architect
124 Safdie Architects
125 Diller Scofidio + Renfro
126 Santos Prescott and Associates
127 Duany Plater-Zyberk & Company
128 JAHN
129 Toshiko Mori Architect
130 Populous
131 Rafael Viñoly Architects
132 Hodgetts + Fung
133 KieranTimberlake
134 STUDIOS Architecture
135 Office dA
136 Reiser + Umemoto RUR Architecture PC
137 Sorg Architects
138 Acconci Studio
139 ATOPIA
140 Bernard Tschumi Architects
141 Selldorf Architects
142 Asymptote Architecture
143 LEESER Architecture
144 Preston Scott Cohen
145 Studio Daniel Libeskind
146 Weiss/Manfredi
147 I.M. Pei Architect
148 AECOM
149 Kennedy and Violich Architecture
150 Stan Allen Architect
151 Louise Braverman, Architect
152 Zago Architecture
153 RoTo Architecture
154 LOT-EK
155 Michael Maltzan Architecture
156 Vincent James Associates Architects
157 Carlos Zapata Studio
158 SHoP
159 Studio Shanghai
160 studio SUMO
161 Hashim Sarkis Studios
162 Slade Architecture
163 OBRA
164 L.E.FT
165 Single Speed Design
166 WORKac
167 Utile Inc.
168 MOS
169 Wodiczko + Bonder
170 Höweler + Yoon Architecture
171 Organization For Permanent Modernity
172 Adrian Smith + Gordon Gill Architecture
173 REX
174 over,under
175 MASS Design Group
176 SO-IL
177 Leong Leong
178 NADAAA

Number of Projects

1   2   3   4   7

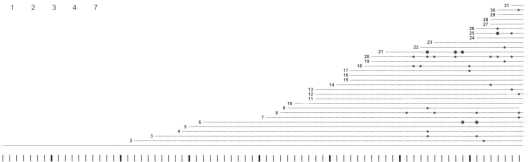

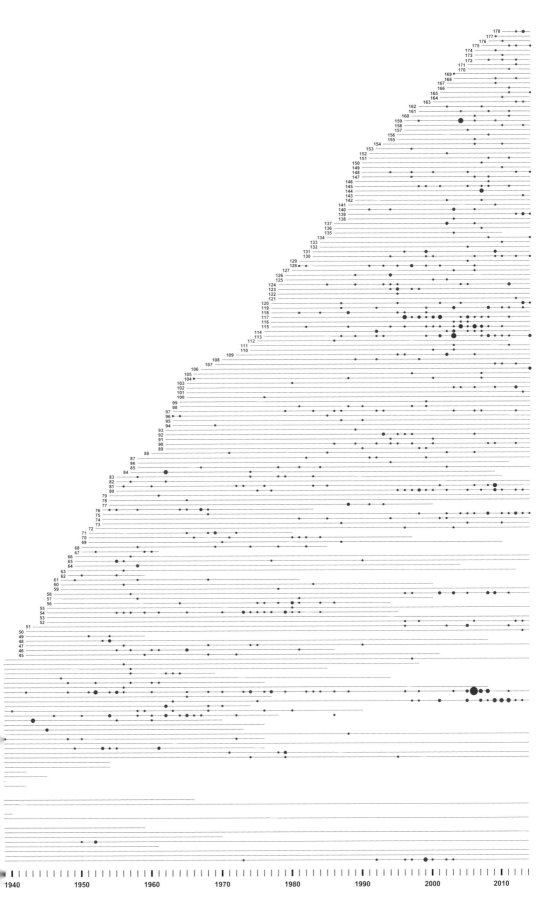

Office*US*: Map

OFFICE*US*

US Pavilion, La Biennale di Venezia
Giardini, Sestiere Castello
30122 Venezia, Italy

Project | **OFFICE***US*

Client | **OFFICE***US*

Site | Venice Biennale, Fundamentals: Absorbing Modernity 1914–2014

Title | Site drawing of OfficeUS depicting location of US architecture offices abroad between 1914–2014 and over 2,300 projects they designed.

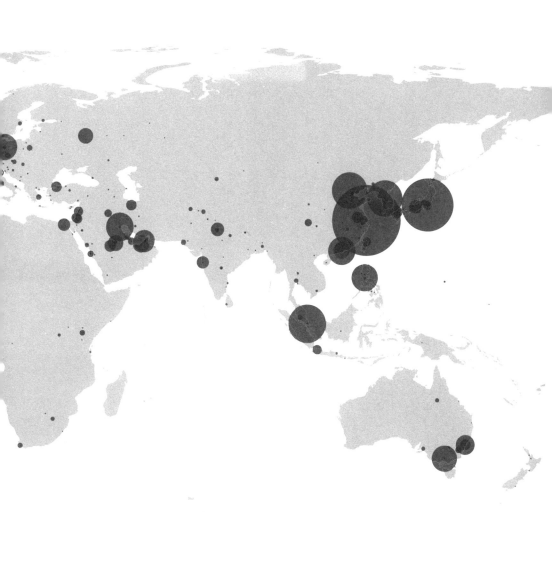

ze indicates the number of projects built in a specific location

'S 2014 Headquarters
Italy

United States of America
2014

Countries
OfficeUS Construction site 1914–2014

Projects
Projects by US architecture offices built abroad, 1914–2014

Offices
US architecture offices building abroad, 1914–2014

Drawn by	Checked by	Scale		File number
GK	EFG			
JW	AM			00
MK	AS			
NJ		Signature	Date	
			06.04.14	

Scale:
0   1,000 Mi   2,000 Mi
0   1,000 Km   2,000 Km   3,000 Km

Office*US*: Manual

Brief excerpts from architecture office manuals (1914–2014)

The Office*US* Manual—a compilation of historical and contemporary source material to be tested, revised, remade, and ultimately completed over the course of the Venice Biennale—will critically examine the procedures and protocols of the architecture office while at the same time guiding the operations of Office*US*.

Manual The purpose of this manual is to supply and provide information and help to new employees entering this organization, and to present members desiring information in regard to procedure. It is not intended as a document of rigid law but more as an elastic guide to office procedure, and is subject to revision from time to time.

Office Manual of John Russell Pope, Architect, 1931

The first requirement to perform any job well is to know the job description. Hence, every design firm should have a written procedural manual that includes such descriptions.

Handbook of Design Office Administration, 1999

Getting Started During the first few years of practice the absence of a system entails but little inconvenience; but as the work grows, a time will come when the methodless man will begin to tell his friends that it is not work but worry that is wearing him out, while the methodical man will welcome the expansion which enables him to make his organization more complete…

Office Management. A Handbook for Architects and Civil Engineers, 1901

Office Structure Partnership: Like a sole proprietorship, a partnership is an unincorporated business that traditionally has been legally indistinguishable from the partners. However, because ambiguities, assumptions, or differences in understanding among partners sometimes lead to legal disputes, many states have enacted "partnership acts" or statutes that establish basic legal principles to govern the relationship among partners and the business relationships between the partnership and other parties.

AIA Best Practices, Legal Structure of Architecture Firms, 2006

Employment at Will Every employee is employed "at will". This means that either the employee or the firm may terminate the employment relationship at any time, with or without cause. Besides simply ending your employment, the firm may change your assignment, pay, benefits, or any other aspect of your employment, with or without cause, and if the change is not acceptable to you, you may end your employment.

Office Manual, 2013

Standards of Conduct The architect's duty as a professional person is higher than an ordinary layperson's duty. Society expects a greater standard of care from a professional person exercising his/her particular skill.

The Architect's Guide to Law and Practice, 1984

Confidentiality In the course of performing professional services for our clients, we are entrusted with confidential client information. It is imperative that all personnel recognize the importance of maintaining the confidentiality of such information. This is not only a professional obligation, but on many projects, it is a contractual obligation as well.

Office Manual, 2013

Drawings The natural tendency of the draftsman to make drawings which are pictures of what will be visible when the work is done, sometimes results in neglect of the intent that a working drawing should be a means and not an end.

Manual of Office Practice for the Architectural Worker, 1924

Etiquette Communications with co-workers, clients, and vendors should be professional at all times. Minimize talking between workspaces or over cubicle walls. Instead, conduct conversations with others in their workspace. When necessary, keep volume to a level that is not disruptive. Refrain from using inappropriate language (swearing). Avoid discussions of your personal life/issues in public conversations.

███ Office Manual, 2010

Storage Architectural records present tremendous storage problems and expense because of their bulk and their size. Although flat storage is ideal for drawings, flat files are expensive and take up floor space.

Records in Architectural Offices. Suggestions for the proper organization, storage, and conservation of Architectural Office Archives, 1981

Attire and Decorum Dress appropriately. This will provide self-confidence and send a message to others that they are dealing with a professional.

Handbook of Design Office Administration, 1999

Overtime Although it is in everyone's best interest to complete work during regular office hours, the nature of the profession of architecture sometimes makes this impossible. The firm expects every member of the staff to be available for overtime work during critical rush periods.

Venturi & Rauch Handbook, 1974

General Correspondence Nothing is a more sure indication of the habits of a man of business than the management of his correspondence. A good man of business will acknowledge the receipt of every letter the same day that is received.

Office Management, A Handbook for Architects and Civil Engineers, 1901

Reception and Visitors Make your reception room speak for you. It is like the introduction, the dust cover of a new book, the jacket on a fine phonograph record. In short, it is the opening salvo in your campaign to conquer any hesitancy apotential client might have about you or your ability. You are an architect, and therefore are expected to know how to design a functional, attractive interior. You don't have to be told about good lighting, attractive colors, interesting materials, or smart and comfortable furniture.

Architecture, a Profession and a Business, 1967

Procrastination Time is a most important factor in all building operations. At no stage of the work should the architect procrastinate in the matter of securing decisions and expediting the progress of the drawings. The contractor is always most willing to place the blame for delay in construction work upon the office of the architect. Responsibility for progress in field construction must always remain with the contractor.

Office Manual of John Russell Pope, Architect, 1931

Clutter Stop! Take a look at what is on the desk or around the room. Is all that "stuff" cluttering your space vital to the tasks at hand? Is it piled there because it has no place to go? Use it, file it, put it away, or throw it away!

Handbook of Design Office Administration, 1999

EXPERTISE

MASS

JOSEPH ALLEN STEIN
ARCHITECT

MARCEL BREUER AND ASSOCIAT

PERKINS

JOHN RUSSELL

+ WILL

Walker & Gillette

McKIM
MEAD &
WHITE

DS+R

POPE

WILLIAM L. PEREIRA

ROBERT A.M. STERN
ARCHITECTS

eduardo catalano

AECOM

MIE

VAN D

R O H

Harrison and Abramovitz

studio**sumo**

SASAKI

VSBA
VENTURI, SCOTT BROWN AND ASSOCIATES

GA

Richard Neutra

moore ruble yudell

OU

GLUCKMAN MAYNER ARCHITECTS

RAFAEL VIÑOLY ARCHITECTS

GehryPartners

CASS
GILBERT

GWATHMEY
SIEGEL
KAUFMAN &
ASSOCIATES
ARCHITECTS llc

Machado and Silvetti
Associates

KIERAN

BERNARD TS
NEW YOR

JOHN M JOHANSEN

EERO SAARINEN AND ASSOCIATES

HENRY KILLAM MURPHY ARCHITECT

KRJDA

THE AUSTIN COMPANY

POPULOUS

SafdieAr

SsD

VJAA

LEO A DALY

DELAN

TOSHIKO MORI ARCHITECT

sh p

utile

EDWARD LARRABEE BARNES

Morris Lapidus

ANTOINE PREDOCK ARCHITECT

PAYETTE

hlw

Kahn

hplusf

Santos Prescott and As

ACCO

STU

STUDIOS
architecture

TOD WILLIAMS BILLIE TSIEN
ARCHITECTS

MOS

MICHAEL
MALTZAN
ARCHITECTURE

Warren & Wetmore

HOLABIRD & ROOT

PER

wodiczko+bonder

CARLOS
ZAPATA
STUDIO

LEONG LEONG ARCH

MICHAEL GRAVES & ASSOCIATES

DMJM

Shepley Bulfinch

JPRA

HSS

STEVEN HOLL ARCHIT

Davis Brody Bond

LOUIS I. KAHN

RU

LOUISE
BRAVERMAN
ARCHITECT

RR

SITE

TOWN

ASYMPTOTE ARCHITECTURE

OBRA ARCHITECTS

Minor

Preston Scott Cohen, Inc.

HARTMAN-COX ARCHITECTS

ERDE

bassetti architects

CZA

CANNONDESIGN

STUDIO SHANGHAI

SOM

HOK
h+k

KPF

KOETTER | KIM & ASSOCIATES INC.

HKS

A S
G G

DPZ **Gensler**

NADAAA

JAHN

SLADE ARCHITECTURE

Richard Meier & Partners
Architects LLP

FENTRESS ARCHITECTS

HSA

R O T O

O

LDORF
HITECTS

F**X**FOWLE W∧TG

m o r p h o s i s

EISENMAN ARCHITECTS

LAKE

TECTS
R I S

ROMA

William B. Tabler
A R C H I T E C T S

Eliot Noyes

L.E.FT ARCHITECTS
WWW.LEFTISH.NET

ORG
ORGANIZATION FOR
PERMANENT
MODERNITY

TAC

Hillier

PJ›AR

ARQUITECTONICA

ELLERBE BECKET

RICH

NIEL·H
RNHAM

CRSS

RTKL

Gp GOETTSCH
PARTNERS

ZAGO ARCHITECTURE

Bohlin Cywinski Jackson

O-IL

IATES

JOHN HEJDUK

R E X *nbbj*

WORK AC

EDWARD DURELL STONE | ARCHITECT

HARRY WEESE

ZGF

Paul R. Williams

I COBB FREED & PARTNERS

Mitchell | Giurgola Architects, LLP

german mccurry

STUDIO DANIEL LIBESKIND

WEISS / MANFREDI
ARCHITECTURE / LANDSCAPE / URBANISM

EPSTEIN

OWS AND HAMILTON

eler + Yoon Architecture

VICTOR GRUEN INTERNATIONAL

PLANNING AND ARCHITECTURE
ENTWURF UND PLANUNG
URBANISME ET ARCHITECTURE

ITHGROUP JJR

eser

PERRY DEAN ROGERS | PARTNERS

integrus
ARCHITECTURE

PAUL RUDOLPH

BTA+

Pelli Clarke Pelli Architects

KVA matx

NG STUBBINS

KMW Architecture

H2L2
a NELSON company

G ASSOCIATES

aki

CLA
CHARLES LUCKMAN ASSOCIATES

SAA

ANTONIN
RAYMOND

LOT-EK

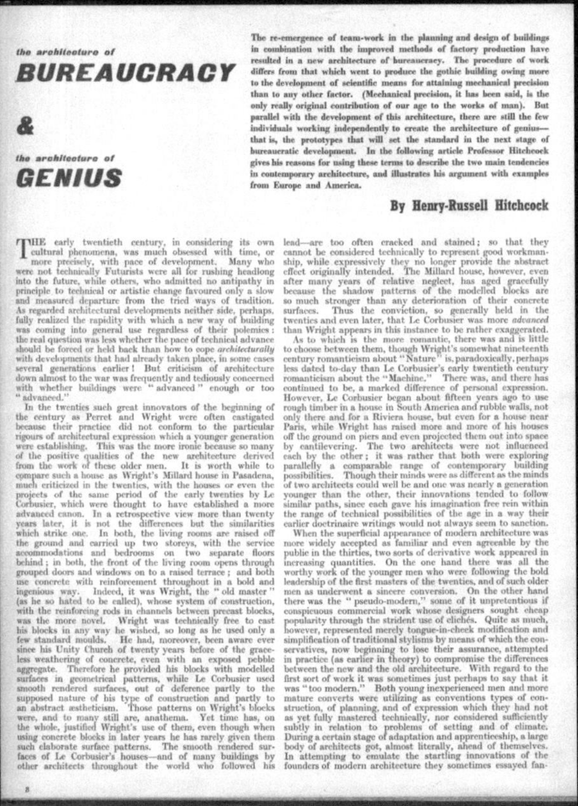

the architecture of
BUREAUCRACY
&
the architecture of
GENIUS

The re-emergence of team-work in the planning and design of buildings in combination with the improved methods of factory production have resulted in a new architecture of bureaucracy. The procedure of work differs from that which went to produce the gothic building owing more to the development of scientific means for attaining mechanical precision than to any other factor. (Mechanical precision, it has been said, is the only really original contribution of our age to the works of man). But parallel with the development of this architecture, there are still the few individuals working independently to create the architecture of genius—that is, the prototypes that will set the standard in the next stage of bureaucratic development. In the following article Professor Hitchcock gives his reasons for using these terms to describe the two main tendencies in contemporary architecture, and illustrates his argument with examples from Europe and America.

By Henry-Russell Hitchcock

THE early twentieth century, in considering its own cultural phenomena, was much obsessed with time, or more precisely, with pace of development. Many who were not technically Futurists were all for rushing headlong into the future, while others, who admitted no antipathy in principle to technical or artistic change favoured only a slow and measured departure from the tried ways of tradition. As regarded architectural developments neither side, perhaps, fully realized the rapidity with which a new way of building was coming into general use regardless of their polemics: the real question was less whether the pace of technical advance should be forced or held back than how to cope *architecturally* with developments that had already taken place, in some cases several generations earlier! But criticism of architecture down almost to the war was frequently and tediously concerned with whether buildings were "advanced" enough or too "advanced."

In the twenties such great innovators of the beginning of the century as Perret and Wright were often castigated because their practice did not conform to the particular rigours of architectural expression which a younger generation were establishing. This was the more ironic because so many of the positive qualities of the new architecture derived from the work of these older men. It is worth while to compare such a house as Wright's Millard house in Pasadena, much criticized in the twenties, with the houses or even the projects of the same period of the early twenties by Le Corbusier, which were thought to have established a more advanced canon. In a retrospective view more than twenty years later, it is not the differences but the similarities which strike one. In both, the living rooms are raised off the ground and carried up two storeys, with the service accommodations and bedrooms on two separate floors behind; in both, the front of the living room opens through grouped doors and windows on to a raised terrace; and both use concrete with reinforcement throughout in a bold and ingenious way. Indeed, it was Wright, the "old master" (as he so hated to be called), whose system of construction, with the reinforcing rods in channels between precast blocks, was the more novel. Wright was technically free to cast his blocks in any way he wished, so long as he used only a few standard moulds. He had, moreover, been aware ever since his Unity Church of twenty years before of the graceless weathering of concrete, even with an exposed pebble aggregate. Therefore he provided his blocks with modelled surfaces in geometrical patterns, while Le Corbusier used smooth rendered surfaces, out of deference partly to the supposed nature of his type of construction and partly to an abstract æstheticism. Those patterns on Wright's blocks were, and to many still are, anathema. Yet time has, on the whole, justified Wright's use of them, even though when using concrete blocks in later years he has rarely given them such elaborate surface patterns. The smooth rendered surfaces of Le Corbusier's houses—and of many buildings by other architects throughout the world who followed his lead—are too often cracked and stained; so that they cannot be considered technically to represent good workmanship, while expressively they no longer provide the abstract effect originally intended. The Millard house, however, even after many years of relative neglect, has aged gracefully because the shadow patterns of the modelled blocks are so much stronger than any deterioration of their concrete surfaces. Thus the conviction, so generally held in the twenties and even later, that Le Corbusier was more *advanced* than Wright appears in this instance to be rather exaggerated.

As to which is the more romantic, there was and is little to choose between them, though Wright's somewhat nineteenth century romanticism about "Nature" is, paradoxically, perhaps less dated to-day than Le Corbusier's early twentieth century romanticism about the "Machine." There was, and there has continued to be, a marked difference of personal expression. However, Le Corbusier began about fifteen years ago to use rough timber in a house in South America and rubble walls, not only there and for a Riviera house, but even for a house near Paris, while Wright has raised more and more of his houses off the ground on piers and even projected them out into space by cantilevering. The two architects were not influenced each by the other; it was rather that both were exploring parallelly a comparable range of contemporary building possibilities. Though their minds were as different as the minds of two architects could well be and one was nearly a generation younger than the other, their innovations tended to follow similar paths, since each gave his imagination free rein within the range of technical possibilities of the age in a way their earlier doctrinaire writings would not always seem to sanction.

When the superficial appearance of modern architecture was more widely accepted as familiar and even agreeable by the public in the thirties, two sorts of derivative work appeared in increasing quantities. On the one hand there was all the worthy work of the younger men who were following the bold leadership of the first masters of the twenties, and of such older men as underwent a sincere conversion. On the other hand there was the "pseudo-modern," some of it unpretentious if conspicuous commercial work whose designers sought cheap popularity through the strident use of clichés. Quite as much, however, represented merely tongue-in-cheek modification and simplification of traditional stylisms by means of which the conservatives, now beginning to lose their assurance, attempted in practice (as earlier in theory) to compromise the differences between the new and the old architecture. With regard to the first sort of work it was sometimes just perhaps to say that it was "too modern." Both young inexperienced men and more mature converts were utilizing as conventions types of construction, of planning, and of expression which they had not as yet fully mastered technically, nor considered sufficiently subtly in relation to problems of setting and of climate. During a certain stage of adaptation and apprenticeship, a large body of architects got, almost literally, ahead of themselves. In attempting to emulate the startling innovations of the founders of modern architecture they sometimes essayed fan-

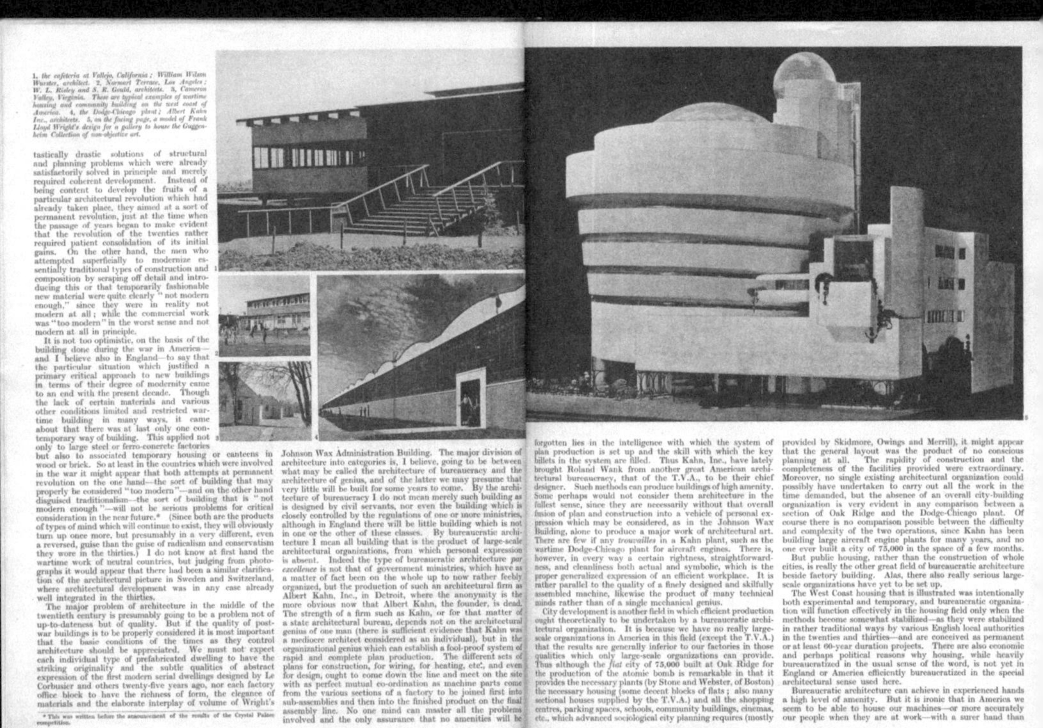

1, the cafeteria at Vallejo, California; William Wilson Wurster, architect. 2, Normart Terrace, Los Angeles; W. L. Risley and S. R. Gould, architects. 3, Cameron Valley, Virginia. These are typical examples of wartime housing and community building on the west coast of America. 4, the Dodge-Chicago plant; Albert Kahn Inc., architects. 5, on the facing page, a model of Frank Lloyd Wright's design for a gallery to house the Guggenheim Collection of non-objective art.

tastically drastic solutions of structural and planning problems which were already satisfactorily solved in principle and merely required coherent development. Instead of being content to develop the fruits of a particular architectural revolution which had already taken place, they aimed at a sort of permanent revolution, just at the time when the passage of years began to make evident that the revolution of the twenties rather required patient consolidation of its initial gains. On the other hand, the men who attempted superficially to modernize essentially traditional types of construction and composition by scraping off detail and introducing this or that temporarily fashionable new material were quite clearly "not modern enough," since they were in reality not modern at all; while the commercial work was "too modern" in the worst sense and not modern at all in principle.

It is not too optimistic, on the basis of the building done during the war in America—and I believe also in England—to say that the particular situation which justified a primary critical approach to new buildings in terms of their degree of modernity came to an end with the present decade. Though the lack of certain materials and various other conditions limited and restricted wartime building in many ways, it came about that there was at last only one contemporary way of building. This applied not only to large steel or ferro-concrete factories but also to associated temporary housing or canteens in wood or brick. So at least in the countries which were involved in the war it might appear that both attempts at permanent revolution on the one hand—the sort of building that may properly be considered "too modern"—and on the other hand disguised traditionalism—the sort of building that is "not modern enough"—will not be serious problems for critical consideration in the near future.* (Since both are the products of types of mind which will continue to exist, they will obviously turn up once more, but presumably in a very different, even a reversed, guise than the guise of radicalism and conservatism they wore in the thirties.) I do not know at first hand the wartime work of neutral countries, but judging from photographs it would appear that there had been a similar clarification of the architectural picture in Sweden and Switzerland, where architectural development was in any case already well integrated in the thirties.

The major problem of architecture in the middle of the twentieth century is presumably going to be a problem not of up-to-dateness but of quality. But if the quality of post-war buildings is to be properly considered it is most important that the basic conditions of the times as they control architecture should be appreciated. We must not expect each individual type of prefabricated dwelling to have the striking originality and the subtle qualities of abstract expression of the first modern serial dwellings designed by Le Corbusier and others twenty-five years ago, nor each factory office block to have the richness of form, the elegance of materials and the elaborate interplay of volume of Wright's Johnson Wax Administration Building. The major division of architecture into categories is, I believe, going to be between what may be called the architecture of bureaucracy and the architecture of genius, and of the latter we may presume that very little will be built for some years to come. By the architecture of bureaucracy I do not mean merely such building as is designed by civil servants, nor even the building which is closely controlled by the regulations of one or more ministries, although in England there will be little building which is not in one or the other of these classes. By bureaucratic architecture I mean all building that is the product of large-scale architectural organizations, from which personal expression is absent. Indeed the type of bureaucratic architecture *par excellence* is not that of government ministries, which have as a matter of fact been on the whole up to now rather feebly organized, but the production of such an architectural firm as Albert Kahn, Inc., in Detroit, where the anonymity is the more obvious now that Albert Kahn, the founder, is dead. The strength of a firm such as Kahn, or for that matter of a state architectural bureau, depends not on the architectural genius of one man (there is sufficient evidence that Kahn was a mediocre architect considered as an individual), but in the organizational genius which can establish a fool-proof system of rapid and complete plan production. The different sets of plans for construction, for wiring, for heating, etc., and even for design, ought to come down the line and meet on the site with as perfect mutual co-ordination as machine parts come from the various sections of a factory to be joined first into sub-assemblies and then into the finished product on the final assembly line. No one mind can master all the problems involved and the only assurance that no amenities will be forgotten lies in the intelligence with which the system of plan production is set up and the skill with which the key billets in the system are filled. Thus Kahn, Inc., have lately brought Roland Wank from another great American architectural bureaucracy, that of the T.V.A., to be their chief designer. Such methods can produce buildings of high amenity. Some perhaps would not consider them architecture in the fullest sense, since they are necessarily without that overall fusion of plan and construction into a vehicle of personal expression which may be considered, as in the Johnson Wax Building, alone to produce a major work of architectural art. There are few if any *trouvailles* in a Kahn plant, such as the wartime Dodge-Chicago plant for aircraft engines. There is, however, in every way a certain rightness, straightforwardness, and cleanliness both actual and symbolic, which is the proper generalized expression of an efficient workplace. It is rather parallel to the quality of a finely designed and skilfully assembled machine, likewise the product of many technical minds rather than of a single mechanical genius.

City development is another field in which efficient production ought theoretically to be undertaken by a bureaucratic architectural organization. It is because we have no really large-scale organizations in America in this field (except the T.V.A.) that the results are generally inferior to our factories in those qualities which only large-scale organizations can provide. Thus although the *fiat* city of 75,000 built at Oak Ridge for the production of the atomic bomb is remarkable in that it provides the necessary plants (by Stone and Webster, of Boston) the necessary housing (some decent blocks of flats; also many sectional houses supplied by the T.V.A.) and all the shopping centres, parking spaces, schools, community buildings, cinemas, etc., which advanced sociological city planning requires (mostly provided by Skidmore, Owings and Merrill), it might appear that the general layout was the product of no conscious planning at all. The rapidity of construction and the completeness of the facilities provided were extraordinary. Moreover, no single existing architectural organization could possibly have undertaken to carry out all the work in the time demanded, but the absence of an overall city-building organization is very evident in any comparison between a section of Oak Ridge and the Dodge-Chicago plant. Of course there is no comparison possible between the difficulty and complexity of the two operations, since Kahn has been building large aircraft engine plants for many years, and no one ever built a city of 75,000 in the space of a few months.

But public housing, rather than the construction of whole cities, is really the other great field of bureaucratic architecture beside factory building. Alas, there also really serious large-scale organizations have yet to be set up.

The West Coast housing that is illustrated was intentionally both experimental and temporary, and bureaucratic organization will function effectively in the housing field only when the methods become somewhat stabilized—as they were stabilized in rather traditional ways by various English local authorities in the twenties and thirties—and are conceived as permanent or at least 60-year duration projects. There are also economic and perhaps political reasons why housing, while heavily bureaucratized in the usual sense of the word, is not yet in England or America efficiently bureaucratized in the special architectural sense used here.

Bureaucratic architecture can achieve in experienced hands a high level of amenity. But it is ironic that in America we seem to be able to house our machines—or more accurately our people when they are at work—with a surer hand than

* This was written before the announcement of the results of the Crystal Palace competition.

Henry-Russell Hitchcock, "The Architecture of Bureaucracy and the Architecture of Genius," *Architectural Review*, January 1947.

MICHAEL KUBO

The Concept of the Architectural Corporation

Despite the increasing presence of large, team-based offices within US architectural practice over the last century, a history of how architects and critics have understood these offices has yet to be written. The nature of group practice has changed from the big businesses and large organizations that accompanied the merger movement at the turn of the twentieth century to the factory producers of the industrial expansion in the 1910s and 1920s, the bureaucratic firms of the postwar boom, and the multinational conglomerates of the neoliberal present. Only after World War II did the term "corporate" come to constitute a topos of architectural discourse, one that refers at once to a specific mode of production, the mentality of its producers, and the perceived qualities of the work produced. Throughout these changes in the scope of architectural organization, architects and historians have speculated on the implications of the large-scale office for the status of architecture as a business, a profession, and a field of cultural production.

   A convenient place to enter this history of critical reception is in midstream, in the years immediately after the World War II, when numerous authors looked to the largest firms of the early twentieth century to comprehend the implications of team-based practices for postwar architectural production. Among the earliest attempts was Henry-Russell Hitchcock's 1947 article, "The Architecture of Bureaucracy and the Architecture of Genius," in which he predicted that the major categories of postwar architecture would be distinguished not by style, but by economy of production.[1] Hitchcock noted that the prewar terms of debate, centered on avant-garde themes of advance or regression, had given way to a "clarification of the architectural picture" in which "it came about that there was at last only one contemporary way of building," namely modernism. Based upon this stylistic consensus, Hitchcock predicted the evolution of a new professional entity to meet the increasing scale and scope of design tasks in a postwar society: the bureaucratic office. "Bureaucratic architecture," he wrote, would include "all building that is the product of large-scale architectural organizations, from which personal expression is absent." In contrast to the speed and competence required for large-scale projects, to which bureaucratic architecture would ideally be suited, Hitchcock counterposed "an entirely different world" of design practice for those monumental or special cultural commissions requiring artistic or creative synthesis, "the world of the architecture of genius." The genius

①
Henry-Russell Hitchcock, "The Architecture of Bureaucracy and the Architecture of Genius," *Architectural Review*, No. 101 (January 1947), 4.

would be the anti-bureaucrat, "the sort of architect who functions as a creative individual rather than as an anonymous member of a team"; his method would be "a particular psychological approach and way of working at architecture which may or may not produce masterpieces."

These two types of practice and their resulting expression—the competent prose of the bureaucrat and the imaginative poetry of the genius—would each have their exclusive domain of professional application. Significantly, Hitchcock already warned that this dichotomy, at once productive and discursive, would require the architectural critic to develop different tools to evaluate the built results of such practices. Henceforth, it would no longer be possible to judge bureaucratic production on the same artistic criteria that had applied to the prewar avant-garde, whether the interpretive framework of signature and authorial intention or the expressive attributes of imagination, creativity, or synthesis.

Frank Lloyd Wright provided the inevitable model of Hitchcock's architectural genius, reinforcing an image maintained through the atelier-like atmosphere Wright cultivated at his Taliesin studios in Arizona and Wisconsin. The office of Albert Kahn represented the bureaucrat, known primarily for factories and offices for Ford Motor Company and other Detroit manufacturers. For Hitchcock, Kahn's office represented "the type of bureaucratic architecture *par excellence*." He praised: "The strength of a firm such as Kahn...[that] depends not on the architectural genius of one man...but in the organizational genius which can establish a fool-proof system of rapid and complete plan production." Such a system, organized in technical divisions from design to engineering to construction, enabled different sets of design information to "meet on the site with as perfect mutual co-ordination as machine parts come from the various sections of a factory to be joined first into sub-assemblies and then into the finished product on the final assembly line."

By 1947, however, Fordist factory production was already an anachronistic model for large-scale, postwar organizations. A year before Hitchcock's text, the sociologist Peter Drucker identified the corporation as the representative American social institution, predicting its emergence as the dominant form for business and other postwar institutions.[2] In contrast to the assembly-line production embodied by Ford Motor Company, Drucker argued that the managerial principles that would typify the coming economic boom would emulate the flexible, distributed model of General Motors, the largest corporation in the world by the 1950s. General Motors' structure consisted of independent automobile divisions combined with coordinated decision making and control between divisions to ensure consistency across the company's product lines. A mix of specialists at different levels within the hierarchy allowed information to travel both upwards and downwards through the production chain, increasing efficiency from the factory floor to the management office. Decentralization, teamwork, and flexibility were, for Drucker, the characteristics that would mark the progressive application of corporate models across both business and institutional domains in the postwar context.

② Peter Drucker, *Concept of the Corporation* (New York: The John Day Company, 1946).

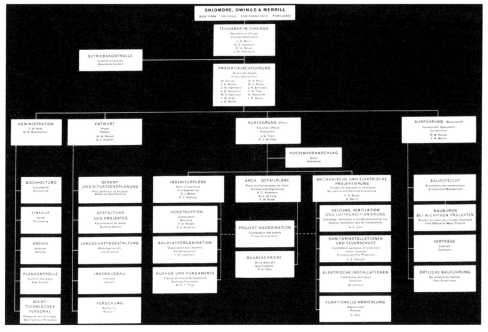

Skidmore, Owings & Merrill, organizational diagram, published in *Bauen + Wohnen*, April 1957.

Such managerial methods found their closest parallel in architectural practice in the offices of Skidmore, Owings & Merrill (SOM), the firm which became uniquely synonymous with the term "corporate" during this period. SOM's success was based on the development of the "package deal," in which large teams of architects and engineers delivered complex projects from site planning and structural engineering to detailed design, facade systems, interiors, budgeting, and administration.[3] Diagrams of the firm's organization published in architectural journals precisely represented Drucker's efficient yet flexible corporation. In practice, the image of SOM as a firm characterized by consistent products rather than by signature architects—one supposedly so anonymous that a partner claimed "it could even be called the ABC Company"[4]—conflicted with the acknowledgment of Gordon Bunshaft as the firm's lead designer, and with his description of his role as office "dictator."[5] Yet the overall impression of a smoothly functioning team was successful enough that *Fortune* magazine extolled SOM's "group design," while *Business Week* marveled at the firm's $2 billion dollars of "design by conference."[6] *Newsweek* made explicit the firm's affinity with Drucker's managerial paradigm, praising SOM for its "enormous and assiduous activity and production—something like a General Motors of the architectural world."[7]

As Hitchcock had situated the emerging architecture of bureaucracy in terms of the prewar model of Albert Kahn's office, so contemporary critics looked to earlier examples of large-scale practice in order to understand this new scale of production. In a special issue of *Bauen + Wohnen* dedicated to SOM in 1957, Sigfried Giedion situated their work within the lineage of Chicago firms like Burnham and Root that had been among

③
William Hartmann, "S.O.M. Organization." *Bauen + Wohnen* Vol. 11, No. 4 (April 1957), 116.

④
"Skidmore, Owings & Merrill, Architects, U.S.A." *Museum of Modern Art Bulletin*, Volume XVIII, No. 1 (Fall 1950), 7.

⑤
"Designers For a Busy World: Mood For Working." *Newsweek* (May 4, 1959), 100.

⑥
"The Architects From Skid's Row," *Fortune* (January 1958), 137-40, 210, 212, 215; "2-Billion Worth of Design by Conference," *Business Week* (Dec. 4, 1954), 96–104.

⑦
"Designers For a Busy World: Mood For Working," 97.

Peter Smithson, "The fine and the folk," *Architectural Design*, August 1965.

the pioneers of the large-scale architectural business model at the turn of the twentieth century.[8] Responding to Hitchcock and Giedion with a view from outside the United States, Peter Smithson placed SOM's genealogy not with the commercial architects of the Chicago School but rather with the New York office of McKim, Mead & White, among the largest architectural firms at the end of the nineteenth century.[9] For Smithson, both firms embodied a lineage of luxurious materials and careful execution inaccessible to foreigners, "that special tradition of concentration on detail which Americans enjoy." Describing the other-worldly impression of "machine-absolute" buildings like SOM's Chase Manhattan Bank, Smithson wrote that they "arouse the strongest cargo-cult feelings in foreigners, and are truly hints of *une architecture autre*." Hitchcock would also link the fetish character of such products with the professionalization of the firms that produced them, suggesting "the acceptance of the skyscraper outside of North America has certainly already led in some cases to the development of architectural offices comparable in scale and organization to the American ones. Thus it is not only the American skyscraper that has come to be adopted abroad but, up to a point at least, the methods of its design and production."[10]

Evident in these descriptions was the need to reconcile the prewar notion of modernism as a cultural avant-garde with the mainstream, corporate organization by which such products were achieved. Giedion's essay had characterized SOM as an "experiment" in merging management and progressive design, by using this scale of organization to convince clients of the value of modernist aesthetics. Nathaniel Owings himself alluded to such ambitions in his account of SOM's early years, claiming

⑧
Sigfried Giedion, "The Experiment of SOM," *Bauen + Wohnen* Vol. 11, No. 4 (April 1957), 113. In his introduction to the first monograph of SOM's work in 1962, Hitchcock placed the firm's heritage with "the inventor and developer of the large architectural office—the 'plan factory', if you will—Daniel Burnham." Hitchcock, in Ernst Danz, *Architecture of Skidmore, Owings & Merrill 1950–1962* (New York: Praeger and London: The Architectural Press, 1962), 8.

⑨
Peter Smithson, "The fine and the folk: An essay on McKim, Mead and White and the American tradition," *Architectural Design* (August 1965), 394–97.

⑩
Henry-Russell Hitchcock,"The Rise to World Prominence of American Architecture," *Zodiac 8: America*, ed. Bruno Alfieri (Milan: 1961), 2.

that "we were not after jobs as such. We were after leverage to influence social and environmental conditions. To work, we must have volume... Volume meant power. We would try to change men's minds."[11] A 1950 exhibition of SOM's work at the Museum of Modern Art had already affirmed the perceived compatibility between the repetitive, reproducible character of modernism and the efficiencies of bureaucratic production, characterizing the firm as one in which designers "work together, animated by two disciplines which they all share—the discipline of modern architecture and the discipline of American organizational methods."[12]

Yet the interest of other young architects in team-based practices after World War II lay less in leveraging big business toward aesthetic ends than in how large-scale involvement could be channeled toward broader cultural goals. Collaboration became the watchword for a generation of architects schooled in the belief that anonymity, teamwork, and the broadest scale of action were the keys to progressive architectural production. Inspired by the massive building projects of the Tennessee Valley Authority under the New Deal, and by the collaborative pedagogy of the prewar Bauhaus, young architects called for new models of collective production that would embrace the emerging fields of planning, engineering, and landscape.[13] For adherents to this ethos, a perceived consensus around the principles of the modern movement after the World War II combined with a commitment to challenge the trope of the genius inherited from the first generation of modernist masters, which was seen as inadequate to address the urgent building problems of their time.[14]

Emblematic of the belief in team-based practice as a social ethos was The Architects Collaborative (TAC). The firm was established in 1945 by seven young architects along with Walter Gropius, the German émigré who led the Bauhaus and later, the Harvard Graduate School of Design. Founded as an experiment in collective production, TAC eventually became the largest dedicated architectural practice in the United States. In the postwar decades the firm's headquarters formed the nucleus of a vibrant professional culture of designers gathered around Harvard Square, numbering into the hundreds—many of them working in offices indebted to the collective atmosphere first established by TAC. Sometimes referred to by its legatees as the "Cambridge School," for members of this scene it was within the structure of practice itself, beyond its visible products, that the postwar evolution of modernism would take place.

The seven young architects who came together to form TAC with Gropius were linked by a network of overlapping personal and professional connections, formed in this shared climate of social and architectural optimism at the start of the postwar building boom. Norman ("Fletch") Fletcher, Louis McMillen, Robert McMillan, and Benjamin Thompson had been classmates at Yale, where they talked about forming what Fletcher called the World Collaborative, an "ideal office" that would combine painting, sculpture, and architecture.[15] John ("Chip") Harkness had worked with Fletcher during the war (both were conscientious objectors) at SOM in New York, and later, with Jean Bodman, for the firm of Saarinen and Swanson in Michigan. Sarah Pillsbury and Bodman

(11)
Nathaniel Alexander Owings, *The Spaces in Between: An Architect's Journey* (Boston: Houghton Mifflin Company, 1973), 66.

(12)
"Skidmore, Owings & Merrill, Architects, U.S.A.", 5.

(13)
Jean Bodman Fletcher's thesis at Harvard, for example, proposed a migrant workers' community and factory in the context of a regional plan for California's Central Valley, integrating flood control, electric power development, and water conservation. See Bodman Fletcher, "There Should Be Regional Planning in Central Valley," *Arts & Architecture* (May 1945), n.p.

(14)
See *An Opinion on Architecture* (Boston: The Century Press, 1941), published by Bruno Zevi and other students of the Harvard Graduate School of Design as a critique of the school's formalist tendencies under Joseph Hudnut. Its authors proclaim, "We see only one solution for the future of architecture as an expressive and social activity: COLLECTIVE WORK among architects, engineers, contractors, and the working class."

(15)
Interview with Norman Fletcher conducted by Perry Neubauer, November 6, 2006. My thanks to Neubauer for providing transcripts of this and other interviews with then-surviving founders of TAC.

"Gropius Appraises Today's Architect,"
Architectural Forum, May 1952.

The Architects Collaborative partners meeting circa 1950. Partners from left to
right: Chip Harkness (with vest), Jean Bodman Fletcher, Norman Fletcher, Walter
Gropius, Louis McMillen. *Source: Perry Neubauer.*

had both studied at the Cambridge School of Architecture and Landscape
Architecture, the first degree-granting graduate school in the United States
designed specifically for women in these fields. Harkness and Pillsbury
had married in 1941, Bodman and Fletcher in 1945. Committed to forming
a practice together after the war, these friends decided that adding an
experienced senior practitioner would help them find their way in the field
and lend stature to the young firm. Coincidence and good timing inter-
vened to bring Gropius, the very figure of Bauhaus pedagogy, on board.[16]
In him, they found an eminent practitioner as well as a highly sympathetic
collaborator, one whose attitude toward the value of teamwork closely
matched their own. Christened The Architects Collaborative, the goal of
its founders was, in Sally Harkness's words, nothing less than "to remake
the world."[17]

TAC represented a model of practice distinct from other prominent
team-based architecture firms of the postwar period like SOM or Caudill
Rowlett Scott (CRS), though all would eventually come to be grouped
together by critics under the rubric of the corporate office. The collaborative ideal at TAC meant something very different from the hierarchy
represented by the work of SOM. Key to the TAC approach was the idea
that teams should consist of generalists able to criticize each other
as equals, rather than parceling tasks among specialized practitioners
according to the managerial principles of efficiency and division of labor.
This structure was formalized through a weekly meeting in which all
the partners gave shared criticism of each others' projects, Gropius among
them. Working at other team-based firms meant suits and ties, a time
clock, and a rigid chain of command; TAC meant corduroy and jeans, wild
(occasionally scandalous) office parties, and a messy environment of
shared investigation closer to an atelier than a corporate office. Embedded
in this environment was Gropius himself, at once simply one among
the partners and the singular figure identified with the outsize legacy
of the Bauhaus. By 1966, when the first major monograph on TAC

(16)
After returning from
wartime medical duty in the
American Field Service,
Harkness received a letter
from Fletcher proposing
a collaborative office on
the same day that Gropius
asked him to teach in the
Master's class at Harvard.
Chip pitched the idea to
his professor, who agreed
to join the firm. Fletcher
later suggested that Louis
Kahn and George Howe
had been considered as
possible collaborators prior
to approaching Gropius.
Interview with Norman
Fletcher conducted by Perry
Neubauer, November 6,
2006, and interview with
John C. Harkness conducted
by Neubauer, December 3,
2006.

(17)
Interview with Sarah
Harkness conducted
by Perry Neubauer,
November 3, 2006.

culminated the first twenty years of the firm's work, the founding partners reiterated their sustained faith in the collectivist model, contributing essays with titles like "TAC's Teamwork," "Collaboration," and "The Idea of Anonymity."[18]

Given Gropius's identification with the Bauhaus pedagogy of team-based work among holistically-trained designers and its postwar translation into schools of architecture in the United States, critics chose to see TAC's organizational model as the application of these same principles in the context of Americanized professional practice. As the chosen voice of TAC's work in the architectural press (though significantly not the primary author of the firm's output), Gropius wrote extensively about the positive impact that collaborative models of management could have on architectural practice. In 1952, on the verge of his retirement from Harvard to focus on the practice, Gropius reiterated the urgent need for "a closely co-operating team together with the engineer, the scientist and the builder," in which "design, construction and economy may again become an entity—a fusion of art, science and business."[19]

Gropius's argument was both ideological and pragmatic. He insisted that collaboration across disciplines would allow the architect to recover the ideal of integration represented by the pre-industrial figure of the master builder in the context of postwar industrial society. These issues of production also directly concerned questions of authorship and the self-image of the producer, issues with which Gropius was intimately familiar through his long engagement with design pedagogy. Students of architecture would have "to learn to collaborate without losing their identity," an approach he had worked to promote through collaborative workshops at the Bauhaus and later at Harvard. The historical task of the next generation of architects, inheritors of the legacy of modernism, would be to overcome "the ideology of the past century" that "has taught us to see in the individual genius the only embodiment of true and pure art."[20] Significantly, Gropius understood that this change in pedagogy would enable new attitudes towards individual self-consciousness for architects in practice, no longer taught to think in terms of singular authorship. He warned that these new team-based production would entail an inevitable confrontation with inherited expectations about the autonomy and importance of the architect, predicting that "*Architects in the future will refuse to be restrained from a natural urge to take actual part in a team effort with the industry to produce buildings and their parts. The emphasis, I believe, will be more and more on the team.*"[21]

Such battles over the scope and authority of architects marked the first in a series of fundamental shifts in the legal and economic conditions of architectural practice in the United States that widened the gulf between increasingly large firms and smaller, boutique practices after the 1950s. These changes included the increased specialization of building types and the expansion of liability protection that architectural firms were required to carry, which encouraged the consolidation and centralization of practice into a small number of large firms. The 1972 agreement of the American Institute of Architects (AIA) with the Department of Justice

(18)
The Architects Collaborative (Teufen: Arthur Niggli, 1966).

(19)
Walter Gropius, "Gropius Appraises Today's Architect," *Architectural Forum*, May 1952, 111. This statement was republished in modified form as "The Architect Within Our Industrial Society" in Gropius, *Scope of Total Architecture* (New York: Harper & Brothers, 1955), 76–90.

(20)
Gropius, "The Architect Within Our Industrial Society," in *Scope of Total Architecture*, 86.

(21)
Ibid., 84. Italics original.

to cease publishing a standard template for architects' fees—a major stake in the AIA's founding charter to promote the interests of US architects as a community of financially disinterested professionals—further exacerbated the need for firms to grow bigger in order to meet the demands of competition on the open market.[22]

By the 1970s, the economies of production represented by team-based offices had become the norm within architectural practice. A scale of operation that before the World War II had been reserved for a handful of firms—including those of Burnham and Root, McKim, Mead & White, and Albert Kahn—formed the typical structure of mainstream architectural production. This expansion of corporate practice was intimately related to the expanding oil economies of the Middle Eastern Gulf States after the World War II. Josep Lluís Sert's US Embassy in Baghdad after 1955 and TAC's commission to design the University of Baghdad in 1957 were among the earliest examples of what would become a growing involvement in the region by US architects. Yamasaki & Associates, CRS, Hellmuth, Obata + Kassabaum (HOK), Daniel, Mann, Johnson & Mendenhall (DMJM), Brown Daltas and Associates, SOM, William L. Pereira & Associates, and many others would follow their lead in subsequent years. These exchanges reached their peak during the boom in crude oil prices from 1973 to 1983, a shift in clientele that formed a direct corollary to the corresponding decline in building practice in the United States.

Faced with such evident entanglements in the politics and economics of architectural practice, contemporary critics chose to abandon any real interpretation of such modes of production, disavowing the call by a previous generation of authors for an analytical framework through which such practices could be evaluated on their own terms. Surveying the legacy of the avant-garde "masters" and their postwar followers, Manfredo Tafuri and Francesco Dal Co took up the dichotomy laid out by Hitchcock in 1947 only to lament a condition in which "a true and proper 'architecture of bureaucracy' settled in everywhere," while the field "came to be dominated not by individual architects intent on communicating their opinions of the world but by large studios in which the tasks were parceled out with virtual assembly-line standards."[23] Such modes of practice, for Tafuri and Dal Co, could only produce buildings "as anonymous as the architectural concerns that build them." By the time of *Transformations in Modern Architecture*, a comprehensive survey of the previous two decades of production held at the Museum of Modern Art in 1979, curator Arthur Drexler could only point (following the historian Peter Collins) to the "archaeologically unclassifiable" variations of late and post-modern production on display—a selection dominated by the work of corporate firms—declaring the result to be "bewildering, profuse, overloaded, contradictory, inconsistent, largely mediocre."[24]

Exhibitions like *Transformations* made evident the ellipsis that had come by this time to obscure such practices in architecture, exacerbated by a neo-avant-garde which framed itself as the rejection of a mainstream professional practice lacking in criticality toward its own

[22]
See Jay Wickersham, "An Accidental Revolution: The Transformation of Architectural Ethics in the 1970s," paper delivered at the Society of Architectural Historians annual meeting, April 2011. My thanks to Wickersham for providing the manuscript of this paper.

[23]
Manfredo Tafuri and Francesco Dal Co, *Modern Architecture/2* (Milan: Electa, 1976), 339.

[24]
Arthur Drexler, *Transformations in Modern Architecture* (New York: Museum of Modern Art, 1979); "Response: Arthur Drexler on Transformations," interview with Drexler conducted by Andrew McNair. *Skyline* (Summer 1979), 6.

conditions of production. Retracing the steps that led to his PhD dissertation at the University of Cambridge, *The Formal Basis of Modern Architecture*, Peter Eisenman conspicuously located his decision to return to the academy in having been "disillusioned with practice" after working for TAC in the summer of 1959.[25] So too, Robert Venturi reacted negatively to his experience in the office of Eero Saarinen & Associates in the 1950s, by then a firm of hundreds responsible for delivering an eclectic range of corporate images for a variety of clients.[26] Latent in such reactions was a shared nostalgia for the ideal of the genius, with an emphasis on difficult, complex, and resistant forms of production as a deliberate counter to the smooth efficiencies represented by the distributed postwar office.

Yet, the critique of the corporate by neo-avant-garde architects and historians, far from producing resistance to the economic dominance of the profession by large-scale offices, only reinforced the widening disparity in the critical attention given to such firms versus smaller, boutique practices. Indeed this lack of attention had much the opposite effect, leaving few models by which to assess the even larger multinational offices that emerged from the 1990s onward. As these entities have increased in size and obscurity, they have become known less through any evaluation in the architectural press than by their market categorization in trade journals as "AEC" firms, providers of architecture as simply one among an immense array of building services.[27] Emblematic of such scope and mega-scale is AECOM, with 45,000 employees, among which some 1,300 are architects. The firm's acronym, rumored to refer only to the range of services it provides—Architecture, Engineering, Construction, Operation, and Maintenance—is quite literally anonymous, evacuated of any message other than the firm's market categorization. Recognizing and reading the work of such distributed bodies today requires a renewal of the call made by Hitchcock for critical tools commensurate with the reality of this production, one which the history of corporate practices and their reception can only suggest.

(25) Peter Eisenman, postscript to *The Formal Basis of Modern Architecture* (PhD Dissertation, Cambridge, 1963), published in 2008 (Basel: Lars Müller).

(26) On Saarinen's firm in this period, see Walter McQuade, "The New Saarinen Office," *Architectural Forum* (April 1962), 113–19.

(27) AEC is the market categorization for firms that provide architecture, engineering, and construction services, as used in the yearly ranking of such offices by trade journals like *Engineering News-Record* and *World Architecture*. SOM would be an AE firm according to this categorization, for example, while TAC, a dedicated architecture practice with no engineers on staff, would be classified as an A firm.

Following:
Frank Lloyd Wright, Taliesin West, drafting room, Scottsdale, AZ, 1950. © Ezra Stoller/Esto.
Skidmore, Owings & Merrill (SOM) offices, Chicago, IL, 1958. © Ezra Stoller/Esto.
The Architects Collaborative (TAC) offices, Cambridge, MA, 1967. © Ezra Stoller/Esto.

PEGGY DEAMER

Office Management

Twenty years on either side of Henry-Russell Hitchcock's 1947
pronouncement distinguishing "genius" from "bureaucratic" practices
are two firms that demonstrate the power of the "bureaucratic" overseas.
In both cases, however, the nature of that power is neither obvious
nor direct; that is, it does not (merely) pertain to the buildings deposited
by these American firms in various countries. Rather, it involves ideologies of the production, not the product, of architecture. Moreover, these
ideologies evolve as they go back and forth between Europe and the
United States and are "American" only in the sense that the United
States initiates and then crystallizes the exchange. The two examples are
atypical of US architectural practices even as they are more "American"
for adopting managerial practices of industrial production outside the
confines of architecture.

The two offices are Albert Kahn Associates in Detroit, whose
office built 521 factories in Russia between 1928 and 1929 and Caudill
Rowell Scott (CRS) whose offices in Texas had built numerous projects
overseas by the time Bill Caudill, one of its founding partners, was sent
to the USSR in 1969 as a member of a US team to examine the results
of Kahn-instigated industrialization. The ideologies that were at play in
these two firms center on Taylorism (Kahn), that very American-born
system of production, and corporatism (CRS), Taylorism's reincarnation
after its post World War II international transformation.

That Taylorism and corporatism had stylistic effects on buildings—
and that these effects were themselves part of a complex set of ideological
exchanges—is known and documented elsewhere. European modernism's infatuation with the machine-age aesthetic is just the tip of an
iceberg that conceals the particular circumstances transforming American
industrial modernity into European cultural modernism.[1] Likewise, the
corporate style of Internationalism, characterized by steel construction
and the glass curtain wall, is, after its Americanization of European
modernism in the 1930s, exported to emerging nations eager to accept
this symbol of progress and modernity from the United States.[2] What is
less documented is how, independent of architecture, Taylorism merged
into corporatism through international exchanges or how both penetrated
architecture at a level deeper than style.

[1]
See Mauro F. Guillen,
*The Taylorized Beauty of
the Mechanical: Scientific
Management and the Rise
of Modernist Architecture*,
(Princeton: Princeton
Architectural Press, 2006).
See also Harm G Schroter,
*Americanization and the
European Economy:
A Compact Survey of
American Economic
Influence in Europe Since
the 1880s* (Dordrecht:
Kluwer Academic Publishers,
2005), especially Chapter
1, "Fordism and Taylorism
Come to Europe".

[2]
See Annabelle Jane
Wharton, *Building the Cold
War: Hilton International
Hotels and Modern
Architecture* (Chicago:
University of Chicago
Press, 2001).

Taylorism and Albert Kahn Associates

Frederick Taylor rose to prominence in 1890 as a leader of a reform movement in shop management centered in the American Society of Mechanical Engineers. His analysis of more efficient movements for segmented tasks was meant to increase productivity for the factory owner, but was also meant to increase wages for the worker who, paid by differential piece rates, would produce more and get more pay for a given portion of time. His was also a system of management (hence its designation as "scientific management"), since the optimized worker, unable to do the work and oversee it at the same time, requires managers to direct the process. Managers in Taylorism are more numerous, more essential, and more qualitatively distinct than in other forms of production.

Scientific management before World War I had an enormous effect on the United States as it was adopted by Henry Ford and applied to his Ford Motor Company's automobile production.[3] Despite the fact that by 1914 the US economy was already larger than that of Britain, France, and Germany combined, pre World War I Europe—where labor was plentiful and cheap but raw material scarce—was operating on the inverse of the American economic model and not ideologically affected by Taylorism and Fordism. After World War I however, as the power of the US economy became equated with state power, not only did European industries study Ford's techniques to revitalize their economies, but governments also adopted Taylorism to support their political policies. As European countries reorganized after World War I, Taylorism emerged in syndicalism, in political parties pushing public-private "scientifically managed" partnerships, in "Soviet" models of factory based communities, and, in newly revolutionized Russia, communism. Lenin, initially opposed to scientific management for its exploitation of labor, became an advocate and initiated policies that eventually found their way into Stalin's first five-year plan.

The effect of Taylorization on American architecture was procedural, although aimed at the construction of a professional, not working, class. Because there was no state sponsorship of architecture, American offices were market, not ideologically, driven.[4] The belief in the non-governmental, private office supplied with salaried, itinerant employees—unlike the European master-apprentice atelier system—ensured that practices were competitive and entrepreneurial. As members engaged in a relatively young profession in the early twentieth century tried to prove its viability vis-à-vis both other American professions and European architectural practices, US architects sought to prove they were neither workers nor businessmen; they strove, rather, to be members of a class equal to their patrons.[5] The American individualism that encouraged the private office also discouraged collectively motivated research that might have led to greater, Taylorized, efficiencies. As with Europe, individual genius, not good management, determined "quality." In this context, Albert Kahn's office was an exception.

Kahn's entry into architecture was itself exceptional. Born in Prussia and having immigrated to the United States when he was eleven

(3)
Fordism, often erroneously equated with Taylorism, is more properly defined by its emphasis on standardization and the setting of wages to balance production power with consumption power.

(4)
The lack of sponsorship is one reason that American scientific management never yielded, as it did in Europe, a more idealistic/nationalistic vision of a transformed society. See Guillen, *op. cit.*

(5)
See Mary N. Woods, *From Craft to Profession: The Practice of Architecture in Nineteenth Century America* (Berkeley: University of California, 1999) and Judith R. Blau, *Architects and Firms: A Sociological Perspective on Architectural Practice* (Cambridge, MA: MIT Press, 1987).

1927

1995

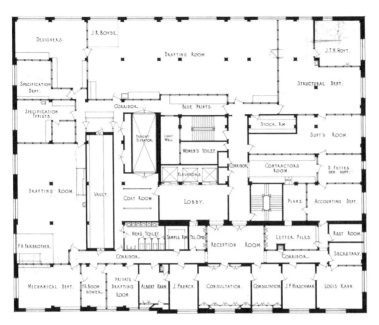

Offices of Albert Kahn, Inc., Floor Plan: Marquette Building; Detroit, Michigan; 1918. *Source: Bentley Historical Library, University of Michigan*

years old, he did not hold a professional architecture degree or attend architecture school. Kahn opened his office in 1895, incorporated in 1918 and in 1940, with more than 500 employees, renamed the firm Albert Kahn Associated Architects and Engineers, Inc. His firm succeeded alongside the birth of the auto industry in Detroit precisely because of his willingness to accept the factory commissions his architectural colleagues scorned. Over the course of 1,000 commissions he received from Henry Ford, Kahn learned not only how to please his client but also how to adopt Fordism into his practice.[6] The same production processes for which he designed factories — Taylorism and Fordism — he incorporated into his own design production.

In addition to the efficiency realized by having in-house civil, mechanical, and structural engineers, the most singular feature of the association was a horizontal, fast-track design approach that bypassed the traditional vertical from-author-to-draftsperson-to-consultant-to-contractor downward passage of work. When a job came in, the Executive Division secured all the necessary material and consultant contracts as well as the material sourcing. At the same time, the engineers and architects in the Technical Division developed their structural blueprints and coordinated specifications. Working drawings for a plant could be prepared and construction facilitated in one month.[7]

The Executive Department was divided into two parts: office management for accounting and administration and construction coordination for bidding and construction management. The Technical Department was divided into four parts: the design department (plans and sections); the architectural department (styling); the structural

⑥
As Henry Russel Hitchcock noted, "Albert Kahn took the lead around 1905, in developing a type of subdivision and flow of work in his office in Detroit comparable to the new methods of mass-production that his motor-car factories were specifically designed to facilitate." Henry Russel Hitchcock, *Architecture: Nineteenth and Twentieth Centuries*, (Harmondsworth: Penguin Books (1958), 547. See also Federico Bucci, *Albert Kahn: Architect of Ford* (New York: Princeton Architectural Press, 1993), 125.

⑦
Bucci, 129.

Construction of the assembly building at Chelyabinsk Tractor Plant, 1930, using the Kahn Truss system.
Source: Chelyabinsk Tractor Museum

department; and the mechanical department, which itself encompassed five subdivisions of sanitation, heating, air conditioning, electrical, and operations diagramming.

Communication was completely rationalized with requests for material, payments, daily relations between department heads, and timetables for the designers all done on identical but functionally differentiated color-coded forms. Every department of the firm had a graph of their work in which the projected progress was indicated in a system of coordinates with a black curve, the actual progress marked with a red curve, the difference in the two indicating the need for immediate remedy.[7] Research and development was an essential part of the firm's operation and was linked to the construction company owned by Albert Kahn's brother, Julius. The Trussed Concrete Steel Company invented and patented the "Kahn System," a unique concrete reinforcement operation consisting of steel-rolled bars with wings that work in tension while the concrete works in compression. Albert Kahn Associates built the first reinforced concrete buildings in Detroit using this system.

Kahn was clear that the head of a successful firm was not its design talent. "There is no place here for the temperamental artist, the clear-headed business man must have charge."[8] The leader "had to be prepared to furnish detailed designs and instructions (to avoid delays and misunderstanding), pay attention to costs, insurance and payroll, oversee the phases of construction, and provide inspection and assistance on the worksite."[9] While Kahn was personally ambitious in his marketing of the firm, he motivated his employees with good salaries, profit sharing, bonuses established according to merit, and a life insurance policy redeemable every five years.

[8] Ibid.,126.

[9] Ibid.

When he incorporated in 1918, Albert Kahn moved his office to the Marquette Building where the layout maximized efficient production. Written up in *Architectural Forum* that year for its innovations,[10] the plan shows that the structural engineers, mechanical engineers, the head designers, and the office manager were each given corner offices with the drafting rooms between. The superintendents' rooms were on either side of the meeting room. Clear glass walls separated the designers' rooms to combine privacy with exposed work habits. Innovative for its time, every office had an external phone, an internal phone, and an intercom.

Ten years after Albert Kahn incorporated, his American Taylorization got the attention of the Russians. In 1928, after canvassing the United States for someone to jumpstart Soviet industrialization, the Russian Amtrog Trading Corporation contacted Kahn and offered him a $4 million contract to build a tractor plant. This first commission led to $2 billion worth of construction contracts and Stalin's appointment of Kahn as the consulting architect to his first and second five-year plans.[11] Kahn's firm prepared all of the architectural and engineering drawings, the road and railway accesses, and provided key personnel including installation expertise. Less than a month after Kahn signed the contract on June 30, 1929, the first engineers, twenty-five in all, arrived in Moscow. What they found was nothing — no expertise, no infrastructure, no pencils, no drafting boards, no blueprint machines, and no ability to understand one another. Farm hands were converted into draftspeople and construction workers, and some 4,000 citizens were trained as Soviet engineers and apprentices. In two years, they had built 521 factories from Kiev to Yakutsk.[12]

Corporatism and CRS

If industrial production and Taylorist management characterized pre-World War II America, corporations and corporatism characterized the United States after World War II. Corporatism evolved from Taylorism in the years immediately after World War II when industrial production became more complex, more consumer oriented, and necessarily more "worker friendly." Corporations were thoroughly American, but the progressive thinkers of corporatism — those that gave it its white-collar allure — were immigrants from Europe. Peter Drucker, known as "the father of corporate thinking," came to America from Austria, bringing with him his European concern for worker alienation. Fearing, as many postwar European intellectuals did, that industrially abused workers would be driven to communism, Drucker envisioned a "harmonious polity" made up of well-managed economic entities — corporations — in which authority was clear but empowering. In 1945, Donaldson Brown, General Motors' business mastermind, asked Drucker to participate in a two-year socio-scientific analysis of the corporation. GM dismissed and refuted the resulting book, *The Concept of the Corporation*, but it made Drucker famous.[13]

Drucker's main thesis was "management by objective," an idea that was less anti-Taylorism than a subtle reassignment. The corporate

[10]
G.C. Baldwin, "The Office of Albert Kahn, Architect, Detroit, Michigan," *Architectural Forum*, vol. 29, no. 5, November 1918, 125–26.

[11]
Hesitant about communism and its supposed infiltration by Jews, Kahn nevertheless felt sorry for the post-Czar Russian population.

[12]
When he retired, Kahn was given a medal for distinguished war service. Because Germany knew relatively little of Russia's instant industrialization, its leaders miscalculation of the ease of invasion was significant in the defeat of Germany in World War II. This and the design and production of factories essential to the war made Kahn, the Tayorist architectural manager, an American hero. "Art: Industry's Architect,"*Time Magazine*, June 29, 1942.

[13]
Drucker suggested that the auto giant might want to re-examine a long list of entrenched policies on customer relations, dealer relations, employee relations, and more.

manager was to focus on the needs of the consumer/client, not the success of the corporation itself; he would set corporate goals but let the workers choose the processes and personal objectives. Understood to be intrinsically capable and willing, the corporate workers—non-unionized (industry and the proletariat no longer the relevant paradigm) and part of a new, expanded middle class—were professionals, scientists, managers, and technicians that, Drucker said, had been created by Taylorism but not properly managed by it. These "knowledge workers" commanded information, not people; they were part of management without being managers. They were, for Drucker, the workers of the "post-capitalist society."[14]

Other immigrants and European-trained sociologists fleshed out the progressive element of corporatism, addressing the need for corporations, prone to self-sustaining lethargy, to embrace change. Teamwork and research were seen by theorists such as Kurt Lewin and Donald Schön as essential components in managing change. Setting far-reaching goals—"problem setting, not problem solving"[15]—ensured that corporations didn't merely do things right, but found the right thing to do. This not only ensured an ethical position but a managerial one as well: workers would buy into the validity of the corporate goal and contribute to the team approach.

Corporate management ideology found its expression in architecture, in stylistic and programmatic terms. The International Style, America's version of Modernism, became synonymous with the new office skyscraper. Lever House by SOM and the Seagram Building by Mies van der Rohe epitomized an American version of "progress." But again, as with Taylorism, effective American corporatism came through the absorption of corporatist methods into the practices of American architectural offices. A new form of architectural office that both embraced corporatism in its structure and produced it in its buildings emerged with Skidmore Owings and Merrill, HOK, Harrison and Abromovitz. Anti-individualist (hence the team names), working in teams, incorporating sets of experts, embracing research and development, dividing the work between design, production, and business—these firms showed their corporate clients that they were one of them.

But another firm, Caudill Rowlett Scott (CRS) embraced corporatism at a more profound level and, like the firm of Albert Kahn Associates, explored "Americanism" at a level deeper than the typical US architectural practice did. All of the aforementioned firms remained partnerships and held onto traditional pyramidal models of design production in which the leaders were the designers, and the leaders of the designers were the partners. CRS in contrast became the true corporate architectural office. Founded in 1946 in College Station, Texas by Bill Caudill, John Rowlett (Caudill's student), Wallie Scott, and William Pena (who didn't want his name included), the firm incorporated in 1957 and became a publicly traded company in 1971.

If Albert Kahn had been exceptional for his willingness to take on factory work and apply design to orphaned programs, CRS was exceptional for concentrating on small local schools and working for

(14) See Peter F. Drucker, *Post-Capitalist Society* (New York: Harper Collins Publisher, Inc., 1993).

(15) See Donald A. Schön's *The Reflective Practitioner: How Professionals Think in Action* (New York: Basic Books, 1959). Kurt Lewin's publications were less widely distributed but very influential in organizational psychology, Gestalt psychology, and field theory.

communities that had barely heard of modernism and could not imagine that an architect from MIT, where Caudill was trained, would do their bidding. Capitalizing on his thesis, "Space for Teaching," Caudill and CRS won its first commission for the Stillwater school district (where Caudill had been a young student and which was the subject of his thesis), convincing a skeptical school board of the virtues of a modern building that prioritized efficient circulation, cross ventilation, and a non-hierarchical distribution of program. Based on its immediate success—the project was seen as revolutionary for its application of modern principles to an ordinary program—and wide publication, CRS went on to design schools, colleges, and universities in twenty-six states and eight countries.

Education was not just a program of choice for CRS. It permeated the ethos of the office and provided—ironically, given the distance of the firm from the large, East Coast corporations—the essential lessons of progressive corporatism. MIT, which not only granted Caudill's degree but which eventually gave CRS work, was home to numerous corporate gurus—Lewin and Schön among them. Caudill[16] and Rowlett both taught at Texas A&M and the majority of their staff had also been their students. Texas A&M, a land grant school, was home to research structuring the emerging military-industrial complex as the United States entered the Cold War. Indeed, education in general at this time was seen as the core of US intellectual and technological domination and, modeling the values of corporatism, emphasized research, teamwork, collaboration, and "objective learning."

CRS's obsession with "programming"—the primary focus of their research—enacted Drucker's "management by objective" with its imperative to serve the client. They had employees "squat" on their clients' sites to understand the issues of the brief, they conducted surveys, and they drew diagrams of functional desires and tested them with clients. Schön's "problem setting, not problem solving" emerged at CRS in the form of the book, *Problem Seeking: An Architectural Program Primer*.

At CRS, the team approach—which was both desirable "since there was not a genius like Frank Lloyd Wright among us, we worked together as a team"[17] and strategic because the specialized knowledge of each member meant they associated with external organizations—formed the basis for its management structure. The Drucker directive to treat employees not as factors in production but as members of the community was an essential part of keeping CRS empathetically bound even as they opened branch offices in more and more cities. All staff shared in the communication of the firm principals—Caudill's "Things that I Believe In" (TBIs) being the most intimate and effective in sharing "objectives"—and compensation, even for the partners, was agreed upon collectively. The principals set the goals but let the staff choose their place in it.

CRS practically invented the concept of architectural research at a time when the profession barely understood the term. Besides government studies in housing and some analyses done by the housing industry, it was virtually unheard of in the design firm.[18] The research permeated every

(16)
Caudill would be Director of the School of Architecture at Rice University from 1961 to 1969.

(17)
The CRS Team and the Business of Architecture, 1.

(18)
The AIA in 1946 established a department of Education and Research, but it was not until a 1959 conference funded by the American National Science Foundation that research on architecture would be distinct from research on building, housing, materials, and systems. I owe much of this discussion to Avigail Sachs' paper, "Marketing through Research: William Caudill and Caudill, Rowlett, Scott (CRS), *The Journal of Architecture*, 13:6, 737–52, December, 2008. http://trace.tennessee.edu/cgi/viewcontent.cgi?article=1001&context=utk_architecpub

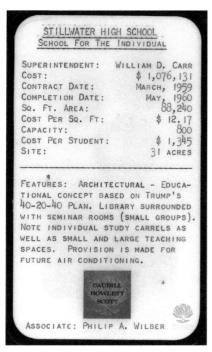

CRS "cards" for discussion with clients, early 1960s. *Source: CRS Center Archives, College of Architecture, Texas A&M University.*

Even children were allowed a voice in the design process during squatters session for Fodrea Community School in Columbus, Indiana, in 1971. *Source: CRS Center Archives, College of Architecture, Texas A&M University.*

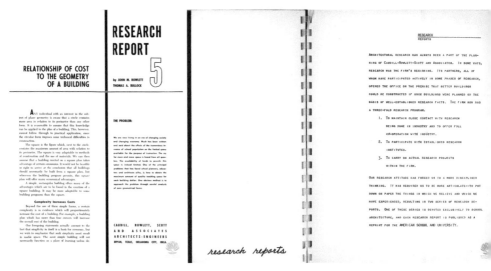

Research in a CRS promotional brochure 1959. The brochure also included descriptions of the firm's building types, examples of CRS designs and a long discussion of the teamwork in the firm. *Source: CRS Center Archives, College of Architecture, Texas A&M University*

Cover of CRSS Capital annual report, 1985. *Source: CRS Center Archives, College of Architecture, Texas A&M University.*

aspect of the firm's work: the business, the design (programming), the clients, the methods of procurement and construction, and the optimization of environmental systems; and it proved to be a highly profitable marketing tool. In the 1950s and 1960s, architects were not allowed to advertise based on their design work but were allowed to disseminate "factual material." CRS research, though centered on their client-driven work, so qualified. The dispersal of their research material, pulled together in publications that were given free to their existing and potential clients, and published in architectural journals as well, served the double purpose of attracting more clients while raising the stature of the firm within the profession. Likewise, the specialists they hired to stay abreast of client and contractor needs guaranteed that marketing was an in-house affair, aiding, as their 1960 Policy Manual stated, better design while promoting external "friendships." Mixing academia and practice for full impact, Caudill instituted the Architectural Division of the Texas Engineering Experiment Station (TEES) at Texas A&M in order to publish the transcribed "reports" of each of his firm's projects.

In 1957, CRS incorporated.[19] In doing so, it became more structured and centralized, dividing into design, production, and supervision, and pushed research into areas of education previously unexplored. The Ford Foundation asked CRS to run a school design program for developing countries under its auspices, taking the firm to South America and India. In 1964, tapped by educational professionals working in Saudi Arabia, CRS designed the King Fahad University of Petroleum and Minerals, a project which would last twenty-five years and land CRS in the Middle East ten years earlier than other US firms. Strategically, CRS paid increased attention to the managerial processes that produced buildings, not just designs. The industrialization of construction that emerged in the 1960s alongside the education sector's move toward fast-track construction made this shift in CRS research both necessary and profitable. Herb Pasteur, a partner at CRS writes to Caudill, then the president of the firm, in a 1969 memo: "The process is becoming more important than the product. The approach is more important than the solution. The process approach should depersonalize architecture. Maybe it would even take architecture away from the architect and give it to the people."[20]

This same year, the US Department of Foreign Affairs delegation to the USSR asked Bill Caudill to participate in assessing that country's industrial housing production. The visit had Caudill and the delegation assessing, in essence, the results of Kahn's work in jump-starting Russian industrialization.[21] The American team's visit was closing the circle of work by its countryman forty-one years earlier.

In the three weeks between August 23 and September 9, and as documented in the report, *Industrialized Building in the Soviet Union (A Report of the US Delegation to the USSR)*, "The group traveled as official representatives of the United States under the US/USSR Exchange agreement for 1968-69 which was administered by the Department of State. The Building Research Division of the National Bureau of Standards,

[19]
I owe Paolo Tombesi for much of the history of the transforming business structure of CRS. His "Capital Gains and Architectural Losses: The Transformational Journey of Caudill Rowlett Scott (1948–1994)," *The Journal of Architecture*, vol 11, no. 2, 2006, 145–68, is an excellent resource. Much of the character of CRS and the specifics of their personal dynamics are from *CRS and the Business of Architecture.*

[20]
Tombesi, 153.

[21]
Although there is no indication that they visited factories designed and built by Kahn—indeed, those factories were largely for tractors and equipment, not housing—it is interesting that the housing factories they did see were specialists in reinforced concrete, the very material that Kahn's brother's firm had devised and that Kahn himself made popular.

US Department of Commerce, was the American Sponsor of the exchange."[22] The delegation consisted of the chair, Dr. James R. Wright, Caudill, and six others from the American construction industry.[23] They found an advanced reinforced concrete prefabrication construction industry that was unable to set standards for onsite work, leaving even the most advanced housing units looking old and worn. They brought back to America a mandate for HUD to step up its affordable housing production. What it meant for CRS was access to the world of international diplomacy. Both the visit to the USSR and CRS's hosting of the Soviet delegates on their reciprocal visit to the United States a few years later were as much the construction of détente as they were the construction of buildings, coming at a time when the relations between the two superpowers were stabilizing as both were weakened by political difficulties elsewhere, the United States in Vietnam and the Russia in China.[24]

Having lost money in 1969 despite it being one of its "best" years, CRS, 247 in number and ranked by *Engineering News and Record* as the sixty-second largest firm in the United States, needed both an infusion of capital and a strategy to make it less vulnerable to market fluctuation. The partners formed a parent company called CRS Design Associates, Inc. (CRSDA) that issued publicly held stock the same year they won the AIA Firm of the Year award. After opening its ownership to investors, the management of CRS became increasingly directed by engineers and financial executives, far from the world of design. Buyouts of companies topped the corporate agenda, bringing out-of-house associated industries in-house. In 1978, CRS restructured again and was renamed "The CRS Group." After additional mergers with and acquisitions of numerous overseas power plants (industries less affected by the fluctuations of the market), in 1994, forty-six years after its founding, CRSS (CRS-Sirrine) sold its never-profitable architectural and engineering divisions to its former rivals, HOK and Jacob Engineering respectively. A year later, the corporation was acquired by American Tractebel, the US subsidiary of Powerfin SA, a member of the Belgian conglomerate active in gas and electric private sectors utilities, for $206 million.

Conclusion

Like Albert Kahn Associates, which both offended Hitchcock as he tried to assign "bureaucratic" firms marginal aesthetic roles in mass-produced housing and also caused him to reconsider canonical American architecture, CRS both disturbs critical sensibility for straying beyond known professional paradigms and also provokes by placing architecture squarely in the American corporate dream.

The fact that both firms were financially motivated is central to a critic's ambivalence; quality, not profit, ensures our profession's gentlemanliness. The emphasis on efficiency, management, and production over aesthetics, object production, and bespoke design indicates Taylorism's inappropriate intrusion on the intimacy of design. And yet the success of both firms rests on equating that efficiency with a self-effacement not directly related to greed and generated more by a desire to serve the client.

[22] James R. Wright, ed., Building Research Division, Institute for Applied Technology, National Bureau of Standards, Washington, DC, 20234, Department of Commerce, Special Publications 334, May 1971.

[23] David Watstein, manager of the Structural Clay Products Institute; W. Burr Bennett, Jr., Executive Director of the Prestressed Concrete Institute; Philip D. Bush, Vice President of Kaiser Engineering; Charles C. Law, Jr., Chief of the Technical Services Branch, Services Design Division, Office of Design and Construction, Public Building Services, General Services Administration; Fred W. Mast, past President of the Associated Contractors of America; and Dr. Charles Orlebeke, Executive Assistant to Secretary Romney, Department of Housing and Urban Design.

[24] Caudill writes in his notebook of that visit, *Memos from Russia 1969: Caudill Rowlett Scott*, "When our Russian friends visited Houston CRS put on a 'progressive dinner' for them in our homes. We had cocktails and snacks at Willie Pena's townhouse, the main course at the Caudill home, and dessert, more snacks and more drinks at the Herb Pasteur home, a moving, swinging affair." 214. This after Caudill had noted that in the three weeks in the USSR, they had never been invited into anyone's house. (*CRS Investigation 15*, 2 Feb 70).

In mastering the specific US programmatic agenda of their respective times, both firms "served" the United States as much as they served themselves and thereby served an Americanism desired by others overseas as well.

More interesting still is the model both firms offer of American architecture's injection into diplomacy. The lesson here is two-fold. One is the new power of a firm to shape international relations. That both firms played a part in the United States' changing relationship with Russia is testimony to architectural practice's newfound agency, one that powers both capitalist ideology and capitalism itself. Both also demonstrate that America alone does not own that ideology. Taylorization transformed into a sociopolitical, not merely economic, model overseas; it gained ideological exposure and then ideological transformation outside of the United States. As Taylorism became equated with proletarianism and proletarianism with communism, European intellectuals rethought the nature of scientific management to match and produce a more "democratic," more middle class, and more cohesive workforce. It was not just the United States that served and was served, it was all of the nations operating under capitalism. And for better or worse, the profession of architecture was integral to its orchestration.

Union Carbide Corporation Headquarters Entry Plaza, 1961 SOM. Natalie de Blois was senior designer on this canonic Park Avenue tower. The building stands over railroad tracks leading out of Grand Central Station, requiring extraordinary spatial and structural innovation and coordination to accommodate access to the building, an underground passage to the station, and the ongoing operations of trains. New York © Ezra Stoller/Esto.

HILARY SAMPLE

Natalie De Blois

An architect, teacher, and activist, Natalie de Blois spent thirty years of her half-century career working in the New York City (1944–62) and Chicago (1962–74) offices of Skidmore, Owings and Merrill (SOM). She was the first designer in the New York City office where she helped define the forms of midcentury corporate modernism, particularly the glass-and-steel office tower typology that housed complex, international organizations.[1] These corporations and the large architectural firms that designed for them adopted the organizational structures they served, reshaping the nature of professional practice. Yet, even as a key author of the architectural language of international corporate modernism, she has largely been excluded from histories of the period, overshadowed by her renowned colleague, architect, and SOM partner Gordon Bunshaft. De Blois's career reflects the difficulties faced by a midcentury American woman professional, and, while she was not the only woman at SOM, her struggles were particularly complex. Despite holding a leadership position within the office, she was never rewarded with partner status. Tracing her career reveals challenges faced by architects of both genders during this time and highlights SOM's rapid transformation into one of the largest architecture offices in the world—one that framed itself as a design firm offering more than technical expertise.

Upon graduating from Columbia University's Graduate School of Architecture, Planning and Preservation in 1944, de Blois briefly interned with Ketchum, Gina & Sharp in New York City before joining the eight-year-old firm of SOM. By 1948, she was working alongside Bunshaft on many seminal projects—Lever House (1952), Hilton Istanbul (1955), Connecticut General Life Insurance Company Headquarters (1956)—and later as the senior designer on the Union Carbide Corporation Headquarters (1960) and Pepsi-Cola Corporation World Headquarters (1960). Three of these projects—Lever House, Pepsi-Cola, and Union Carbide—stand on Park Avenue in New York City.

At a time when American and multinational corporations began to occupy urban centers with high-rise headquarters, de Blois helped develop the modern style that would typify the genre. Her designs transformed the basic elements of the corporate tower, with innovative office layouts, and re-engineered the workspace of (largely women) secretaries. Each of the Park Avenue buildings achieved high performance in a minimal facade through a careful calibration of glass, silicone, stainless

①
SOM Journal 2, Hatje Cantz, Natalie de Blois Interviewed by Detlef Mertins, June 17, 2004, Chicago; https://www.somchina.cn/publication/natalie-de-blois-interviewed-detlef-mertins

1944

1984

Lever House Ground Floor Courtyard, SOM, 1952 New York. © Ezra Stoller/Esto.

steel, spandrel panels, fireproofing, and maintenance systems. The glass facade became a symbol of the new work environment and new social order.[2] Social organization was also reconfigured at the ground, where de Blois connected the otherwise insular building type to the city, opening it to the street edge and integrating plazas, landscape, open-air court-yards, and colonnades. In each of her buildings, the engagement of the pedestrian level with the urban context was innovative, with Lever House lifting to invite the public into an unexpected courtyard, Pepsi-Cola hovering effortlessly above the sidewalk, and Union Carbide dramatizing workers' everyday experience with a giant red escalator funneling them into the office floors above. All three buildings lifted the facade allowing the sidewalk to slip beneath the bulk of the building, reinterpreting the Manhattan grid.

At Lever House, de Blois was the lead designer of the low-lying courtyard building, which takes up much of the site, strengthening the view of the tower's south facade as if it were a billboard for the inter-national manufacturer of soaps and detergents. As an early paradigm of privately owned public space in New York City, the raised second floor and hollowed out ground floor eliminated the usual retail storefronts, subverting the need for an artificially illuminated entry lobby in favor of an exterior social space. De Blois, who would later speak of her interest in urban planning, was prescient in her efforts to seek an integral relationship between architecture and the city.

One of the many parallels between de Blois's working world and the corporate world SOM designed was the gender inequality: she was a professionally marginalized figure who primarily provided visions for

(2)
Michelle Murphy, "Building Ladies" in *Sick Building Syndrome, and the Problem of Uncertainty: Environmental Politics, Technoscience, and Women Workers.* Duke University Press, 2006, 45.

worlds in which women were marginalized more generally. De Blois designed the modern American workplace, where women, who largely played supportive roles, were visible in the open-plan configurations, but invisible within the corporations' higher ranks. This inversion of spatial visibility and power appears in de Blois's Lever House and Union Carbide headquarters. Behind the glazed and taut curtain walls, female secretaries sat within the open floor plan, while male managers occupied private offices with city views. Corporations around the globe adopted these towers, replicating both the internal organizational structure of the US corporation and its physical form, appearance, and gender politics. While de Blois strove to design new work standards that would increase productivity and work flow, she also produced a new social environment and collective. It is now possible to reflect on these spaces as restricting advancement, just as de Blois was unable to break through the "glass ceiling." Through these projects—and others that de Blois led between 1953 and 1960—she encountered not only the challenges of headquarters design but also the corporate politics of the clients she served—politics much like she experienced at SOM. The 1955 SOM newsletter featured scenes of the New York office with de Blois at her drafting desk, the only woman in the image.[3] However, when Betty Blum in 2004, asked her if she thought she was treated fairly, she seemed unfazed: "Yes, for what I am, I was treated fairly...Being a woman architect is not the important thing to me. I've always been singled out because I'm the one who did large buildings, but architecture is a building profession."[4]

While indeed it was a "building profession," during these years at SOM, de Blois became not only a licensed architect but also a "design architect" within the design department, a distinction that emerged in the New York office the early 1950s. In an interview, conducted in 2004, de Blois describes returning to the New York office after completing a Fulbright Fellowship in Paris and working for a year (1952–53) in Bad Godesberg, Germany, where she led SOM's office and held the title "chief of design."[5] Because of her leadership position in the German office, and her continued working relationship with Bunshaft, de Blois would retain an equivalent position when she returned to New York in 1953. On the separation of design and production into different departments and rooms, she became one of very few employees in the New York office to work as a design architect. Within this newly formed design department she worked on Connecticut General and Union Carbide — two of the most important projects of her career.[6]

A small leather-bound photo album, with Bunshaft's name embossed in gold letters, documenting a site visit to the then-nearly completed Connecticut General headquarters offers a glimpse into de Blois' world. Ezra Stoller, the famous photographer, recorded the meeting between the president of Connecticut General, Frazer B. Wilde, and the architects, Bunshaft, de Blois, and William Brown, a managing partner at SOM, who had gathered, among other reasons, to discuss a mock-up of Florence Knoll's modern furniture for the open-plan workspaces. In this setting, De Blois is seen seated with a blazer, skirt, and heels, hair trim,

(3)
SOM Newsletter October 15, 1955, 2.

(4)
Oral History of Natalie De Blois, Interviewed by Betty J. Blum; Compiled under the auspices of the Chicago Architects Oral History Project; The Ernest R. Graham Study Center for Architectural Drawings, Department of Architecture, The Art Institute of Chicago Copyright © 2004 The Art Institute of Chicago; 62.

(5)
SOM Newsletter no. 9 December 15, 1954, 2.

(6)
Oral History of Natalie De Blois, Interviewed by Betty J. Blum; Compiled under the auspices of the Chicago Architects Oral History Project; The Ernest R. Graham Study Center for Architectural Drawings Department of Architecture The Art Institute of Chicago Copyright © 2004 The Art Institute of Chicago; 66.

Following four spreads: © ESTO, Source: Gordon Bunshaft Archive, Avery Library, Columbia University.

Connecticut General Life Insurance Bloomfield, CT. SOM. Women primarily occupied the interior open plan desks, 1957 © Ezra Stoller/Esto.

and without the glasses that she typically wore in most photographs. This album, which Stoller made for Bunshaft, includes rare images of her at a job site with the partners and client, even though she worked closely with them and frequently met with clients without Bunshaft. In a 2004 interview with Detlef Mertins, for example, she recalls a meeting for the "Kennedy International Airport" project that was preceded by Bunshaft's critique of her outfit: "You can't come to the meeting unless you go home first and change your clothes. I don't like green."[7] Although supported by Bunshaft professionally, she recalled that his personal treatment of her was typical of the times.[8] The photos capture de Blois's shifting presence, in the margins, off center, and obscured. Nonetheless, she is present — a testament to her involvement and recognition as an architect by Bunshaft — to give her approval for the design of the female workers' furniture and to review the construction in general.

　　Connecticut General, among the first corporate headquarters to be built in a suburban setting, is a stark contrast to de Blois's designs for urban headquarters buildings. The shift in site from a densely populated city, with its many amenities, to a comparatively sparsely settled suburban context resulted in a rethinking of the corporate headquarters program, which involved, for example, the formation of a women's committee that worked directly with de Blois to write an expanded program, including a library, billiard room, food store, dry cleaner, medical department, and cafeteria.[9] The first floor contained some of these uses, which were located adjacent to open-air courtyards designed by Isamu Noguchi and, in one case, by de Blois, at Bunshaft's request.[10] As at Lever House, a significant amount of space was dedicated to open-plan work areas, which

[7] https://www.somchina.cn/publication/natalie-de-blois-interviewed-detlef-mertins

[8] https://www.somchina.cn/publication/natalie-de-blois-interviewed-detlef-mertins

[9] Blum, *Oral History of Natalie De Blois*, 66.

[10] https://www.somchina.cn/publication/natalie-de-blois-interviewed-detlef-mertins

were primarily occupied by women and never located more than thirty feet from a window.

Returning to the Stoller photo album, the space, though still under construction, displays the mocked-up work environment with open plan desks, enclosed offices with clerestories, and partition walls aligned with the ceiling grid.[11] Here it is possible to see the inside of a private office as well as the large open space for the administrative staff. On the first page of the album, President Wilde,, hands on hips, stands on an unfinished concrete floor. A wheel barrow and ladder in the background indicate that the project is still under construction. De Blois is in several photographs, looking quite serious; in one image she is seated at a large circular meeting table in conversation with her colleagues. These images expand the narrative of her role within SOM, as most published photographs present her sitting behind a drafting desk. At Connecticut General she is dressed as a professional, an architect, yet a woman—whose influential project is nearing completion.

In his autobiography, Nathaniel Owings, a founding partner of SOM, wrote that de Blois's "mind and hands worked marvels in design— and only she and God would ever know just how many great solutions, with the imprimatur of one of the male heroes of SOM, owed much more to her than was attributed by either SOM or the client."[12] And that was in part due to the system of production at SOM, which was devoted to optimizing the organization of labor forces not only for its clients but also for its own architectural practice. Led by Bunshaft, the New York City office developed a strict structure of production based on tasks and skills involved with design and technologies. As Bunshaft explained in an interview, "They were not dreamers. SOM exists today because they could service the needs of the building public. Half the jobs they get, nobody else could do it. SOM grew with the times. They were always there to grow...The firm is hungry for talent. Talent moves up the ladder, and there's no head man."[13] A group portrait taken for a meeting of partners and associate partners in the Chicago office in 1958 illustrates the so-called "flat pyramid" that Bunshaft described. This aggregation of talented partners and associate partners was the rationale for how the firm "succeeded" and was "flexible."[14] While there was "no head man" in the photo, there were no women either; de Blois, despite being a senior designer on the Connecticut General, Union Carbide, and Pepsi-Cola projects, was not a part of the "flat pyramid." The streamlined approach to design and its detailing enabled a proficiency of building; even today the office's structure is a legacy of this early division of work.[15] This organizational model enabled de Blois to oversee and significantly contribute (although largely anonymously) to so many prominent projects.

While there were intentional slights and what would today be considered discrimination, it is significant to understand the context of SOM's corporate structure. De Blois was not promoted to the "pyramid" until 1964, when she became an associate partner, nearly twenty years after joining in the New York office. In 1974, she resigned without a pension from SOM's Chicago office, where she had relocated twelve years

(11)
"Well, we did a full-scale mock-up just to study the window wall, the partition system, lighting and furniture systems. At that time, there was no office furniture that looked right in that space. I mean, the furniture that you could buy was all big, heavy, with rounded corners. So it was important to bring in somebody who could design compatible furniture and see that it was built, for the modern building that we were designing." Blum, *Oral History of Natalie De Blois*, 60.

(12)
Nathaniel Alexander Owings. *The Spaces in Between: An Architect's Journey.* Boston: Houghton Mifflin, 1973. Print. http://www.nytimes.com/2013/08/01/nyregion/an-architect-whose-work-stood-out-even-if-she-didnt.html?_r=1&

(13)
SOM Journal 3, Hatje Cantz, 165.

(14)
Ibid., 165.

(15)
Author's experience between 1996–99 in the New York City SOM office design department.

SOM's Chicago office, Partners and Associate Partners, 1958. *Source: Skidmore, Owings & Merrill, Photographer: Austen Field.*

earlier, and moved to Houston to begin a new chapter of her career and life.[16] There, in the wake of the oil boom, she joined several former Chicago SOM employees at Neuhaus & Taylor. This same year she became a Fellow of the American Institute of Architects, at a time when there were only twelve women registered architects in the Chicago AIA chapter.[17]

In 1988, long after she had left SOM and while she was teaching as an adjunct professor at the University of Texas at Austin (1980–93), de Blois was invited to visit SOM's New York office. The photograph taken for the occasion shows de Blois slightly hunched, lean, and with precisely cropped hair. She is flanked by a group of young men dressed in the late 1980s corporate uniform of crisp white shirts, a holdover from the 1950s mantra "to build a business you must first build men."[18] In the midtown Manhattan office, they stand in front of a travertine wall, the same material found in SOM's offices worldwide.[19] The smiling men are de Blois's former students turned SOM employees. She was their mentor, as she was to others in the profession. This photo — the poses, expressions, and setting — portrays her story as an educator and demonstrates that modern architecture firms were built through a more diverse intellect and experience than history tends to illustrate. When asked what her greatest contribution to architecture was, de Blois replied: "To the field of architecture? Well, I think probably, it's in being an architect who actually worked on buildings, and as a mentor for other women."[20]

This image, snapped the same year Bunshaft received the Pritzker Prize, captures her complex struggle. De Blois repeatedly dismissed concern for being a woman architect, she was "one-hundred percent against the idea that there was a difference between what a man or a woman brings to architecture."[21] For her, it was the work, the architecture that mattered. At the end of her career the projects that she admired the most were the Pepsi-Cola and Connecticut General headquarters, not

[16] Blum, *Oral History of Natalie De Blois* 114, 137.

[17] Ibid.,112.

[18] Reinhold Martin, "Computer Architectures, Saarinen's Patterns, IBM's Brains." *Anxious Modernisms*, Cambridge: The MIT Press, 2000, 148.

[19] Office located on 42nd Street in the Daily News building, upon leaving the lobby, the design department was the first visible part of the office. An open floor plan was filled with desks and computers.

[20] Blum, *Oral History of Natalie De Blois*, 141.

[21] Ibid., 139.

Natalie de Blois with SOM employees, 1988. *Source: Skidmore, Owings & Merrill.*

the towers. "I had no great love for high-rise buildings, I mean, it's a commercial thing; it's an economic question, beyond my control.[22]

De Blois's legacy is multifaceted, from her steadfast focus on architecture to her late-career efforts to address the challenges facing young women architects, the latter a seeming contradiction to the interviews she gave. She was a founding member of the Chicago Women in Architecture group and spent more than a decade on the AIA's Task Force for Women in Architecture where she worked toward producing opportunities for and reflecting on the needs of women architectural students.

Without a careful rereading of the past, and some necessary rewriting of it, architecture's culture will remain overwhelmingly exclusionary and devoid of the many women architects and designers who operate within it. De Blois's career spanned a time of rapid change in the American workplace, and her development as an architect was shaped by the complexity of shifting practice, as well as her progressive views about practice, particularly women's issues. Despite instances of discrimination and sexism, she received credit as the senior designer of iconic projects such as Union Carbide and Pepsi-Cola and public credit.[23] A 1958 *Fortune* magazine article "Architects from Skid's Row," includes a photograph of de Blois—alongside partner Bill Brown—listing her as a "senior designer,"for a skyscraper and overseeing five junior designers.[24]

While postwar US corporate architecture incorporated ultra-flat facades to reveal a progressive internal structure, more often than not it produced an organizational structure so rigid that its imagery became a system used against the very nature of progress itself. Despite being complicit in designing these "standards" and creating a new framework for environments of control, de Blois was subject to such "standards" herself. While much has been made of de Blois's inability to break through the "glass ceiling," her legacy is not about the inequities. It is this: she was an architect (making architecture) ahead of her time.

[22]
Ibid., 140.

[23]
https://www.somchina.cn/publication/natalie-de-blois-interviewed-detlef-mertins

[24]
Fortune Magazine, "Architects from Skid's Row," January 1958.

BEATRIZ COLOMINA

The Office in the Boudoir

The office has moved into the bed. In what is probably now a conservative estimate, *The Wall Street Journal* reported in 2012 that eighty percent of young New York City professionals work regularly from bed. The fantasy of the home office has given way to the reality of the bed office. The very meaning of the word "office" has been transformed. Millions of dispersed beds are displacing concentrated office buildings. The boudoir is defeating the tower. Networked electronic technologies have removed any limit to what can be done in bed. It is not just that the bed office has been made possible by new media. Rather, new media is designed to extend a one hundred year old dream of domestic connectivity to millions of people. The history of the office building has been shadowed by a secret history of the supercharged bed.

How did we get here?

In his famous short text "Louis-Philippe, or the Interior," Walter Benjamin wrote of the splitting of work and home in the nineteenth century:

> Under Louis-Philippe, the private citizen enters the stage of history...For the private person, living space becomes, for the first time, antithetical to the place of work. The former is constituted by the interior; the office is its complement. The private person who squares his accounts with reality in his office demands that his interior be maintained in his illusions...From this spring the phantasmagorias of the interior. For the private individual the private environment represents the universe. In it he gathers remote places and the past. His living room is a box in the world theater.[1]

Industrialization brought the eight hour shift and the radical separation between home and office or factory, rest and work, night and day. Postindustrialization collapses work back into the home and takes it further into the bedroom and into the bed itself. Phantasmagoria is no longer lining the room in wallpaper, fabric, images, and objects. It is now in the electronic devices. The whole universe is concentrated on a small screen with the bed floating in an infinite sea of information. To lie down is not to rest but to move, as the bed is now a site of action. But the voluntary invalid has no need for legs. The bed has become the ultimate prosthetic and a whole new industry is devoted to providing contraptions to facilitate work while lying down: reading, writing, texting,

Facing page: Hugh Hefner at work with array of stimulants. Playboy Mansion, Chicago. © Burt Glinn/Magnum Photos.

1953

① Walter Benjamin, "Louis-Philippe, or the Interior," in *Reflections: Essays, Aphorisms, Autobiographical Writings*, ed. Peter Demetz, translation by Edmud Jephcott (New York: Schoken Books, 1978), 154.

2014

recording, broadcasting, listening, talking, and of course, eating, drinking, sleeping, or making love, activities which of late seem to have been turned into work itself. Waiters in restaurants in the United States ask if you are "still working on that" before removing your plate or your glass. And endless advice is being dispensed about how to "work" on your personal relationships or "schedule" sex with your partner. Sleep too, is hard work for millions, with the psycho-pharmaceutical industry dispensing new drugs every year and an army of sleep experts providing advice on how to achieve this apparently ever more elusive goal — of course, all in the name of higher productivity. Everything done in the bed has become work.

This philosophy was already embodied in the figure of Hugh Hefner, who famously almost never left his bed, let alone his house. He literally moved his office to his bed in 1960 when he moved into the Playboy Mansion at 1340 North State Parkway, Chicago, turning it into the epicenter of a global empire and his silk pajamas and dressing gown into his business attire. "I don't go out of the house at all!!!...I am a contemporary recluse," he told Tom Wolfe, guessing that the last time he was out had been three and a half months before and that in the last two years he had been out of the house only nine times.[2] Fascinated, Wolfe described him as "the tender-tympany green heart of an artichoke."[3]

Playboy turns the bed into a workplace. From the mid-1950s on, the bed becomes increasingly sophisticated, outfitted with all sorts of entertainment and communication devices as a kind of control room. The magazine devoted many articles to the design of the perfect bed. Hefner acted as the model with his famous round bed in the Playboy Mansion in Chicago. The bed was first introduced as a feature in the "Playboy Townhouse" article of 1962, which presents a detailed unrealized project in plans, sections, and renderings that had been originally commissioned to be Hefner's own house. Not by chance, the only piece of the design to be realized was the bed, which was installed in the Mansion. The bed is a house in and of itself. Its rotating and vibrating structure is packed with a small fridge, hi-fi, telephone, filing cabinets, bar, microphone, Dictaphone, video cameras, headphones, TV, breakfast table, work surfaces, and a control panel for all light fixtures for the man who never wants to leave. The bed was Hefner's office, his place of business — where he conducted interviews, made his phone calls, selected images, adjusted layouts, edited texts, ate, drank, and consulted with playmates.

Hefner was not alone. The bed may have been the ultimate US office at midcentury. In an interview in the *Paris Review* in 1957, Truman Capote is asked: "What are some of your writing habits? Do you use a desk? Do you write on a machine?" To which he answers:

> I am a completely horizontal author. I can't think unless I'm lying down, either in bed or stretched on a couch and with a cigarette and a coffee handy. I've got to be puffing and sipping. As the afternoon wears on, I shift from coffee to mint tea to sherry to martinis. No, I don't use a typewriter. Not in the beginning.

[2] Tom Wolfe, "King of the Status Dropouts," *The Pump House Gang* (New York: Farrar, Straus & Giroux, 1965).

[3] Ibid., 63.

The epicenter of the universe: Playboy Mansion, Chicago. © Burt Glinn/Magnum Photos.

I write my first version in longhand. Then I do a complete revision, also in longhand...Then I type a third draft on yellow paper...No, I don't get out of bed to do this. I balance the machine on my knees. Sure, it works fine; I can manage a hundred words a minute.[4]

④
"Truman Capote, The Art of Fiction No. 17," interviewed by Patti Hill, *The Paris Review* n. 16, Spring-Summer 1957.

From morning to afternoon to evening, the drinks, the paper, and the equipment change, but his position on the bed does not.

Even architects set up office in bed at midcentury. Richard Neutra started working the moment he woke up, with elaborate equipment enabling him to design, write, or even interview in bed. As his son Dion Neutra revealed:

Dad's best time for creative thinking was early in the morning, long before any activity had started in the office below. He often stayed in bed working with ideas and designs, even extending into appointments which had been made earlier. His one concession to convention was to put on a tie over his night shirt when receiving visitors while still propped up in bed![5]

⑤
Dion Neutra, "The Neutra Genius: Innovation & Vision," *Modernism* [Vol.1 No. 3], December 1998.

Neutra's bed in the VDL house in Silver Lake, Los Angeles included two public phones, three communication stations to talk with other rooms in the house, the office below, and even another office 500 meters away, three different call bells, drafting boards and easels that folded down over the bed, electric lights, and a radio-gramophone

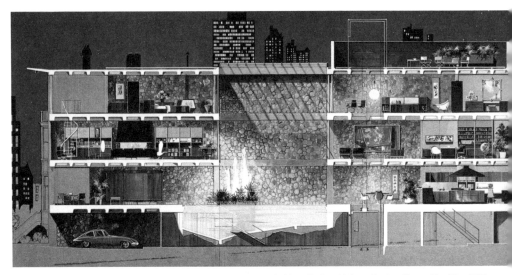

Slice of the New Bachelor Life: The Playboy Townhouse cut-away view. Architect: R. Donald Jaye, drawing: Humen Tan, May 1962 *Playboy.* © Playboy Enterprises International, Inc.

Rotating Architecture: Playboy Townhouse Bedroom with Hefner's Bed.
Architect: R. Donald Jaye, drawing: Humen Tan, May 1962 *Playboy.* © Playboy
Enterprises International, Inc.

controlled from a dashboard overhead. A bedside table rolling on casters held the tape recorder, electric clock, and storage compartments for drawing and writing equipment so that he could, as Neutra put it in a letter to his sister, "use every minute from morning to late night."[6]

Postwar America inaugurated the high performance bed as an epicenter of productivity: a new form of industrialization that was exported globally and has now become available to an international army of dispersed but interconnected producers. A new kind of factory without walls is constructed by compact electronics and extra pillows for the 24/7 generation.

The kind of equipment that Hefner envisioned (some of which, like the answering machine, didn't yet exist) is now expanded for the internet and social media generation, who not only work in bed but socialize in bed, exercise in bed, read the news in bed, and entertain sexual relationships with people miles away from their beds. The Playboy fantasy of the "nice girl next door" is more likely realized today with someone on another continent than in the same building or neighborhood. A person you may have never seen before and may never see again—and it is anybody's guess if she is real—exists in some place and time—or an electronic construction. Does it matter? As in the 2013 film *HER*, a moving depiction of life in the soft, uterine state that is a corollary to our new mobile technologies, HER is an operating system that turns out to be a more satisfying partner than a person. The protagonist lies in bed with HER, chatting, arguing, and making love.

If, according to critic Jonathan Crary, capitalism is the end of sleep, colonizing every minute of our lives for production and consumption,[7] the actions of the voluntary recluse are not so voluntary in the end. It may be worth noting that Communism had its own ideas of bringing the bed to the work place. In 1929, at the height of Stalin's first five year plan, with the working day extended and mass exhaustion of factory workers in the face of staggering production quotas, the Soviet government organized a competition for a new city of rest for 100,000 workers. Konstantin Melnikov presented the "Sonata of Sleep," a new building type for collective sleep, with mechanized beds to rock the workers to unconsciousness and slanted floors to eliminate the need for pillows. Centralized control booths with sleep attendants would regulate temperature, humidity, smell, and even sounds to maximize sleep. The inspiration was symptomatically American. Melnikov had read about a military academy in Pensacola, Florida that taught language to sleeping cadets. Sleep itself had become part of the industrial process.

In today's Attention Deficit Disorder society, we have discovered that we work better in short bursts punctuated by rest. Today many companies provide sleeping pods in the office to maximize productivity. Bed and office are never far apart in the 24/7 world. Special self-enclosed beds have been designed for office spaces, turned into compact sealed capsules—mini space ships—that can be used in isolation, or gathered together in clusters, or lined up in rows for synchronized sleep. They are a part of work rather than its opposite.

(6)
Neutra to Verena Saslavsky, December 4, 1953, Dione Neutra Papers, quoted in Thomas S. Hines, *Richard Neutral and the Search for Modern Architecture: A Biography and History* (Los Angeles: University of California Press, 1982), 251.

(7)
Jonathan Crary, 24/7: *Late Capitalism and the Ends of Sleep* (Verso, 2013).

Between the bed inserted into the office and the office inserted into the bed, a whole new horizontal architecture has taken over. It is magnified by the "flat" networks of social media that have themselves been fully integrated into the professional, business, and industrial environment in a collapse of traditional distinctions between private and public, work and play, rest, and action. The bed itself with its ever more sophisticated mattress, linings, and technical attachments is the basis of an intrauterine environment that combines the sense of deep interiority with the sense of hyper connectivity to the outside. Not by chance, Hefner's round bed was a kind of flying saucer hovering in space in a room without windows, as if in orbit, with the TV hanging above as a reference to planet earth. It is a circle, the classical image of the universe. The bed today has also become a portable universe, equipped with every possible technology of communication. A midcentury fantasy has turned into a mass-reality.

What is the architecture of this new space and time?

In the 1960s and 1970s experimental architects devoted themselves to the equipment of the new mobile nomads in a whole galaxy of lightweight, portable interiors with soft reclining spaces as the core of a complex of prosthetic extensions. All of these projects can be understood as high performance beds complete with media, artificial atmospheres, color, light, smell… a kind of POP Psychedelic Melnikov with the worker now sleeping inside the control booth. Reyner Banham wrote about the nude Jane Fonda flying through space in her fur-lined horizontal bubble in the same breath that he enthusiastically embraced the architecture of Playboy. It was just a matter of time before John Lennon and Yoko Ono held a week-long "Bed-In for Peace" in the Amsterdam Hilton Hotel during their honeymoon in March 1969. The idea for "Bed-In" came from "Sit-In" protests and was intended as a non-violent protest against war and to promote world peace. "Make love, not war" was the slogan of the day but to the disappointment of journalists, John and Yoko were fully dressed in their pajamas, sitting in bed, as John put it, like angels. The bed has taken over from the street as the site of protest. They invited the world's press into their room every day between 9am and 9pm, treating the bed as an office in which they worked while journalists streamed in and images streamed out.

What is the nature of this new interior that we have decided collectively to check ourselves into? What is the architecture of this prison in which night and day, work and play, are no longer differentiated and we are permanently under surveillance, even as we sleep in the control booth? New media turns us all into inmates, constantly under surveillance, even as we celebrate endless connectivity. Each of us has become "a contemporary recluse" as Hefner put it half a century ago.

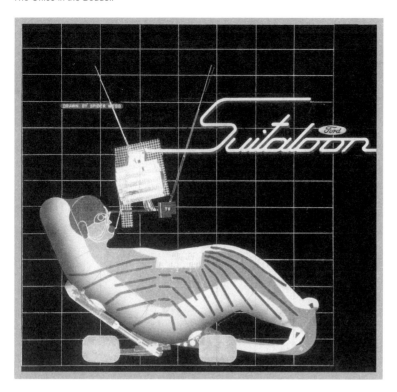

The electronic bed: Michael Webb, Suitaloon. *Michael Webb © Archigram 1968–79.*

Instant bed, the Napmaster. *Source: Nathan Sayers for MetroNaps.*

A
new
world
to work in

ACTION OFFICE ®

If you're a stand-up worker, come in and see
Action Office. If you're a sit-down worker,
come in and see Action Office. If you like to
straddle or perch while you work, come in
and see Action Office.
You see, we made Action Office just for you.

Researched and developed by Robert Propst,
Director of Herman Miller's Research Divisi•
Design by George Nelson.

Action Office advertisement, 1965. *Source: HermanMiller.*

BRANDEN HOOKWAY

Mobility as Management: The Action Office

Soon after receiving the 1965 Alcoa Industrial Design Award for his work on Herman Miller's Action Office, the first office furniture system, George Nelson wrote that design had neglected the knowledge worker:

> In a factory, a semi-literate laborer may be backed up by $100,000 worth of machinery, but nobody makes that kind of investment in a white-collar worker...I think the executive is the most downtrodden guy in business today. He gets a room with sofas and a place for a photograph of the wife and kids, but nobody cares if his office helps him do his job. He has none of the advantages of privacy or public exposure, and has all the disadvantages of both...At the same time, his plush corner office cuts him off from easy contact with the people who work for him...Action Office furniture is a response to these opinions. It expresses our feelings that the office today is not just a desk but a collection of work stations, a place to get the job done.[1]

While Nelson was responsible for designing the components of the first Action Office, Robert Probst developed the concept. His role is given only passing acknowledgment in Alcoa's award with the mention: "Mr. Nelson's designs were based on detailed behavioral studies undertaken by Robert Probst, director of Herman Miller's product research laboratory."[2] Hugh De Pree, then president of Herman Miller, would later recall, "Some thought it a case of poetic injustice" that the award went to Nelson without mentioning Probst's "basic work" on Action Office.[3] More inventor than designer, Probst began consulting for Herman Miller in 1958 after a chance meeting at the Aspen Design Conference. He joined the company full-time in 1960 to found its first research division, with the expected participation of Nelson and Charles and Ray Eames.[4] Probst's initial design proposals ranged from a laser beam construction level, to seating ideas using netting and waffle springs, to a livestock identification program and an artificial heart valve. By 1961 "The Action Office"—presented as the problem of designing "the office environment and equipment" to enhance self-sufficiency, memory, balanced physical activity, and "the generative process that leads to decision"—had taken priority among the research division's ongoing projects.[5]

Action Office frames knowledge work and its organization as a multi-faceted problem. Its elements describe an ergonomics of use. Work

1958

1971

(1) George Nelson, "Experts Speak: What's Wrong with Office Design," *Today's Secretary* (Feb 1966): 46, 83.

(2) Rukk, Kiek and McAuliffe, Inc. for Alcoa, "George Nelson... has received the 1965 Alcoa Industrial Design Award," news release, November 30, 1965.

(3) Hugh De Pree, *Business as Unusual: The People and Principles at Herman Miller* (Zeeland, MI: Herman Miller, 1992), 87.

(4) Herman Miller employee communication, August 31, 1960, Herman Miller Archives, Pubs709.

(5) D. J. De Pree, notes on Bob Probst's Presentation to the Management Group on October 25, 1961, Herman Miller Archives, Hrd45.

surfaces, display areas, shelf organizers, and task lighting are arranged to enhance the visibility of work in progress, with the idea that providing quick and intuitive access to information would augment decision-making. To mitigate the effects of sedentary office work on health and productivity, the components are set at a range of low and high heights to promote movement between sitting and standing postures throughout the workday. Along these lines, the sole chair specified in the launch of Action Office in 1965 is a "perch chair" compatible with the higher range of work surface heights. Yet what is most essential to the conceptualization of Action Office is how its elements come together as a re-configurable environment. Each element not only relates to its immediate user, but also works with other elements to allow for a wide variety of social spaces, circulation pathways, and privacy requirements, so as to constitute a system that could be calibrated to the changing needs of an organization. As systems furniture, the whole was meant to be greater than its individual elements. Hence Probst's observation in a 1962 report that, "we are not really selling furniture or equipment as much as an improved working environment."[6] In defining this environment, Probst tested potential elements and arrangements in consultation with psychologists, medical doctors, executives, and specialists in industrial engineering and human relations. He commissioned studies of Action Office prototypes by the Department of Psychology at Michigan State University in 1962 and the industrial psychology consulting firm Dunlap and Associates in 1965. A 1966 paper by Probst published in the journal *Human Factors* cites these studies in describing psychology's influence on the conceptualization of Action Office. He also cites two cognitive psychologists: George Armitage Miller, whose "work on information and memory greatly influenced Action Office concepts of information assembly, identification, and limitation in offices;" and Ulric Neisser, whose "work on visual search," or the cognitive processes involved in recognizing patterns in visual perception, "reinforces the proposals to emphasize visual display."[7]

The aim of Action Office was to facilitate a kind of spatial information processing, with the office system functioning as an interface between knowledge worker and organization. For its user, Action Office would be a kinesthetic work environment offering comfortable and intuitive access to a visual and informational search space. For organizations, it would provide means of integrating workers into a reconfigurable diagram of interpersonal relationships and workflow. Already by 1962, Probst viewed Action Office as less an office design than a system for designing offices. It was intended as a responsive environment in which the capacity to modify spatial relationships would also become the means to maintain vital connections between worker, task, and organization. He proposed that Action Office marketing include the development of a consulting service with expertise in "human factors engineering (job and task analysis), total business organization insight and perspective, and space planning."[8]

The first iteration of Action Office was completed in December 1964. While it enjoyed a successful launch in 1965, disappointing sales and high production costs soon convinced De Pree that Action Office "did

⑥
Robert Probst, report on the Action Office, October 8, 1962, Herman Miller Archives, Ao63.

⑦
Robert Probst, "The Action Office," in *Human Factors* (August 1966): 304.

⑧
Probst, report on the Action Office.

not live up to Probst's concepts." He cited the elegance of its design as part of its failure: "the feedback from our sales people was that we had produced 'another marshmallow sofa'—a product that was beautiful and exciting, but didn't work."[9] The 1964 Action Office comprised furniture elements and matched accessories, united by a distinctive design vocabulary. Its cast aluminum bases, which were the basis of Nelson's Alcoa award, were also the primary reason that Action Office proved expensive and difficult to produce. Its elements, specified with options in size and finish, included high and low desks with varied drawer configurations; conference tables and desks; work tables and mobile side tables; specialized desks for display, typewriting, and phone communications; and storage units configurable with shelves, shelving organizers, display panels, file bins, and a perch chair.

The unresolved tension between Nelson's object design and Probst's system concept is evident in the first Action Office brochure. Formatted as a loose-leaf 16-sheet folio in a clothbound slipcover featuring highly produced color photographs and perspective line drawings of its furniture elements, the brochure only included one image of multiple Action Office elements configured together. Yet while the images depict Action Office as a collection of design objects, the brochure text describes a system whose elements are addressed only passingly as "equipment," "components," or an "expression" of "Herman Miller standards for practical elegance and long term usefulness." Instead, Action Office is described as an ambient "working climate," or as having the "capability to create working climates based on a grasp of environmental forces and their effects on humans." Framed as a remedy to the "wasteland" of the contemporary office that "saps vitality, blocks talent, frustrates accomplishment," Action Office would recognize "change as a continuous rather than an occasional force" and provide a "delicate balance between protection from distraction and awareness of the currents of company activity."[10]

Herman Miller immediately sought to mitigate this disjunction between system and object, by not only publishing material demonstrating the possible configurations of the existing system, but also starting development on a second version of the product. "Action Office 2" would be a lower-cost and more conceptually developed version of the original product, which would remain in production as an "executive" version dubbed "Action Office 1." De Pree relates that the development of Action Office 2 only renewed "friction between the Nelson office and Probst's research division" where "each group was working on a different basis, with little interaction." This situation was resolved through a competition in which both groups were given three months to develop their respective proposals, on which basis the conceptual and design development of Action Office 2 was assigned exclusively to Probst.[11]

Action Office 2 gained "considerable additional impetus" from a space planning technique developed in Germany.[12] *Bürolandschaft,* or office landscaping, was the product of a management consultancy directed by the brothers Wolfgang and Eberhard Schnelle. The first office landscape was produced in 1960 for a mail-order publishing division of

(9)
De Pree, *Business as Unusual*, 87.

(10)
"A World to Work In: The Action Office," product brochure (Zeeland, MI: Herman Miller, 1964).

(11)
De Pree, *Business as Unusual*, 88.

(12)
Probst, "The Action Office," 303.

the Bertelsmann media conglomerate. By 1964, articles and a monograph on office landscaping had been published in English. Like Probst, the Schnelle brothers had been influenced by "human factors" or "developmental" management theories addressing how human relationships affect worker productivity, as well as by cybernetics, the postwar science of communication and control. The Schnelle brothers would call their planning method *Organisationskybernetik* and publish materials on cybernetics under the imprint Verlag Schnelle. Office landscaping began with a careful tracking of communications and information flow across all levels of an office organization, systematically transforming this data into an open office plan of seemingly chaotic clustering of desks and low partitions. Like the Action Office, the office landscape conceived of management as a process of influencing relationships at the scale of the task and in real time.

Probst met Wolfgang Schnelle in 1967 at a seminar on office landscaping in Stockholm. In an report on this seminar published in *Office Design* magazine, Probst focuses on Schnelle's presentation and in particular on issues that either align with or depart from the concepts behind Action Office. These comparisons address building form ("very emphatic about large space efficiencies"), planning methods ("a continuous debugging process by management and planners that must be carried out continuously in any large organization"), and factors in acoustic control, illumination, and climate. As Probst recounted, communication in the managed environment bore political implications for Schnelle: "the old authoritarian hierarchy stratifications, which insulate and separate individuals and groups illogically, are the enemies of communication and fluency," while "the new model recognizes the complexity of tasks and the need for sensitive meshing of people to express and gain larger objectives."[13] Probst concluded critically: the office landscape "is already over-methodized and locked into a too limited concept of organizational form," while its furniture is "especially lacking" in "any components that would handle information display" or "integrate communications devices." Following on this latter point in a brief discussion with Schnelle, Probst reported, "he expressed the opinion that furniture companies as such are not a primary factor in the office landscape programs."[14]

Nonetheless, Probst's exposure to office landscaping lead him to rethink the relationship between architecture and furniture, and to the idea of configuring Action Office 2 around a system of panel walls. "Even by 1964," Probst wrote, "it had become clear that furniture and wall function could no longer be isolated functionally. Interior walls had been dominated by the building, and furniture, in turn, had been dominated by the walls. Consequently, a pedestal wall concept emerged which integrated combinations of furniture and wall components that could be rearranged, as needed, into highly varied groupings."[15] Action Office 2 panels were manufactured in twelve, twenty-four, and forty-eight inch modular widths and at heights of sixty-two and eighty inches. They locked together quickly and easily using an Allen wrench, and could be configured either free-form or in a rectilinear or hexagonal grid. While

(13)
Robert Probst, "The Landscape is Based on Thorough and Technical Data," in *Office Design Magazine* (September 1967): 25, 26.

(14)
Ibid., 27, 28.

(15)
Ibid.

Action Office configuration including worktable, communications center, storage and display unit, and high desk, 1964. *Source: HermanMiller.*

First Action Office 2 installation,at the C&S Bank, 1969. *Source: HermanMiller.*

some remained freestanding, most of the furniture types designed for Action Office 1 were redesigned to be panel hung. A utilitarian approach to materials and details considerably reduced the cost of the components. The brochures published to accompany Action Office 2 focused primarily on functionality, configurations, planning methods, and the relation of these to an emergent knowledge economy.

Action Office 2 was launched in 1968 to near instant success, undeterred by furniture design that Charles Eames described as "honest ugly."[16] Soon after, Herman Miller became a publicly traded company, and Knoll, Steelcase, Haworth, and others launched their own competing office systems furniture lines. Action Office 2 led into Herman Miller's next significant product, the task chair. William Stumpf, designer of Herman Miller's 1976 Ergon chair and co-designer with Donald Chadwick of the 1984 Equa Chair and the 1992 Aeron chair, first met Probst at a talk on the Action Office in 1968. Stumpf began working for Herman Miller in 1970, following Probst's proposal that he be hired to work on seating "to develop either the waffle spring or the net seat, or both, into a super comfort low cost contract seat for the educational market."[17]

Action Office 2's innovation lay in the formlessness of its system, rather than the form of its objects. It was less a completed design than a technique for managing the space of work. As Probst's colleague recalled, while one "inventoried desks and chairs," one *"managed facilities and systems furniture."*[18] The idea that office space should be continually managed was reflected in Probst's introduction of Action Office 2 in the 1968 book *The Office: A Facility Based on Change*. While Probst designed the elements of Action Office 2 with mobility in mind, he advocated beginning with a process of "facility simulation." This process involved speculative exploration or "pre-gaming" of possible office configurations through scale models and computer-aided design before

⑯
Joe Schwartz, *How Design Happened at Herman Miller* (Zeeland, MI: Herman Miller, 2006), 46.

⑰
Robert Probst, "Waffle or Net Seating for Education: A Proposal to Herman Miller Inc.," proposal, June 1970.

⑱
Joe Schwartz, *How Design Happened at Herman Miller* (Zeeland, MI: Herman Miller, 2006), 53.

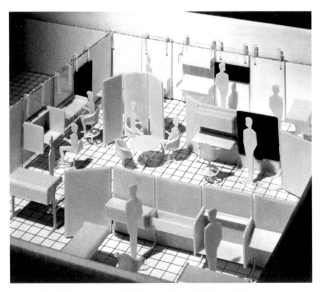

Office layout "simulation" using the Action Office 2 Model Kit, 1969.
Source: HermanMiller.

Cover image, 1964 Action Office brochure.
Source: HermanMiller.

arriving at a furniture layout.[19] The aim was a fluid relation between conceptual tool and spatial elaboration. In 1969, Herman Miller marketed an elaborate scale model kit of Action Office 2 as a visualization and presentation tool for salespeople and facilities managers. The use of scale models to explore and photographically document potential office configurations was considered faster and more convincing than the hand-drawn schematic plans and renderings they would replace—"your Polaroid now becomes your pencil," read one advertising release.[20] Yet, Probst continued to advocate the development of computer tools as "the one really promising avenue" for facility planning. In a 1971 proposal he argued that "traditional interior floor plan drawing…is too ponderous, slow, unresponsive, and not in the hands of the actual decision makers," and that while scale model kits are "the next best answer…for the large facility this approach becomes impractical to manipulate."[21]

    As an object of design, Action Office might best be located in virtual problem space—as a space of hard-coded potentiality continuously open to a combinatorics of adaptation and reconfiguration, an office user interface. Here Action Office anticipates another form of desktop configuration. A 1984 Action Office brochure would include a case study on Apple Computer, Inc., which "has been using the Action Office System almost since the day the company headquarters moved from Steven Jobs' parents' garage." In the words of one Apple facility designer, "flexibility is one of the good things about the Herman Miller system…the work stations we set up never look the same the next day."[22] In this formlessness, the Action Office, like the office landscape, could be seen as a concrete spatialization of a lineage of management theories stretching from the present back through the twentieth century. The formlessness of the postwar office presented a challenge to architecture as a discipline. For a principal of the space planning firm JFN Associates writing in 1969, systems furniture and office landscaping have "shaken lots of conventional architects and office designers who have been thinking only in terms of 1920 Bauhaus and 1960 Skidmore, Owings & Merrill rectangular grid space, solutions that are neat and orderly looking."[23] Office design increasingly fell under the purview of space planning, management consulting, facilities management, lighting and acoustic design, and industrial design, with the role of architecture limited to providing enclosure. Like the postwar city, the postwar office became a touchstone in arguing what properly belonged to architecture. For some, architecture would gravitate toward the expanded field of environmental design, seeking to "improve the connections between science and technology on one hand, and the humanities and social sciences on the other."[24] For others, architecture's encounter with information and management constituted "a crisis of the ideological function of architecture," to be warded off through critical theory or behind the reconstructed historical boundaries of architectural autonomy.[25]

(19)
Robert Probst, *The Office: A Facility Based on Change* (Zeeland, MI: Herman Miller, 1968), 39–40.

(20)
Molly Thiss, advertising release, August 12, 1969, Herman Miller Archives, no number.

(21)
Robert Probst, "A Proposal for the Development of a Facility Simulation and Gaming Tool using a Computer Based Graphics Method," report, June 14, 1971, Herman Miller Archives, Pubs8091.

(22)
Action Office System, brochure (Zeeland, MI: Herman Miller, 1984), 15.

(23)
Douglas Wheeler-Nicholson, "Maybe: An Americanization of the Open Plan," in "Office Landscape Layout: Pro and Con" in *The Office Magazine* (July 1969): n.p.

(24)
Robert L. Geddes quoted in Robert Venturi, *Complexity and Contradiction in Architecture* (New York: Museum of Modern Art, 1966), 14.

(25)
Manfredo Tafuri, *Architecture and Utopia: Design and Capitalist Development,* trans. Barbara Luigia La Penta (Cambridge, MA: MIT Press, 1976), 181.

EXCHANGE

OfficeUS: Émigrés

Within OfficeUS are a significant number of architects who themselves emigrated to the United States. Mapping the emigration routes of these architects (only those who came as adults) in conjunction with their exported projects reveals the global reach and impact of these transplanted architects. Highlighted are projects exported back to their home country as a kind of return emigration, often in a very different political and cultural climate.
—Amanda Reeser Lawrence

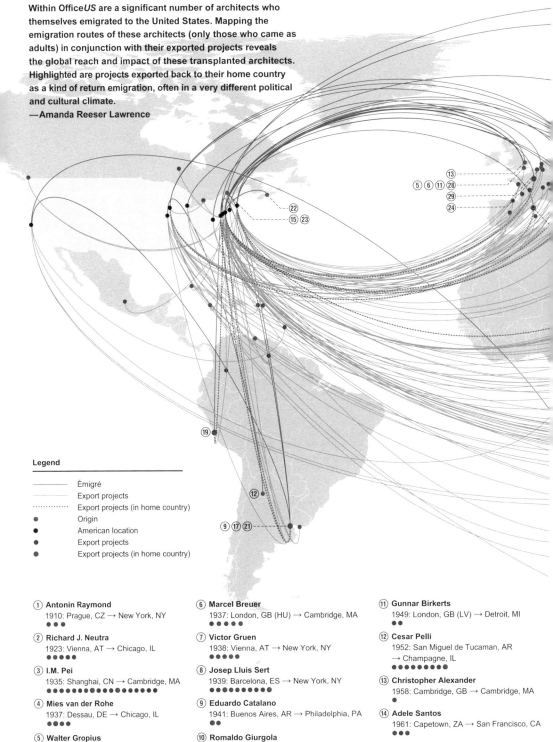

Legend

——————— Émigré
——————— Export projects
.... Export projects (in home country)
● Origin
● American location
● Export projects
● Export projects (in home country)

① **Antonin Raymond**
1910: Prague, CZ → New York, NY
● ● ●

② **Richard J. Neutra**
1923: Vienna, AT → Chicago, IL
● ● ● ● ●

③ **I.M. Pei**
1935: Shanghai, CN → Cambridge, MA
● ● ● ● ● ● ● ● ● ● ● ● ● ● ● ●

④ **Mies van der Rohe**
1937: Dessau, DE → Chicago, IL
● ● ● ●

⑤ **Walter Gropius**
1937: London, GB (DE)
→ Cambridge, MA
● ● ● ● ● ● ● ● ● ● ● ● ● ● ● ● ● ●

⑥ **Marcel Breuer**
1937: London, GB (HU) → Cambridge, MA
● ● ● ● ●

⑦ **Victor Gruen**
1938: Vienna, AT → New York, NY
● ● ● ● ●

⑧ **Josep Lluis Sert**
1939: Barcelona, ES → New York, NY
● ● ● ● ● ● ● ● ● ●

⑨ **Eduardo Catalano**
1941: Buenos Aires, AR → Philadelphia, PA
● ●

⑩ **Romaldo Giurgola**
1949: Rome, IT → New York, NY
● ● ● ● ●

⑪ **Gunnar Birkerts**
1949: London, GB (LV) → Detroit, MI
● ●

⑫ **Cesar Pelli**
1952: San Miguel de Tucaman, AR
→ Champagne, IL
● ● ● ● ● ● ● ● ●

⑬ **Christopher Alexander**
1958: Cambridge, GB → Cambridge, MA
●

⑭ **Adele Santos**
1961: Capetown, ZA → San Francisco, CA
● ● ●

⑮ **Moshe Safdie**
1964: Montreal, CA (IL) → Philadelphia, PA
● ● ● ● ● ● ● ● ●

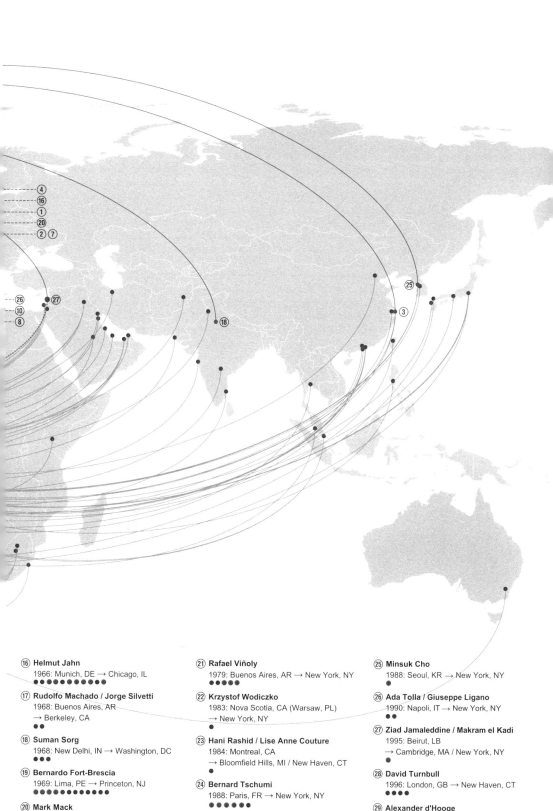

⑯ **Helmut Jahn**
1966: Munich, DE → Chicago, IL
●●●●●●●●

⑰ **Rudolfo Machado / Jorge Silvetti**
1968: Buenos Aires, AR
→ Berkeley, CA
●●

⑱ **Suman Sorg**
1968: New Delhi, IN → Washington, DC
●●●

⑲ **Bernardo Fort-Brescia**
1969: Lima, PE → Princeton, NJ
●●●●●●●●●●●

⑳ **Mark Mack**
1973: Judenburg, AT → New York, NY
●●●●●●

㉑ **Rafael Viñoly**
1979: Buenos Aires, AR → New York, NY
●●●●●

㉒ **Krzystof Wodiczko**
1983: Nova Scotia, CA (Warsaw, PL)
→ New York, NY
●

㉓ **Hani Rashid / Lise Anne Couture**
1984: Montreal, CA
→ Bloomfield Hills, MI / New Haven, CT

㉔ **Bernard Tschumi**
1988: Paris, FR → New York, NY
●●●●●●

㉕ **Minsuk Cho**
1988: Seoul, KR → New York, NY
●

㉖ **Ada Tolla / Giuseppe Ligano**
1990: Napoli, IT → New York, NY
●●

㉗ **Ziad Jamaleddine / Makram el Kadi**
1995: Beirut, LB
→ Cambridge, MA / New York, NY

㉘ **David Turnbull**
1996: London, GB → New Haven, CT
●●●●

㉙ **Alexander d'Hooge**
2005: Leuven, BE → Cambridge, MA
●

Chicago to Canberra:
Walter Burley Griffin & Marion Mahony

Marion Mahony, Frank Lloyd Wright's first employee, was also the first registered woman architect in the United States. From 1895 to 1903, she worked in the Oak Park studio, developing her distinctive rendering style and producing drawings often attributed to Wright. There, in 1901, she met landscape architect Walter Burley Griffin, and a decade later they became design and life partners. In 1906, Griffin established an independent practice, and Mahony joined him in 1911. In 1914, they moved to Australia, having won The Federal Capital Competition to design a master plan for the nation's new capital city in Canberra.

Griffin wrote, "I have planned an ideal city—a city that meets my ideal of the city of the future."[1] Despite his grand ambitions and the federal government's promises that the project would be built, only small sectors of the plan were realized due its radicality and economic strain created by the outbreak of World War II. In 1920, he resigned from the project, but the partners remained in Australia because they had established successful practices in Sydney and Melbourne. In 1921, the wake of Canberra, Griffin purchased a 650-acre plot of land in North Sydney to develop (later to be know as Castlecrag) for which he designed fifty houses and built sixteen.

By the late 1920s, the Australian economy suffered the effects of the Depression. Mahony and Griffin partnered with a long time client, Nisson Leonard-Kanevskya, an engineer and businessman who capitalized on the national government program to construct incinerators across the country as a means to manage the growing populations' waste.

Between 1929 and 1938, Griffin and Mahony designed thirteen incinerators in collaboration with Leonard Kanevskya's Reverberatory Incinerator and Engineering Company. The team worked closely together providing local governments with a complete architectural and engineering package of industrial function wrapped in decorative envelopes that belied their pragmatic program.
— Ashley Schafer

Talia Freedman and Levi Bedall were invaluable research assistants for this article.

① "American Designs Splendid New Capital for Australia, *The New York Times*, Sunday, June 2, 1912

Marion Mahony
Source: the New York State Historical Society

Walter Burley Griffin in 1912
Source: State Library of New South Wales

Australia becomes a Commonwealth and names Canberra the new capital

1895

1895 Frank Lloyd Wright hires Marion Mahony to work in the Oak Park studio. She is his first employee

1898 Mahony becomes first woman registered architect in the US

1901 Walter Burley Griffin begins working for Wright

1906

COMMONWEALTH OF AVSTRALIA
FEDERAL CAPITAL COMPETITION

CITY AND ENVIRONS.

Commonwealth of Australia Federal Capital competition:
City and Environs. *Source: National Archives of Australia*

Newman College at the University of Melbourne
Source: the National Library of Australia

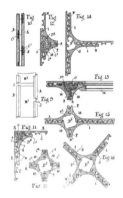

Knitlock Construction 1917 Patent
Source: P.Y. Navaretti

1909
Wright moves to Germany, leaving the Chicago office in the hands of Herman von Holst and Mahony

1911
Mahony and Griffin marry

Mahony and Griffin win the competition to design Canberra

1914
Mahony and Griffin design the town plan for the city of Griffith and Leeton, outside of Canberra

Mahony and Griffin move to Australia to oversee Canberra project

1915
Griffin designs Newman College at the University of Melbourne

1917
Mahony and Griffins' Chicago office closes

Griffin patents Knitlock masonry technique

1920

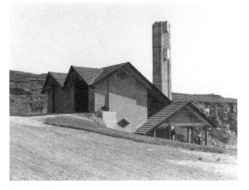

Waratah Victoria
Source: the National Library of Australia

Randwick NSW
Source: Diane Betts

Ku-ring-gai NSW
Source: the National Library of Australia

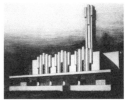

Glebe NSW
Source: the National Library of Australia

Leonard Building
Source: the National Library of Australia

Castlecrag Masterplan
Source: the National Library of Australia

Essendon Victoria
Source: Mati Maldre

1920

1921
Mahony and Griffin begin to develop plan for Castlecrag

Mahony and Griffin buy a plot of land on the Sydney Harbor and plan the Castlecrag Community. The Griffins build 16 houses from 1921 to 1934

1923
Nisson Leonard-Kanevskya, owner of Reverberatory Incinerator & Engineering Company (REICo), commissions Griffin to design Leonard House

1925
Mahony and Griffin move to Castlecrag, just outside of Sydney, and continue development of the suburb

1929
US stock market crashes
Australia enters depression due to heavy dependence on export

1930

Pyrmont NSW
Source: Diane Betts

Leichhardt NSW
Source: Diane Betts

Hindmarsh, South Australia
Source: Mati Maldre

Thebarton, South Australia
Source: Mati Maldre

Willoughby NSW
Source: Mati Maldre

Brunswick Victoria
Source: Diane Betts

Ipswich South Australia
Source: Mati Maldre

Canberra Australian Capital Territory
Source: Mati Maldre

1934

1935
Griffin moves to India to work on Lucknow University Library. 41 commissions follow.

1937
Griffin dies, Mahony returns to the US

1938

1939
Australia enters WWII

1945

Frank Gilbreth, Route Model, N. E. Butt Co., Providence, Rhode Island, 1912. Source: "A New Development in Factory Study: The Use of the Route Model as a Method of Investigation" *Industrial Engineering* XII No. 2, 1913, 58.

Frank Gilbreth, Stereochronocyclograph, Auergesellschaft Co., Berlin, Germany, 1914. *Source: Gilbreth Library of Management, Purdue University.*

Between 1896 and 1915, Frank Gilbreth synthesized techniques from economics, physiology, and engineering into a graphic projection system for describing objects and processes in space-time. The route model, which used masonry string to schedule and route processes through a construction or manufacturing site, and the stereochronocyclograph, which measured the ergonomic performance of work stations using light bulbs, photography, and film, were developed simultaneously in New England and Germany.

IVAN RUPNIK

Exporting Space-Time: American Industrial Engineering Tools and European Modernism

Export: 1900–1917

In May 1900, Frederick Taylor, the father of industrial engineering, burst onto the European engineering scene in a cloud of sparks, steel shavings, and propaganda at the International Exhibition in Paris. Bethlehem Steel, the foundry for which Taylor had been consulting since 1898, had chosen to exhibit a single artifact—their new high-speed cutting tool. This tool had already created quite a buzz across the Atlantic, demonstrating cutting rates and depths exceeding anything else on the market. Taylor himself insisted that the company not present the tools alone, as nearly all of the other American manufactures at the *Bois de Vincennes* would, but instead, transplant a portion of the foundry from Pennsylvania to the Continent, no matter the expense. By fabricating the tools on site, Taylor distinguished Bethlehem's tools from those of the other companies at the show and established himself as a master not of the production of machine-made products or tools, but of industrial engineering methods.[1] In his writings, Taylor explains that these air-hardening steel tools were developed through the "scientific study and analysis of all of the methods and implementations of use."[2] He also quantified that these tools were the byproduct of 30–50,000 experiments in multiple industries over twenty-six years, for which 800,000 pounds of steel and millions of dollars were expended.[3] This precise experimental derivation of standard methods and norms, often referred to as the "laboratory method," would be used by Taylor and disciples to distinguish his approach, named "scientific management" in 1910, from the "methodological organization of work" of "systematic management," from which this new industrial engineering approach evolved. Taylor insisted that industries develop their own standard methods experimentally, rather than rely on rules of thumb or academically-derived theories.[4]

Taylor distinguished "scientific" management, the dual gathering of data and application of that data, as an "art," as compared to engineering, an "exact science."[5] Unlike the mechanical and civil engineering disciplines that emerged during the Industrial Revolution, which dealt with the "materials and forces of nature," industrial engineers were faced with the much messier task of engineering "men and capital."[6] While Taylor sought to provide more accurate studies of human labor, he emphasized the imperfection of experimentally-derived standard methods, and encouraged his readers to test them in their own practice as quickly as possible. He also reinforced the tentative and even site-specific nature of

(1)
Robert Kanigel, *The One Best Way* (Cambridge: The MIT Press, 1997), 337.

(2)
Frederick Taylor, *The Principles of Scientific Management* (New York: Harper, 1911), 25.

(3)
Taylor emphasized the experimental nature of his approach starting with *Shop Management* (New York: Harper, 1911(1903)). For more on Taylor's work at Bethlehem Steel see David Nelson, "Scientific Management, Systematic Management, and Labor, 1880–1915" *Business History Review*, (Winter, 1974), 487–505.

(4)
Taylor's own writings were often less clear than those of his advocates. Henry La Chatelier, the French chemist who witnessed the Paris demonstration in 1900, wrote one of the most salient explanations of Taylor's approach in "Le Système Taylor," *Bulletin de la Société d'Encouragement pour l'Industrie Nationale*, 113 (March 1914), 280–318.

(5)
Taylor, *Shop Management*, 63.

(6)
Lindy Biggs, *The Rational Factory* (Baltimore: Johns Hopkins University Press, 1996), 40.

these methods, stating that they could prove "most beneficent" in one case, and "disastrous" in another; the development of methods could approach science but their implementation would remain an art.[7]

Taylor found the dream of a fully hybridized space of knowledge and material production elusive in his own work and struggled with relating the "laboratory method," as well as the raw data of his 50,000 experiments, outside of the Taylor Circle, his closest collaborators who often understood aspects of this work better than Taylor himself did.[8] Taylor's ability to communicate these methods was largely hampered by his own unique aesthetic sensibility; Taylor had the ability to visualize the world as a series of numerical patterns and was commonly frustrated with the inability of others to do so. This may explain why his own data collection, visualization and collections, line and bar graphs, as well as his instruction cards—scheduling tools, which documented particular tasks down to the second—did not attain a more widespread implementation. Taylor stated that the instruction card was to the art of management what the drawing was to engineering, the discipline's primary medium. Similar to a drawing, the instruction card could "vary in size and form according to the information" being conveyed.[9] For Taylor, these simple charts contained an analogous visual spectacle to the performance he had staged in Paris; however, for most people, even his closest associates, they remained quite opaque. Lacking Taylor's innate numerical aesthetic, Henry Gantt developed the first new industrial engineering projection tool, the "graphic daily balance in manufacture," around 1901.[10] It was used to track individual worker performance against experimentally-derived standards, evaluating the standard as much as the individual. By 1914, it was modified to track the interdependencies between various subtasks in a given process. This new instrument, known today as the Gantt chart, reflected deeper differences between Taylor, who would "plough right through" perceived obstacles, and Gantt, who was more adaptive to particular conditions. Instead of warping a space of production to fit a management system, Gantt argued that there were as many "distinct scientific managements" as there were "different shops."[11]

Like the instruction card, the Gantt chart focused primarily on scheduling processes in time.[12] It was Frank Gilbreth, a master mason turned industrial engineer, who pioneered the "precise visualization" and projection of processes "in space and time," between 1900 and 1917.[13] Where Taylor saw numbers, Gilbreth saw motions; not only could he look at a brick wall and deduce how the bricks had been fired, he could also determine where the bricklayer had been trained. He described bricklaying as the "work of a juggler," stating that the mason could "see (his) work grow," leaving behind a personal "monument."[14] This admiration for vernacular construction, shared by most progressive architects at the time, could not have been more different from Taylor's, and yet the underlying principles, particularly the "laboratory idea," were identical.[15]

Despite his early experiences as a bricklayer, Gilbreth's interest in Taylor's principles was motivated by his work in reinforced concrete.[16] Here, as in all of his work, Gilbreth applied his affinity for the visual-

[7] Taylor, *Principles of Scientific Management*, 128.

[8] Ibid., 132.

[9] For a discussion of Gantt's success in comparison to Taylor, see Nelson, 503–04.

[10] See S. G. Walesh, *Engineering Your Future: The Non-Technical Side of Professional Practice in Engineering and Other Technical Fields* (Hoboken: Wiley, 2000), 145.

[11] Horace Drury, *Scientific Management* (New York: Columbia University, 1915), 95–6.

[12] A Gantt chart was used to plan and manage the construction of the Langwies Viaduct (1912–14) in Switzerland. Tom Peters, *Building the Nineteenth Century* (Cambridge: The MIT Press, 1996), 291.

[13] Sigfried Giedion credited Frank Gilbreth, the "master of motion studies," with precisely investigating the "form of movement" in "space and time" in *Mechanization Takes Command* (New York: Norton Press, 1974 (1948)), 47.

[14] Frank Gilbreth, "The Packet System," unpublished manuscript, Gilbreth Library of Management, Purdue University. Box 34, Folder 0247 (November 02, 1914).

[15] An interest in evolution more then revolution dominated the discourse of *Deutscher Werkbund*, as argued by a number of scholars, including Stanford Anderson, Francesco Passanti, Laurent Stalder, and Erik Ghenoiu.

ization of motion, developing a series of new projection instruments ranging from construction plant drawings to site plans—which tracked both machines and materials on site—to models of the various construction phases, which were built in his office, photographed, and sent to the site at various intervals.[17] In contrast to Taylor's numerical concrete-curing charts, Gilbreth provided a graphic technique he called "accounting without books."[18]

Unlike Taylor and Gantt, who primarily consulted for other companies, Gilbreth owned his own contracting business, affording him the ability to apply his principles fully. He was also more successful in documenting and relating his variations and adaptations of industrial engineering techniques to the building site through a series of manuals published in 1908 and 1909. Here Gilbreth contrasted the "manufacturer," for whom the factory was a controlled space of off-site production that simplified his work and allowed him to focus on scheduling in time, with the "contractor," whose sites of production were numerous, varied, and more difficult to control, and therefore required a greater "completeness of organization" and more attention to routing in space as well as time.[19] When Gilbreth and his wife and partner, Lillian Gilbreth, shifted from contracting to industrial consulting, it would be these space-time projection tools, developed on the construction site, that would distinguish their approach in manufacturing from that of other members of the Taylor Circle, and it would be these same tools that would later attract the attention of European architects.

One of Gilbreth's most powerful and effective projection tools, the "route model," was developed between the building site and the factory in North America and Germany, where he was consulting. Gilbreth had used physical models as a variation of construction plant drawings—projection instruments that allowed engineers to plan and manage the distribution of materials, machines, and workers in relation to the position of the structure being built—as early as 1904.[20] His first route models, built for work at the New England Butt Company, in 1912, and the *Auergesellschaft* Company in Berlin, in 1913, differed from his earlier models in that they considered the assembly of a structure as well as its continued operation and inhabitation.[21] Like Taylor, Gilbreth would later emphasize that this technique resulted from experiments conducted within industries, and like the Gantt chart, this tool allowed for the "visualization of the entire plant at a single glance," albeit now in space as well as time. Gilbreth used colored string to route various manufacturing processes through the structural frame, seeking to "shorten the course" of a given task, not through the micro-management of a single worker, as Taylor had done, but through the restructuring of the architecture of work itself.[22] The larger route model of the entire factory was linked to smaller work station models, drawn templates made of white cardboard that documented the spatial and temporal volume of any given task. These miniature building sites had first been used by Gilbreth in construction and were informed by his early patents for an adjustable scaffold system in 1895. Gilbreth would develop progress photos of the various

(16)
F. Taylor and S. Thompson, *A Treatise on Concrete, Plain and Reinforced* (New York: Wiley, 1905).

(17)
"Progress photos" are the first systematic use of photography to plan, manage, and document construction, according to Peters, 392.

(18)
Gilbreth, *Field System* (New York: Clark, 1908), 12.

(19)
Ibid., 4–6.

(20)
Frank Gilbreth used construction plant drawings as early as 1902, two of which were included in his *Concrete System* (New York: The Engineering News, 1908), 8, 10, 52, and in S. E. Thompson, *Reinforced Concrete in Factory Construction* (New York: Portland Cement Co., 1907), 228.

(21)
Route models, first developed for construction, were used by Gilbreth as a "method of investigating the conditions obtaining in any given factory as regards the passage of material through the different processes." Discussed in "A New Development in Factory Study: The Use of the Route Model as a Method of Investigation" *Industrial Engineering and the Engineering Digest* XIII 2 (February, 1913), 61.

(22)
Workstations were articulated as "templates of white cardboard, representing the plan area occupied by each tool, or the space devoted to any single purpose in the shop." Ibid. 61.

configurations of these models to help plan production processes, just as he had of his construction sites a decade before. Cyclographic studies were the last step in this process, serving as a precise measurement of the performance of newly introduced ergonomic instruments—scaffold-like structures for industrial production—as well as an evaluation of the overall collective organization of the factory, essentially treated as a four-dimensional building site.[23] Despite the Gilbreths' prolific work on the development of new projection tools, adapted from construction to manufacturing and ideal for the planning of production, as well as occupation, few American architects showed interest in these techniques until the mid-1920s. European architects would be the first to use these new projection tools, starting around 1918.

Import: 1918–1930

Around 1913, after a series of highly publicized strikes in America and France and the translation of Taylor's *Principles* into German, European architects became interested in American industrial engineering.[24] With the space of off-site factory production already claimed, architects looked to apply these techniques to an emerging design problem: worker's housing settlements. Peter Behrens, who had come into contact with the Taylor System at the *Allgemeine Elektricitäts-Gesellschaft* (AEG), would take a lead in this effort with the publication of *Toward Economical Building: A Contribution to the Settlement Question* in 1918.[25] While Behrens's manual on settlement design was the first to discuss "scientific management," much of his "economical" techniques relied on the visual planning and site engineering principles published by Raymond Unwin in his *Town Planning in Practice* (1909).[26]

While Behrens may have been the first European architect to witness the use of industrial engineering tools, one of his former employees, Le Corbusier, outpaced him in his comprehension of Taylor and Gilbreth's work, the work of Raymond Unwin, and the synthesis of these ideas into settlement building. Le Corbusier, who first saw the Taylor System in Berlin in 1910, had the opportunity to work with American engineers on a series of industrial buildings in 1917 and would publish his first text on *taylorisme* in 1918, going so far as to equate it to *la vie moderne*.[27] In these early writings, Le Corbusier made an important distinction that escaped many later scholars, namely that while the nineteenth century was the age of the machine (and that the machine essentially destroyed the individual skilled artisan), twentieth-century industrialization would be defined by "synthesis and order," the organization of collective "practical work."[28] *Taylorisme* promised the kind of organicism symbolic of the Gothic, or that of the age of Pericles; its tools would finally assist in the production of a modern *village integrale* that Le Corbusier had been searching for in various vernacular traditions since 1910.[29]

Le Corbusier had been preoccupied with settlement design since he was first exposed to industrial engineering as well as to the Garden City movement.[30] Like Behrens, Le Corbusier's own design system, the Dom-ino System, borrowed heavily from Unwin's *Town Planning in*

[23] The Gilbreths developed cyclographs, generated by photographing the motions of an individual wearing a custom light-emitting element in 1912. First published in "Chronocyclegraph Motion Devices for Measuring Achievement," *Proceedings of the Second Pan-American Congress*, Washington D.C. (January 3, 1916), 1–14.

[24] Taylor devoted a significant portion of *Principles* to Gilbreth's work on motion study in construction.

[25] *Vom Sparsamen Bauen: Ein Beitrag zur Siedlungsfrage* (Berlin: Bauwelt, 1918), 60-61, co authored with Heinrich de Fries was the first published use of the term "scientific management" by an architect.

[26] Unwin's manual, *Town Planning in Practice* (London: T Fisher Unwin, 1911(1909), ix, promised to make available the "principles of organization" used by industry for the planning of "urban communities."

[27] A. Ozenfant and C.-E. Jeanneret, *Après le Cubisme* [After Cubism] (Paris, 1918), 26–28. Here Le Corbusier essentially equates *l' esprit nouveau* and *taylorisme*. For a history of this period see A. Brooks, *Le Corbusier's Formative Years* (Chicago: University Of Chicago Press, 1999), 485–86.

[28] Ozenfant and Jeanneret, 26–7.

[29] For Le Corbusier's interest in the vernacular see F. Passanti, "The Vernacular, Modernism, and

Practice at the settlement scale, while his standard reinforced concrete frame reflected the influence of industrial engineering theories and methods. Like the tentative standards of industrial engineers, Le Corbusier's Dom-ino System evolved with each iteration between 1914 and 1926, when Le Corbusier completed the first phase of his own "laboratory of standardization, industrialization, taylorization" at Pessac.[31] His work at Pessac, and in subsequent *plan libre* houses, resembles Gilbreth's route models with their structural frames, lack of roofs or facades, and their free floating work stations. Although Le Corbusier may have been one of the first European architects to closely study and incorporate aspects of industrial engineering into his own design approach, this pioneering work presumably suffered due to a lack of "accounting without books."[32] Ultimately, American industrial engineering, as well as the pioneering work of Le Corbusier, would find a more receptive atmosphere for experimentation in Weimar Germany.

Le Corbusier's understanding of industrial engineering was also informed by the writings and lectures of Hermann Muthesius.[33] Two years after Behrens's and Le Corbusier's texts, the Werkbund's founder would integrate Taylor's and, particularly, Gilbreth's work into his own theoretical discourse. Muthesius abandoned his earlier term of *typisierung* (typification), put forth in 1914, for a new term, *typenbau*; directly translated as "type building" but used to mean "building with types," the shift in terminology demonstrating the absorption of Unwin's design techniques, which the German architect had used at Hellerau, as well as "building types," or better stated, "evolving types" through site-specific experiments.[34] While Muthesius's writings had never been clearer than in this settlement design manual, *Kleinhaus und Kleinsiedlung*, he had provided a model of this approach as early as 1904–05, in his account of Norman Shaw's Bedford Park, a project he described as "the master's experiment" and the "means to the end" of evolving new "small house" typologies.[35] Muthesius concluded his analysis of type-building with an overview of Gilbreth's work, speculating on how this approach could be adapted to Germany's cooperatively owned construction companies, the *Bauhütten*, where workers (not only owners and managers) were involved in the organization of building. A year later, Martin Wagner, Muthesius's former student, began disseminating Gilbreth's work through the official journal of the *Bauhütten* association, *Soziale Bauwirtschaft*.[36]

As editor of *Soziale Bauwirtschaft* and *Wohnungswirstscaft*, Wagner provided the German-speaking architectural community the most extensive survey of American industrial engineering available in Europe. Wagner also included his own work, the work of various *Bauhütten*, as well as the work of American construction firms and architects, including John Conzelman, whose prefabricated row houses in Youngstown, Ohio (1917–19) first combined Unwin's and Gilbreth's methods at the scale of an entire settlement. However, Wagner and his close collaborator Bruno Taut warned their readers not to "focus on the architecture" of these American settlements, publishing only construction photos.[37] Furthermore, Taut began to use Gilbreth's routing studies to compare his own unit

Le Corbusier," *Journal of the Society of Art Historians* Vol. 56 No.4 (1997), 438–51.

㉚
Brooks, 220–22.

㉛
From a June 13, 1926 speech by Le Corbusier, published and discussed in Philippe Baudon, *Pessac de Le Corbusier: 1927–1967* (Paris: Bordas, 1969 (1985)), 146–48.

㉜
For more on Pessac see Bryan Taylor, *Le Corbusier at Pessac*, (Exh. cat., Harvard University, Cambridge, October-November 1972).

㉝
Brooks, 221.

㉞
In 1918, Muthesius replaced typification with *typenbau* (type building), explaining the concept through Classical, vernacular, and industrial examples in *Kleinhaus und Kleinsiedlung* (The Small House and the Small Settlement). In the second, significantly expanded, edition (Berlin: Bruckmann, 1920), he added a chapter titled "Wirtschaftliche Baubetriebsformen" (Systematically Managed Building Methods), 332–34, which linked Taylor's and Gilbreth's work to type building.

㉟
H. Muthesius, *The English House, Volume I: Development*. trans. Janet Seligman (1904; reprint London: Frances Lincoln Ltd., 2007), 135–37.

㊱
Between 1921 and 1925, dozens of articles on industrial engineering were published in *Soziale Bauwirtschaft*, the magazine Martin Wagner edited, with particular focus on Gilbreth's work.

Frank Gilbreth, Progress photos, Lowell Lab, MIT, 1902, Boston, Massachusetts. *Source: Bricklaying System (1909), 22–25.*

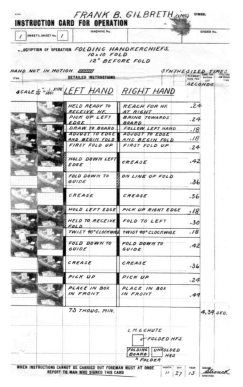

While Frederick Taylor, Henry Gantt, and other early industrial engineers focused primarily on projecting processes in time, Gilbreth's experience in construction led him to consider space as well as time, and to engage a broader palette of existing projection tools, including architectural drawings, as well as photography and film. He used progress photos (above) to document and manage the spatial arrangement of his construction sites; this technique provided the basis for his motion-study work in industry, as seen in his instruction cards (left), which included micro-motion studies, visual coding of motion types, as well as packet drawings, showing the position of workers, materials, and finished goods.

Frank and Lillian Gilbreth, "Instruction Card for Operation," Herman Auckam Company, 1912. *Source: Gilbreth Library of Management, Purdue University.*

ter Gropius, Progress photos, RFG "Experimental Settlement," Dessau, Germany, 1928.
rce: "Report on the Experimental Settlement in Dessau", RFG II No. 2 (April, 1929),110–13.

Walter Gropius employed many of Gilbreth's techniques, including progress photos (above) and micro-motion studies (left) as part of the design, construction, and operation of the Bauhaus school, masters' houses, and settlement at Torten between 1925 and 1928. Like Gilbreth, Gropius used motion study for planning as well as analysis.

er Gropius, Micro-motion studies of crane lowering beam and of opening 'boswik' grill,
sau, Germany, 1926. Source: Bauhaus Builds Dessau (1930),103, 175.

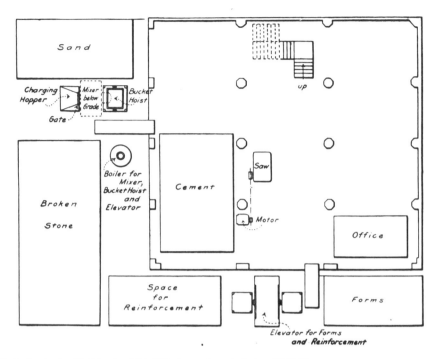

Frank Gilbreth, Construction Plant Drawing, 1904–1906. *Source: Concrete System (1908), 08.*

Frank Gilbreth, Gilbreth System Packet Scaffold, 1895-1908,
*Bricklaying System (1909), 80. Source: Gilbreth Library of
Management, Purdue University.*

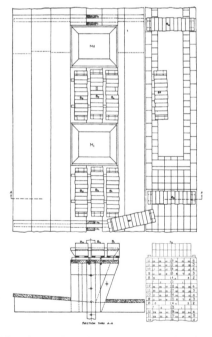

Gilbreth developed construction plant drawings, modified site plans and floor plans, to plan and manage the position of machines,
raw materials, and laborers in relation to a structure being erected, starting around 1900. His route models were four-dimensional versions
of this projection type. The Gilbreth or Packet scaffold, a miniature mountable factory, was designed using the same principles.

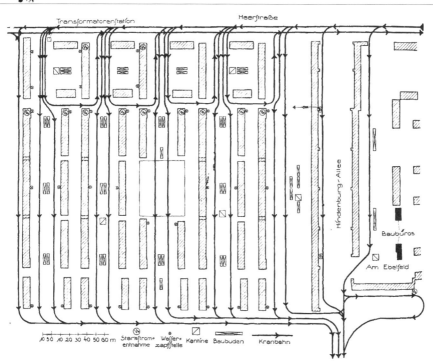

st May, Building Site Organization Plan, Praunheim Settlement, 1928. *Source: "Report on the Experimental Settlement in Dessau,"* G II No. 4 (April, 1929), 94.

st May, Frankfurt System of Panel Assembly, gress Photos and Assembly Drawing, 5–1928. *Source: "Report on the erimental Settlement in Dessau", RFG II No. April, 1929) 46–9; Das Neue Frankfurt 03 30), 57.*

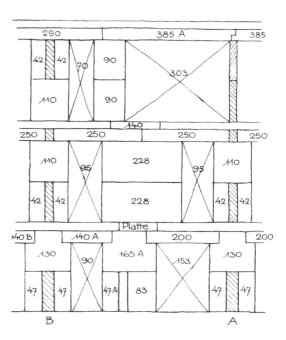

ween 1926 and 1928, Gropius and Ernst May combined Gilbreth's construction organization with Raymond Unwin's visual and site ning techniques in Dessau and Frankfurt. May developed a new concrete masonry unit around issues of on-site assembly through the of progress photos and construction plant drawings at various scales, from the Frankfurt region to the individual work station.

organizations with those of existing unit types; these diagrams would be published in American architectural journals long before Gilbreth's own work was given any attention.[38] Wagner and Taut's work culminated in the *Hufeisensiedlung* in Berlin (1925–33). While this settlement reflected Taut's aesthetic and Wagner's organizational talents, demonstrating mastery of Unwin's and Gilbreth's manuals, it was two other German architects, Walther Gropius and Ernst May, who, building on their work, would begin not only to utilize these techniques but to invent new ones.

Like Le Corbusier, Gropius first encountered the Taylor System at Behrens's office around 1910. However, he would not have the opportunity to use industrial engineering tools until 1925, when he began work on the Bauhaus Settlement at Torten, near Dessau. Gropius took Muthesius's notion of the settlement as the ideal laboratory for architectural experimentation to its logical conclusion as early as 1923, when he literally placed the *versuchsplatz* (experimental building site) at the center of Bauhaus pedagogy; the opportunity to finally realize this outdoor classroom was arguably one of the most decisive factors in moving the school to Dessau. Gropius's work benefited from Wagner's journals and Unwin's and Gilbreth's manuals. He also used new projection techniques developed at that time to *schedule* and *route* New York's high-rises. American architects and engineers, following Gilbreth's example, combined simplified sections of high-rises with line and bar graph techniques, generating a modified Gantt chart, which Gropius would call a *zeit plan* or time plan. At Torten, Gropius developed his own time plans for a more complex spatial and temporal condition, the horizontal settlement. Whereas the American examples relied on the repetitive nature of high-rise floors, translating them into the sub-tasks of a given process, Gropius's sub-tasks were his unit-types, organized along the settlement's streets.[39]

The high cost of experimentation at Torten led Gropius to lobby for governmental support. This effort led to the establishment of the *Imperial Research Society for Systematic Management in Building and Dwelling* (RFG).[40] The RFG disseminated industrial engineering tools for the systematic management of building sites and housing, and encouraged the experimental derivation of standards through four "experimental settlements."[41] Through this program, German architects came close to realizing the goal of scientific management, the fusion of the spaces of intellectual and material work. In this effort, they referenced the work of the German Engineering Association, which had developed a unique program in 1917 wherein individual industrial plants would submit their own standards for practice to the NADI committee to be synthesized into national standards, known as DIN-Norms.[42] Gilbreth praised the program in 1922, coining the term "superstandards" for DIN-Norms, in order to distinguish them from tentative standards developed by individual factories. He hoped that America would develop a similar program, with more of a focus on the "standardization of methods" instead of products.[43] In his 1920 text linking Taylor and Gilbreth's work to settlement design, Hermann Muthesius would also enthusiastically

[37] M. Wagner, "Der Rationelle Wohnungsbau," 159–63, and B. Taut, "Die industrielle herstellung von wohnungen" 159–163, both in *Wohnungwirstschaft* 1 No. 7/8 (1 December 1924), focused on industrial engineering principles applied to settlement design. In their discussion of Atterbury and Conzelman, they borrowed from H. Whipple, ed., *Concrete Houses: How They Were Built* (Detroit: Concrete Cement Age, 1920), 36–51.

[38] For more on German work in American architectural journals, see Hyungmin Pai, *The Portfolio and the Diagram* (Cambridge: MIT Press, 2006), 178.

[39] Gropius attributed his "time plans" to high-rise construction in "Erfolge der Baubetriebsorganisation in Amerika (The Success of Building Management Organization in America)" *RFG Technical Symposium in Berlin* Proceedings, 15–17 April 1929. He discussed the Bank of New York and Graybar buildings, which used drawings similar to Gilbreth's route models and drawings. During the postwar period, Soviet engineers would call these drawings *tsiklogrammy* or cyclographs.

[40] *Reichsforschungsgesellschaft für Wirtschaftlichkeit im Bau- und Wohnungswesen* (RFG). I have translated *Wirtschaftlichkeit* as "systematic" instead of "economic" or "efficient." For more on the RFG program (1927–1931) see A. Schwarting Die Siedlung *Dessau-Törten: Rationalität als ästhetisches Programm.* (Dresden: Thelem, 2010), 233–40.

endorse this program for its rigorous empirical approach to the evolution of types. Muthesius also warned about the potential of a new academicism of rationalistically deduced "generally valid elementary forms" developing in municipal and federal planning institutes, one that ignored the "spatial and temporal contingency" of types. He continued to advocate for the settlement, and not the institute or the academy, as the ideal space of architectural inquiry.[44]

Of the four RFG-sponsored projects, Ernst May's Praunheim Settlement (1926–29) most comprehensively captured Gilbreth's industrial techniques, Unwin's visual and site planning, and Le Corbusier and Gropius's more recent work, which he first published in his journal, *Das Neue Frankfurt*, in 1926. May cleverly exceeded the goals of the RFG by converting Praunheim from one experiment to three; the first at the scale of multi-unit building, the second at the scale of a street, and the last at the scale of a small settlement, one that combined considerations for both "building" and "dwelling" within a single projection document and each phase informing the next. His Frankfurt System panels were first fabricated under controlled factory conditions but were later moved to a large dock at Frankfurt harbor that had connections to transportation infrastructure which proved more critical than ideal off-site conditions. He would also apply the same organizational principles to brick and concrete panel construction. When presenting his work in 1929, May echoed Muthesius and Taylor, explaining that the 16 unit types at Praunheim were "evolved" for a specific space and time.[45]

By 1930 a worsening economic and, later, political situation prematurely ended the work of the RFG. May took his experimentally derived data and experience to the Soviet Union. There he would summarize much of his experience in a "type project" for Moscow in 1932. Although this particular project was never built, the drawing set provided the basis for the industrialized housing delivery work in postwar USSR.[46] Gropius published a veritable survey of Gilbreth's techniques used at the Bauhaus in *Bauhaus Builds Dessau* (1930). He and Wagner immigrated to the United States, finding a country deeply influenced by industrial engineering but a discipline that was still more interested in academic composition. One of the first American architects to match the European interest in American industrial engineering tools was Charles Eames, who in 1944 also saw their greatest application in the design of settlements. By that time he could already rely on a full palette of architectural projection techniques informed by interwar transatlantic and trans-disciplinary exchange, although he and his partner, Ray, applied them at the product design scale.[47] During the postwar period, the application of what Gilbreth called the "Office System," the management of the space of intellectual labor, as opposed to the "Field System," the management of the space of construction or fabrication, became more widespread in large American architectural offices like Skidmore, Owings & Merrill (SOM), at the same time that many industrial engineering practices had become fully integrated into American industries, like Du Pont, where new projection tools,

[41] Experimental settlements were subsidized in Dessau, Stuttgart, Frankfurt, and Munich.

[42] NADI (*Normenausschuß der deutschen Industrie*). DIN-Norm is an acronym for a NADI norm.

[43] Frank and Lillian Gilbreth, "Superstandards: Their Derivation, Significance and Value," *Bulletin of Taylor Society* VII No. 3 (June 1922), 107–09.

[44] Muthesius, (1920), 320–24, 326.

[45] "Bericht uber die Versuchssiedlung in Frankfurt A. M.-Praunheim" *RFG* II No. 4 (April 1929). May stated that "we have evolved a total of 18 types" in a lecture titled "Housing Policy of Frankfurt" given on January 12, 1929. The English text is May's own translation.

[46] Postwar Soviet housing construction was deeply influenced by this project. See Eve Blau and Edward Kaufman, ed., *Architecture and Its Image: Four Centuries of Architectural Representations* (Montreal: Canadian Centre for Architecture, 1989), 213–14.

[47] A discussion of the challenge faced by Gropius and other émigré architects in adapting to the significantly different disciplinary roles they encountered in the United States. Margaret Crawford, "Can Architects Be Socially Responsible?" *Out of Site: A Social Criticism of Architecture*, edited by Diane Ghirardo, (San Francisco: Bay Press, 1990), 27–46.

like Critical Path Planning, would evolve from the work of Gantt and Gilbreth.[48] By that time, these approaches had become thoroughly embedded in the corporate culture of private industry as well as public administration, transcending not only the Atlantic but also the Iron Curtain. By 1948, when Sigfried Giedion discovered Taylor and the Gilbreths, few professionals, including architects, referred to them by name, though many of their theories and tools were fully integrated into everyday practice. Despite the prevalence of their methods within architectural practice, many others, particularly the ability to experimentally derive standards and to truly project process in space and time, remained as elusive as they had been for US industrial engineering pioneers at the turn of the century and European architects during the interwar period.

[48] Critical path planning, developed in 1956, the first new instrument to challenge the predominance of the Gantt chart, was also influenced by Gilbreth's work. For more on this see "Electronics in Military Engineering" *Institute of Electrical and Electronics Engineers Conference Proceedings* Vol. 8 (1964), 442.

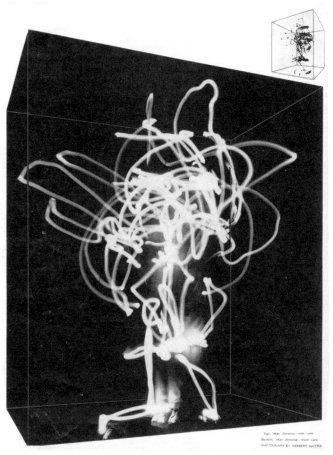

The enthusiasm shown by European modernists for the work of industrial engineering and Frank and Lillian Gilbreth's motion-study techniques during the 1920s was finally matched in the United States by Charles Eames and John Entenza, who included a number of Herbert Matters's motion studies (above) that were directly influenced by the Gilbreths, in their 1944 article "What is a House?" There followed a short renaissance of interest in the Gilbreths by Laszlo Moholy-Nagy and Sigfried Giedion, exactly three decades after they had drawn the attention of Peter Behrens, Le Corbusier, Martin Wagner, and Hermann Muthesius. Source: *Charles Eames, John Entenza, and Herbert Matter, "What is a House?" Arts and Architecture Prefabrication Issue (July 1944), 36.*

CLAIRE ZIMMERMAN

Albert Kahn's Territories

If the end of the Cold War marked the decline of territoriality as a defining characteristic of modern global affairs, then American architect Albert Kahn may be the quintessential architect of a territorial age.[1] During that phantom war, the United States and the Soviet Union further developed arsenals begun during World War II, transforming them from repositories for combat into assets of global influence. As an architect of both "the arsenal of democracy" and that of the USSR under Joseph Stalin, Kahn's work underwrote both sides of the Cold War long after the architect's death in 1942. Kahn's territory was centered on the American powerhouse, Detroit, but at its periphery lay a branch office established in Moscow in 1929. At the geographical edge of Kahn's domain, that office nevertheless developed over five hundred factories to assist in Soviet industrialization, sixty years after the late industrialization of Germany, and well over a hundred years after that of Great Britain and France.[2] The Kahn firm's Soviet factories produced goods that ranged from textiles to turbines, as part of Stalin's First Five Year Plan (1928–32) to rapidly industrialize a gigantic agrarian nation that was lagging behind Europe and the United States in economic and political power.[3] Despite the well-warranted attention that this extraordinary historical episode has received in recent years, it tells only part of the story of Kahn's global impact. In addition to the Soviet contract, Kahn's work traveled to other sites around the world, and not through building commissions alone. At least three other export activities of the Kahn enterprise merit consideration, in addition to that of building design. The production and dissemination of building components, the production and circulation of photographic images, and the export of products made or assembled in Kahn's factories join the buildings themselves to demonstrate how American territory expanded through instruments of design. I speculate here about the role that each has played in the history of the twentieth century, whether already well known, or still poorly understood, in a preliminary sketch of Albert Kahn in modern architecture.

　　To begin by disaggregating Kahn's manner of practicing architecture from that of contemporaries such as Frank Lloyd Wright suggests possible explanations for the simultaneous rise (due to volume) and fall (due to lack of artistry) of Kahn's international reputation. His work was frequently depicted in publications on modern building or on Fordism, but often without name credit. By contrast, Kahn's firm bore his name

[1]
See Charles Maier, "Consigning the Twentieth Century to History: Alternative Narratives for the Modern Era," *The American Historical Review* 105: 3 (June, 2000), 807–31; Reinhart Koselleck, *Future's Past: On the Semantics of Historical Time* trans. K. Tribe (New York: Columbia University Press, 2004 [1979]); Saskia Sassen, *Territory, Authority, Rights: from Medieval to Global Assemblages* (Princeton: Princeton University Press, 2006).

[2]
Sonia Melnikova-Raich, "The Soviet Problem with Two 'unknowns:' How An American Architect and a Soviet Negotiator jump started the industrialization of Russia," *IA Journal of Industrial Archaeology* 36:2 (2010/2013) 57–80.

[3]
Jean-Louis Cohen, *Architecture in Uniform* (New Haven: Yale University Press, 2011), 81–140; Anatole Senkevich, Jr., "Albert Kahn's Great Soviet Venture as Architect of the First Five-Year Plan, 1929-1932," *Dimensions* 10 (1996), 34–49; Dmitrij Chmel'nickij, "Der Kampf um die sowjetsche Architektur: Ausländische Architekten in der UdSSR der Stalin-Ära," *Osteuropa* 55: 9 (Stuttgart: Deutsche Verlags Anstalt, 2005), 91–111.

THE FIVE YEAR PLAN OF ECONOMIC DEVELOPMENT OF THE U.S.S.R.

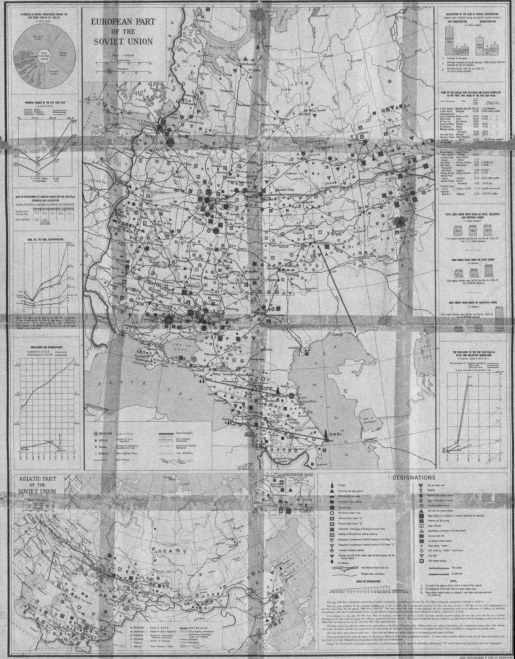

"The Five Year Plan of Economic Development of the U.S.S.R." by John Bartholomew & Son, Ltd., Edinburgh, 1929.
Source: Albert Kahn Papers, Bentley Historical Library, University of Michigan.

alone until 1940, when it was changed to "Albert Kahn Associates" in preparation for the handover that was anticipated to accompany the founder's looming retirement (in fact, he died on the job, in the middle of World War II). As many have noted, Kahn authored a process, not a personal language of architecture with a distinctive artistic signature.[4] One of the questions confronting the global export of Kahn's work concerns how the procedures of the firm intersected with the market for new building beyond United States territory and with the increasingly frequent challenge of "remote building" in the late nineteenth and early twentieth centuries.[5]

In an essay on Kahn's work, George Nelson cited the *Observer* critic, Frederick Towndrow, to the effect that "a great architecture is anonymous, communal, and international."[6] Nelson echoed these claims in relation to Kahn's work, noting that "Kahn invariably says 'we' when referring to his work," and that the buildings themselves contain "no idea of personal authorship."[7] Carl Condit repeated a similar claim when he wrote that Kahn had "to develop design by anonymous teams, in which each specialist contributed his particular skill or knowledge to the final unified result. The method and the product together constituted a subrevolution in architecture."[8] Best known, perhaps, is Henry-Russell Hitchcock, who called Kahn "the architect of bureaucracy," a lasting epithet that cast him in sharp contrast to Wright, genius architect.[9] Elsewhere I have detailed how interwar ideological battles provoked the need to distinguish new and experimental from well-built conventional work. Specifically, Hitchcock's introduction of the phrase "a high level of amenity" to describe Kahn's work suggested that the notion of architectural *quality* could be parsed to protect experimental work, such as Wright's, from accusations of poor construction or underdeveloped new building technology. Good design was no longer the same as good building.[10] More importantly, perhaps, the way that historians and critics characterized Kahn's architecture reflected an implicitly internationalist focus, in that regional character or indigenous construction were replaced by anonymity, generality, and ubiquity. This understanding of Kahn's work contrasts with the architect's loyalty to American industry, to architects of the American Renaissance such as Henry Bacon and Charles McKim, and to the successful prosecution of World War II to which he contributed measurably.

The architect's name, then, subsumes an array of operations beyond building design and construction, expanding the title "Architect" into something more generalized than building designer. The Kahn office organization, as Peggy Deamer relates elsewhere in this volume, is as notable as is the firm's expansion into related businesses, an expansion that is revealed in Kahn's published and unpublished archives.[11] But Kahn had an unusual edge as he expanded his professional organization. Julius Kahn, whose engineering degree at the University of Michigan was financed by his elder brother, established a company that supplied the Kahn architectural firm with building products for expanding technologies such as reinforced concrete. Similarly, in 1893, Kahn and his sister Molly Kahn Fuchs co-founded Multicolor, a reprographics firm that

(4)
See Peggy Deamer's essay in this volume for more information on Kahn's office organization.

(5)
I use this term to describe the distance between an architect's home office and the building site, when that distance increases beyond local or regional scale.

(6)
Frederick Towndrow, *Architecture in the Balance: An Approach to the Art of Scientific Humanism*, (New York: Frederick A. Stokes, 1934), 177.

(7)
George Nelson, *Industrial Architecture of Albert Kahn, Inc* (New York: Architectural Book Pub. Co., 1939).

(8)
Carl Condit, review of Grant Hildebrand, *Designing for Industry*, in *Technology and Culture* 16:2 (April 1975), 313–15.

(9)
Henry-Russell Hitchcock, "The Architecture of Bureaucracy and the Architecture of Genius," *Architectural Review* (January 1947), 3–6.

(10)
See Claire Zimmerman, *Photographic Architecture in the Twentieth Century* (Minneapolis: University of Minnesota Press, 2014); also see idem, "The Labors of Albert Kahn," *Visual Culture and Archives*, Bentley Historical Library: http://deepblue.lib.umich. edu/handle/2027.42/99758 (accessed 2/7/14) For the German context, see Barbara Miller Lane, *Architecture and Politics in Germany*, 1918–1945 (Cambridge, Mass.: Harvard University Press, 1968/1985) and Richard Pommer and Christian Otto, *Weissenhof 1927*

pioneered rapid reproduction of architectural drawings. Fuchs handled the reprographic needs of her brother's architecture office, streamlining work and lowering costs.[12] Kahn's brother Moritz ran the Moscow office; his brother Louis was second-in-command at Albert Kahn Associates, and took over the firm after Albert's death. A fourth brother, Felix, strayed a little further afield, establishing a contracting company based in San Francisco. To call "Albert Kahn" a distributed force rather than a single author is therefore quite correct, as he extended his reach through the professional activities of members of his own family.[13]

1. Building Products

Kahn and his brother Julius made an early territorial excursion into the building products industry around 1902. As Frank Sedlar has noted, Julius Kahn's building products firm developed from a proprietary system of reinforced concrete that he incorporated as "The Trussed Concrete Steel Company," or Truscon, with Albert's financial backing. A promotional brochure for Truscon notes that the company produced "Kahn Building Products, which have been used in over fifteen thousand structures of all types in every part of the world."[14] Julius Kahn soon branched out from the design and production of a reinforcement bar for concrete construction into a broad palette of construction components that he marketed as off-the-shelf building products. The "Kahn Bar," Truscon rib-lath, rib studs, corner bead, concrete reinforcement, and prefabricated metal window frames were some of the Truscon products that were used widely in early twentieth-century construction projects worldwide.[15] Truscon products were used in civic buildings in Cuba and Venezuela, in Frank Lloyd Wright's work in Japan, in the Boots "Wets" factory (completed by Owen Williams in 1932 in England) and in Kahn's own family home in Detroit, to name a few specific sites. Sedlar is currently exploring the early activities of this company, identifying the products marketed by the firm and documenting their use in a wide range of Kahn buildings and other projects around the world. Albert Kahn's role here was tri-fold; first as part owner, then as client and underwriter of Truscon, he demonstrated his own expansive definition of the architect's role in American business and society.[16] Backing his brother's innovations and proving a reliable consumer of Truscon products, Kahn was only one of the wide range of architects and builders served by the company in the United States and abroad.

2. Photographs

The Truscon palette of building products, its influence on the building industry since, and the buildings made possible through its techniques are little known today. Not so the photographs of the factories that Albert Kahn built for Detroit manufacturers in the first three decades of the twentieth century, precursors of "the big three" auto companies today. Photographs of American industrial achievements, as Reyner Banham noted years ago, frequently appeared on the European scene in the nineteen teens and twenties. As is now well known, Walter Gropius

and the modern movement in architecture (Chicago: University of Chicago Press, 1991).

⑪
G. C. Baldwin, "The Offices of Albert Kahn, Architect, Detroit, Michigan," *Architectural Forum* 29, no. (1918), 125–30.

⑫
Albert Kahn Papers, Archives of American Art, Box 6.

⑬
This metaphor expanded into the firm's self-promotion as a "family;" although such a metaphor is commonly used in businesses of all kinds, it acquires a particular valence in this case.

⑭
See Frank Sedlar, "Engineering Industrial Architecture: The Trussed Concrete Steel Company and Albert Kahn," unpublished manuscript. This work is currently under development for publication. Also see Joseph Siry, "The Architecture of Earthquake Resistance: Julius Kahn's Truscon Company and Frank Lloyd Wright's Imperial Hotel," *Journal of the Society of Architectural Historians* 67:1 (2008), 78-105; and Chris Meister, "Albert Kahn's Partners in Industrial Architecture," *Journal of the Society of Architectural Historians* 72:1 (2013), 78–95.

⑮
Rib Lath for Stucco and Plaster in Sidings, Partitions, Ceilings and Furring and Rib Studs for Hollow Walls and Partitions (Kahn Building Products, Trussed Concrete Steel Company, n.d.), 3.

⑯
Albert Kahn, "Architecture and Business," typescript, Albert Kahn Papers, Bentley Historical Library, University of Michigan (henceforth, BHL).

published photographs of Kahn's factories in the 1913 issue of the German Werkbund yearbook. Others appeared in Werner Lindner's *Die Ingenieurbauten in ihre guten Gestaltung* (1923), in Adolf Behne's *The Modern Functional Building* (1926), and in other Weimar publications on American developments in architecture and other fields.[17] Photographic images of Kahn's factories, often attributed to Henry Ford with no mention of Kahn's name, concretized Fordist abstraction, giving capitalism a particular shape and affect. The seemingly endless glass expanses of the "Crystal Palace" in Highland Park, or the glass-sheathed monster sheds at River Rouge—the places where Ford produced parts and cars—appeared in photographs as signifiers for invisible abstractions such as American imperialism, capitalism as a market system, and mass production as the visible result of that system. Photographs of buildings or machines hosted other associations as well, connoting efficiency, functionalism, and the notion of progressive development. But while such associations adhered in photographic images, their relationship to buildings remained unverified.[18]

The "photographic architecture" of pre-World War I and interwar America as it appeared in the European press thus constitutes the second manner in which Kahn's work traveled outside the United States. In contrast to the building products of Truscon, this photographic architecture—by which I mean the appearance of architecture in and through photographic images and the agency of that appearance—had a sizable impact on the development of European modernist ideas.[19] Nikolaus Pevsner distinguished two phases of modern designer-architects in his *Pioneers of the Modern Movement* of 1936: the New Traditionalists and the New Pioneers. For both of these groups (the first included Peter Behrens, the second Walter Gropius), the factories of US industry represented an architectural beacon—to keep in sight, but also hold at a distance. As others have noted, US industrial buildings provided European architects with a counter-model: raw building awaiting the disciplining force provided by Enlightenment tradition.[20] Photographs of Kahn's architecture were the raw material for decades of European architectural production, where modernity was sublated into something called "modernism," worthy of architecture's long historical pedigree. The nearly invisible but extensive export of Truscon products shaped developing construction practices and with them larger technological systems; by contrast, highly visible but physically flimsy photographic images projected "frontiers of Utopia" to architects, clients, and publics throughout the industrializing world.[21]

3. Buildings

Buildings by the Kahn firm were also transported to international sites through construction drawings, full-scale building components, and with the aid of architectural experts from Detroit. The factories built to support the industrialization of the USSR are the best known of these. Their significance lies in their volume and impact on the Soviet economy, not in specific architectural qualities, which remain nearly invisible for

[17] Walter Gropius, "Der Entwicklung moderner Industriebaukunst," *Die Kunst in Industrie und Handel* 1:12; Deutscher Werkbund: *Jahrbuch des Deutschen Werkbundes* (Jena: Diederichs [1913]), 17–22; Werner Lindner, *Die Ingenieurbauten in ihre guten Gestaltung* (1923); Adolf Behne's *Die moderne Zweckbau*, or *The Modern Functional Building* (1926). Also see Reyner Banham, *Concrete Atlantis* (Cambridge, Mass.: MIT Press, 1986) and Jean-Louis Cohen, *Scenes of the World to Come: European Architecture and the American Challenge, 1893–1960* (Paris: Flammarion, 1995).

[18] See Hans Belting, *An Anthropology of Images: Picture, Medium, Body* (Princeton: Princeton University Press, 2011 [2001]), 5; Jacques Ranciere, "Introduction," *The Future of the Image* (London: Verso, 2007 [2003]).

[19] "Beyond Visibility: Modern Architecture in the Photographic Image," in *Photographic Architecture in the Twentieth Century*, op. cit.

[20] Jean-Louis Cohen, op. cit.

[21] Louis Marin, "Frontiers of Utopia: Past and Present," *Critical Inquiry* 19: 3 (Spring 1993), 397–420. See Marin's essay for continuity in the narrative of "Amerikanismus" cited here.

ALBERT KAHN
Seamless Steal Tubes, Detroit

Page from Adolf Behne, *Der moderne Zweckbau* (Munich: Drei Masken Verlag, 1926), showing Detroit Seamless Steel Tubes Company Plant, Detroit, by Albert Kahn Architects.

Abb. 115. Maschinenhaus IX der Fried. Krupp A.-G., Essen

Abb. 116. Fabrik in Nordamerika

Page from Werner Lindner, *Die Ingenieurbauten in ihre guten Gestaltung* (Berlin: Wasmuth, 1923), with Highland Park Plant, Detroit (the "Crystal Palace"), 1910, by Albert Kahn Architects.

several reasons. Kahn signed a contract with the Soviet Union in May 1929 that enabled the firm to evade some of the negative impact of the Great Depression as it unfolded from October of the same year. The first of these factories was constructed of steel trusses manufactured in the United States and shipped to the USSR. In photographs taken upon completion, the Soviet factories resemble similar buildings in Detroit, mass-produced in construction and design. Although other international projects by the firm were more or less globally distributed from Canada to Argentina, and Cuba to Shanghai, these Soviet buildings are almost certainly the most dramatic example of the impact that American exports of architecture had on the global economy before World War II.

Shortly after his death, an article in the *Bulletin* of the Michigan Society recalls Kahn's contribution to the war's Eastern Front, accompanied by a telegram sent to Kahn's widow, in which the architect Viktor Vesnin noted that "MR. ALBERT KAHN. . . . RENDERED US GREAT

SERVICE IN DESIGNING A NUMBER OF LARGE PLANTS AND
HELPED US TO ASSIMILATE THE AMERICAN EXPERIENCE IN
THE SPHERE OF BUILDING INDUSTRY."[22] Although Kahn's Russian
plants were theoretically built for tractor, not tank production, it was
Kahn's suspicion that over-designed building foundations, an unnecessary
cost that he resisted, suggested the Soviets had planned to use the buildings
for munitions production from the beginning, despite their engineers'
claims to the contrary. "My brother Moritz and I suspected something
because of their insistence on heavier foundations than were needed.
They merely smiled when we suggested lighter construction and said we
did not understand their 'weather.' We agreed then that they were
planning armament buildings." These remarks were recorded in 1942,
after the German invasion that began in June 1941, the infamous
"Operation Barbarossa."[23]

Kahn's work in the Soviet Union had developed just after Henry
Ford's second public endorsement of The International Jew in 1928.[24]
Ford thus declared his political views on "the Jewish question" publicly,
at the same time employing a German-Jewish immigrant and son of a
rabbi as his architect. Kahn claims to have had qualms about contributing
to the Soviet cause, but quickly overcame them, according to his
personal correspondence with family members (Ford was equally willing
to support the spread of his production technology to the Soviet Union,
political differences notwithstanding).[25] Kahn's correspondence shows how
the transfer of technology to the Soviet Union and good business practice
for his firm tended in the same direction at this time. In this case, the
territorial expansion of American business and the enhancement of Soviet
industry constitutes a manner of informal foreign policy between the
United States and Russia that contrasts starkly with international relations
between the two countries throughout the years of the Cold War.

If the Soviet factories played a role in World War II, as manufac-
turing facilities of the Fordson tractor transformed for munitions production,
Kahn also designed factories or parts thereof from Argentina to Denmark.
American manufacturers commissioned most of these buildings, and
indeed, not all were factories. The Ford Motor Company alone commissioned projects in Argentina, Brazil, Canada, Denmark, England,
Japan, Mexico, and Uruguay. Other clients included the Fisher brothers
(Fisher Body), General Motors, Intasio Building, the Kelsey-Hayes
Wheel Company, the Packard Motor Company, and Norsk Industries. Kahn
undertook a range of Canadian projects across the border from Detroit.
The United States Navy commissioned projects from Alaska to Hawaii;
the firm worked on bases in San Juan and Guantánamo Bay. All of these
comprise just over three percent of the total project list recorded in the
firm's database until 1942.[26]

4. Armaments

And finally, a fourth export product that resulted from Kahn's professional
efforts was materiél for the European and Pacific theaters of World War II.
Kahn's participation in military supply was decisive, as the firm moved

[22]
The full message reads:
"SOVIET ENGINEERS
BUILDERS ARCHITECTS
SEND YOU THEIR
SINCERE SYMPATHY
IN CONNECTION
WITH THE DEATH OF
YOUR HUSBAND, MR.
ALBERT KAHN, WHO
RENDERED US GREAT
SERVICE IN DESIGNING
A NUMBER OF LARGE
PLANTS AND HELPED
US TO ASSIMILATE THE
AMERICAN EXPERIENCE
IN THE SPHERE OF
BUILDING INDUSTRY."
Albert Kahn Papers,
Archives of American Art.

[23]
See "Ten Years Ago" from
Malcolm Bingay's Column,
'Good Morning,' Detroit
Free Press, July 16, 1942.
Reprinted in Michigan
Society of Architects Bulletin
16 (March 30, 1943), 195;
Melnikova-Raich, op. cit.

[24]
Fordwerke GmbH Köln
(Ford Cologne) was
founded in 1930, and would
be turned to armaments
production before the
Detroit factories, with the
use of forced labor. For
Ford's research into the
history of its Cologne plant,
see http://www.upi.com/
Business_News/Security-
Industry/2001/12/06/
Nazi-atrocities-at-
Ford-Werke-studied/
UPI-36841007666227/
(accessed January 24,
2013).

[25]
Albert Kahn Papers,
Archives of American Art,
Box 6.

[26]
BHL

FORD BOMBER - EARLY STAGE OF MANUFACTURING AREA ERECTION - SUMMER 1941

FORD BOMBER · STEEL FOR SUB·ASSEMBLY BAYS   1941

FORD MOTOR COMPANY   NO. 75550
              Airplane Parts Manufacture Building
Albert Kahn-Associated Architects & Engineers Inc.
Ypsilanti   Michigan

Whitehead & Kales   Structural Steel
J.A Utley Co.   Foundations
Arrow Roofing Sheet Metal Works   Roof Sheet Metal Work
U.S Gypsum Co.   Steel Deck Roof
Gargaro   Storm Sewers & Water Lines
                                     Runway Paving
Julius Porth & Son Co.
Bryant & Detwiler   General Contractor

View *Looking East in 130' Bay*
Btry. Col., R&P
Date *11-19-41* Photo No. *661*

LOOKING WEST ON NORTH SIDE OF BLDG. 1.5.42 #287

Willow Run Bomber plant under construction, Albert Kahn and Associates, Architects, 1941.
Source: Albert Kahn Papers, Bentley Historical Library, University of Michigan.

swiftly to build armament factories to fill government orders; some came on line in record time, ahead of schedule and under budget.[27] Tanks and planes assembled in Kahn's rapidly built factories were projected to alter the course of the war, to be employed by allied invasion forces as they reclaimed Europe.[28] Ford's Willow Run bomber plant, designed in 1941, is currently the most visible emblem of this sort of export—in part because of its partial demolition in the winter of 2014, following the 2010 closure of the GM plant that was still operating in a small fraction of the immense space. Kahn planned ninety acres enclosed under one roof, turned through ninety degrees to avoid a county line that would have made the plant liable for tax in two counties.[29] A building designed to extrude product down an assembly line (in this case, the planes were assembled at stations and moved slowly down the floor of the building) contained a turntable on which B-24 "Liberator" bombers rotated before continuing their movement out the massive doors of the plant. Promotional material on Willow Run and its plane suggests that Kahn's efficiency in producing this building meant that B-24s went into service sooner than anticipated, playing a decisive role in the final two years of the war.[30]

To move through the list enumerated above in reverse order, materiél, photographic images, and buildings are well known in twentieth-century history, illustrating how architecture and politics intersect and constitute one another. The production of armaments was part of the practical politics of warfare. The Soviet factories and other Kahn export buildings were integral to expanding industrialization and were part of the political project of both state and corporate multi-nationalism. The factories were, at the same time, important to Stalin's regime, with its heavy emphasis on modernization. And finally, the photographs of US industrial architecture were enlisted to promote intensified industrialization and greater productive efficiency elsewhere. Left- and right-leaning governments admired them, and not only because support for technological progress was strong across the political spectrum. Because they were photographs, they served varied ideological purposes, according to captioning, accompanying text, and qualities of the photographs themselves (as distinct from those of the buildings they depicted). All three of these modes of export are well known individually, yet combined they expand our understanding of Kahn's global impact, suggesting a similarly inclusive frame of reference for other instances of architectural export.

From the historian's perspective, the first manner of Kahn export mentioned in this account, that of the building products industry that aided ubiquitous, consistent construction systems throughout the world, remains a mystery today. We know little about Truscon's influence on domestic and international building production throughout the rest of the twentieth century. Today's building products industry developed in the wake of the early standardization of products offered by Julius and used regularly by Albert; to what degree these early efforts were decisive, we do not yet know. The Kahn brothers systematized a set of building practices just as other infrastructures coordinated the American environment in

27
Albert Kahn, "Architecture in the National Defense Program," typescript April 1941 and idem., typescript November 28, 1941, both Albert Kahn Papers, BHL.

28
"Special Defense Issue devoted to the work of Albert Kahn Associated Architects and Engineers, Incorporated," *Michigan Society of Architects Bulletin* 12/30/41; *Albert Kahn Memorial Issue, Weekly Bulletin of the Michigan Society of Architects* vol. 17 (March 30, 1943).

29
See Albert Kahn, typescript November 28, 1941, 11, Albert Kahn Papers, BHL. The Crystal Palace in London covered 18 acres; the palace complex at Versailles encloses 16.5 acres in a variety of spaces.

30
Albert Kahn, Architect of Modern Times" (dir. Dieter Marcello, 1993), 38:10. Promotional videos on Willow Run include "B-24 Willow Run Assemby Plant," http://www.youtube.com/watch?v=iKlt6rNciTo (accessed Feb. 20, 2014)

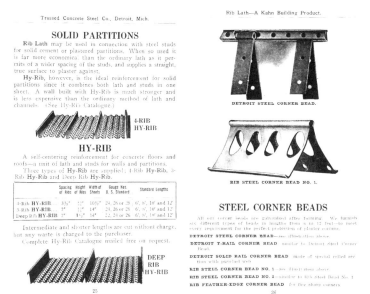

Pages from product catalogue, Kahn Building Products, Trussed Concrete Steel Company.

similar ways. The market for products such as rib lath or steel sash, products that could be used in a wide variety of applications, had the effect of democratizing building practices in line with market forces across the board, with obsolescence and technical innovation incorporated into the development model from the beginning. Whether this democratizing potential was a primary motivation or not, such products would be subject to regular technical improvement in a climate favorably disposed to innovation, based on a market model that favored rapid turnover and promoted obsolescence. Architecture partakes of this systematization, as do other manners of building in the United States. But the history of this export product awaits further exploration, as Truscon's proprietary "Kahn bar" was displaced by yet more ubiquitous and generalized concrete reinforcement systems. Architects and engineers carefully designed systems of building and the components with which to execute them, giving rise to a *lingua franca* of construction materials that rapidly escaped their designers' hands.

The Kahn firm's export products may be yet more numerous than those described here: those of Truscon ("Kahn Building Systems"), those related to printed matter, buildings commissioned by clients, and building contents. These four, however, show how American architecture (or any architecture) defined its territories in the twentieth century—not only, or even primarily, through buildings on sites, but rather through diffused operations that expanded the architect's role in an increasingly connected world.

Acknowledgments
My thanks to Nancy Bartlett, Sally Bund, Nancy Deromedi, and Karen Jania of the Bentley Historical Library, to Frank Sedlar and the other students in a workshop on Albert Kahn in Winter 2013, and to Sonia Melnikova-Raich, who shared the results of her research before they appeared in press. I also thank Amanda Lawrence, Ana Miljački, and Ashley Schafer for their helpful comments on this preliminary sketch for a larger work on Albert Kahn.

COMPLETED AUTOMOBILES

Photomontage from *USSR in Construction*, No.1, 1933. Published from 1930-41 in Russian, German, English, and French, *USSR in Construction* was a propaganda journal intended to inform readers abroad of the development of Russia into a leading industrial power under Stalin's first and second Five Year Plans *Source: Houghton Library, Harvard University.*

Panoramic view of the Chelyabinsk Tractor Plant, 1933. *Source: Chelyabinsk Tractor Plant Museum.*

OfficeUSSR

In the brief period between May 8, 1929, and April 29, 1932, an unprecedented transfer of expertise, materials, and technology to the Russian government was undertaken and facilitated by the firm of architect Albert Kahn.

This extraordinary exchange, which ran counter to the official diplomatic policies of the United States, was initiated by the Soviets in 1928 after a group of high-ranking Soviet officials undertook a tour of the American industrial scene. Stalin had just announced his first Five Year Plan, which collectivized farms and brought Russian industry under state control. His government was intent on rapidly increasing industrial production in order to catch up to its western counterparts, address Russian military weakness that had become evident during World War I, and develop self-sufficiency.

Chief among Kahn's growing body of industrial projects, the River Rouge Plant (1917–1928) convinced the Soviets to commission Kahn's firm to act as consulting architects to the Soviet government and to give him their first contract, for the Stalingrad Tractor Plant. River Rouge, and the subsequent Russian projects it inspired, embodied Kahn's idea of the "beautiful factory": a single-story complex tightly designed around the flow of materials and labor, with abundant natural light from the sides and above.

By April of 1932, when the contract with Russia was dissolved, Kahn's firm had helped establish an office in Moscow with branches in at least eight other cities, which jointly employed over 2,000 people, and also provided a training program for the design, engineering, and construction of factories through which many more Russians passed. The Kahn organization was directly responsible for over 520 new Russian factories whose products included automobile parts, tractors, freight cars, airplane parts, steel, aluminum, heavy machinery, and power, and ultimately tanks that some have suggested helped turn the tide of World War II.
— Megan Miller

Map and diagram of the Ford River Rouge Plant, 1941. *Source: The Collections of The Henry Ford.*

*"There must be a study of the flow of materials to develop
a scheme simple and direct for the transportation and
handling of materials without the need for crossing or
retracing of production...There is absolutely no need for
dark interiors. If the plan adopted necessitates such, then the
plan is not right. Nor is it right if it be complex, difficult to
read, or follow."*

—

Albert Kahn, 1939[1]

[1] Albert Kahn, "Industrial Architecture," *Weekly Bulletin of the Michigan Society of Architects*, 13 (November 7 1939), 8.

THE KAHN ORGANIZATION

A thoroughly integrated organization of design specialists, with two divisions and six major departments and more than 600 employees, has made it possible for Albert Kahn to make impressive speed records in the construction of tremendous war production plants

CHIEF ADMINISTRATOR

ASSISTANT ADMINISTRATOR

PROJECT ADMINISTRATORS

TECHNICAL DIVISIONS

EXECUTIVE DIVISION

ARCHITECTURAL DEPARTMENT — STRUCTURAL DEPARTMENT — MECHANICAL DEPARTMENTS — ESTIMATING DEPARTMENT — CONSTRUCTION COORDINATION — OFFICE MANAGEMENT

CHIEF ARCHITECT / CHIEF DESIGNER / STEEL DESIGN / CONCRETE DESIGN / SANITARY ENGINEERING / HEATING ENGINEERING / VENTILATING AIR CONDITIONING / PROCESS ENGINEERING / ELECTRICAL ENGINEERING / CHIEF ESTIMATOR / DEPARTMENT CHIEF / CHIEF ACCOUNTANT

JOB CAPTAINS / ASSISTANTS / JOB CAPTAINS / JOB CAPTAINS / JOB CAPTAINS / JOB CAPTAINS / JOB CAPTAINS / JOB CAPTAINS / JOB CAPTAINS / ASSISTANTS / OBTAINING TENDERS / CHIEF SUPERINTENDENT / ACCOUNTANTS

ASSISTANTS / DETAILERS / DRAFTING / DRAFTING / DRAFTING / DRAFTING / DRAFTING / DRAFTING / DRAFTING / STENOGRAPHERS / AWARDING CONTRACTS / ASSISTANT SUPERINTENDENT / STENOGRAPHERS

DETAILERS / CHECKING / CHECKING / CHECKING / CHECKING / CHECKING / CHECKING / CHECKING / EXPEDITING CONSTRUCTION / RESIDENT CLERKS OF WORK / FILING

CHECKING / SPECIFICATIONS / SPECIFICATIONS / SPECIFICATIONS / SPECIFICATIONS / CHECKING CONTRACT ACCOUNTS / DRAWINGS / CORRESPONDENCE

SPECIFICATIONS / CHIEF OF SPECIFICATIONS DEPARTMENT / ASSISTANTS / TYPISTS / ISSUING CERTIFICATES / MAILING

Diagram of the Kahn Organization, 1942 (reprinted from *Architectural Record* Vol. 91 No. 6, June 1942).

Photo of American specialists inside Chelyabinsk Tractor Plant, 1932.

"*No one designer will have all of the technical knowledge required for this type of work; hence, to serve the best interests of his client, he will surround himself with a group of men—architectural draftsmen, process engineers, structural, electrical, power, sanitary, heating, ventilating and air conditioning engineers. His staff will embody specification writers, field superintendents, cost accountants, expediter and job managers. The cooperation of the members of such a staff in one organization, under one roof, and under the guidance of one principal, produces efficient buildings, economically and expeditiously constructed.*"

—

Albert Kahn, 1936 [2]

(2)
Albert Kahn, *Industrial and Commercial Buildings*, (Detroit, Albert Kahn Inc., 1936) 3.

Aerial view of Ford Rouge Plant, circa 1945. *Source: The Collections of The Henry Ford.*

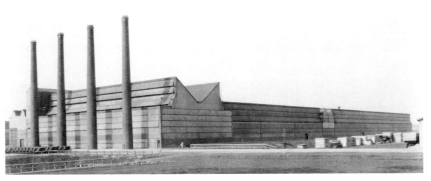

Exterior view of the Glass Plant at Ford Rouge, 1927. *Source: The Collections of The Henry Ford.*

1895

1895
Albert Kahn
opens first office

05.26.1896
Czar Nicholas
II, last czar of
Russia, crowned

06.04.1896
Henry Ford
completes first
gas powered car

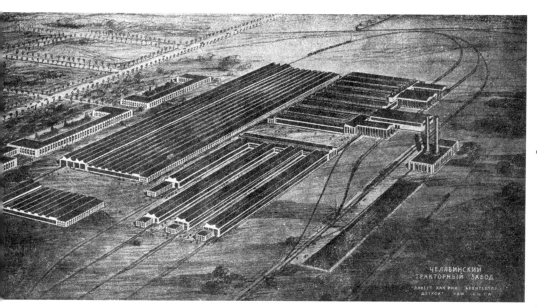

Axonometric rendering of the Chelyabinsk Tractor Plant by Albert Kahn Architects and Engineers, circa 1930. *Source: Bentley Historical Library, University of Michigan.*

Exterior view of the Chelyabinsk Tractor Plant, 1933. *Source: Chelyabinsk Tractor Plant Museum.*

Kahn designs
first industrial
building

1903
Julius Kahn
becomes chief
engineer at AKA

1905

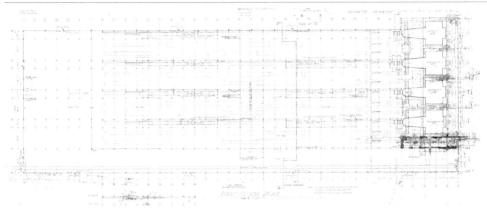

Glass Plant at Ford Rouge, Plan, 1922, by Albert Kahn Architects and Engineers. *Source: Bentley Historical Library, University of Michigan.*

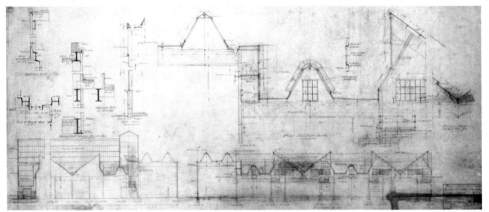

Glass Plant at Ford Rouge, Building sections, 1922, by Albert Kahn Architects and Engineers. *Source: Bentley Historical Library, University of Michigan.*

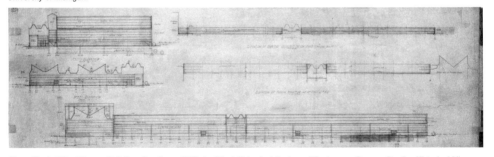

Glass Plant at Ford Rouge, Building elevations, 1922, by Albert Kahn Architects and Engineers. *Source: Bentley Historical Library, University of Michigan.*

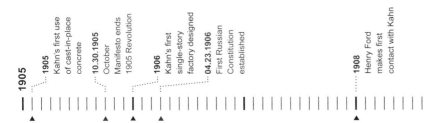

1905

1905 Kahn's first use of cast-in-place concrete

10.30.1905 October Manifesto ends

1905 Revolution

1906 Kahn's first single-story factory designed

04.23.1906 First Russian Constitution established

1908 Henry Ford makes first contact with Kahn

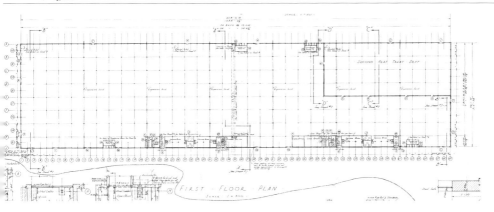

alingrad Tractor Plant Assembly Building, Plan, 1929, by Albert Kahn Architects and Engineers. *Source: Bentley Historical rary, University of Michigan.*

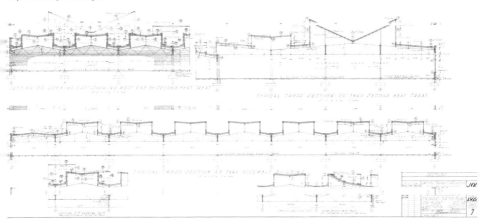

lingrad Tractor Plant Assembly Building, Building sections, 1929, by Albert Kahn Architects and Engineers. *Source: Bentley torical Library, University of Michigan.*

lingrad Tractor Plant Assembly Building, Building elevations, 1929, by Albert Kahn Architects and Engineers. *Source: Bentley torical Library, University of Michigan.*

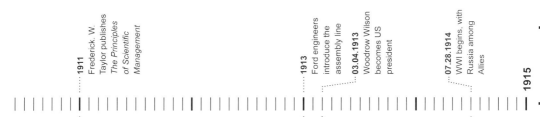

1911
Frederick. W. Taylor publishes *The Principles of Scientific Management*

1913
Ford engineers introduce the assembly line

03.04.1913
Woodrow Wilson becomes US president

07.28.1914
WWI begins, with Russia among Allies

1915

135

Photo documentation of steel erection at Ford Rouge, 1923. *Source: Bentley Historical Library, University of Michigan.*

1915

1917
Construction
of Ford Rouge
Plant begins

03.03.1917
Czar Nicholas II
deposed

10.24.1917
October
Revolution:
Bolsheviks
installed

12.1917
US breaks
off diplomatic
relations with
Russia

1918
Kahn moves
office to top
of Marquette
building

...oto documentation of steel truss for the assembly building at the Stalingrad Tractor Plant, fabricated by McClintic-Marshall Products in New ...k before being shipped to the USSR. *Source: Bentley Historical Library, University of Michigan.*

...oto documentation of foundation construction using horses at the Stalingrad Tractor Plant site. *Source: Bentley Historical Library, ...versity of Michigan.*

1921
American Tractor Brigades arrive in Russia

1921
Fordson tractor production begins at Rouge Plant

03.04.1921
Warren G. Harding becomes US president

04.1922
Joseph Stalin elected General Secretary of the Communist Party

12.28.1922
USSR established

03.04.1923
Domestic tractor industry is formally established in USSR

01.21.1924
Vladamir Lenin dies; Stalin appointed successor

1925

MICHIGAN MANUFACTURER AND FINANCIAL RECORD

DETROIT MICHIGAN — APRIL 19-1930

VOLUME FORTY-FIVE — NUMBER SIXTEEN

Detroit Engineers Direct
Soviet Industrial Revival

Michigan enterprise, a dominant factor in the prosperity of America, today is engaged in the execution of a gigantic program designed to rebuild the entire economic structure of the vast Russian Republic with 155,000,000 inhabitants, a land stretching across two continents, fabulously rich in natural resources. Michigan executives, engineers and skilled laborers, recruited largely in Detroit, are on the ground directing the application of many phases of the Soviet five-year economic plan, while huge amounts of Michigan equipment and supplies, shipped to Russia in recent years, are being put to use in connection with the rehabilitation.

Business relations of the Soviet Union and the state of Michigan are bound together mainly in the development of Soviet automobile and tractor industries, but Michigan factories are furnishing a large share of the machine tools, forge and foundry equipment, farm machinery, office equipment and other items of capital investment necessary to the five-year plan. The Amtorg Trading Corporation, fiscal agents of the Soviet government in the United States, estimates contracts aggregating $10,000,000 in two years, have been placed with upward of 80 Michigan plants with the prospect of a substantial increase in orders as the five-year plan approaches realization.

One of the outstanding projects in the five-year plan is the construction at Nizhni-Novgorod, 273 miles east of Moscow, of an automobile plant and model industrial city of 50,000 inhabitants, patterned after Detroit. The Ford Motor Company is under contract to provide complete technical assistance in building the plant, which is to duplicate on a small scale the 1,100-acre River Rouge plant of the Ford company. The plans are designed for ultimate capacity output of 140,000 passenger cars and trucks annually.

S. S. Dybetz, president of Autostroy (the Soviet Automobile Construction Bureau), and a group of 120 engineers, foremen and office assistants, are now stationed at Dearborn drafting specifications for equipment to be installed in the Soviet factory. This group plans to return to Russia within the coming year to oversee the completion of the plant.

The Austin Company, Cleveland engineering firm, is in charge of construction at Nizhni-Novgorod. Headed by G. A. Bryant, Jr., vice-president, 15 Austin officials were to sail for Russia this month to be on the spot for the beginning of construction work on the motor car plant. More than 100 engineers and draftsmen at the Austin headquarters in Cleveland spent the winter preparing drawings for the project. Most of the preliminary work will have been completed when the Austin party reaches Nizhni-Novgorod. This includes dredging the Oka river to provide dock facilities for landing supplies in addition to assembling

ALBERT KAHN

President of Albert Kahn, Inc., Detroit, consulting architects and engineers for the Soviet Supreme Economic Council. Mr. Kahn has an international reputation as an architect. He designed the General Motors, Fisher, First National Bank buildings and Ford laboratory. His firm drew plans for the Soviet tractor plant nearing completion at Stalingrad, Russia.

materials and erecting shelter for 8,000 workers who will be employed on the job.

The big problem before Russian engineers is that of scaling down specifications of the equipment in use at the River Rouge plant. The Ford works is geared to produce as high as 10,000 cars and trucks daily, while the Soviet plant at capacity will turn out less than 10 per cent of this volume. Practically all equipment to go in the Soviet plant must come from America and much of it has already been ordered. Blast furnaces and steel mills, under construction in Russia, are to furnish steel for the Soviet automotive industry.

A Detroit firm, Albert Kahn, Inc., architects and engineers, have been engaged by the Soviet Supreme Economic Council as general consulting engineers to prepare plans and designs for industrial projects. Work awarded Kahn will total $2,000,000,000 this year. This firm, which has designed plants for Ford, Hudson and Packard, furnished plans for a $25,000,000 tractor plant nearing completion at Stalingrad, located in the lower Volga region of the Soviet Union. This plant is to manufacture 50,000

tractors annually of 15-30 horsepower type.

Construction at Stalingrad was in charge of John Calder, Detroit engineer, and the speed with which the building was erected is said to equal the best records established by American contractors. It was March, 1929, that a delegation of Soviet engineers arrived in the United States to assist in laying out designs for the factory. The building now awaits the arrival and installation of equipment ordered in this country. Production of tractors is due to get under way in Russia this year.

A. J. Brandt, Detroit engineer, recently returned from a stay of several months in the Soviet Union, where he acted as consultant in laying out Russian automotive plants. Mr. Brandt, former vice-president of the Oakland Motor Car Company, is chief engineer of the American Austin Motor Company which is now going into production of a so-called "bantam" automobile.

In addition to Ford and Kahn, the Timken-Detroit Axle Company is to furnish technical assistance to the Soviet motor car industry.

The Soviet Union is not only calling upon Michigan manufacturers for technical help in building Russian factories, but it is purchasing large quantities of motor cars, trucks and tractors as well as other equipment.

In the sale of finished motor cars to the Soviets, the Ford company has the inside track. The contract which provides for the use of Ford patents and designs by the Soviet automobile industry calls for the purchase by Russia of $30,000,000 in Ford products in five years. This contract, which runs nine years, was signed at Dearborn a year ago by Henry Ford and two representatives of Russia, V. U. Meshlauk, vice-chairman of the Soviet Supreme Economic Council, and S. G. Bron, chairman of Amtorg Trading Corporation. A substantial part of the contract has been fulfilled by Russia within the past year.

Other Michigan automobile manufacturers have held contracts with the Soviet Union during the past five years, including General Motors, Dodge, Packard, Chrysler, and the Continental Motors Corporation. Important orders have been filled by the Long Manufacturing Company and the Champion Spark Plug Company, both of Detroit, and the A. C. Spark Plug Company, of Flint. The Long company makes clutches.

Another group of purchases made in Michigan for the Soviet Union, principally by the Amtorg Trading Corporation, is that of machine tools, forge and foundry equipment. Among the companies belonging to this category, the following may be mentioned: the Lock Pattern Works, the Osborn Manufacturing Company and the Cartwright Die Tool Company, of Detroit; E. W. Bliss Company, of Hastings; and Wickes Brothers, of Saginaw.

While the automobile and tractor industry of

US press clippings from the scrapbooks of Albert Kahn Architects and Engineers, 1930–31.
Source: Bentley Historical Library, University of Michigan.

Detroiters Helping To Build Vast Plant Which Soviet Hopes Will Convert Nation to Bolshevism and Enable It To Outdo U. S.

1925

04 to 08.1926
Ford experts spend five months in USSR

05.01.1926
Ford adopts forty-hour work week

10.01.1928
Stalin announces First Five-Year Plan

03.04.1929
Herbert Hoover becomes US president

05.08.1929
Kahn contracted to build

The entire plant resembles one gigantic machine, all parts of which function in strict harmony with the others...All production is arranged not only in the space of the plant but also in the space of time, and therefore the extent of each article not in space but in time is of leading significance to every worker in the factory.

«WE ARE BECOMING A COUNTRY OF METAL, A COUNTRY OF AUTOMOBILIZATION». STALIN

Stamping presses.

It is true that simple village lads and maidens who go to work in a factory (and continue to do so now) do not become skilled workers right away. In time, however, they do acquire skill and they master the process of production even before they swap their bast-shoes for leather footwear. Our tractor factories are the best evidence of this. The automobile plant in Gorky (formerly Nijni-Novgorod) is also a shop where new people are forged, and he who was yesterday a colhoz farmer, to-day controls the levers of a machine and learns to master the process of production by attending special technical courses.

Soviet press images from *USSR in Construction* No.1, 1933. *Source: Houghton Library, Harvard University.*

Stock market crash begins Great Depression

01.09.1930 Kahn's firm contracted to consult on all USSR industrial projects

04.15.1930 Kahn's Moscow headquarters open

07.07.1930 Design of Chelyabinsk is completed in Detroit office

04.29.1932 Kahn's Moscow unit stops work

12.31.1932 Stalin declares First Five-Year Plan "fulfilled"

03.04.1933 Franklin D. Roosevelt becomes US president

11.16.1933 US establishes diplomatic relations with USSR

1935

Railroad Cars and Fordson Tractor Parts at Rouge Plant, interior, 1921. *Source: The Henry Ford.*

1935

05.26.1937
The Battle at the
Overpass takes
place at the
Rouge Plant

1939
Tank production
begins at
Chelyabinsk
Plant

Interior photograph: Forge shop at the Chelyabinsk Tractor Plant, 1930s. *Source: the Chelyabinsk Tractor Plant Museum.*

06.22.1941
Hitler invades Russia

Late 1942
German Army storms Stalingrad Plant

12.08.1942
Albert Kahn dies

02.02.1943
Red Army defeats German Army in Battle of Stalingrad

1945

Office*US*: World Currencies

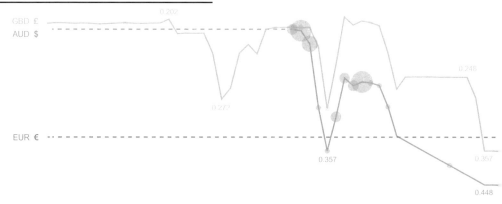

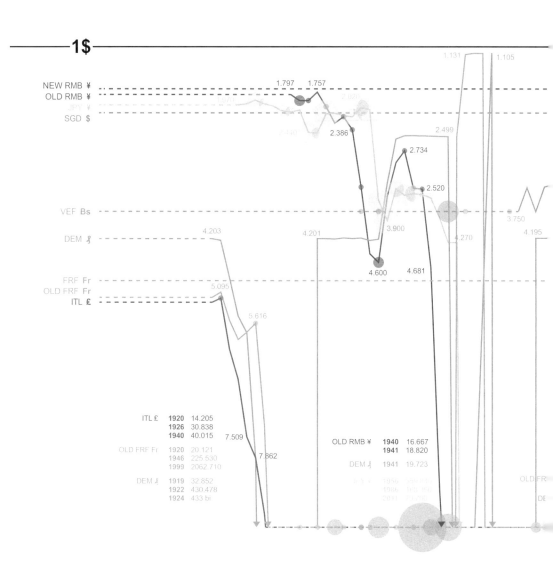

GBD £
AUD $

0.202

0.272

EUR €

0.357

0.248

0.357

0.448

1$

NEW RMB ¥
OLD RMB ¥
JPY ¥
SGD $

1.797   1.757

2.386

2.734

2.520

1.131   1.105

2.499

VEF Bs

3.900

3.750

DEM ℳ

4.203

4.201

4.270

4.195

FRF Fr
OLD FRF Fr
ITL £

5.095

4.600   4.681

5.616

7.509

7.862

ITL £	1920	14.205
	1926	30.838
	1940	40.015

OLD FRF Fr	1920	20.121
	1946	225.530
	1999	2062.710

DEM ℳ	1919	32.852
	1922	430.478
	1924	433 bi

| OLD RMB ¥ | 1940 | 16.667 |
| | 1941 | 18.820 |

| DEM ℳ | 1941 | 19.723 |

OLD FR

DE

1900   1910   1920   1930   1940   1950

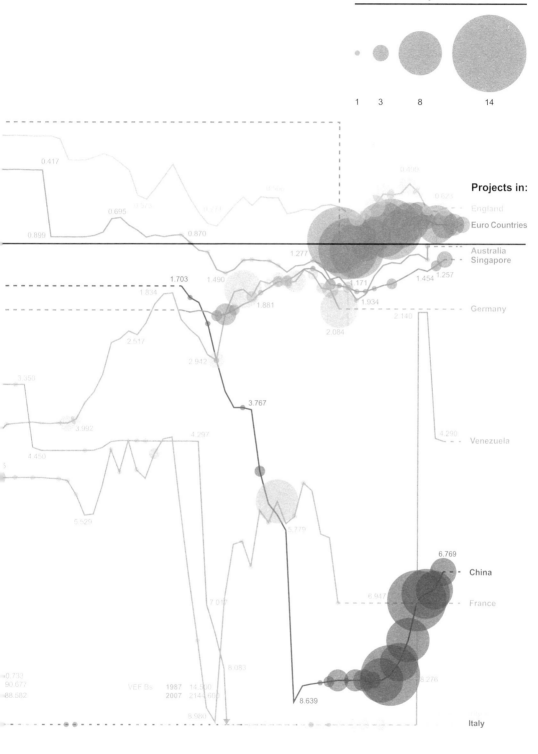

Number of Projects

1 3 8 14

Projects in:

England
Euro Countries

Australia
Singapore

Germany

Venezuela

China

France

Italy

0.417
0.695
0.573
0.774
0.499
0.623
0.899
0.870
1.277
1.703
1.490
1.834
1.881
2.084
1.171
1.934
1.454 1.257
2.140
2.517
2.942
3.350
3.767
3.992
4.297
4.290
4.450
5
5.529
5.779
6.769
6.947
7.017
8.083
-0.733
90.677
88.582
VEF Bs 1987 14.500
2007 214.600
8.639
8.276
8.980

1970   1980   1990   2000   2010

KELLER EASTERLING

The Management

Modern architects of the early twentieth century dreamed of architecture and urbanism as a shared global platform. Modular proportional systems, flexible joints, minimum requirements for dwelling, and prefabrication technologies were among the proposals offered in projects, books, exhibitions, or conferences like the meetings of the International Congresses of Modern Architecture (1928–59). Spatial variables, it was hoped, would shape a universal language.

Yet the titanic, utopian dreams of avant-garde modern architecture were no match for the plodding bureaucracies of consensus that attended two other languages or platforms born in the twentieth century—those of standards and management protocols. More ubiquitous than any modernist spatial proposals, these practices shaped a contemporary Esperanto.

Standards
Beginning in the last half of the nineteenth century, the history of standard making parallels the history of international organization. International organizations form to coordinate infrastructure, for instance, liaise between allies at war, make peace, confront social issues, or organize reconstruction in the aftermath of the world wars. The International Telecommunications Union of 1865, the International Civil Aviation Authority of 1903, the International Electrotechnical Commission of 1906, the International Monetary Fund and World Bank, both of 1944, the North American Treaty Organization of 1949, and the Organisation for Economic Co-operation and Development of 1961 are among thousands of organizations that today address countless issues and problems around the world. Ballooning in numbers after World War II, many convene UN-style congresses with headquarters in Geneva, the Vatican City of international organization.

If legislation or law is the currency of governments, standard making is the currency of international organizations. Technical standards ensure, for instance, that bullets will be uniform in size, railway's gauges will be compatible from one country to another, radio signals can be received globally, or Internet protocols can be shared. Standards supply the calibrations and compacts for the world, the non-binding soft law of commercial and extrastate exchanges.

Founded in 1947, the International Organization for Standardization (ISO) is a nongovernmental organization that coordinates all this global standard making. Lying at the crossroads of many nongovernmental organizations, ISO determines standards for virtually everything, be it credit card thickness, film speed, screw threads, lubricants, container-locking mechanisms, dashboard pictograms, or JPEGs. While most people have never heard of ISO, everyone is subject to its careful and seemingly innocuous diligence. Whether food, garments, or vehicles, almost every object is bristling with ISO standards that allow it to be manufactured and distributed around the world. Since the making and handling of every component of a building must comply with standards, architects too are, through the construction and fabrication organizations with which they associate, unwitting subjects of the ISO parliament.

Management

During the same postwar Pax Americana, the world began to share a fascination with US corporate management styles. In 1944, a *Fortune* article, "The Doctors of Management," reported that business advising had itself become a big business. The number of consulting firms grew from 100 in 1930 to 400 in 1940, and the number of professional organizations and business schools reflected serious interest in management practices.[1] Firms like Booz Allen Hamilton and McKinsey & Company had long been in business.[2] Using Alfred P. Sloan Jr.'s leadership of General Motors as paradigm, Peter Drucker's 1946 book, *Concept of the Corporation*, profiled the corporation as an agile, intelligent, and trans-national player—an emergent social and political institution.[3] *Concept of the Corporation* and subsequent books would introduce a number of durable terms such as "privatization" or "knowledge worker."[4]

By 1950 there were approximately 1,000 management firms in the United States. They portrayed themselves as viable partners to the nation, a "contractor state" consulting on governance, defense, cold war tactics, and the space race. They joined the Organisation for Economic Co-operation and Development, the International Monetary Fund, the World Bank and other intergovernmental organizations—the new organs of global coordination and cooperation. Many offices relocated to Washington, DC, and their consultants moved fluidly through the ranks of authority, advising both businesses and governments domestically and abroad. The enactment of the Marshall Plan extended their influence globally as they were awarded an increasing number of overseas contracts. Even the Bank of England was "McKinseyed."[5] By the 1960s these consultants, attired in conservative dress, had become legendary characters haunting the Yale Club and the University Club in Manhattan.

This was the corporate culture that US architecture firms like Skidmore, Owings & Merrill (SOM) reflected as they too developed a global practice through military and government contracts. In 1942 SOM designed Oak Ridge, Tennessee, where the atomic bomb was built. After the war SOM's Istanbul Hilton (1951), partly funded by the Marshall Plan, and the Tel Aviv Hilton (1965) became symbols of the cold war era.[6] SOM mirrored its clients in dress and demeanor. The firm also adopted a similar organizational structure and, like its clients, was often referred to with a list or acronym of the partners' last names. The

(1)
Christopher D. McKenna, *The World's Newest Profession: Management Consulting in the Twentieth Century* (London: Cambridge University Press, 2006), 18, 47, 62; John Micklethwait and Adrian Wooldridge, *The Witch Doctors : Making Sense of the Management Gurus* (New York: Times Books, 1996).

(2)
Booz Allen Hamilton had its first incarnation in 1919, and McKinsey & Company appeared in 1926. McKenna, *The World's Newest Profession*, 47.

(3)
Peter F. Drucker, *Concept of the Corporation* (New York: The John Day Company, 1946), xiii, xi.

(4)
John Micklethwait and Adrian Woodridge, in their analysis of contemporary management culture, suggest that Drucker incorporated not only structural and human relations thinking but also notions of scientific management with the sense that the successful executive was one who set deliberate objectives and met them. In other words, there was still something to chart— still a kind of obsessive management accounting that could quantify benchmarks and goals. Micklethwait and Woodridge, *The Witch Doctors*, 77, 74, 67–83.

(5)
McKenna, *The World's Newest Profession*, 62, 181–86. Like Drucker, McKinsey adopted the authority of the academic with its own journal, the *McKinsey Quarterly*. Micklethwait and Woodridge, *The Witch Doctors*, 54.

Hilton-style international modernism of SOM and similar firms became a customary offering for the headquarters and installations of the multinational corporation.

"Quality Management"

The histories of standards and management practices that were coordinating and accessorizing the postwar built environment had long been intertwined. Both shared early-twentieth-century intelligence about scientific management techniques, and in the late twentieth century they would take a consolidating turn toward each other that moved the center of influence away from the United States.

US management practices significantly transformed as they circulated through other countries, especially postwar Japan. After the war General MacArthur enlisted US management experts to consult with the Japanese about improving their trade and economy. *Concept of the Corporation* was a best seller in Japan, but, in dialogue with theorists from the United States, the Japanese focused on a strain of management thinking known as "quality management." Evolving from "quality inspection," quality management incorporated sophisticated techniques for gathering data about products so that, for instance, each item off the assembly line did not have to be individually inspected. Some of the same data-gathering techniques also influenced "quality assurance," a practice of determining customer satisfaction. Checklists and mottoes such as POSDCORB (an acronym for Planning, Organizing, Staffing, Directing, Coordinating, Reporting, and Budgeting) or PDCA (short for Plan, Do, Check, and Act) fueled quality management techniques. Like other forms of management including Drucker's, those techniques successfully migrated from the shop floor to the boardroom to influence structural practices and human capital as well as the dispositions of organizations.

Exceeding the expectations of their US tutors, Japanese management developed what would be called Total Quality Management (TQM), a strain of quality management thinking that improved on the US techniques. By including an ethos about *kaizen,* or continual improvement, TQM lent an almost spiritual rigor and devotion to the techniques. To the obsessive checklists, the Japanese added incantatory slogans and mantras about striving and eliminating error (e.g. "You are surrounded by mountains of treasures." Meaning: There are many problems from which to learn.[7] Or a management expert might look for "the 5 Ws and the 1 H." Meaning: One needs to ask "why" at least five times to determine the cause of a problem and then decide "How" to fix it.) Other, more recognizable hallmarks of this style also included *kan ban,* or just-in-time production. As Japanese production techniques markedly improved by the 1970s, and as Japanese TQM practices became more popular around the world, they challenged the supposedly dominant US techniques to become the new global paradigm.

Responding to the global popularity of quality management techniques in the 1980s, ISO made a surprising move. This organization

(6)
Annabel Jane Wharton, *Building the Cold War: Hilton International Hotels and Modern Culture (Chicago: University of Chicago Press, 2001), 19–22, 114.

(7)
Ibid. 79. Mauro F. Guillén, *Models of Management: Work, Authority, and Organization in a Comparative Perspective.*

that long developed highly technical standards decided to create a completely different form of standard—a management standard. In addition to addressing highly determinate specifications, ISO addressed the indeterminate, even mysterious term "quality." Satisfying the habits of ISO members who were already proponents of global management principles, ISO introduced a nontechnical, quality management standard called ISO 9000. With this standard the organization hoped to achieve universal contact, bringing more and more players into the ISO fold.

Today almost every major industry in the world has adopted quality management practices, and most major global organizations speak in the jargon and managementese of ISO 9000. But in some ways no one really knows what the standard is because it has no specific content. ISO 9000 establishes principles of quality management—a procedure for managing any industry to better satisfy customers and improve both production and market status. Quality standards do not dictate technical specifications for a product but rather offer management guidelines for a process or quality system. A certification and auditing process that directs corporations to assess themselves based on a short list of principles that are interpreted differently for every industry, whether it is food service or automobile manufacturing. Using systematic, almost obsessive, processes of data gathering and feedback, ISO 9000 promises to deliver a well-run company, with strong supplier relations and enhanced customer satisfaction.[8] For instance, ISO 9000 is responsible for the voice on the other end of the telephone line announcing, "Your call is being recorded for quality assurance purposes."

While the contemporary quality management culture initially absorbed Japanese and European influences, the United States still contributes special management tropes, largely from popular culture. The motivational slogans of quality mix with the self-help advice of gurus like Steve Covey *(The Seven Habits of Highly Effective People)* or Tom Peters. The Tom Peters website offers a sample of his helpful advice, including lists such as "The Top 50 'Have-Yous,'" "100 Ways to Succeed/ Make Money," or "The 209 Irreducibles.[9] The United States also offers sister management techniques like Motorola's Six Sigma program, introduced in 1988, and now broadly applied to many different kinds of organizations. One can become a black belt in Six Sigma management. Like promises in spiritual cults or recipes for celebrity, all these practices continually refresh their message with new content, maintaining a forward movement that is satisfying perhaps precisely because it cycles through familiar territory with only slight variations. All this content must be constantly boiled down to essential steps that can be absorbed instantly. The result is a welter of books, seminars, lectures, heroes, bibles, acronyms, upbeat jargon, steps, takeaways, executive summaries, and "go-to" concepts.

Organizations wear their ISO certification as a seal of approval. ISO 9000 compliance is even, as soft law, a condition of entering the European Union. ISO has continued to develop other families of quality management standards like ISO 14000, related to the environment, or ISO 26000, related to social responsibility. Since these standards are

[8]
Staffan Furusten, "The Knowledge Base of Standards," in *A World of Standards*, ed. Nils Brunsson, Bengt Jacobsson, and associates (London: Oxford University Press, 2000), 71–78.

[9]
"Free Stuff," Iom Peters, accessed February, 15, 2014, http://www. tompeters.com/freestuff/ index.php

non-binding the environmental standard, for instance, does not specify emissions levels, but instead directs an organization to assess its own environmental consciousness. While the satisfaction of the customer registers as important information in quality management standards, there is no standard related to labor conditions or other complex issues. ISO management standards may increase awareness of important issues like those related to the environment, but they also lubricate the workings of global corporations and potentially even inoculate them against labor or environmental scrutiny. Finally, management standards may be universally appealing because they are largely meaningless.

Architecture directly or indirectly adopts the quality management habit. While some architecture firms are actually ISO 9000 certified, most all associate with ISO 9000-certified corporate clients, construction companies, or fabricators for whom quality is the essential nonsensical shibboleth. Just as a global activist group like Social Accountability International piggybacks on ISO habits by presenting its SA8000 principles using a similar template, architecture groups like Leadership in Energy and Environmental Design or Social Economic Environmental Design also format their practice using management structures and a management patois.

More important, independent of architects, the prevailing standards and management checklists have helped shape some of the most dominant and contagious spatial products — everything from shopping malls and golf courses to resorts, automated ports, and even entire cities. Growing rampantly and outpacing law, these formulas generate some of the most profound changes to the globalizing world.

The utopian dreams of modern architecture failed for good reason. As Bruno Latour has argued, "We have never been modern."[10] Ideas are coexistent rather than successive, and there is no singular redemptive spatial platform. Yet perhaps another kind of nonmodern spatial variable might now contribute enormously to global governance. Spatial variables that introduce neither standards nor prescriptions but rather new interdependencies and relationships have the currency of something like spatial software. These variables can manipulate (or hack) the dominant formulas that make most of the space in the world.

[10] *We Have Never Been Modern* (Cambridge: Harvard University Press, 1993).

This essay is adapted from a section of Keller Easterling's forthcoming book *Extrastatecraft: The Powers of Infrastructure Space* (Verso, 2014).

BARRY BERGDOLL

Breuer as a Global Architect

1928

Today it is a commonplace that New York is home to an overwhelming majority of the most famed and inventive US architectural offices, while also home to streetscapes and a skyline crafted largely by an entirely different set of architects little known outside the real estate profession.

From the 1950s until recently, there has been a paradoxical divide: the architects who attract professional attention, set new themes and challenges, and make the prestige of some of America's most sought-after architecture schools have left very little impact on the shape and image of the nation's largest city. Rather, New York's signature firms seem to be in the business of exporting designs, not only to the suburbs and across the country, but also to places as far away as Beijing, Seoul, or Rio de Janeiro. Even the alliance under former Mayor Michael Bloomberg between international star practitioners and Manhattan's luxury residential real estate developers was largely comprised of imported stars. International architects like Jean Nouvel or Jacques Herzog and Pierre De Meuron or the Los Angeles architect Neil Denari are shaping the city more than renowned American firms such as Steven Holl, whose projects are today easier to admire in China than in Chelsea. While this broader phenomenon awaits its historian, this essay looks at one case study of a New York office that grew to international importance in the 1950s and 1960s and largely changed the face of the city. Marcel Breuer (1902–81) was one of many European émigrés of the 1930s who by the 1960s were exporting American design and office practices to postwar Europe and the wider American sphere of economic and cultural influence after World War II.

For the most part the American office model — including the architectural office model — that succeeded in the export markets that developed rapidly with American political and commercial dominance in the capitalist world in the postwar decades followed the models that first emerged in the years around 1900 in firms such as McKim, Mead & White. The model was perfected after the war by Skidmore, Owings & Merrill (SOM), which had offices in New York, Chicago, San Francisco, and more recently London.[1] Already in 1947, Henry-Russell Hitchcock had defined the dichotomy of both office organization and architectural approach in an article penned for the London-based *Architectural Review,* "The Architecture of Bureaucracy and the Architecture of Genius."[2] Eight years later, returning from a trip to nearly a dozen Latin

1974

①
Mary Woods, *From Craft to Profession: The Practice of Architecture in Nineteenth-Century America.* (Berkeley: University of California Press, 1999). Reinhold Martin, *The Organizational Complex, Architecture, Media, and Corporate Space* (Cambridge, Mass.: MIT Press, 2005).

②
Henry-Russell Hitchcock, "The Architecture of Bureaucracy and the Architecture of Genius," *Architectural Review* 101 (January 1947): 3–6.

149

The House in the Museum Garden, The Museum of Modern Art, New York, 1949, Marcel Breuer. *Source: The Museum of Modern Art, New York.*

American countries for a survey at the Museum of Modern Art of ten years of practice south of the border, "Latin American Architecture Since 1955," it seemed to America's most widely traveled architectural historian that the anonymity of the new architecture lining Latin America's new boulevards confirmed that the United States had emerged as a major exporter of a suitable normative background architecture for city building. Specifically, he noted the role that American architectural education played in the formation of many of the architects. "Modern Architecture in Latin America has come of age and this major flowering has much to contribute to the rest of the world… Because of the quantity of current Latin American building exceeds our own, the appearance there of predominantly 'modern' cities gives us the opportunity to observe effects which we ourselves still only anticipate," Hitchcock writes. Parallel to the work of SOM, whose early commission for the Venezuelan Pavilion at the New York World's Fair (1939) brought it notice, Hitchcock found abundant evidence in Latin American cities of his ideal of the architecture of bureaucracy, a normalization of the international style. "A very considerable proportion of the best Latin American architects ... Particularly those under forty, owe at least the final stages of their professional education to the architecture schools of the United States … Even the influence of the great masters, Wright and Gropius, and Mies, are rarely very noticeable, which is more surprising since no single Latin American architect as yet, except Niemeyer, has established so sharply personal a style that his influence on his colleagues is worthy of a comment. In a sense there is in present day Latin America—outside Brazil and Mexico at least—something approaching Gropius's idea of an impersonal anonymous architecture. Even national characteristics are often better explained by different climatic conditions on different materials and methods of construction than by deeper cultural currents."[3]

By the end of the 1950s the emerging American political and economic hegemony had constructed an ever-greater zone of influence. The expertise in city planning that had been a French market niche maintained by the expertise, for instance, of Alfred Hubert Donat Agache in Brazil, Jean-Claude-Nicolas Forestier in Cuba, and others in the early decades of the century, notably as Paul Lester Wiener and Town Planning Associates' work extended throughout Latin America. During this period the New York office of Marcel Breuer catapulted from a practice largely centered on the rapidly expanding suburban market for single-family houses in the wake of the baby boom and returning soldiers from the war benefiting from housing subsidies, toward a large-scale international practice. Notably, his practice changed more dramatically perhaps than other émigrés, including Walter Gropius and Mies van der Rohe who emigrated around the same time during the early years of the Hitler regime.[4]

In the mid-1930s Breuer experienced a peripatetic few years when the rise of Hitler made practice in Berlin, where he had opened an office in 1928, impossible for this Jewish-born Hungarian architect. After unsuccessful starts in Budapest, Zürich, and then London Breuer emigrated to the United States, following his old master Gropius to Harvard University. Together they practiced from a small office in Cambridge, Massachusetts, Breuer teaching as well at Harvard's Graduate School of Design and working on the collaboration's small but steady stream of single-family house projects, most of which were in New England. By 1942 Breuer determined to strike out again on his own, and in 1946 with a single commission to lure him, moved to New York to set up an office, comprised at first of just himself and the occasional draftsmen, often volunteers and former students. He was poised to ride New York's wave of postwar expansion and internationalization, even if this took forms much more diverse than he could imagine in 1946. It would appear that Breuer's was the rare case of an office that transformed within a few years from designing mostly small-scale projects for individual private clients to focusing primarily on corporate and government jobs, often for large complexes with multiple buildings, many developing into international operations with similar American business and architectural structures on several continents. In 1946 he occupied a single floor of a New York City brownstone; by the end of his career he operated from several floors of a Madison Avenue office building in a rapidly transforming midtown Manhattan.

Already by 1959 Breuer, whose major calling card a decade earlier was the aura lent by his model of a suburban butterfly-roofed binuclear house at the Museum of Modern Art[5] (1949), was running an international

(3)
Henry-Russell Hitchcock, *Latin American Architecture Since 1945.* (New York: The Museum of Modern Art, 1955), 20.

(4)
William Jordy, "The Aftermath of the Bauhaus in America: Gropius, Mies, and Breuer," in *The Intellectual Migration: Europe and America, 1930–1960,* ed. Donald Fleming and Bernard Bailyn, (Cambridge, Mass.: MIT Press, 1969); reprinted in *"Symbolic Essence" and other writings on Modern Architecture and American Culture,* ed. Mardges Bacon, (New Haven: Yale University Press, 2005), 187–224.

(5)
Introduced with great fanfare in the garden of the Museum of Modern Art.

Torin Corporation, Penrith, Australia, 1973–74, Marcel Breuer and Herbert Beckhard, Architects; Harry Seidler and Associates, Associated Architects. *Source: Marcel Breuer Papers, Special Collections Research Center, Syracuse University Libraries.*

Torin Corporation, Nivelles, Belgium, 1962–69, Marcel Breuer and Hamilton P. Smith. *Source: Marcel Breuer Papers, Special Collections Research Center, Syracuse University Libraries.*

practice. The office was engaged in building a university campus and major church building for the world's largest Benedictine monastery, working for the Torin Corporation's expanding international business, advising the New Haven Railroad network on architecture and design, designing an embassy for the United States State Department in The Hague and collaborating on the headquarters for UNESCO in Paris with the Italian engineer Pier Luigi Nervi and the French architect Bernard Zehrfuss. They opened a site architecture office in Paris, Breuer's first effort at working on two continents. Just twenty years after his arrival in America at the tail end of the Depression, Breuer had realized works across the extended suburbs of New York City, as well as in Detroit, Kansas City, Kansas and Minnesota, which included a portfolio of school buildings, public libraries, university buildings, factories, and department stores. In addition, his practice was on the verge of globalization, with realized projects in France, the Netherlands, Germany, Argentina, and projects pending in Venezuela and Switzerland. In the 1960s, the French practice would expand considerably with large-scale planning projects for both housing and a ski resort, while commissions would arrive for buildings in England and Italy. In the 1970s he would join the call for projects in the Near East, with unrealized projects in Iran and Afghanistan, as well as a final building in Australia for the Torin Corporation. But of the some 250 buildings and projects his office produced, it was not until 1957 that he was entrusted with a project in New York City — new buildings for the (former) campus of Hunter College in the Bronx. These and the Whitney Museum (1964–66) on Madison Avenue, built when Breuer was in his early sixties, would be his only contributions to the face of New York City.[6]

The rapid change of scale and the development of a multinational practice, although not infrequent in New York offices in the 1950s, is particularly interesting in Breuer's case. The expansion of his office took place during a period in which Breuer cultivated two seemingly opposed approaches to architecture: an interest in the individual building as a highly articulated composition with an artistic signature, and a fascination with the possibility of harnessing advances in new materials and industrial production for prefabricated construction. Both these attitudes were inherited from the Bauhaus, where Breuer trained both in the intuitive Vorkurs (preliminary course) pioneered by Johannes Itten and in the prefabricated housing research that preoccupied Gropius in his Weimar and Dessau years. The dream of the prefabricated house was imported to America, the very country Gropius had toured in 1928 in search of models for factory-produced dwellings. While the two collaborated on several potentially prefabricated projects, notably the Aluminum City Terrace project in New Kensington, Pennsylvania (1941–42) — housing sponsored by the Federal Works Agency for defense workers at the outset of the United States' involvement in World War II — they would go their separate ways after this project. Gropius partnered with the newly emigrated German prefabrication pioneer Konrad Wachsmann to develop the Packaged House System. Breuer pursued government contracts,

(6)
The most comprehensive work on Breuer, complete with a catalogue of the work, is Isabelle Hyman, *Marcel Breuer, Architect: The Career and the Buildings.* (New York: Harry N. Abrams, Inc. 2001).

View of Assembly Building (right) and Secretariat (left), UNESCO Headquarters, Paris, France, 1954–58, Marcel Breuer, Pier Luigi Nervi, and Bernard Zehrfuss. *Source: Marcel Breuer Papers, Special Collections Research Center, Syracuse University Libraries.*

industrial research possibilities, and independent research working with his Harvard students on various housing prototypes. His work looked not only at exploiting new materials but also at new forms of delivery. The Plas-2-Point House prototype (1943) used a plastic laminated plywood developed with the Monsanto chemical company in a design inspired by the lightweight frame and skin of an airplane wing and also investigated possible delivery by fork lift or bulldozer of the lightweight Plas-2-Point type.[7] But after the war and United States government's retreat from subsidies of prefabrication ventures in favor of returning GIs mortgage and loan subsidies, Breuer's approach shifted. A series of Veteran House projects from 1945 and several magazine-sponsored postwar house competitions in 1945–46 yielded to a practice split between one-off houses for individual clients and replies to inquiries of those interested in a replica of the first, and most influential, of the House in the Garden series visited by many thousands in the summer of 1949.

　　Not only did Breuer provide the architectural services for several exact copies of this house in New Jersey and New York (Lauck House, Princeton, 1950; Foote House, Chappaqua, 1950), but he also replied to many builders who attempted to replicate the house based on the construction details included in MoMA's *Bulletin.*[8] Reyner Banham described Breuer's rising fortunes in these years as he became "almost the favorite [architect] of the progressive establishment."[9]

　　Fate, rather than planning, would transform his practice almost overnight in 1953. Opening a letter from a Benedictine monastery in

(7)
Gilbert Herbert, *Dream of the Factory-Made House, Walter Gropius and Konrad Wachsmann* (Cambridge, Mass.: MIT Press, 1984); see also Barry Bergdoll and Peter Christensen, ed., *Home Delivery: Fabricating the Modern Dwelling* (New York: The Museum of Modern Art, 2008).

(8)
I have found copies as far away as Anchorage, Alaska, probably designed in conjunction with Breuer's work on airport buildings for Anchorage and Fairbanks in 1949–53.

(9)
Reyner Banham, *Age of the Masters: A Personal View of Modern Architecture,* revised edition (Tonbridge: Whitefriars Press, 1975), 26.

Collegeville, Minnesota, in mid-March, Breuer could scarcely have imagined that within the next five years the design of a monastery church for the world's largest Benedictine order would make the Catholic Church, along with the United Nations, the mainstays of his expanding practice. Nor could he have imagined in 1936, when he and his English partner F.R.S. Yorke designed a utopian Garden City of the Future in response to a commission by the British Concrete and Cement Association, that he would someday be able to build many of the building types proposed. Little could Breuer have expected that the chance to realize an interlocking complex of buildings, defining a whole community and exploiting reinforced concrete to generate previously unknown building forms, should come from a Benedictine abbey then housed in vaguely neo-Romanesque buildings on the shores of a sylvan lake some eighty miles northwest of Minneapolis. This, combined with the UNESCO commission, would catapult Breuer to a whole new level of practice. The UNESCO project opened a protracted battle not over the possibility of modernism's monumentality, but over the place of a monumental modernity in the representational system of monuments that demarcated Paris's skyline. The search for sculpturally expressive monumental forms played off against serial normality—something anathema to the Bauhaus in which he had trained—and the heroic exploration of modern engineering— something only hinted at in the cantilevered seats he had tooled in the Bauhaus workshops – would become the major themes of his work for the next three decades. This was as much the case in the contrast between the powerful canted forms of the Assembly Building at UNESCO and the sheer curtain wall of the Y-shaped administrative building raised on powerful concrete piloti (clearly inspired by Le Corbusier at Marseilles). Or in the contrast between the similarly formed Church with its sculptural bell banner against the repetitive cells of the monastery block and later of the student residence halls on the campus of St. John's Abbey and University in Minnesota.

In these vast projects Breuer would develop his own version of a collaborative practice, quite different from the model of the collective that Gropius would develop as the ideology and practice of The Architect's Collaborative in Cambridge, Massachusetts. As the Breuer office grew he took on associates—Herbert Beckhard, Hamilton Smith, and Robert Gatje were the first—but rather than develop a corporate structure he sought to create an atelier system. In most cases, Breuer remained involved in each project, working with only one associate on each project, even as he was developing a new formal vocabulary in consultation with form-giving structural engineers: Nervi in Paris and in Collegeville, Minnesota, later the Hungarian-born Paul Weidlinger and his office in New York. With Weidlinger Breuer would develop some of his most startling designs, notably his New York projects: the Whitney Museum, with its reverse ziggurat cantilevers, and the cantilevered double lecture hall for New York University perched on the cliff over the Harlem River at University Heights in the Bronx. As much as this design owed to distant memories of Melnikov's worker's clubs of thirty years earlier,

El Recreo Urban Center, Caracas Venezuela, 1958-60, Marcel Breuer, Ernesto Fuenmayor Nava, and Manuel Sayago; Herbert Beckhard, Associate. *Source: Marcel Breuer Papers, Special Collections Research Center, Syracuse University Libraries.*

NYU's Begrish Hall (1959–61) would become something of an international model in its own right, emulated in theme and variation as far away as the Polytechnic University in Quito, Ecuador, with Oswaldo de la Torre's 1965 El Teatro Politéchnio.[10] By then a line of export had been opened to South America as well as to Europe.

    With UNESCO Breuer entered the export market that was growing with US influence in the decades of the Cold War. There had been an earlier attempt, when Breuer had considered moving to Argentina to accept the invitation of a former Harvard pupil, Eduardo Catalano, to give lectures and perhaps help start, as dean, a new architecture school in Buenos Aires. Also pending was an invitation from the Colombian government to consult on aspects of the master planning for rapidly growing Bogotá. A double issue of the Argentine magazine *Nuestra Arquitectura*— September and November 1947—was dedicated to his work preparing the way for his reception in South America and, declaring that although "Breuer no cree en la existencia del Estilo Internacional," he nonetheless offered a "linguaje archquitectonico," which "abre neuvos horizonetes y sirve para confirmer la sencillez natural de los hombres con valores positivos."[11] And although the rise of Juan Perón's government probably contributed to the abandonment of this possible return to academia just two years after Breuer had left Harvard, it did open a bicontinental exchange of influence that can be traced in both Breuer's South and North American work in the 1950s. The influence can be seen not least in the thin-shell parabola vaults developed with Catalano for the Hunter College Library in the Bronx (1957–60). Breuer left behind his first building on foreign soil, the Ariston Club at Mar del Plata, a clover-leaf shaped dance

(10)
Quito: 30 años de arquitectura moderna, 1950–1980, 200–01.

(11)
Eduardo Catalano, "El Linguaje Arquitectonico de Marcel Breuer," in *Nuestra Arquitectura*

hall and bar clad in wood and cantilevered off a rectangular base, finished by Catalano and Francisco Coire in 1947–48 after Breuer's departure. It adapted a pavilion project Breuer and Yorke had imagined in the Concrete City of the Future project a decade earlier, although Breuer in fact never saw the Ariston Club built. Today it is abandoned and slowly falling into ruin, a metaphor perhaps for Breuer's first trip to South America. Likewise, his master plan proposals for Bogotá, completed in December 1947, on the same trip and including a medical city to be designed by Breuer, would remain on paper, as would the better known master plan that Le Corbusier drew up for the Colombian capital three years later.

Despite the exponential growth of his office after 1953, Breuer retained something of a studio-like structure, led by the former Bauhaus meister. And numerous visits to his office by foreigners record the interest in his model, even as a countervailing one to SOM or to I.M. Pei, whose office was growing with its association with the real estate developer William Zeckendorf. The Breuer biographer Isabelle Hyman notes a 1964 visit by Japanese architects interested in how American offices were structured, comparing the models of SOM, Mies van der Rohe, Paul Rudolph, Pei, and Breuer. By May 1955 the office was so large — with twenty draftsmen in addition to the associates — that it was moved to the heart of commercial midtown on 57th Street at Lexington Avenue; a decade later they moved west on 57th Street to the corner of Madison Avenue. Influence began to flow back and forth across the Atlantic. When the firm completed the De Bijenkorf department store buildings on the Coolsingel in Rotterdam (1955-57), Lewis Mumford, who had condemned Breuer's work on UNESCO, recommended the Dutch commission to architects on both sides of the Atlantic as "one of the best office-building facades I have seen anywhere."[12] The Rotterdam store was possible because Breuer was frequently in Paris working on UNESCO.

⑫
Lewis Mumford, "The Cave, The City and the Flower," reprinted *Highway and the City.* (New York: Harcourt, Brace & World, 1963), 39–40.

But the UNESCO commission had not only increased Breuer's prestige at home, leading to many new and larger US commissions, it had also shown him that practice on multiple continents was possible in the age of jet travel and of phone and telegram communication. In 1958, the end of Pérez Jiménez's dictatorship opened a new chapter in Venezuela and tempted many US-based architects south. The skyline of Caracas began to transform with US-style office buildings. Breuer, working with an associate, Herbert Beckhard, developed a project for a beach resort on the Caribbean coast at Tanaguarena within months of the ascendancy of the new democratic government. The next year, the prospect of a 22-acre downtown real estate development, El Recreo, in Caracas, led Breuer to open a Caracas office led by Beckhard. Within a year, Breuer closed the office and Beckhard was on his way back to New York, plagued by disputes with the local architects over the project credits published in *Architectural Record* magazine. But a few years later, he opened a second office as the firm gained a foothold in the French urban expansions of the 1960s, sustained by the private commission to develop a ski resort in the French Alps near Chamonix at Flaine. This project was spearheaded by Eric Boissonnas, a French executive at the Schlumberger international oil

Cantilevered terrace at the south end of the Hotel Le Flaine, Haute-Savoie, France, 1970, Marcel Breuer and Robert F. Gatje. Yves Guillemaut, photographer. *Source: Marcel Breuer Papers, Archives of American Art, Smithsonian Institution.*

company who had come to know Breuer during his years living between Paris, Texas, and New Canaan, Connecticut. By 1964 the resort project had achieved such dimensions that Breuer sent another associate, Robert Gatje, to set up a Paris office, staying for two years before handing over the reins to Mario Jossa, the first member of Marcel Breuer and Associates to work exclusively abroad. (Jossa would continue the office for many years after Breuer's death in 1981). The French office developed plans for a vast resort town along the Aquitaine coast between Bordeaux and Biarritz, never executed, as well as housing for the Zone d'urbanisation en priorité at Bayonne, built from 1966 to 1973. On the strength of Flaine they were invited to design hotels and ski resorts as far away as Afghanistan and Iran, never to be realized. In France, Breuer would also build for IBM, at La Gaude, outside Nice, one of the most convincing of the egg-crate-reinforced concrete integrated facades he developed for laboratories, offices, government buildings, and universities worldwide in the 1960s and 1970s.[13] No less were the thirteen buildings for the Torin Corporation that Breuer built in Connecticut, California, Ontario, England, Belgium, Germany, and even Australia, from an association that had begun with the company executive Rufus Stillman. Stillman's admiration for the House in the Garden at MoMA led him to commission the first of three houses he would build for his growing, and then shrinking, family in Litchfield,

(13) On IBM La Gaude see Robert F. Gatje, *Marcel Breuer, A Memoir.* (New York: Monacelli Press, 2000), 100ff.

Construction View, IBM Research Center, La Gaude, France, 1960–64, Marcel Breuer and Robert F. Gatje. *Source: Marcel Breuer Papers, Special Collections Research Center, Syracuse University Libraries.*

Connecticut, from 1950 to 1974, as well as schools for the Litchfield County school system. Worldwide influence came as much through personal relationships—Stillman and Boissonnas—in a world of trans-national corporations, as it did through such official programs as the United States embassy building program in the 1950s or de Gaulle's decentralization program, which led to the location of IBM-France in a rural site outside Nice. Likewise, Breuer sought until his retirement in 1976 to maintain a close-knit office of associates rather than partners. As Gatje recalls in his lively memories of his longtime employer and mentor, Breuer demanded no financial contribution to become an association, merely the promise of a decade of loyalty—an offer, it seems, that was not made to the numerous women who worked in the firm over the years, from Barbara Neski to Margaret Helfand. By the time he retired in the mid-1970s, amid the controversy over his project for a speculative tower over New York's Grand Central Terminal, Breuer's work was largely abroad, the economic downturn of the 1970s having made New York City a veri-table ghost town for projects by New York architects. His alliance with local real estate had failed, but his international influence was a product of a network of corporations and friendships that spanned the globe.

Petroleum Power:
Architecture and Oil

1944 ◄·········
Bretton Woods system of international financial exchange begins

1948 Bechtel completes Trans-Arabian Pipeline (Tapline) linking Gulf oil fields to the Mediterranean

Standard Oil of New Jersey, Socony-Vacuum Oil join Socal and Texaco as owners of Arabian-American Oil Company (ARAMCO)

1950

The work of the largest US offices after World War II frequently followed the path of oil. As newly wealthy states sought to place themselves on the world stage, US architects chased the specter of petroleum-fueled development and the speculative finance economy to which it gave rise, first in Venezuela and Colombia (the first major sources of foreign oil) and then in the Middle Eastern Gulf states after the 1950s. The following timeline and map show oil-related projects by US architects from the end of World War II through the First Gulf War, including universities, embassies, airports, military cities, workers' housing, and offices towers, all directly financed by oil companies or by governments and banks made rich by national oil revenue.

Often enabled by engineering giants like Bechtel or contracted through federal entities like the US Army Corps of Engineers, these exchanges reached their peak during the boom in crude oil prices from 1973 to 1983, a shift in clientele that formed a direct corollary to the corresponding decline in building practice in the United States. The volatility of this involvement became evident after the economic fallout of the Iran-Iraq War, the Iranian Revolution, the collapse of the black-market Souk al Manakh stock exchange in Kuwait, and the beginning of OPEC quotas on oil production contributed to the slow demise of US firms like TAC and CRS which had expanded on oil-related commissions in these states.
— Michael Kubo

● Commissioned by U.S. State Department, Foreign Buildings Operations Office

● Commissioned by U.S. Army Corps of Engineers

Oil Price per Barrel, Real (2008 dollars)

Town Plan for Creole Petroleum Corporation (Standard Oil of New Jersey), Amuay Bay, Venezuela
Skidmore, Owings and Merrill

Shell Caribbean Petroleum Corporation Headquarters, Caracas, Venezeula
Badgeley and Bradbury

United States Embassy ●
Tehran, Iran
Ides Van der Gracht (Foreign Buildings Operations Office)

Creole Petroleum Corporation (Standard Oil of New Jersey) Headquarters, Caracas, Venezuela
Lathrop Douglass

Iraq Development
Board created to spend
70% of national oil
revenue on development

1953 1953 August 19: Coup in
Iran orchestrated by UK
and US governments;
US-supported Pahlavi
dynasty assumes power

1955 Turkey, Iraq, Pakistan
and Iran form Baghdad
Pact with UK and US to
prevent communist
encroachment in the
Middle East

1951

Iran's oil industry
nationalized from
Anglo-Iranian Oil
Company

1945

1991

Standard Oil Vacuum
Company Facilities
and Housing,
Sumatra, Indonesia
Skidmore, Owings and
Merrill

Sucre Building, Mobil
Oil Corporation
Headquarters,
Caracas, Venezuela
Donald Hatch
and Associates

Medical Center,
Shiraz, Iran
Edmund Jay Whiting

Neighborhood Unit in
Pomona, Maracaibo,
Venezuela
Town Planning
Associates

Hotel del Lago for
Employees of Creole
Petroleum Corporation
(Standard Oil of New
Jersey), Maracaibo,
Venezuela
Holabird, Root and
Burgee

United States
Embassy ●
Baghdad, Iraq
Sert, Jackson and
Gourley

1951

1952

1955

1958　July 14
Coup in Iraq;
pro-Western
Hashemite monarchy
overthrown

1959　Iraq leaves
Baghdad Pact

1960　Organization of
Petroleum Exporting
Countries (OPEC)
begins in Baghdad with
Iran, Iraq, Saudi Arabia,
Kuwait and Venezuela
as founding members

1961 ···

Oil Company Offices,
Bogotá, Colombia
Lathrop Douglass

United States
Embassy ●
Caracas, Venezeula
Donald Hatch
and Associates

Civil Air Terminal ●
Dhahran, Saudi Arabia
Yamasaki and
Associates

University of Baghdad,
Baghdad, Iraq
The Architects
Collaborative

United States
Embassy ●
Tabriz, Iran
Edward Larabee
Barnes Associates

1957

1958

Iraqi oil industry
nationalized

Kuwait becomes
independent state

1965

US signs treaty for US
Army Corps of
Engineers to supervise
and contract military
facilities in Saudi Arabia

Jeddah International
Airport, Jeddah,
Saudi Arabia
Edward Durell Stone

Riyadh International
Airport, Riyadh,
Saudi Arabia
Edward Durell Stone

Master Plan of Tehran,
Tehran, Iran
Victor Gruen
International

Kuwait Fund for Arab
Economic Development,
Kuwait City, Kuwait
The Architects
Collaborative

King Faisal Military
Cantonment ●
Khamis Mushayt,
Saudi Arabia
BATMED (Frank E.
Basil Inc., The
Architects Collaborative,
Metcalf & Eddy Inc.)

King Fahd University
of Petroleum and
Minerals, Dhahran,
Saudi Arabia
Caudill, Rowlett, Scott
(CRS Inc.)

Palace of Princess
Fatemah, Tehran, Iran
Brown Daltas and
Associates

Arabian-American Oil
Company (ARAMCO)
Office Building,
Dhahran, Saudi Arabia
Skidmore, Owings and
Merrill

Television Broadcast
Stations ●
Jeddah, Riyadh, Medina,
Buraydah, Taif and
Mecca, Saudi Arabia
Frank E. Basil Inc.

King Abdulaziz Military
Cantonment ●
Tabuk, Saudi Arabia
BATMED (Frank E.
Basil Inc., The
Architects Collaborative,
Metcalf & Eddy Inc.)

1962

1964

1965

▲

Souk al Manakh,
Kuwait City, Kuwait
The Architects
Collaborative

Souk al Safat,
Kuwait City, Kuwait
The Architects
Collaborative

Royal Saudi Air Force
Headquarters Building ●
Riyadh, Saudi Arabia
Smith, Hinchman and
Grylls

Photogrammetry
Building, Ministry of
Petroleum and Minera
Riyadh, Saudi Arabia
CRS Group

Ministry of Defense ar
Aviation Executive
Office Building ●
Riyadh, Saudi Arabia
Brown Daltas and
Associates

Saudi Officers Club ●
Riyadh, Saudi Arabia
Brown Daltas and
Associates

National Library,
Abu Dhabi,
United Arab Emirates
The Architects
Collaborative

Souk al Wataniya,
Kuwait City, Kuwait
The Architects
Collaborative

Tehran International
Airport, Tehran, Iran
William L. Pereira
and Associates

Union Oil New Town,
Indonesia
Leo A Daly

1971

1972

▲

1973 OPEC oil embargo begins

Iranzamin School, Tehran, Iran
Perkins and Will

Hajj Terminal, Jeddah International Airport, Jeddah, Saudi Arabia
Skidmore, Owings and Merrill

Commercial Parking Garages, Kuwait City, Kuwait
Skidmore, Owings and Merrill

Infantry Center and School and Field Artillery Center and School Master Plans, Khamis Mushayt Military Cantonment ●
Khamis Mushayt, Saudi Arabia
Perkins and Will

Imperial Medical Center (Iran University of Medical Sciences), Tehran, Iran
William L. Pereira and Associates

King Saud University, Riyadh, Saudi Arabia
HOK+4 Consortium (Hellmuth, Obata + Kassabaum; CRS Group; Gollins Melvin Ward Partnership [UK]; Syska & Hennessy, Inc.; Dames & Moore)

Saudi Arabian National Guard Headquarters ●
Riyadh, Saudi Arabia
Leo A Daly / Saudi Consulting House

King Faisal Naval Base ●
Jeddah, Saudi Arabia
Frank E. Basil Inc.

King Abdulaziz Naval Base ●
Jubail, Saudi Arabia
Frank E. Basil Inc.

Airborne and Physical Training School Complex, Khamis Mushayt Military Cantonment ●
Khamis Mushayt, Saudi Arabia
Sverdrup and Parcel

King Khalid Military City ●
Saudi Arabia
Brown Daltas and Associates

Arabian-American Oil Company (ARAMCO) Workers' Housing, Dhahran, Saudi Arabia
CRS Group

1975 Kuwait Oil Company nationalized

King Abdul Aziz Military City ●
Riyadh, Saudi Arabia
CRS Group

Sewage Treatment Plant, Khamis Mushayt Military Cantonment ●
Khamis Mushayt, Saudi Arabia
Perkins and Will

Headquarters of the Royal Saudi Naval Forces ●
Riyadh, Saudi Arabia
Frank E. Basil Inc.

Joint Banking Centre, Kuwait City, Kuwait
Skidmore, Owings and Merrill

1976 Bechtel, Ralph M. Parsons contracted to design Jubail and Yanbu industrial port cities

King Fahd International Airport ●
Dammam, Saudi Arabia
Yamasaki and Associates

Master Plan for Yanbu New Town, Yanbu, Saudi Arabia
Skidmore, Owings and Merrill

Jeddah Master Plan Comprehensive Study, Jeddah, Saudi Arabia
Sert, Jackson and Associates with SaudConsult and RMJM

King Khaled International Airport, Riyadh, Saudi Arabia
Hellmuth, Obata + Kassabaum

National Commercial Bank, Jeddah, Saudi Arabia
Skidmore, Owings and Merrill

Ministry of Defense and Aviation Headquarters ●
Riyadh, Saudi Arabia
Hudgins-Thompson Ball and Associates

Technical Institute, Shiraz, Iran
Hugh Stubbins and Associates

Saudi Arabian National Center for Science and Technology Master Plan, Riyadh, Saudi Arabia
Sert, Jackson and Associates

Instituto Tecnológico Venezolano del Petróleo (INTEVEP) Laboratories, Caracas, Venezuela
William L. Pereira and Associates

Armed Services Headquarters, Indonesia, Jakarta
William L. Pereira and Associates

Jubail Industrial City Master Plan, Jubail, Saudi Arabia
The Architects Collaborative

1973　1974　1975　1976　1977

1979 Iranian Revolution; Pahlavi monarchy overthrown

Saddam Hussein comes to power in Iraq, launches major building program in Baghdad

1980 Iran-Iraq war begins

Saudi Arabian government acquires 100% percent ownership stake of ARAMCO

1981 East–West Pipeline linking Jubail and Yanbu industrial port cities completed

1982 Oil glut; first OPEC quotas on oil production

Souq al Manakh black-market stock exchange collapses in Kuwait

Iran Hostage Crisis

Ministry of Foreign Affairs Housing, Riyadh, Saudi Arabia
CRS Group

Royal Navy Hospital, Jubail, Saudi Arabia
Page Southerland Page

Saddam International Airport, Baghdad, Iraq
William L. Pereira and Associates

Monetary Agency Head Office, Riyadh, Saudi Arabia
Yamasaki and Associates

Saudi Arabian Airlines Communications and Data Processing Facility, Jeddah, Saudi Arabia
Leo A Daly / Saudi Consulting House

Khulafa Street Development, Baghdad, Iraq
The Architects Collaborative

Kuwait Institute for Scientific Research, Kuwait City, Kuwait
The Architects Collaborative

Al-Ahli Bank, Kuwait City, Kuwait
Skidmore, Owings and Merrill

Al-Jubail Petrochemical Company Headquarters, Jubail, Saudi Arabia
Leo A Daly / Saudi Consulting House

Residential District, Yanbu New Town, Yanbu, Saudi Arabia
Leo A Daly / Saudi Consulting House

SABIC Petrochemical Company Headquarters, Riyadh, Saudi Arabia
Leo A Daly / Saudi Consulting House

Residential District, Yanbu New Town, Yanbu, Saudi Arabia
CRS Group

United States Embassy ●
Riyadh, Saudi Arabia
CRS Group

Institute of Public Administration, Riyadh, Saudi Arabia
The Architects Collaborative

Arabian-American Oil Company (ARAMCO) Administration Building, Dhahran, Saudi Arabia
CRS Group

National Methanol and SADAF Administration Buildings, Jubail, Saudi Arabia
CRS Group

Ruwais New Town for Abu Dhabi National Oil Company, Abu Dhabi, United Arab Emirates
CRS Group

Kuwait News Agency, Kuwait City, Kuwait
The Architects Collaborative

1978   1979   1980   1981   1982

100

1990 Iraq invades Kuwait   1991

First Gulf War

80

60

0

Kuwait Foundation for
the Advancement of
Science, Kuwait City,
Kuwait
The Architects
Collaborative

King Faisal
Air Force Base ●
Tabuk, Saudi Arabia
Frank E. Basil Inc.

United Gulf Bank
Building, Manama,
Bahrain
Skidmore, Owings and
Merrill

Residential District,
Yanbu New Town,
Yanbu, Saudi Arabia
The Architects
Collaborative

Government Conference
Center, Jeddah, Saudi
Arabia
Wiliam B. Tabler
Architects

Public Authority for
Civil Information,
Kuwait City, Kuwait
The Architects
Collaborative

1984

1986

The Casablanca Solar House, by John I. Yellott and Charles Shaw, exhibited at the United States Department of Commerce Trade Fairs in Morocco in 1958, had a sloping roof to maximize solar incidence on an array of phase-change solar heating panels. *Source: Department of Archives and Special Collections, Arizona State University, International Solar Energy Society Archive.*

John I. Yellott began sketching a desert solar house when he toured with the United States Department of Commerce Trade Fair in 1957. *Sourc Department of Archives and Special Collections, Arizona State University, John I. Yellott Collection.*

DANIEL A. BARBER

The Casablanca Solar House: Energy and Technological Exchange in the Cold War

From the late 1940s to the late 1950s, alternative forms of energy were on the minds of many American architects, engineers, and policy makers. With the war over, and with little knowledge of the extensive oil reserves in the Middle East, they were concerned about energy sources for future growth. Discussions led to experiments in solar energy for house heating, in wind farms, in cultivating algae as a food source, in the design and use of shading devices, and in a range of other alternative energy systems that are being explored again today.

One such experiment was a house built for the United States Department of Commerce Trade Fair in Casablanca in 1958. The Casablanca house was a solar house intended for workers in new factories being built far from the labor force of the city. It was an off-the-grid house: heated, cooled, and ventilated exclusively by solar energy. Instead of photovoltaics (which did not come into widespread use until the mid-1970s), the panels on the Casablanca house used water, chemical compounds, and pebbles as heat storage mediums — experimental processes that, in the period, appeared to offer an alternative trajectory for the development of energy technologies.

The house combined local materials and imported technology — a model, in built form, for the global exchange of technological and design knowledge that was characteristic of this alternative energy discourse. The large stone aggregate in the concrete walls came from nearby quarries, and served to protect the interior from the harsh sun. The house was, technically, a shed: with no ceiling or partition walls, these thick piers supported the multi-faceted roof. The roof's multiple angles allowed panels to be oriented towards the ideal solar incidence for their latitude; the flexibility in the designed roof line suggested that similar houses could operate in other climates that required other angles of incidence.

The Casablanca house used an innovative method to absorb, store, and use solar energy. In so doing it exhibited a number of technologies exported and exchanged in the period. The solar panels themselves were being proposed for a range of uses and regional conditions. These panels were multi-layered: on the top, two panes of glass allowed solar radiation to penetrate, while also providing some insulation to keep radiation in. Behind the glass was an intermediate air space to collect the heated air. The backing was a metal plate, painted with a black coating that had also been the subject of much analysis and experimentation to maximize its radiation-

1948

1959

absorptive capacity—these "carbon black" treatments were used for solar ovens, solar water heaters, and solar desalination plants in many developing regions.

As the sun heated the air in the intermediate air space, this air was blown by fans into a series of interior columns. These columns held one of two heat storage devices—the first used smooth pebbles to absorb heat for a brief time before releasing it into the room. The second was more complex and significantly more effective: it involved canisters filled with chemical solutions that had phase-change properties. These solutions would liquefy as they were warmed by the solar-heated air, storing the heat in this liquid state. As the surrounding air cooled, the solutions recrystallized and, in the process, released the stored heat. This heat could be radiated from the storage canister, or blown into the room with electric fans. The house also had a solar-assisted cooling system: in hot weather air could be drawn over a chemical refrigerant and cooled before being blown into the room. The phase-change chemical salts could also absorb heat in the room on a hot day. There was a separate group of panels for direct solar water heating.

Phase-change systems were the subject of intensive experimentation in the immediate postwar period, with houses near Boston, Tel-Aviv, and Phoenix all using them effectively for heat absorption and storage. The system at Casablanca drew on these precedents and attempted to simplify the system for better integration into design methods for ease of installation and use. The use of pebbles as heat storage also had a number of precedents in Denver, outside Tucson, and in South Africa. Both of these storage systems exhibited technological effectiveness and ease in exportation. To a great extent, it was the idea, rather than the materials themselves, that needed to circulate. Technological exchange in solar house heating primarily required the exchange of knowledge, and relied on the circulation of experts through systems of influence, such as that provided by the trade fairs.

The design and technology of the Casablanca house was developed by John I. Yellott and Charles M. Shaw. Yellott was a mechanical engineer and expert on solar technology who had been traveling with the Department of Commerce fairs periodically starting in 1956; Shaw was an architect and the general contractor for the fair. Yellott was also the executive secretary of the Association for Applied Solar Energy (AFASE), an organization founded in Phoenix, Arizona, in 1954, which was one of the first international non-governmental organizations (INGOs) to take on a recognizably *environmental* set of issues. The AFASE encouraged government agencies and industry leaders to support research in solar technologies and had identified developing countries as vibrant arenas to further the goal of realizing an effective solar home.

As Yellott indicated in an article entitled "Solar Energy: Its Domestic and Foreign Implications," written around the time the Casablanca house was built, the AFASE's arguments for the importance of solar technology were focused on a careful reading of the uneven geographic distribution of energy resources, and the need to develop new technological research

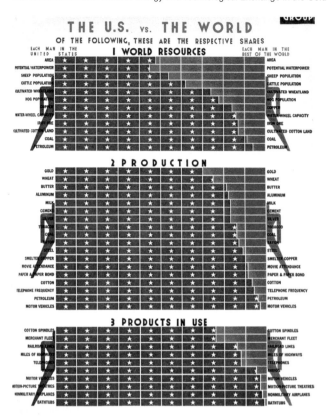

When R. Buckminster Fuller was the science and technology consultant to *Fortune* from 1936 to 1942; he produced the chart showing "The U.S. vs. The World" in terms of resource use for *Fortune*'s tenth anniversary issue in 1940.

in order to secure reliable energy.[1] Yellott's article was based on a number of presentations at the AFASE's "World Symposium on Applied Solar Energy," held in 1955, and was rooted in a dynamic discussion of energy, economy, and politics occurring since the end of World War II. Architecture had an important role in this discussion, both because the technology of solar heating was seen as an immediate way to improve the quality of life in a number of regions and climates (impacting a large percentage of the global population), and also because attention to the design of the house brought cultural and social concerns into the center of these political and economic discussions. Then, as now, government agencies and INGOs saw technology as a salve to geopolitical complications, for better or worse. For a number of scientists, policy makers, economists, and others, the design of the solar house was an experimental site of great geopolitical consequence.

Thus the Casablanca solar house is evidence of a new perspective, emergent right after World War II, in which ideas and decisions about design and technology were intricately interconnected with economic policies, geopolitical alliances, and the possibility of new social formations.[2] Solar advocates and government agents framed alternative energy in

①
John I. Yellott, "Solar Energy: Its Domestic and Foreign Implications," *The Analysts Journal*, vol. 14, no. 1 (February 1958): 15–20.

②
This general process has been described by Michel Foucault as that of "governmentalization," through which architecture can be seen as one of many "arts of governance"—not governance per se, but a managerial disposition to the care of the population, coextensive with the cultural sphere. See Michel Foucault, *The Birth of Biopolitics: Lectures at the College de France, 1978–79* (New York: Palgrave Macmillan, 2008), 217–26.

two ways: First, as an "income source" rather than a "capital deposit"; that is, the technological development of solar energy held the possibility of expanding on an almost infinite source instead of depleting a finite one. Second, renewables were seen as a "complementary resource"— a complement to other, fossil fuel-derived sources, and a complement to a range of economic and foreign policy initiatives playing out across the sun-drenched global south. The strategy was especially potent in the context of the Cold War, allowing for an exchange by which developing regions could receive technical assistance from the United States, thereby encouraging political affiliation, while simultaneously opening new geographic regions to the exploration for and exploitation of fossil fuels by American energy corporations. The house in Casablanca, entangled with government policies, technological trajectories, and concerns over the resource-depleted future didn't *do* all of these things, but it clarified the outlines and the stakes of the discussion. Its awkward form stands as evidence that alternative energy technologies were seen as viable in the immediate postwar period—and that many different relationships between energy, technology, and social systems were still seen to be possible.

Although we tend to think of the period following World War II as one of endless consumer growth, in fact the industrial engine for that growth, and the energy that would power it, had to be produced, experimented with, and argued for. Growth in the United States after the war was predicated on industrial expansion, full employment for returning soldiers, and a dramatic increase of the housing stock, all of which required a reliable source of energy.[3] The source of this energy was not immediately evident and there was concern that, with American oil reserves seemingly depleted by the war, fossil fuels would not be adequate.[4] The economic, political, and technological demands of developing a reliable energy source—oil, solar, or otherwise—were significant, as were the social challenges to adapting to a new global energy regime.[5]

Though much of the initial investigation into energy availability occurred in the United States, it was immediately seen as a global issue. The relationship between the United States and global energy consumption was out of balance even before the war. R. Buckminster Fuller identified this in a 1940 chart developed for *Fortune* magazine comparing "The U.S. vs. The World" in terms of energy use.[6] This data visualization indicated that the amount of energy being used far exceeded regionally available resources—an issue of special concern, as the accompanying map indicated, for the heavily populated and economically powerful East Coast of the United States.

As American policy makers, corporate researchers, economists, and others started to look around after the war, many saw this concern over energy as an opportunity to reconsider the relationship between energy, technology, and social systems.[7] Prominent industry research projects and government reports explored how to prepare for the future using different sources according to varying degrees of energy availability. Studies were written, maps drawn, and charts projected into the future in order to assess the potentials and pitfalls of these different energy trajectories.[8]

[3]
See Chester Bowles, *Tomorrow Without Fear* (New York: Simon and Schuster, 1946), 49 and Craufurd D. Goodwin, *Energy Policy in Perspective: Today's Problems, Yesterday's Solutions* (Washington, D.C.: The Brookings Institution, 1981), 5ff.

[4]
Harold Ickes, "We're Running Out of Oil!," *American Magazine* (December 1943), 38. Almost eighty percent of the oil used by the Allies was drilled from the Gulf of Mexico region.

[5]
Timothy Mitchell has recently identified both "the rapid construction of lifestyles in the United States organized around the consumption of extraordinary quantities of energy" and "the new apparatus of peacetime 'national security'" as tactics in the production of scarcity, and thus as justification for securing consistent energy availability. Timothy Mitchell, *Carbon Democracy: Political Power in the Age of Oil* (New York: Verso, 2011), 41.

[6]
R. Buckminster Fuller, "U.S. Industrialization" *Fortune* 21 (February, 1940): 50–57.

[7]
On opportunities embedded in technological trajectories, see Andrew Barry, "Technological Zones," *The European Journal of Social Theory* 9:2 (2006): 239–53.

[8]
See Julius Krug, et. al., *National Resources and Foreign Aid* (Washington, D.C.: Government Printing Office, 1947); Farrington Daniels, "Solar Energy," *Science* 109, no. 2821 (1949): 51–57; Harold J. Barnett, *Energy Uses and Supplies: 1939, 1947, 1965*

Eugene Ayres, a research executive for Gulf Oil, was one of these energy forecasters who became convinced that renewable sources were the best solution. Ayres was suspicious of fossil fuel resources not so much because of an anticipated doomsday date of depletion—which he saw as being far enough in the future that adequate preparations could be made—but because of the basic principle that investing in renewables would allow for wholly different kinds of economic equations. Renewables, or "income sources" as he termed them, were not subject to an economic model of extraction to depletion (however extended by technological innovation), but one of investment towards expansion.[9]

Ayres insisted that the "host of technologists" working on finding new energy supplies should "focus their efforts on income sources."[10] A chart illustrating "some possibilities in our future energy picture" indicated that research streams developed in the present would have consequences for the near and long term future—the possible extension of known fuel reserves would fluctuate according to different scenarios of alternative energy research. Technological research was itself a powerful resource, not only allowing existing energy to be used more efficiently but also allowing new sources to be developed.

Ayres focused this rethinking of energy and economy on the solar house. At a conference on "Space Heating with Solar Energy" held at the Massachusetts Institute of Technology (MIT) in 1949, he gave an opening presentation that detailed the importance of design in this context. The Solar Energy Research Fund at MIT, led by the Department of Mechanical Engineering, had built two houses, and would build two more by the end of the 1950s. The most successful, MIT Solar House III of 1949, used a bank of water-based solar collectors atop a symmetrically sloping roof.[11] The collectors were connected to a radiant ceiling system, and stored the heated water in a heavily insulated tank in the roof structure. It worked well and was lived in by a graduate student's family until 1953. At the symposium Ayres also pointed to another house, built in Dover, Massachusetts, in 1948, designed by the architect Eleanor Raymond and the engineer Maria Telkes—the first house to use the phase-change system that would later be implemented in Casablanca.

The 1949 conference was held largely to invite architects to join the discussion on solar technology. Lawrence Anderson, a professor in the MIT Architecture department, based his senior design studio on the problem, and brought new design proposals into the MIT project. Anderson modeled solar incidence modeled solar incidence in relationship to building shape and orientation, while the engineers refined the storage of heat and worked out how to best distribute it to the house. Anderson later developed these schematics into an "idealized house" that rejected both "convention and practicality of construction" in order to "have maximum collector area with optimum tilt and minimum non-irradiated area."[12] The house had the full south façade "at optimum tilt"; in section, the north side was a semicircle, partially buried in an artificial berm to increase insulation and provide a basement heat-storage area.

Anderson's "idealized house" captured the tenor of much of this

(Washington, D.C.: Bureau of Mines, 1950); Palmer Putnam, *Energy in the Future* (New York: Reinhold, 1953); Hubbert M. King, *Nuclear Energy and the Fossil Fuels* (Houston, TX: Exploration and Research Division, Shell Development Company, 1956).

⑨
Eugene Ayres, "Major Sources of Energy" *Addresses and Reports Delivered at the Twenty-Eighth Annual Meeting, Chicago, Illinois, November 8 to 11, 1948* (New York: American Petroleum Institute, 1948), 109–44.

⑩
Eugene Ayres and Charles A. Scarlott, *Energy Sources: The Wealth of the World* (New York: McGraw Hill, 1952).

⑪
Eugene Ayres, "Windows," *Scientific American* (February, 1951): 60–65.

⑫
Lawrence B. Anderson, Hoyt C. Hottel, and Austin Whillier, "Solar Heating Design Problems," *Solar Energy Research*, eds. Farrington Daniels and John Duffie (Madison, WI: University of Wisconsin Press, 1955), 47–56; 49. Written in 1953.

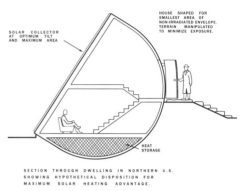

Lawrence Anderson and his students produced a number of typological studies, models, and diagrams, including the "Section of an Idealized Solar House" (above, right) to assess the best design parameters for maximized solar heating.

Following years of analyses, Lawrence Anderson designed the fourth MIT solar house in 1958 with his former student Robert Pelletier. The house was built into a hill to increase insulation, with a south-facing roof to absorb solar radiation. The solar system could be switched off in the summer; in mid-winter an auxiliary system could be engaged.

solar house discussion—that design had the capacity to make a passive heating system more effective and should be considered among the technologies making existing energy supplied more efficient. He insisted that the basic premise from which an appropriate solar design can emerge required an implicit architectural understanding of the technological problem of solar energy. "Every architect," he wrote, "should know how to design for the most favorable climatic response of his enclosure so that, other factors being equal, he will minimize summer discomfort, require less fuel during temperature extremes, or extend the zones in which no mechanical equipment is required."[13] Anderson pursued typological studies of solar technology with his students. In 1957, with his former student Robert Pelletier, Anderson designed and built MIT Solar House IV, which had a sloped roof at the optimum angle and was built into a hillside to maximize insulation. It also included a solar stove, where the family that lived there cooked hot dogs in the summer.

The solar heating discussion in the late 1940s and early 1950s had many other consequences, a number of which can be read in the Casablanca house. Around the same time as the MIT conference, policy and industry interest in solar house heating technology increased. At the United Nations Scientific Conference on the Conservation and Utilization of Resources—a wide ranging, three-week conference addressing a number of global resource concerns held in 1949—both the MIT House III and the Raymond/Telkes house were discussed at length. Solar house heating was seen to be one of a number of means by which the conference intended to integrate concerns of "less developed countries" into the research practices of the "economically advanced countries."[14] This integration—of American technological experiments, new forms of energy, and the needs of developing economies—was also the explicit project of a 1952 report by President Truman's "Materials Policy Commission." The commission had been formed to analyze "the combined material requirements and supplies of the entire free non-Communist world," as well as the government policies and corporate practices affecting them, in order to outline a system of extraction and distribution that could provide for the "common welfare, common growth, and common security of these countries."[15]

The issue was not only to map existing resources, but also to develop a new global system of energy use and supply, coordinated by the United States. The policy question in 1952 was how to encourage private capital to flow into underdeveloped countries at a rate sufficient to develop the resource deposits that industrialized nations required, and to do so while expanding the economic and political influence of the United States.[16] Technological efforts to use resources more efficiently, and in particular to encourage the use of income sources, were seen as an important element of how the United States could encourage a country's political affiliation in the midst of Cold War tensions.[17] Concerns over resources were also political issues regarding territorial control and global economic systems, in which issues of technological and design expertise were intricately embedded.

[13]
Ibid., 48.

[14]
United Nations Department of Exact and Natural Sciences, "Memorandum on The Scientific Conference on Resource Conservation and Utilization," (Lake Success, NY: UNESCO, 10 November 1948), 4.

[15]
President's Materials Policy Commission, *Resources for Freedom: Summary of Volume I of a Report to the President* (Washington, D.C.: US Government Printing Office, 1952), 2–4.

[16]
Alfred E. Eckes, *The United States and the Global Struggle for Minerals* (Austin, TX: University of Texas Press, 1979), 185.

[17]
See David S. Painter, *Oil and the American Century: The Political Economy of the U.S. Foreign Oil Policy, 1941–1954* (Baltimore, MD: Johns Hopkins University Press, 1986).

These concerns came to the fore in the organization of the Association for Applied Solar Energy (AFASE), and especially in its sponsorship of the Casablanca house. The AFASE was founded by economists and technological researchers who had been part of Truman's Materials Policy Commission, with financial and logistical support from the Ford Foundation and the Stanford Research Institute.[18] Following Ayres' imperative, the AFASE was interested in how to direct research streams into renewable resources—not out of a fear of impending scarcity, but out of the assumption that such research would eventually bear fruit, and would make economic sense over the long term.

Like Ayres, the AFASE was very interested in the potential of the solar house. A solar house competition, led by Anderson, was envisioned as a prominent part of the World Symposium on Applied Solar Energy, a showcase of solar technology held in the summer of 1955. While the competition ended up being too costly as a first step, discussion of the design and technology of solar housing took up a large part of the conference. After the World Symposium, the solar house was again identified as a promising site for research. At the same meeting John I. Yellott—the co-designer of the Casablanca house—was named executive secretary of the Association. Yellott had already been involved with the design of solar buildings in Madras, India, and Albuquerque, New Mexico, and was anxious to continue these experiments.

The United States Department of Commerce Trade Fairs offered Yellott an ideal opportunity. The fairs were already heavily loaded with concerns over the exchange of technology, economics, and politics. United States involvement in the fairs had been initiated by Eisenhower in 1955 to encourage "two-way trade and better understanding of the United States."[19] Positioned as a battleground in the Cold War, Eisenhower saw the trade fairs as an opportunity to demonstrate how American ingenuity could improve quality of life and accelerate economic development, especially in countries under threat of Communist influence. As the *New York Times* indicated, Eisenhower was sending these "official exhibitions…[to] places where the United States sees political advantage to be gained among the people or with their government."[20] The AFASE was one of many beneficiaries of "seed money" that the federal government distributed to corporations and agencies to work on projects especially for the fair.

The solar exposition that Yellott had developed—largely drawing on the technology exhibited at the World Symposium—included solar ovens and stoves, solar water desalination, solar algae growth, solar furnaces, solar clocks, and many other systems and devices. It proved to be such a popular aspect of the fair that Yellott proposed, with the architect Shaw, to build a solar house that could simultaneously demonstrate the potential of solar heating and cooling as well as house this range of experimental devices. In Casablanca from May 4th to the 19th, 1957, and then in Tunis from October 19th to November 3rd of the same year, Yellott's popular exposition was given center stage, with the solar house right next to a geodesic dome. Local industrialists along with

[18]
The Commission was dissolved after issuing its report, though many working on the project formed the think-tank Resources for the Future. This group, which still exists today, hosted the conference "The Nation Looks at its Resources: The Midcentury Conference on Resources for the Future" in 1954. The idea for the AFASE was hatched in a panel on solar energy.

[19]
"U.S. Expands Role in Trade Exhibits" in the *New York Times* (January 3, 1957).

[20]
Ibid. According to the *Times* the fairs featured "typical American homes, voting machines, 'atoms for peace' applications, US farm production, 'do-it-yourself' workshops, American art and design, electronic devices and automated factories."

visiting corporate and government leaders were led through the exhibition. Demonstrations were made both to indicate the potential of solar technologies and to suggest their relevance to a range of social and economic concerns. Not unlike other demonstration houses of the postwar period, the Casablanca house was a site for the exchange of ideas — ideas about architecture, and, in this case, about how design methods and strategies could be integrated with a range of economic and political aspirations.

The Casablanca solar house stands out not only for its willingness to alter its design dramatically to maximize radiation exposure, but also for its clear expression of the potentials and pitfalls of the emergent postwar energy condition. While the immediate concern over resource scarcity largely had dissolved by the mid-1950s as US economic, military, and diplomatic power managed to secure foreign oil resources for the growing demands of domestic industries, the persistent dynamism of the solar energy discourse late into the decade suggests some of the tensions that lay beneath these new systems of economic and energy exchange. The promise of the solar house, as a complementary resource, was simultaneously economic, social, and political, and was also rooted in an anxiety about how shifts in the global energy metabolism could have negative and unanticipated consequences in the future. As one writer put it, anticipating much of the environmentalist tensions of the 1970s: "there is more than one way of saving ourselves from a future in which the world is long on population and short on everything else."[21] In other words, while by the late 1950s much of the rhetoric around "income energy" experimentation was focused on its applicability to developing economies, implicit in the discourse was how these strategies would, eventually, be imported back to developed northern economies to save them from themselves.

Soon after Yellott returned to the United States, the AFASE finally initiated a competition to design a demonstration solar house.[22] Entries were received from around the world and the winning house was built outside Phoenix in 1959. The competition stands, like the Casablanca house, as an important symbol of the increasingly global character of architecture in the 1950s — and as a symbol that this global engagement was in large part based on the capacity of design innovation to intersect with a number of professional fields and social concerns. Inside the carefully designed panels and piers of the Casablanca solar house, a space was created not only for the exchange of energy and design technologies, but also for the exchange of anxieties and aspirations about the inevitable complications of energy futures.

[21] Eric Hodgins, "Power from the Sun," *Fortune* 43 (September, 1953), 194.

[22] John I. Yellott, *Living With the Sun: Volume I: Sixty Plans Selected From the Entries in the 1957 International Architectural Competition to Design a Solar-Heated Residence.* (Phoenix, AZ: The Association for Applied Solar Energy, 1958) and Daniel A. Barber, *A House in the Sun: Modern Architecture and Solar Energy in the Cold War* (New York: Oxford University Press, forthcoming 2015)

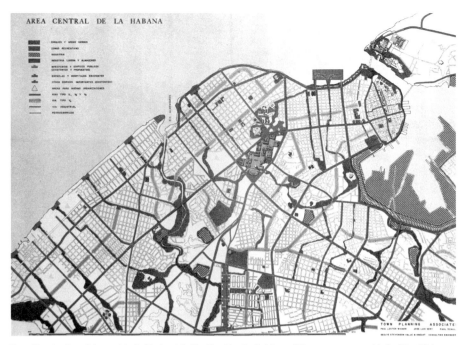

Town Planning Associates and Junta Nacional de Planificación, Central Area of Havana as proposed in the Plan Piloto de la Habana, 1955–58. The plan proposes the superimposition of a network of roads to organize the city into sectors. A second network of lineal paths connects parks and open spaces. Both networks are grafted onto the existing elements of the city. *Source: the Frances Loeb Library, Harvard Graduate School of Design.*

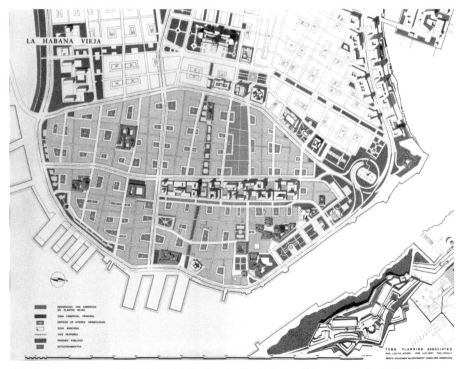

Town Planning Associates and Junta Nacional de Planificación, Plan for Habana Vieja as proposed in the Plan Piloto de la Habana, 1955–58. The plan proposes to maintain the block arrangement of the colonial quarter of the city, with the exception of the strip of tower blocks seen at the center of the plan. Blocks are to be renovated and rebuilt, but with existing historical buildings incorporated physically and conceptually into the overall fabric of renovation. *Source: the Frances Loeb Library, Harvard Graduate School of Design.*

TIMOTHY HYDE

The Master Plan as Midcentury Export

For the past half century, the geographical proximity of the United States and Cuba has been accompanied by a geopolitical remoteness, with the long established US embargo preventing almost any significant cultural, technological, or material exchange between the two nations. However, prior to the Cuban Revolution in 1959, their geographical proximity was fully exploited in an encompassing spectrum of exchanges now embodied by a series of well-rehearsed clichés representing the Caribbean island as a playground for inhibited North American tourists, with an economy of mafia money laundering and a dictatorial politics stage managed by Washington. The history of Cuba following its independence from Spain at the end of the nineteenth century was far more complex than such clichés allow, but it is certainly true that for several decades, innumerable instances of trade, influence, and solicitation bound the United States and Cuba together.

In this regard, Cuba might be seen as simply a more overt example of the general tendencies latent in relations between the United States and Latin America. President James Monroe had declared in 1823 that the United States would consider the American hemisphere a privileged territory no longer open to the colonialism of the European powers, establishing a doctrine that was subsequently substantiated by economic investment, political opportunism, cultural expansionism, and later, by military engagement. With the founding of hemispheric institutional bodies, first the Pan-American Union and then the Organization of American States, the physical territory of exchange was formalized as a political sphere, supported and strengthened by the mechanisms of trade and treaties. Architectural practices were included among the instruments of exchange, and although European influence remained present in aesthetic matters, North American firms received commissions for buildings, urban plans, and engineering projects throughout Latin America.

In Cuba, a survey of commissions in just the first sixty years of the twentieth century would list a substantial number of prominent US offices: McKim, Mead & White; Bertram Goodhue; Schultze & Weaver; Carrère & Hastings; Skidmore, Owings & Merrill; Welton Becket & Associates; Harrison & Abramovitz; as well as the engineering firm Purdy & Henderson.[1] Clients for their work included the Cuban government, American and Cuban companies, and individual citizens. Like other urban and national contexts in Latin America undergoing rapid modernization,

1955

1959

①
See Eduardo Luis Rodríguez, *La Habana: arquitectura del siglo XX* (Barcelona: Blume, 1998) and Francisco Gómez Díaz, *De Forestier a Sert: ciudad y arquitectura en La Habana (1925–1960)* (Barcelona: Abada Editores, 2008).

Cuba often presented problems or demands different from those of analogous settings in North America. With Cuba's persistent political instability giving rise to a succession of authoritarian governments, large and small firms frequently carried out the projects of modernization under the direct sponsorship of influential patrons—politicians or companies—often without the restraints of transparent financing or established zoning that accompanied similar projects in the United States.[2]

Havana, the largest city in Cuba and its political, financial, and cultural capital, confronted the urgencies of modernization throughout the first decades of the twentieth century. The city's infrastructure of roads and sewers was inadequate to support the physical expansion that accompanied an increasing urban population; civic institutions such as the university required larger, contemporary facilities, as did all three branches of the national government. A number of projects (many carried out by US construction firms) provided partial redress, with a new National Capitol building, new roadways, and elements of a master plan conceived by the French urbanist J.C.N. Forestier all contributing to the improvement of the city.[3] Yet by the late 1940s, it was still evident to many planners and architects that Havana possessed the "physiognomy of a provincial city."[4] Indeed, what was clear to these planners and architects was that Cuba confronted a central problem of modernity: how to design the modern city?

Modern theories of planning and urbanism arrived in Cuba through a variety of sources and mediums. Many Cuban professionals were educated at American universities and maintained professional ties to colleagues; many American practitioners traveled to Cuba for work, as consultants, to deliver lectures, or as visitors to the architectural programs at Cuban universities. Another significant conduit for the transmission of ideas about planning and urbanism were the professional journals that circulated in the United States and Cuba. *Arquitectura,* published by the Colegio de Arquitectos in Havana, frequently printed translations of articles by American professionals and academics. Among the ideas that entered into circulation in Cuba through these routes were the principles of the City Beautiful movement, the progressive planning discourse centered around the University of Pennsylvania, and the Congrès International d'Architecture Moderne (CIAM) discourse on the city which, although European in origin, also arrived as a North American export.

The vehicle for this latter export was the New York firm, Town Planning Associates, headed by the architects José Luis Sert and Paul Lester Wiener. Sert had spent several months in Cuba in 1939, while awaiting a visa to enter the United States as a refugee. He renewed his contacts with Cuban architects a decade later, as Town Planning Associates worked on a private commission for a hotel on the island and entered into a government-sponsored competition for new housing. In 1955, the Cuban government retained Town Planning Associates as consultants to the newly formed national planning board, the Junta Nacional de Planificación (JNP). Although it was to advise the JNP on a range of tasks, Town Planning Associates focused its consultancy

② On the history of Cuban architecture and urbanism examined in relation to political and economic development see Timothy Hyde, *Constitutional Modernism: Architecture and Civil Society in Cuba, 1933–1959* (Minneapolis: University of Minnesota Press, 2013).

③ See Jean-François Lejeune, "The City as Landscape: Jean Claude Nicolas Forestier and the Great Urban Works of Havana, 1925–1930," *The Journal of Decorative and Propaganda Arts,* no. 22 (1996).

④ José R. San Martín, *Memoria del plan de obras del gobierno del Dr. Ramón Grau San Martín* (Havana: Ministerio de Obras Publicas, 1947). (unpaginated)

on the formulation of master plans for several Cuban cities, Havana most prominent among them. The firm was well suited to its role; founded in 1942 by Sert and Wiener, Town Planning Associates had, by 1955, worked on urban designs, master plans, and architectural projects in several Latin American nations including Brazil, Colombia, and Peru.[5] The firm offered to its government clients an expertise in contemporary urban planning as well as participation in an international discourse on the modern city. Sert was an established member of CIAM and the author of *Can Our Cities Survive?*, a book that aimed to translate the CIAM principles that originated in the context of the pre- and postwar European city to the different circumstances of cities in the Americas.[6]

The Plan Piloto de la Habana, the master plan for the city of Havana devised by the JNP and Town Planning Associates between 1955 and 1958, was the result.[7] Although the plan would never be implemented—it was set aside after the 1959 Revolution introduced new political programs and social institutions—it reflected a theory of the city, to be enacted in Cuba on the basis of ideas drawn from North American settings. This master plan aimed to regulate the physical order of the entire city from its historic core to the new districts expanding toward the west and the south, with older colonial quarters and new speculative developments integrated into a system of sectors and a network of roads classified according to a hierarchy of speeds and use. Residential densities, commercial activities, public spaces, and civic functions were all subject to a framework of norms or standards that could be seen most vividly in the proposed reconfiguration of the old colonial core of the city, Havana Vieja. Here the dense historical fabric of the city confronted the projective ambitions of new urban arrangements. In accordance with constitutional requirements that the state endeavor to sustain national culture, several buildings in Havana Vieja had already been legally designated historical monuments. A 1944 decree protected not only monuments like the Cathedral, but also included buildings facing onto the Cathedral Plaza and adjacent streets. But in 1955, the authoritarian ruler of Cuba Fulgencio Batista signed another decree giving broad legal sanction for the "Rehabilitation of Ancient Havana." Although this new decree did not obviate the perquisites of the older law, it did mark a clear change in emphasis from preservation to development.

Given the acknowledged presence of significant historical elements in the district, the development of Habana Vieja presented a quite distinct theoretical problem of the modern city. The CIAM principles of the modern city had largely evaded the question of existing historic dimensions of the city, eliding the discussion of monuments and patrimony in favor of analytical distribution of the functions of the city. However, in the postwar United States, the question was posed through two emerging perspectives: urban renewal and historic districting. Through the lens of urban renewal (which developed in the United States following the passage of the Federal Housing Act of 1949) the wholesale reconstruction of central districts was seen as an ameliorator to urban decline apparent in both physical and social conditions. A concurrent practice increasingly adopted during the

(5)
See José Luis Sert and Paul Lester Wiener, "The Work of Town Planning Associates in Latin America 1945–1956," *Architectural Design* 27, no. 6 (1957) and Eric Mumford, "CIAM and Latin America," in *Sert, arquitecto en Nueva York*, ed. Xavier Costa and Guido Hartray (Barcelona: ACTAR, 1997).

(6)
José Luis Sert, *Can Our Cities Survive? An ABC of Urban Problems, Their Analysis, Their Solutions* (Cambridge: Harvard University Press, 1942).

(7)
Town Planning Associates, *Plan piloto de la Habana* (New York: Wittenborn Art Books, 1959). When employed as technical terms, the definition of "pilot plan" was distinct from that of "master plan" (with the pilot plan more general and the master plan more prescriptive in its details), but both technical usages were in this context subsumed under the theoretical category of the master plan.

1950s—the establishment of historic districts in city centers—provided a contrasting lens through which the preservation of historic urban centers and their buildings were regarded as a brake against urban deterioration. Neither approach possessed, in the early 1950s, a clear privilege over the domain of city planning. In the United States, the two perspectives were quite separate, opposed to one another as arguments about the valuation of existing urban areas with distinctive historical forms.

Although in Cuba the precepts of modernist planning discourse would have been implicitly set against preservation, the concept of the historic district nevertheless had self-evident applicability to Habana Vieja.[8] The formulation of the proposal for Habana Vieja also included both perspectives. In a preliminary sketch, Wiener outlined a new development program over the existing blocks of Habana Vieja, designating a new six-block area to become a financial sector to accommodate the banks that had long been the principal commerce in the area. He also marked three historic sites: the Cathedral Plaza, the Plaza de Armas, and the Plaza Vieja. Subsequent sketches showed several more blocks reconfigured as high-rise buildings set back in superblocks, with the area of new blocks extended much closer to the historical monuments. In these sketches, Wiener directly addressed the significance of the colonial fabric by proposing a "Historic Zone" that would buffer historic buildings from the redeveloped area. In a composite drawing compiled from these studies the area of redevelopment extended to the edges of the historic plazas, contravening the earlier legal terms of their protection. While it reveals that the dense existing fabric of Habana Vieja was largely to be demolished and replaced with superblocks, towers, and high-rise slabs, some further sketches hint that he was still giving consideration to historic elements. Wiener traced several studies that tested different arrangements and scales of street and block, some of which began to recuperate existing dimensions. Another sketch rendered the historic zone in sufficient detail to imply an intention to integrate these buildings into the new urban order.

These intentions coalesced in the final plan devised by Sert and the Cuban architect Mario Romañach, who worked in the JNP as the director of the plan for Havana. They proposed reducing the vast array of superblocks to a linear band and proposed low-rise blocks with open courts for the remaining area. This configuration maintained the courses of almost all of the streets, and therefore the block perimeters as well, so that the existing configuration would persist in the relation of figure and ground. Alternate streets would be widened to ease traffic while the others, reserved for pedestrians, would "preserve the scale and charm of the old streets."[9] Typical diagrams indicated existing property lines maintained after rehabilitation, allowing the irregular colonial era plots to coexist with the more regular geometry of new courtyards. The architects also acknowledged the need to preserve certain historic clusters as urban entities. Their detailed drawing suggested how these historic clusters might coexist with the new arrangement by being integrated within blocks, just as the remaining lots might accommodate combinations of new constructions and rehabilitated buildings.

⑧
A precedent for the rehabilitation of Habana Vieja was present in the nearby US commonwealth of Puerto Rico, in San Juan Antiguo, the colonial district of that capital city. Planning work undertaken in Puerto Rico had a direct influence in Cuba and there was almost certainly an awareness in Cuba of the San Juan example. Proposals for the rehabilitation of San Juan Antiguo included both urban renewal *and* historic districting. See Nathaniel S. Keith and Carl Feiss, "A Report on the Renewal Possibilities of the Historic Triangle of the City of San Juan," (Washington, D.C.: 1955). For the relevant legislation, see Junta de Planificación de Puerto Rico, *Reglamento de zonas antiguas e históricas* (San Juan: Junta de Planificación de Puerto Rico, 1955).

⑨
Town Planning Associates, *Plan piloto de la Habana* (New York: Wittenborn Art Books, 1959), 32.

Above: Collage of photographs compiled by Town Planning Associates and Junta Nacional de Planificación to demonstrate the deteriorated conditions of existing buildings and streets in existing Habana Vieja. *Source: the Frances Loeb Library, Harvard Graduate School of Design.*

Left: Photograph of El Templete collected by Town Planning Associates. The documentation of this historic monument stood in deliberate contrast to the documentation of the dilapidated buildings shown in the photographs above. The contrasting images both influenced the planning concepts resolved in the proposed renovation of Habana Vieja. *Source: the Frances Loeb Library, Harvard Graduate School of Design.*

Elsewhere in the environs of Havana that the Pilot Plan was to regulate, Town Planning Associates and their Cuban colleagues in the JNP proposed a prototypical neighborhood sector that was organized into *cuadras*, or blocks, each filled with single-story attached dwellings to create an even fabric of patio houses. Although its orthogonal form contrasted with the irregular outlines of the cuadras that were to be retained in Habana Vieja, the block structure was an underlying conceptual premise that tied together the parts of the Pilot Plan. At once physical form, legal specification, and social hierarchy, the block pattern claimed a genealogical link to the colonial cities founded under the statutes of the Laws of the Indies.[10] Like the Laws of the Indies, the Pilot Plan asserted the imposition of a normative order upon the future contingencies of the city. Unlike its historical predecessor, however, the Pilot Plan also aimed to absorb into that order the variances and complexities of an already existing city. The framing of real historic monuments within normative *cuadra* was not simply a gesture of preservation, but a legitimation of their participation in the future city of Havana.

The coordination of the real and the normative, the existing and the projected, through the device of the master plan was the core theoretical assertion of the Pilot Plan for Havana. It was also the resulting composite of theories of planning and urbanism imported into Cuba from the United States during the first half of the twentieth century.

Within this discursive exchange between the two nations, not only ideas circulated but also theoretical problems and dilemmas. Between the centuries-old city of Havana and the conception of the modern city lay an array of incommensurables. Such differences could not be resolved by proposing a model city or a new beginning, which would have repressed existing forms and meanings; nor could they be resolved through idiosyncratic or irreducible adaptations, which would have constrained the projected future with the exigencies of the past. Instead, the array of incommensurables was to be addressed and reconciled through the invention of new and transformative interpretations of theoretical or conceptual principles beyond their US sources in the adjacent territory of Cuba.

[10] See Jean-François Lejeune, ed. *Cruelty & Utopia: Cities and Landscapes of Latin America* (New York: Princeton Architectural Press, 2005).

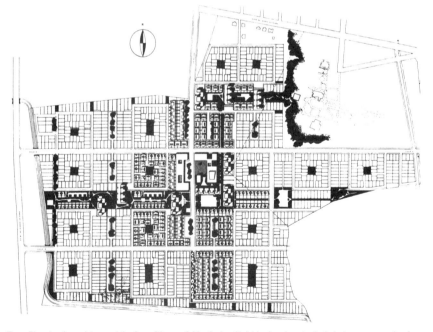

Town Planning Associates and Junta Nacional de Planificación, Typical block configurations for Habana Vieja proposed in the Plan Piloto de la Habana, 1955–58. The diagrams incorporate the logic of the "impermanent constitution" by their inclusion of typicality in the overall cuadra form and contingency in the maintenance of irregular property lines. *Source: Frances Loeb Library, Harvard Graduate School of Design.*

Town Planning Associates and the firm of Arroyo & Menéndez, Neighborhood sector included as an example of a typical housing arrangement in the Plan Piloto de la Habana, 1955–58. The site plan shows the priority given to the cuadra arrangement as the pattern of urban form. *Source: Frances Loeb Library, Harvard Graduate School of Design.*

Exporting Vertical Ambition

The skyscraper is a quintessentially US typology. Since its emergence as a building type in nineteenth-century Chicago, the ambition to build higher has primarily been an American endeavor. For the first hundred years of its development, the United States designed and built the world's tallest skyscrapers. In 1996 the Petronas Towers in Kuala Lumpur were completed and became the tallest buildings in the world at the time. They ushered in a new era of skyscraper construction where Asia and most recently the Middle East are home to the record-breaking tower. Nevertheless, these structures are still being designed and engineered primarily by a handful of US-based architecture firms. This shift represents not just the export of American engineering knowledge and technology, but also the export of the ambition and competitive spirit to win the race to the top.
— Fred Tang

Of the fifteen current tallest towers in the world, eight are US exports—designed by US firms and built abroad. The other seven (in gray) were either built in the United States or by non-US architects.

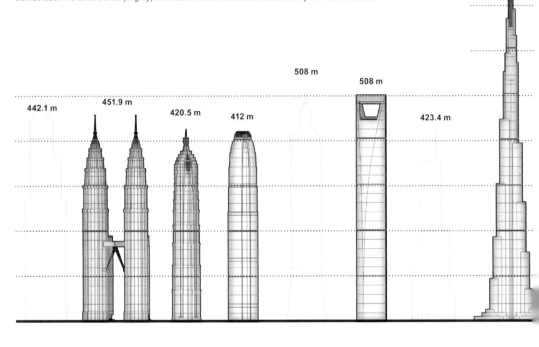

828 m

442.1 m 451.9 m 420.5 m 412 m 508 m 508 m 423.4 m

1974	1996	1998	2003	2004	2008	2009	2010
Sears Tower	Petronas Towers	Jin Mao Tower	Two International Finance Center	Taipei 101	Shanghai World Financial Center	Trump International Tower	Burj Khalifa
Chicago, USA	Kuala Lumpur, Malaysia	Shanghai, China	Hong Kong, China	Taipei, Taiwan	Shanghai, China	Chicago, USA	Dubai, UAE
Skidmore, Owings & Merrill	Pelli Clarke Pelli	Skidmore, Owings & Merrill	Pelli Clarke Pelli	C. Y. Lee & Partners	Kohn Pedersen Fox Associates	Skidmore, Owings & Merrill	Skidmore, Owings & Merrill

1996   1998   2003   2004

Record Breakers: The World's Tallest Building 1914–2014

USA   ## Asia

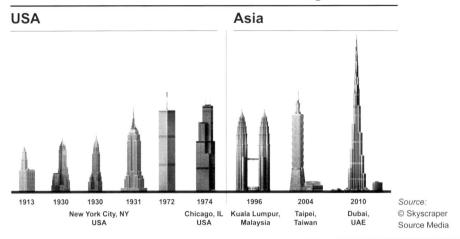

1913	1930	1930	1931	1972	1974	1996	2004	2010
		New York City, NY USA			Chicago, IL USA	Kuala Lumpur, Malaysia	Taipei, Taiwan	Dubai, UAE

Source:
© Skyscraper
Source Media

601 m

484 m

450 m

427.5 m

441.8 m

412.6 m

414 m

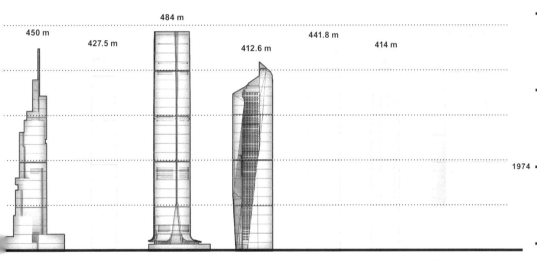

1974

Drawn by Juney Lee.

2010	2010	2010	2011	2012	2012	2012
Nanjing Greenland Financial Center	Guangzhou International Finance Center	**Kowloon International Commerce Center**	**Al Hamra Tower**	KK100	Princess Tower	Makkah Royal Clock Tower Hotel
Nanjing, China	Guangzhou China	**Hong Kong, China**	**Kuwait City, Kuwait**	Shenzhen, China	Dubai, UAE	Mecca, Saudi Arabia
Skidmore, Owings & Merrill	Wilkinson Eyre Architects	**Kohn Pedersen Fox Associates**	**Skidmore, Owings & Merrill**	Tony Farrell and Partners	Eng. Adnan Saffarini	Dar Al Handasah

2008	2009	2010	2011	2012

1996

2014

Petronas Towers

Location	Kuala Lumpur, Malaysia
Architect	Cesar Pelli and Associates
Completion	1996
Height	451.9 meters
Floors	88 floors
Elevators	39
Structure	Reinforced concrete core and perimeter mega-columns

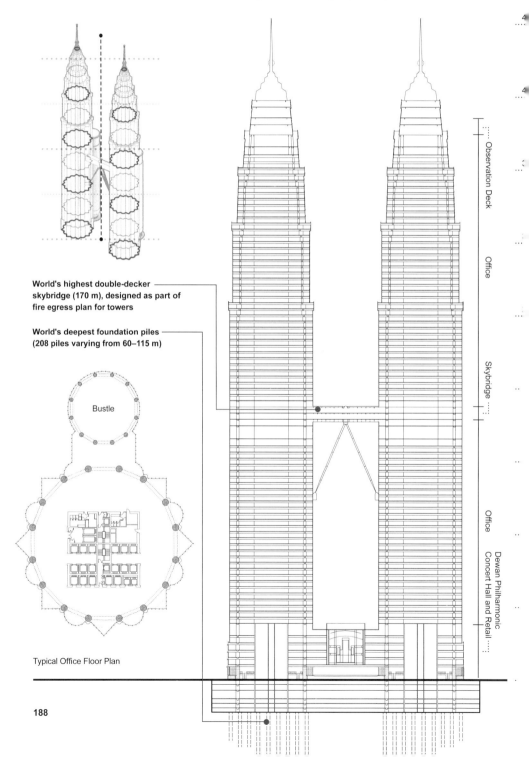

World's highest double-decker skybridge (170 m), designed as part of fire egress plan for towers

World's deepest foundation piles (208 piles varying from 60–115 m)

Bustle

Typical Office Floor Plan

Observation Deck

Office

Skybridge

Office

Dewan Philharmonic Concert Hall and Retail

Jin Mao Tower

Location	Shanghai, China
Architect	Skidmore, Owings & Merrill
Completion	1998
Height	420.5 meters
Floors	88 floors
Elevators	61
Structure	Composite system of reinforced concrete and steel

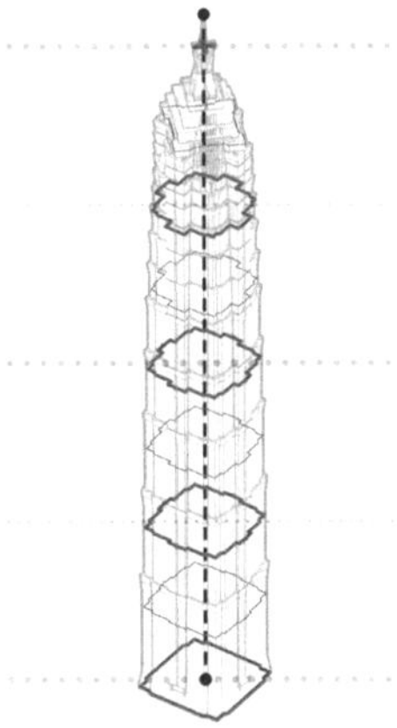

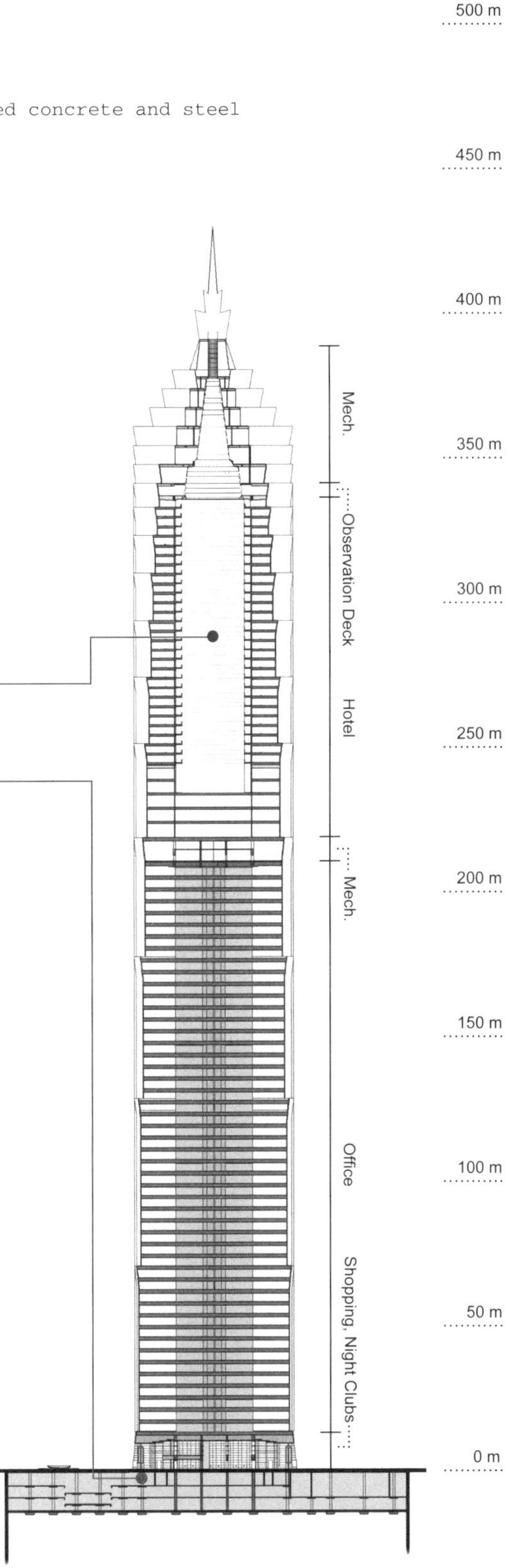

500 m

450 m

400 m

350 m

Mech.

Observation Deck

300 m

Hotel atrium begins at floor 56 and
spans 29 floors (142 m tall)

Hotel

250 m

World's longest laundry chute
(400 m) with custom buffers to
slow speed

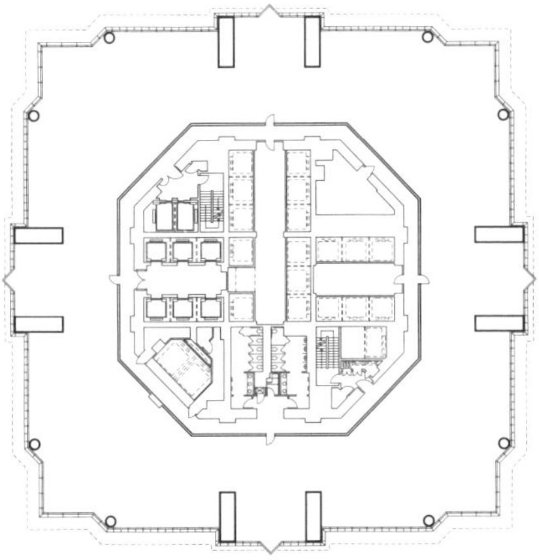

Mech.

200 m

150 m

Office

100 m

50 m

Shopping, Night Clubs

Typical Office Floor Plan

0 m

2 International Finance Center

Location	Hong Kong, China
Architect	Pelli Clarke Pelli
Completion	2003
Height	412 meters
Floors	88 floors
Elevators	62
Structure	Reinforced concrete mega columns with outriggers

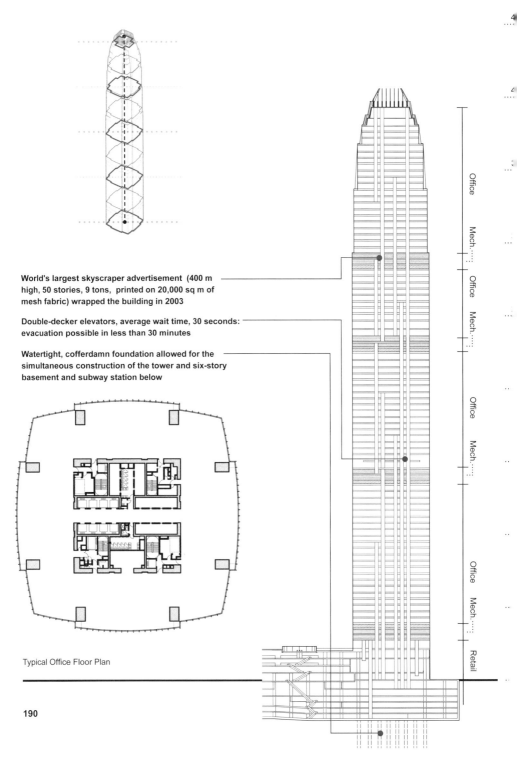

World's largest skyscraper advertisement (400 m high, 50 stories, 9 tons, printed on 20,000 sq m of mesh fabric) wrapped the building in 2003

Double-decker elevators, average wait time, 30 seconds: evacuation possible in less than 30 minutes

Watertight, cofferdamn foundation allowed for the simultaneous construction of the tower and six-story basement and subway station below

Typical Office Floor Plan

Shanghai World Financial Center

Location	Shanghai, China
Architect	Kohn Pedersen Fox
Completion	2007
Height	492 meters
Floors	101 floors
Elevators	91
Structure	Diagonally braced super-structural frame with outrigger belt trusses

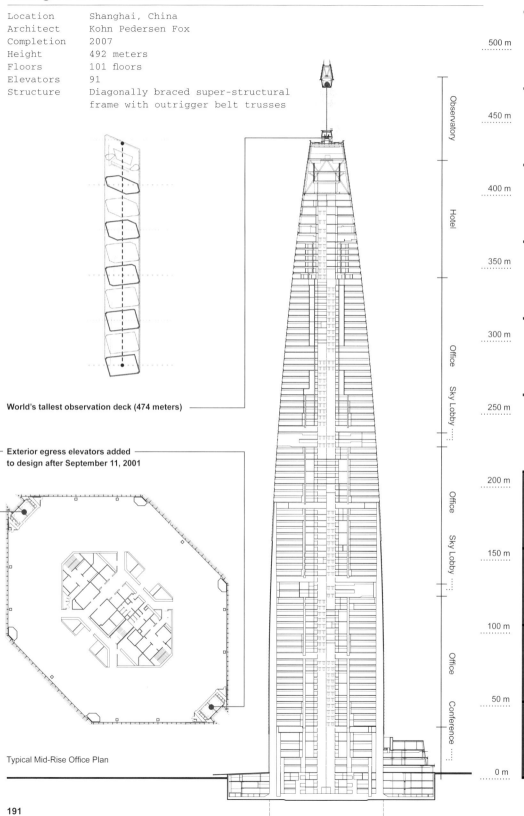

World's tallest observation deck (474 meters)

Exterior egress elevators added to design after September 11, 2001

Typical Mid-Rise Office Plan

Observatory

Hotel

Office

Sky Lobby

Office

Sky Lobby

Office

Conference

500 m
450 m
400 m
350 m
300 m
250 m
200 m
150 m
100 m
50 m
0 m

Burj Khalifa

Location	Dubai, UAE
Architect	Skidmore, Owings & Merrill
Completion	2010
Height	828 meters
Floors	163 floors
Elevators	58
Structure	Reinforced concrete buttressed core

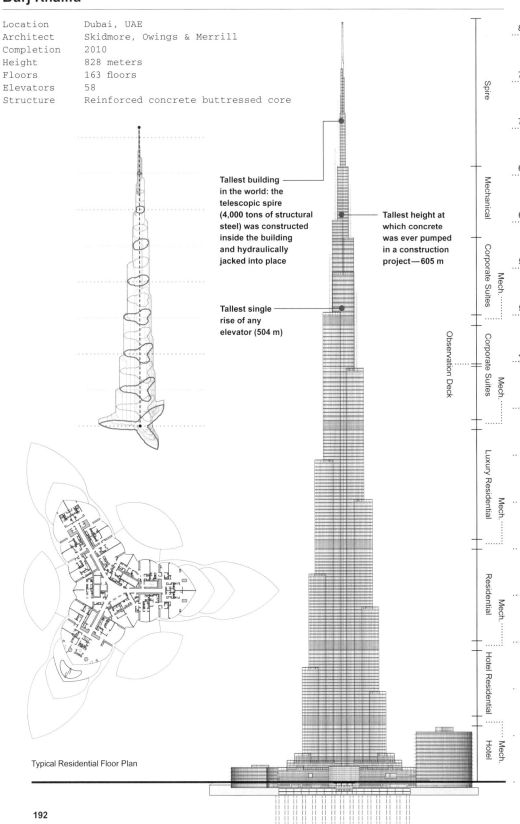

Tallest building in the world: the telescopic spire (4,000 tons of structural steel) was constructed inside the building and hydraulically jacked into place

Tallest height at which concrete was ever pumped in a construction project—605 m

Tallest single rise of any elevator (504 m)

Spire

Mechanical

Corporate Suites

Mech.

Corporate Suites

Mech.

Luxury Residential

Mech.

Residential

Mech.

Hotel Residential

Mech.

Hotel

Observation Deck

Typical Residential Floor Plan

Nanjing Greenland Financial Center

Location	Nanjing, China
Architect	Skidmore, Owings & Merrill
Completion	2010
Height	450 meters
Floors	89 floors
Elevators	54
Structure	Reinforced concrete shear core walls and exterior composite columns

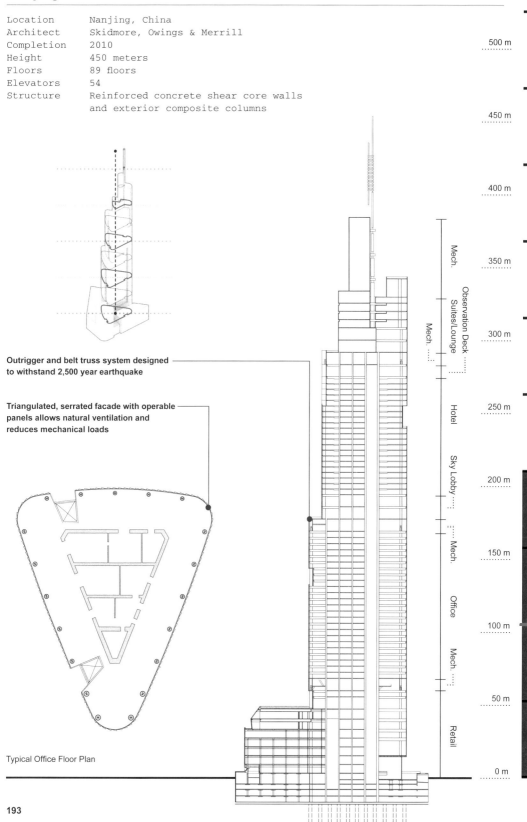

Outrigger and belt truss system designed to withstand 2,500 year earthquake

Triangulated, serrated facade with operable panels allows natural ventilation and reduces mechanical loads

Typical Office Floor Plan

500 m
450 m
400 m
350 m
300 m
250 m
200 m
150 m
100 m
50 m
0 m

Mech.
Observation Deck
Suites/Lounge
Mech.
Hotel
Sky Lobby
Mech.
Mech.
Office
Mech.
Retail

Kowloon International Commerce Centre

Location	Hong Kong, China
Architect	Kohn Pederson Fox
Completion	2010
Height	484 meters
Floors	118 floors
Elevators	83
Structure	Reinforced concrete mega columns

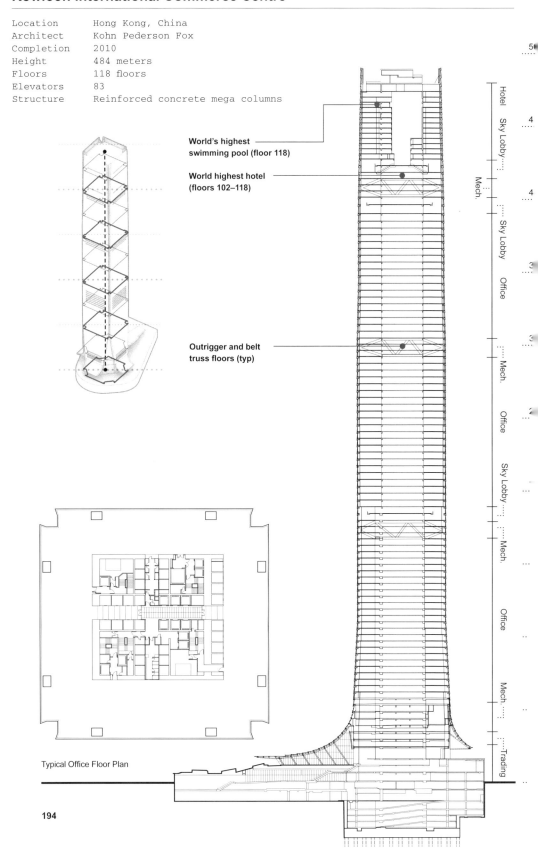

World's highest swimming pool (floor 118)

World highest hotel (floors 102–118)

Outrigger and belt truss floors (typ)

Typical Office Floor Plan

Hotel

Sky Lobby

Mech.

Sky Lobby

Office

Mech.

Office

Sky Lobby

Mech.

Office

Mech.

Trading

Al Hamra Tower

Location	Kuwait City, Kuwait
Architect	Skidmore, Owings & Merrill
Completion	2011
Height	412.6 meters
Floors	77 floors
Elevators	43
Structure	Reinforced concrete shear wall with perimeter moment resisting frame

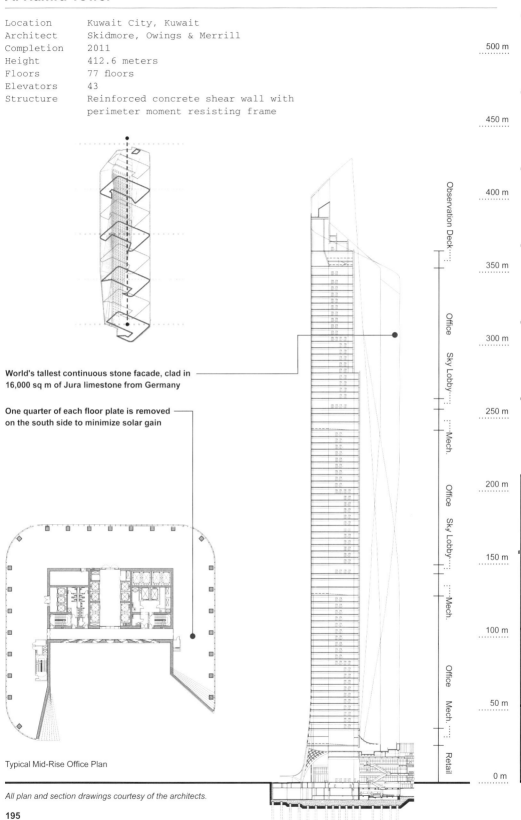

World's tallest continuous stone facade, clad in 16,000 sq m of Jura limestone from Germany

One quarter of each floor plate is removed on the south side to minimize solar gain

Typical Mid-Rise Office Plan

All plan and section drawings courtesy of the architects.

Office*US*: Museums as Cultural Capital

A compendium of museums designed by US architects abroad
since 1914, 85% were commissioned after 1991.

1. Sert, Jackson and Gourley • Fondation Maeght
2. The Office of Ludwig Mies van der Rohe • Neue Nationalgalerie
3. Richard Meier and Partners • Museum for the Decorative Arts
4. Pei Cobb Freed & Partners • Louvre Renovation
5. Venturi, Scott Brown • Sainsbury Wing, National Gallery
6. Edward Durell Stone • Museo de Antropología de Xalapa
7. Richard Meier and Partners • Museum of Contemporary Art
8. Frank O. Gehry & Associates • Vitra Design Museum
9. Frank O. Gehry & Associates • Guggenheim Museum
10. Richard Meier and Partners Architects • Arp Museum
11. Steven Holl Architects • Kiasma Museum of Contemporary Art
12. Michael Graves and Associates • Taiwan National Museum
13. Richard Meier and Partners Architects • Ara Pacis Museum
14. Kohn, Pedersen, Fox • Rodin Pavilion at Samsung Plaza
15. I. M. Pei Architect • Miho Museum
16. Studio Daniel Libeskind • Felix Nussbaum Haus
17. Studio Daniel Libeskind • Jewish Museum
18. Eisenman Architects • City of Culture
19. Studio Daniel Libeskind • Imperial War Museum North
20. RTKL • Shanghai Museum of Science and Technology
21. Bernard Tschumi Architects • Acropolis Museum
22. Studio Daniel Libeskind • Danish Jewish Museum
23. Hellmuth, Obata + Kassabaum • Darwin Centre Museum
24. Frank O. Gehry & Associates • Biomuseo

1914

1958 ①

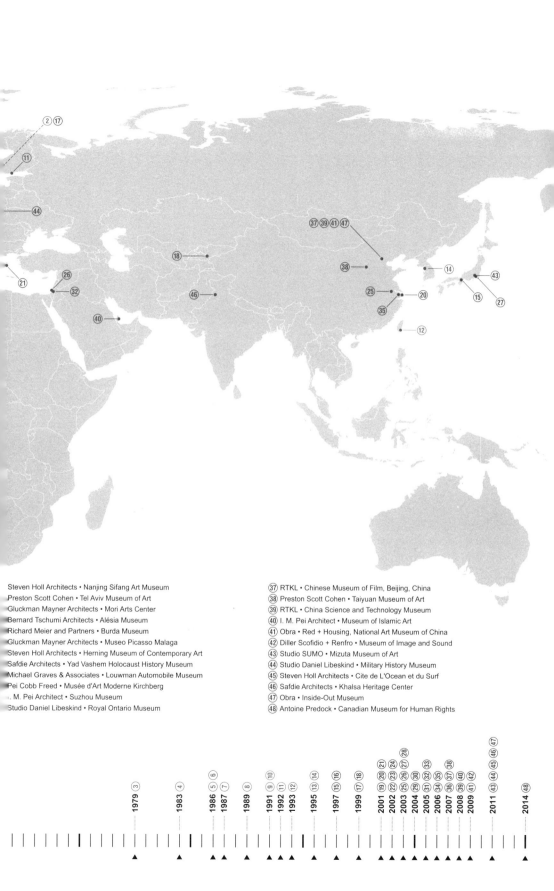

Steven Holl Architects • Nanjing Sifang Art Museum
Preston Scott Cohen • Tel Aviv Museum of Art
Gluckman Mayner Architects • Mori Arts Center
Bernard Tschumi Architects • Alésia Museum
Richard Meier and Partners • Burda Museum
Gluckman Mayner Architects • Museo Picasso Malaga
Steven Holl Architects • Herning Museum of Contemporary Art
Safdie Architects • Yad Vashem Holocaust History Museum
Michael Graves & Associates • Louwman Automobile Museum
Pei Cobb Freed • Musée d'Art Moderne Kirchberg
I. M. Pei Architect • Suzhou Museum
Studio Daniel Libeskind • Royal Ontario Museum

(37) RTKL • Chinese Museum of Film, Beijing, China
(38) Preston Scott Cohen • Taiyuan Museum of Art
(39) RTKL • China Science and Technology Museum
(40) I. M. Pei Architect • Museum of Islamic Art
(41) Obra • Red + Housing, National Art Museum of China
(42) Diller Scofidio + Renfro • Museum of Image and Sound
(43) Studio SUMO • Mizuta Museum of Art
(44) Studio Daniel Libeskind • Military History Museum
(45) Steven Holl Architects • Cite de L'Ocean et du Surf
(46) Safdie Architects • Khalsa Heritage Center
(47) Obra • Inside-Out Museum
(48) Antoine Predock • Canadian Museum for Human Rights

EXPORT

JORGE OTERO-PAILOS

Public Architecture After America's Withdrawal: On the Preservation of US Embassies

Fifty years after the United States completed its most politically ambitious embassy construction program, designed by America's best modernist architects, the State Department has embarked upon a new program with equal potential to transform the world's perception of American architecture. Through its Overseas Building Operations (OBO), the US government is quietly selling off its modernist embassies to the highest bidder, and using the money to build new, larger, and more heavily protected structures. The majority of new buildings built since 2001, having been designed with a single-minded focus on security, aspire to be as impervious as Guantanamo, and indeed the two can also be compared in terms of their lack of architectural distinction.[1] The decommissioning and sale of the old embassies, many of which are masterpieces of American midcentury modernism, are consistent with the State Department's general disregard for architectural culture. However, in foreign countries with strong preservation administrations, measures are being put in place to protect decommissioned US embassies from demolition, and to adapt them to new uses. These adaptations offer creative opportunities for architects to redefine American architecture abroad, and to provide a counter-narrative to the over-determined expression of new embassies as strongholds. To read these two narratives side by side requires that we expand the definition of architectural creativity, beyond the normative notion that it requires making new buildings, to include the possibility of creating contemporary architecture from existing buildings.

US Office

Save for the brief exceptional period, between 1948 and 1960, when modernist embassies were built, the US has not considered architecture a major diplomatic asset. Today, the Department of State views architecture primarily as a target for terrorism and a diplomatic liability. The US government, under constant public pressure to appear thrifty, has a long record of painting architecture as an unnecessary expense. From the origins of the republic to the early twentieth century, the US did not have a building program abroad. Decisions about where to house embassies and consulates were often left to the personal taste of US diplomats, who were also expected to pay for their own residences and offices. Ambassadors were predictably wealthy individuals who could afford the

Facing page: John MacLane Johansen, Chancery of the US Embassy in Dublin (1956–64). *Source: Brioscú Collection, Irish Architectural Archive.*

① Notable exceptions are the highly refined architectural designs by Kieran Timberlake and Tod Williams Billie Tsien Architects for US embassies in London and Mexico City respectively.

1948

2014

honor of representing their country. Their architectural choices were regarded, at least within government, more as a reflection of their personal refinement than as symbols of the United States. Lower ranking consuls, who handled passports, visas, and other such transactions, were often businessmen of more limited means working abroad. They also had to provide their own offices, but were allowed to pay themselves a salary through the collection of fees. The situation changed in the early twentieth century with the passing of the Lowden Act (1911), which provided a modest yearly budget of half a million dollars per year for the State Department to purchase or build embassies. The Porter Act (1926) doubled the yearly budget and established the Foreign Service Buildings Commission (FSBC) to select sites, set priorities, and create an architectural policy for diplomatic buildings.[2]

In general, the FSBC defaulted to buying existing buildings, mostly aristocratic palaces, large enough to house ambassadorial and consular offices under one roof. When new buildings were necessary, the Commission at first tasked architects to design in the local palatial style, following the example of Frank Packard's US embassy in Rio de Janeiro (1923), a sober Portuguese Neo-Colonial styled palace, or J.E. Campbell's Spanish Revival Embassy in Mexico City (1925). One of the FSBC's most prominent construction projects was the US embassy in Paris (1929–32), designed by the New York firm of Delano & Aldrich. A contextual palace that expressed reverence for the surrounding architecture of the Place de la Concorde and the French Beaux Arts style, the building lacked any reference to the transformations that the Beaux Arts underwent in US cities like Chicago, St. Louis or New York.

In other words, when the US started building its embassies, it was not a given that they should appear overtly American in architectural expression. Certainly, buildings had to appear dignified, but government officials did not immediately recognize architecture as an instrument of national representation. In part, this had to do with the fact that, technically speaking (and governmental discourse is particularly technical), an embassy is a group of people, not a building. The word embassy denotes the mission or deputation sent by one state into another to represent it. An embassy can be theoretically housed anywhere, but in practice the building must meet certain criteria. Its physical location must be aligned with the country's political ambitions. Historically FSBC typically tried to locate embassies in the center of cities, next to other embassies, to convey the sense that the United States was one among many powerful nations.

The head of the embassy is of course the ambassador, a title that derives from the Latin *ambactus*, meaning servant. Ambassadors are civil servants whose principal service is to represent their country's government before foreign governments. They stand at the political threshold between the state's inside and its outside, transferring messages to and fro. Their mode of representation is verbal, not visual. Ambassadors are trained to think that their words represent the state, not the style of the room in which they happen to be sitting. They don't conceive of their ability to represent the US as being shaped by whether they have an

[2]
Ron Robin, *Enclaves of America: The Rhetoric of American Political Architecture Abroad, 1900–1965* (Princeton: Princeton University Press, 1992), 22, 70.

"American-looking" architectural stage or not. So one can understand why building in an "American" style was not a priority.

American Architecture

The fact that US embassy buildings exist in wide array of architectural styles, from many different periods, suggests that the meaning and historical significance of US embassies cannot be reduced to their mode of architectural expression. Chancery design has mostly followed the architectural styles in vogue. From the 1880s to the late 1920s, it was French Beaux Arts. Then in the 1930s, American architectural discourse became overtly nationalistic. Influential architects and historians, especially Talbot Hamlin and Fiske Kimball, stoked the idea that a distinctly American architecture had unfolded independent of Europe, while in dialogue with it.[3] Suddenly, the French Beaux Arts appeared foreign and affected, and Neo-Colonial styles came into vogue as autochthonous outgrowths of the first European settlers (thus Neo-Georgian in the East, and Neo-Plateresque or Spanish Revival in Florida and the Southwest). The assertion of Neo-Colonial styles as emblems of American-ness was a deeply political move. It hid deep anxieties among dominant WASP culture about the perceived fracturing social effects of massive immigration. J.D. Rockefeller, Jr. experimented with archi-tecture as a didactic instrument of cultural assimilation through his highly acclaimed restoration of Colonial Williamsburg, where he launched pioneering education programs in the 1930s to subtly teach visitors about Protestant ethics and values. Neo-Colonial became a common choice in practically every building type from federal post offices to private residences. In turn, the FSBC adopted what was fashionable domestically as its model for building new embassies abroad. Among the many examples of Neo-Colonial chanceries, Jay Morgan's design for the American consulate in Yokohama (1932) is one of the most overtly didactic: a replica of the White House. Interestingly, Neo-Colonial became such an over-determined emblem of American archi-tecture that when the Grand Central Art Galleries, a private artists' cooperative, commissioned Delano & Aldrich to design the US Pavilion at the Venice Biennale (1930), they produced a scaled-down version of a Neo-Georgian plantation mansion.

Embassy construction expanded dramatically in the two decades after World War II due to a peculiar combination of domestic and foreign factors that have been thoroughly documented in Jane Loeffler's canonical history of that period.[4] With decolonization and the Cold War came a struggle to solidify foreign allies and court new non-aligned countries such as India, Egypt, and others. US diplomacy efforts expanded from restricted dialogue between diplomats to persuading the broader foreign public of America's virtues. The United States Information Agency became a separate agency in 1953 with a mission to engage in "public diplomacy." It exercised soft power through cultural initiatives and broad-casting programs such as the Voice of America. The USIA's foreign arm, the United States Information Service (USIS), was attached to embassy

(3) See Fiske Kimball, *American Architecture*, (Indianapolis and New York: Bobbs-Merrill Co., 1928); and Talbot Hamlin, *The American Spirit in Architecture*, (New Haven: Yale University Press, 1926).

(4) Jane Loeffler, *The Architecture of Diplomacy: Building America's Embassies*, (New York: Princeton Architectural Press, 1998).

Harrison & Abramovitz, Chancery of the US Embassy in Rio de Janeiro (1952).
Since 1960, when Brazil's capital moved to Brasilia, the building serves as the
US Consulate. *Source: The US State Department.*

missions, and imposed its own requirements, not only for extra office
space, but also for a separate entrance, distinct from the traditional
entrances for consular and ambassadorial services. It also demanded
public amenities such as libraries and movie theaters where foreigners
could come and learn about American culture and business opportunities.
Under normal circumstances, the enormous cost of the new building
program would have made its approval in Congress difficult. But Fredrick
A. Larkin, the Chief of FBO, shrewdly found a way to use war debt to
pay for the new construction, thus circumventing the need for tax dollars
and Congressional oversight.[5] They set up the Architectural Advisory
Committee, which initially included Ralph Walker, Henry Shepley and
Pietro Belluschi, to identify and select established and emerging architects for the dozens of commissions that had to be quickly awarded
and built.

⑤
Ibid., 4, 107.

　　　As in the 1930s, architects solved the question of how to represent
America by building in the style that was domestically in vogue at the
time: modernism. Midcentury chanceries were consistently modernist.
Their outward resemblance to the corporate office buildings and state
government centers built during the 1950s and 1960s begs the question of
what architectural qualities defined midcentury modern US embassies.

Gates

One of the defining characteristics of modern embassies was that they expressed a new engagement with the public. It is important not to confuse the change of style from Beaux Arts to modernism with this new commitment. Embassies have always been built in the prevalent style; postwar, that style was modernism. The modern style is certainly common for postwar embassies, but their stylistic contemporaneity is actually an element of continuity rather than rupture with their prewar predecessors. It is also important not to attribute adjectives typically associated with modernism, such as openness and transparency, to the embassies. Modernist embassies had indeed more glass than Beaux Arts designs, but the glass was not used to invite the public in by exhibiting the embassy's interiors to the street in the manner of Skidmore, Owings & Merrill's Manufacturers Hanover Bank (New York, 1953–54). Rather, larger operable windows were used conventionally to create better natural illumination and ventilation in offices that were heated but not cooled mechanically. For instance, Harrison & Abramovitz's US Embassy in Rio de Janeiro (1952) is relatively opaque at the ground level, with the windowless free-form wall that makes up the library blocking much the view from the street into the lobby. The twelve story travertine-clad tower opens up at the top with a double height loggia meant to look out, rather than in.

In order to ascertain the common characteristic features that represent the postwar turn toward the public in embassy design, we first must look to the client's brief, and only then turn to the individual solutions that each architect proposed for it. Prosaically, the Department of State required an increase in the number of public entrances, from one to three, in order to expand its connection to the public. Ambassadorial, consular, and USIS programs were each to have independent public access to the building. Each entrance, needless to say, represented separate but related aspects of American diplomacy. The matter-of-factness of the requirement has resulted in its significance to postwar embassy design being underestimated, if not entirely unnoticed. Critics and historians have instead emphasized the style of the buildings as the primary bearer of ideological meaning. But as we shall see, embassy entrances are highly symbolic, and even operate as synecdoches for the entire embassy, as gates conceal, reveal and otherwise help negotiate between inside and outside, two realms that in speaking about diplomatic buildings cannot be reduced to interior and exterior, but must be recognized as entirely different political, social and economic realities.

Eero Saarinen's tiny embassy in Oslo (1955–59), is one of the most masterful solutions to the Department of State's new postwar requirements. The required two additional entrances were to be symbolically secondary to the traditional ambassadorial grand entrance. Saarinen was given a triangular site, with one side on a high street across from Norway's Royal Palace, and the opposing vertex a full story downhill. Saarinen followed the plot, designing a triangular five-story building with a relentless pre-cast black concrete and labradorite façade made of a

Eero Saarinen and Associates, USIS entrance to the chancery of the US Embassy in Oslo.
Source: Yale University Manuscripts and Archives.

single repeated module. The entrances would be almost impossible to
identify if it were not for the canopies floating in front of the façade. For
the main ambassadorial entrance, he put a large white canopy supported
by a central flagstaff on the center of the high street façade. The canopy
carried the US flag above and a sculpture of the bald eagle below, which
were the only outward national symbols in an otherwise anonymous
office building. The central entrance led to a ceremonial diamond shaped
atrium spanning the top four floors and topped by a faceted plaster roof
framed in glass. The obvious solution would have been to put the other
two entrances at the center of the other two sides, and to assign a different
program to each edge of the building. But Saarinen rightly felt that
tucking the other two entrances towards the back of the building would
have diminished their symbolic importance. Instead, he moved them
to each of the vertices flanking the main façade, so that all three are accessible from the high street. Only the ambassadorial entrance is visible in
frontal elevation from the Royal Palace, but the other two are the first
thing pedestrians see from the sidewalk approaching the building. Thus
the building maintains an official face of ambassadorial diplomacy
towards official government institutions, but also creates new openings
for the public to enter the embassy. The USIS entrance was open during
regular business hours to allow the public to enter and browse the

Marcel Breuer, Chancery of the US Embassy in The Hague (1956–59). *Source: Marcel Breuer Archive, Syracuse University.*

library and it featured an open cafeteria and auditorium where American films would be regularly screened.

The open doors of postwar embassies were literal, not just visual effects. Today, that sort of access is unthinkable. The Oslo embassy is entirely closed off behind a continuous high fence. The two secondary entrances have been closed, and the building now can only be accessed through a single gate, a detached pavilion in front of the building with airport-like security. The plan is to sell the building and to follow OBO's general strategy to build isolated suburban embassies with single point access and on a site of sufficient size to set buildings back from the street beyond a hypothetical blast zone. OBO's argument is that moving US embassies from urban centers to suburban peripheries enables embassies to better keep their employees safe. The diminution in entrance gate requirements signals a profound change in how the State Department conceives its diplomatic office. We are back to a prewar definition of diplomacy as closed-door discussions among government officials. The public is tolerated for quick bureaucratic transactions, but no longer invited.

Chancery

The number and architectural expression of gates is of central importance in defining the character of an embassy building. Consider the fact that a major aspect of embassy work is to protect the gate. An embassy is a gate-keeping mission. This gate can be understood literally, as in the need to secure access to the building, but it also functions symbolically. An embassy regulates the official information to which foreign governments have access. The US government makes recourse to a precise architectural term, a chancel, to describe the symbolic gate that embassies must keep. Thus, the buildings in which embassies conduct their daily office affairs are formally called chanceries.

In Christian religious architecture, the chancel is the part of the Church near the altar reserved for the clergy and separated from the public by a screened gate. Chancel comes from the Latin *cancelli* meaning grate or crossbars, and indeed such gates separated judges from the public in ancient Roman basilicas. The chancel is no ordinary gate. It divides two different orders of things: the sacred and profane, the forensic and the circumstantial, the domestic and the foreign. In medieval Churches it separated Latin, the priestly language, from the *vulgate anonyme*—just as in embassies it separates domestic from foreign languages. Significantly, the chancel had openings through the grating, symbolizing the possibility of communication. But communication was also dangerous, as contact between these two realities could be polluting. Any communication had to be highly mediated through a third party, the chancellor, whose job was to sit at the gate to control the flow and nature of messages, and where appropriate, carry them, that is translate them, from one side to the other. Today, chancellor can be an ecclesiastical, political, academic, or institutional title. The chancery is the office of the chancellor, who, in the case of US embassies, is the ambassador.

We can now refine the theory that embassies can be housed anywhere to include a caveat: so long as there are gates that can be guarded, allowing only authorized people and information to cross, and marking a relatively porous threshold between inside and outside. A chancery cannot officiate without a physical and symbolic chancel from which to regulate how outsiders access and perceive institutionalized power. Arguably, it need not look like a door. It could be any object, a canopy as in the Oslo example or an entire building. What matters is that it be recognized and treated like a gate behind which another set of rules applies. The symbolic power of the chancel derives from the privilege that receiving states grant embassies (i.e. the group of people) to be immune from the jurisdiction of local law. This treatment extends to the embassy's objects: embassy cars are allowed to park illegally without being ticketed; diplomatic pouches are never opened at border crossings; and more importantly for our purposes, chanceries are granted extraterritorial status and are often exempt from certain local building codes. The chancery is a very special type of office: it objectifies, and therefore symbolizes, the possibility of communication across the chancel, between entirely different systems of law and government. How one enters and exits a chancery, who is invited and excluded, and the degree of porosity of the gate, not just visual but physical bodily access, is in sum the core architectural symbolic expression of diplomacy.

Harry Weese, Chancery of the US Embassy in Accra (1956–59). *Source: The State Department.*

The Architect's Collaborative, Walter Gropius design architect, Chancery of the US Embassy in Athens (1956–59).
© Elizabeth Gill Lui 2005.

Desire

Even modernist embassies were visually rather closed off from the street, even if architecturally they symbolized a diplomatic turn towards the foreign public. Perhaps because they were relatively closed off, and especially because since 2001 they have been entirely off limits, the foreign public desires renewed access to these structures. The threat is that as the US government vacates its modernist embassies the desire for access will result in attempts to impose our contemporary ideas of what a public-oriented building should be onto these structures. It is not unthinkable that their rather opaque facades will be "contemporanized" with transparent glass storefronts that force the interiors upon pedestrians. In most cases, this sort of exhibitionist adaptation will be tantamount to destroying the historic significance of the buildings. But in order to do justice to the buildings, architects will have to rethink contemporary ideas of how notions of the public can be expressed architecturally without relying on glass as a default, for being public is not necessarily being transparent, and is in fact often the opposite.

The vulnerable position in which modernist US embassies find themselves today cannot be overstated. When, in 2009, the State Department agreed to sell the US embassy in London, designed by Eero Saarinen between 1956 and 1960, the architectural press expressed its shock, not at the divestment of the US government from an architectural masterpiece, as one would have imagined, but rather at the fact that it was sold to a Qatari developer and not to the London-based developer Chelsfield.[6] Harry Weese's embassy in Accra (1955–59) was simply demolished and replaced with a building built (one cannot say designed) by Framaco International Inc., a construction management and procurement company that provides the US government with "turnkey" solutions, in joint venture with Turkish International Contractors Metis and Epik.[7] In one notable compensatory exception, the Department of State, through OBO's new Excellence in Diplomatic Facilities initiative, seems to have committed to preserving one example of the United Sates' modern architectural heritage: in 2013 they entrusted Ann Beha with the rehabilitation of the embassy in Athens, originally designed by Walter Gropius and The Architect's Collaborative (1956–61).[8]

Preservationists in some host countries have stepped in to try to safeguard the embassies that the Department of State is selling. In anticipation of the sale of the London Embassy, English Heritage listed it as a Grade II building in the UK's Statutory List of Buildings of Special Architectural or Historic Interest, which will offer it some measure of protection against demolition, but not against radical alterations. In Oslo, the *Byantikvar's* office has begun a dialogue with embassy officials to list Saarinen's building as protected heritage—the trick being that they cannot offer legal protection to the building while the US remains the owner, as its property is technically not Norway. DoCoMoMo is lobbying to prevent the demolition of Marcel Breuer's embassy in The Hague (1957–59), and seems to have persuaded at least the city's alderman for culture, who would like to see it turned into a hotel and museum by

⑥
"US Embassy in Shock Sale to Qatari Diar," in *Architect's Journal* (November 3, 2009), http://www.architectsjournal.co.uk/news/daily-news/us-embassy-in-shock-sale-to-qatari-diar/5210373.article

⑦
http://www.framaco.com/newsawards.php (accessed January 10, 2014).

⑧
http://www.state.gov/r/pa/prs/ps/2013/11/217694.htm (accessed December 20, 2013).

Eero Saarinen and Associates, Chancery of the US Embassy London, England.
Source: Yale University Manuscripts and Archives.

2018, The Hague's year as Cultural Capital of Europe. But the fate of
other extraordinary buildings such as John Johansen's embassy in Dublin
(1956–64) is even less certain.

      What will be preserved, if anything, will be part of the buildings'
façades. The flags and the bald eagles will be removed for sure. The
façades will be blamed for being too closed off, too gate-like, and in need
of partial demolition to accommodate contemporary notions of public
architecture. The interiors will be "adaptively reused," which means that
the buildings will be eviscerated of their characteristic spaces to serve
new uses, like a hotel spa (do we really need another one?). All this will
be done in the name of preserving the architecture. But what do we mean
by architecture? The building and its architecture are related but not
identical. Building satisfies need, architecture satisfies desire. Buildings
are measured in quantities like square feet and dollars. Architecture
is measured in qualities like spatiality, temporality, luminosity, memora-
bility, publicity, and diplomacy. For the architecture of US embassies to
endure the transformations to accommodate the buildings' next functions
requires not just a mode of creativity bent on remaking everything in
the image of contemporary taste, but also one that is focused on rekindling
desire for alternative forms of public architecture. The vanishing
modernist US embassies can help us shape that new conception of public
architecture. But this is a tall order, for in order to grasp their radical
potential we need to transcend the contemporary view that the future is
to be created in our image, and consider the possibility that some of its
defining features are already in existence.

Embassies: Under Pressure

U. S. Legation Office Building
Tangier, Morocco

Hugh Stubbins Associates,
Architects

While this rendering is rather dominated by the arches at the entrance, other features will perhaps contribute more to the overall expression: pierced concrete sun screens shading the large glass areas of the three-story building, marble facing at the ends, an arcaded patio landscaped with water pools and orange trees. The Consular Court at ground level will have a surround of glass at the ceiling line with a shade of colorful mosaic tile. The three-story building is roughly in the center of a one-and-a-half-acre site, is surrounded by one-story elements which with it form the entrance court on one side and an enclosed patio on the other. Open arcades provide circulation at ground level. One-story buildings are wall bearing, with stucco finish.

ARCHITECTURE TO REPRESENT AMERICA ABROAD

Regional Expressions of American Architectural Thinking are Sought for State Department Buildings

THE NEW PROGRAM for State Department buildings in foreign countries might be characterized as a significant experiment in regional architecture for diplomatic objectives. Really now just getting to the first-look stage, the refurbished operation has a panel of famous architects to guide it and a clear statement of purposes. A score or so American architects have had plans for various buildings approved, and an appropriation decision is now in the making.

Objectives are given as two: (1) to represent American architecture abroad; (2) to adapt itself to local conditions and cultures so deftly that it is welcomed, not

criticized, by its hosts. Here is a clear mandate to develop a sympathetic, regional expression of our own architectural thinking, all to a purpose whose importance transcends the normal challenges in design.

This was the need that led to the formation of the rotating Architectural Advisory Panel for the Foreign Buildings Operation, consisting of: Pietro Belluschi, F.A.I.A., dean of the School of Architecture and Planning, Massachusetts Institute of Technology; Henry Shepley, F.A.I.A., of Shepley, Bulfinch, Richardson & Abbott, Boston; and Ralph Walker, F.A.I.A., of Voorhees, Walker, Smith & Smith, New York. The panel is

ARCHITECTURAL RECORD MAY 1955 187

Architectural Record article from 1955.

"Overseas the state department accepts the proposition that good architecture is good government," reads a statement in a 1957 issue of *Architectural Forum,* echoing the widespread sentiment at the time. The massive construction of embassies that followed the World War II was fueled in part by foreign credits, most often paid in materials, and thus skipping the lengthy congressional budget discussions. But just as the overseas face presented by embassies to come out of the most prolific US embassy-construction era was imagined as the projection of "assurance, importance, tact and vitality" of the country itself, the same buildings eventually began receiving reverse projections in direct response to US

foreign policy. Open and hospitable, often shrouded in an exotic regionalist interpretation of screens or louvers, embassies built in the period following World War II became easy targets with devastating consequences. In the 1968 attack on the US Embassy in Saigon — designed by Curtis and Davis Architects from New Orleans and completed in 1966 — attackers blew a hole through the fragile exterior wall surrounding the compound, entered and killed 22 and wounded 188. The Saigon embassy remained a target until the end of the Vietnam War. In direct correlation to patterns of discontent about US foreign policy in the aftermath of the Vietnam War, there were 243 attacks and attempted attacks on US diplomatic installations abroad in the period between 1975 and 1984.

Following the 1983 Beirut suicide bombings, security became a critical issue for FBO. The Department of State submitted to Congress a series of design recommendations and security upgrades for existing and new embassies known as the Inman report. Named after the former head of NSA, retired Navy Admiral Bobby R. Inman who chaired the security commission, the Inman report set in motion a powerful architectural makeover of the US presentation abroad. It called for the replacement of 126 posts, and required all diplomatic facilities to be collected into a single compound outside of city centers, and surrounded by tall walls. The buildings were allowed minimal glazing and recommended to use certified blast resistant material. However, these changes did not decrease the intensity of attacks. According to the US Government Accountability Office (GAO), from 1987 to 1997, after the Inman report was adopted, the US diplomatic facilities overseas were attacked on more than 200 occasions. By far the bloodiest of those took place in 1998 when the US embassies in Nairobi and Dar-es-Salaam where simultaneously attacked, resulting in 224 deaths. Following these attacks, the Crowe Report of 1999 re-emphasized security and the Inman points, which had been rarely implemented in the previous fourteen years due to prohibitive costs. In 2001 Colin Powell appointed a new head of FBO, a retired General Charles Williams, who proceeded by renaming FBO into Overseas Buildings Operations (OBO). Williams invited the engineering and construction firm URS Corporation to advise on the production of the standard embassy design

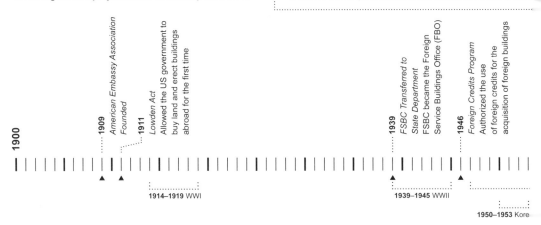

American Embassy Association Founded — **1909**

Lowden Act Allowed the US government to buy land and erect buildings abroad for the first time — **1911**

1900

1914–1919 WWI

1939 FSBC Transferred to State Department FSBC became the Foreign Service Buildings Office (FBO)

1946 Foreign Credits Program Authorized the use of foreign credits for the acquisition of foreign buildings

1939–1945 WWII

1950–1953 Kore

Marginalizing thus the existing Architectural Advisory Board and the architectural values it stood for, three sizes of the 'Standard Embassy Design' were developed from RTKL's latest embassy for Kampala. The key aim for this prototype was to meet the increasingly stricter security requirements while simultaneously reducing costs through common design features and integrated project delivery methods.

While serving on the Senate Foreign Relations Committee in 2009, John Kerry criticized the results of security improvements and implementation of the standard embassy design: "We are building some of the ugliest embassies I've ever seen...I cringe when I see what we're doing." In response to the criticism of both the US foreign policy and of the new crop of US embassies, the Department of State launched a Design Excellence Program in early 2010. Welcomed by architects and architectural critics equally, the later named Excellence in Diplomatic Facilities program revives the debate between inherently conflicting desires of stringent security and the message of openness by offering increasingly vague guidelines including "renewed preference for urban sites" and "cohesive design for site and structure." Though the Excellence Program once again embraces architecture as a "political art," its practical guidelines still limit access to the embassy building, preserving the endless waiting line in front of every US embassy.

- Margaret Arbanas and Ana Miljački

Key Sources:
Jane Loeffler, *The Architecture of Diplomacy: Building America's Embassies* (New York: Princeton Architectural Press, 1998).
Ron Robin, *Enclaves of America. The Rhetoric of American Political Architecture Abroad, 1900–1965* (Princeton, NJ: Princeton University Press, 1992).
AIA Best Practices, Adapting Standard Embassy Design to Specific Sites Contributed by the US Department of State and the US General Services Administration Revised May 2007 (http://www.aia.org/aiaucmp/groups/ek_members/documents/pdf/aiap017590.pdf, last accessed February 9, 2014).
Architecture to represent America Abroad," *Architectural Record*, May 1955.

Standard Embassy Design, 2005

Drawing and information adapted from source: *AIA Best Practices*, pub. 06.04.05 "Adapting Standard Embassy Design to Specific Sites," June 2005, revised May 2007

Small

Approximate size: 4,300 gross m²

Medium

Approximate size: 4,300-7,400 gross m²

Large

Approximate size: > 7,400 gross m²

1914

1948

1985
Inman Report
Sets new security regulations for the design of diplomatic posts.
100 ft setback
• Consolidate all facilities in one secure compound
• Purchase land for expansion within compound.
• 15% maximum glazed surface
• Isolated locations preferred to dense urban areas
• Controlled access to the compound
• No-climb walls and fences
• Anti-ram barriers
• Blast resistant construction

1999
The Crow Report
Elevates Security over all other considerations, restating the Inman Report recommendations, resulting in the Standard Embassy plan

2005
Standard Embassy Design Issued

2006
Secure Fence Act
Act authorizes and provides funding for the physical construction of 700 miles of fencing on the US-Mexico border

2011
Design Excellence Program
Reasserts the role of design in the conception and function of the embassy

2015

1947-1991 Cold War

1965–1973 Vietnam War

2001–Present
War on Terror & Afghanistan War

2003–2011 Iraq War

2014

1905 Beijing (Peking) SAT **1920** San Salvador SAT **1922** Rio de Janeiro Frank L. Packard
Aires, Argentina; June 4, 1926: US Embassy Bombing, Montevideo, Uruguay **1928** Ottawa Cass Gilbert
1936 Helsinki Harrie T. Lindeberg **1938** Monrovia SAT **1939** Havana FBO (Paul Franz Jaquet)
Halldorsson and S.Thordarsson **1945** Ciudad Trujillo SAT Lima FBO(Paul Franz Jaquet) Port-au-Pr
Renzi **1948** Ankara Eggers & Higgins Brussels FBO(Alan Jacobs) Rio de Janeiro Harrison & Abramovitz T
Havana Harrison & Abramovitz **1951** Copenhagen Rapson & van der Meulen Stockholm Rapson & va
Owings, & Merrill (SOM) Dusseldorf SOM with Apel Frankfurt SOM with Apel Le Havre Rapson & v
Stuttgart SOM with Apel Tokyo Raymond & Rado **1953** Jakarta Raymond & Rado Port of Spain N
Bernardi & Emmons Kinshasa (Leopoldville) Weed, Russell, Johnson Lagos Weed, Russell, Johnsor
Josep Lluis Sert Karachi Neutra & Alexander Oslo Eero Saarinen Port-au-Prince Don Hatch Quito V
Basra Harris Amstrong Belgrade Carl Koch Hamburg SOM with Apel London Eero Saarinen Manila
Tangier Hugh Stubbins Tehran Homsey & Homsey The Hague Marcel Breuer Mexico City Page S
Southwestern Architects Canberra Milton Grigg Caracas Donald Hatch Dublin John Johansen M
Emmons Warsaw Welton Becket Associates **1958** Fukuoka G.T. Rockrise Kabul O'Connor & Kilha
Lundy Madras Burk, Lebreton & Lamantia Montevideo I.M. Pei San Salvador Hellmuth, Obatta & l
US Embassy Bombing, Libreville, Gabon **1965** Madras Ginocchio Cromwell Carter Neyland New Delh
Cunningham **1967** Bogotá Mitchell & Giurgola Warsaw FBO (Sal diGiacomo) March 30, 1965: US En
Beauchamp & Marvel **1971** Brasilia Henningson, Durham & Richardson Nairobi A. Epstein & Son
1972 Dakar Madison & Madison International Wellington Robert Beatty 1972: American Diplomatic N
Oudens + Knoop **1978** Budapest Fry & Welch Associates Jakarta Wilkes & Faulkner Lisbon Free
Embassy Attack, Kuala Lumpur, Malaysia; November 4, 1979: US Embassy Attack, Tehran, Iran; Novem
Kuala Lumpur Hartman-Cox La Paz Esherich, Homsey, Dodge & Davis Riyadh Caudill, Rowlett,
Osaka Tatsuya Okura **1982** Cairo Metcalf & Associates Giza (Cairo) Metcalf & Associates **1983** I
Beirut, Lebanon; December 12, 1983: US Embassy Truck Bombing, Kuwait; **1984** Mogadishu Oudens +
Bombing, Beirut, Lebanon; **1985** San José Torres, Beauchamp & Marvel **1986** Saana CRS-Sirrine
1987 Cairo TAC Bogotá Integrus Architecture Nicosia Kohn, Pedersen, Fox San Salvador CRS
Amman Perry, Dean, Rogers, & Partners June 21, 1988: US Embassy Attack, Beirut, Lebanon; Septem
Gunnar Birkets **1992** Kuwait RTKL Associates, Inc Lima Arquitectonica July 27, 1993: US Embassy
Associates **1995** Ashgabat FBO with consulting Architects **1996** Bishkek FBO with consulting Arc
Moscow HOK **2001** Luanda Zagaff **2002** Kampala RTKL Associates, Inc. Phnom Pehn Page S
Dushanbe Kullman Industries Tashkent Karn, Charuhas, Chapman & Twohey Tbilisi HOK Yaound
Consulate Truck Bombing, Karachi, Pakistan; October 12, 2002: US Consulate Attack, Denpasar, Indone
Zagreb HOK Algiers Integrus Architecture Astana Karn, Charuhas, Chapman & Twohey Frankfu
Nairobi Beglin Woods Architects Katmandu Sorg Architects Accra SOM Belmopan HOK Beijin
Embassy Attack, Tashkent, Uzbekistan; December 6, 2004: US Diplomatic Compound Attack, Jeddah, S
Port-au-Prince Karn, Charuhas, Chapman & Twohey **2006** Libreville Sorg Architects Surabaya S
Karachi; September 12, 2006: US Embassy Attack, Damascus, Syria; January 10, 2007: US Embassy
Embassy Attack, Sana'a, Yemen; July 9, 2008: US Consulate Attack, Istanbul, Turkey; September 17, 2l
Page Sarajevo Integrus Architecture April 5, 2010: US Consulate Attack, Peshawar, Pakistan **2011**
July 11, 2011: US Embassy Attack, Damascus ; October 28, 2011: US Embassy Attack, Sarajevo, Bosnia
September 3, 2012: US Consulate Attack, Peshawar, Pakistan; September 11, 2012: US Embassy Attac
Tunis, Tunisia **2013** London Kieran Timberlake Belgrade ZGF February 1, 2013: US Embassy Attack,

co City J.E.Campbell **1926** Tokyo Raymond & Magonigle **May 16, 1926: US Embassy Bombing, Buenos**
a Wyeth & Sullivan **1930** Seville SAT **1931** Amoy Elliott Hazzard **1932** Yokohama Jay Morgan
evideo FBO(Paul Franz Jaquet) **1941** Canberra FBO(Paul Franz Jaquet) Reykjavík Gisli
r FBO(Jaquet) **1946** Canberra FBO(Paul Franz Jaquet) **1947** Naples Geroge Howe with Mario di
des van der Gracht) Dhahran FBO **1949** Tokyo Raymond & Rado **1950** Antwerp Leon Stynen
n **1952** Jiddah FBO Managua FBO Boulogne Rapson & van der Meulen Bremen Skidmore,
n Madrid Garrigues & Middlehurst Munich SOM with Apel Neuilly Rapson & van der Meulen
re **1954** Asunción Keyes, Smith & Satterlee Dakar Moore & Hutchins Hong Kong Wurster,
Edward Durell Stone Port of Spain Mence & Moore Tegucwigalpa Michael Hare **1955** Baghdad
Seoul Ernest Kump Vienna Henry Hill **1956** Accra Harry Weese Athens Walter Gropius/TAC
w Manila A. L. Aydelott Nagoya Cochran, Stephenson & Wing Rabat Ketchum, Gina & Sharp
age **1957** Canberra Milton Grigg Caracas Donald Hatch Dublin John Johansen Mexico City
outhwestern Architects New Delhi Edward Durell Stone Santiago Paul Thiry Singapore Jones &
vard Larrabee Barnes **January 27, 1958: US Embassy Attack, Ankara, Turkey 1961** Colombo Victor
HOK) **1964** Mogadishu Holden, Egan, Wilson, Corser Niamey Robert Beatty **March 5, 1964:**
Cromwell Carter Neyland Saigon Curtis & Davis **1966** Islamabad Geddes, Brecher, Qualls,
ng, Saigon, Vietnam **1970** Buenos Aires Eduardo Catalano Guatemala City-Reed, Torres,
Cesar Pelli and Gruen Associates **September 26, 1971: US Embassy Attack, Phnom Penh, Cambodia**
, Manila, Philippines **1973** Geneva OMNIPLAN, Harrell & Hamilton **1974** Seoul Zo Za Yong and
tti Tokyo Harry Weese **August 19, 1974: US Embassy Attack, Nicosia, Cyprus; August 4, 1975: US**
US Embassy Attack, Islamabad, Pakistan; December 2, 1979: US Embassy Attack, Tripoli, Libya 1980
baatar Ulaanbaatar CitBuilding Office Architects **1981** Manama ROMA Muscat Polshek & Partners
nn, McKinnell & Wood Georgetown Alan Y. Taniguchi **April 18, 1983: US Embassy Car Bombing,**
ber **1984: US Embassy Car Bombing, Bogota, Colombia; September 20, 1984: US Embassy Truck**
: **US Embassy Car Bombing, Lisbon, Portugal; May 14, 1986: US Embassy Attack, Jakarta, Indonesia**
Santiago The Leonard Parker Associates **June 9, 1987: US Embassy Attack, Rome, Italy 1988**
US Embassy RPG Attack, Bogota, Colombia; 1990: US Embassy Attack, Tel Aviv, Israel **1991** Caracas
ima, Peru **1994** Ottawa SOM Bangkok Kallmann, McKinnell & Wood Singapore The Stubbins
Berlin Moore Ruble Yudell **April 24, 1999: US Consulate Car Bombing, Yekaterinburg, Russia 2000**
e Kabul Sorg Architects Abidjan CMSS/HOK/Bradley/Parker & Associates Abuja DMJM/Berger
e **January 22, 2002: US Government Information Center Attack, Calcutta, India; June 14, 2002: US**
2002: US Embassy Bombing, Lima, Peru 2003 Dar es Salaam HOK Nairobi HOK Nairobi HOK
on Karn, Charuhas, Chapman & Twohey **February 28, 2003: US Embassy Attack, Islamabad 2004**
SOM Managua Page Southerland Page Panama City EYP Rangoon SOM **June 30, 2004: US**
05 Bridgetown Sorg Architects Conakry Integrus Architecture Cape Town ZGF Cape Town ZGF
Surabaya Sorg Architects Bamako Integrus Architecture **March 2, 2006: US Consulate Car Bombing,**
, Greece **2008** Bayan Sorg Architects Brazzaville Page Southerland Page **March 18, 2008: US**
sy Attack, Sana'a, Yemen **2009** Dubai Page Southerland Page **2010** Khartoum Page Southerland
Page Southerland Page Ouagadougou Page Southerland Page Tijuana Integrus Architecture
ni Page Southerland Page Karachi Page Southerland Page Monrovia Page Southerland Page
ya; **September 11, 2012: US Embassy Attack, Sana'a, Yemen; September 14, 2012: US Embassy Attack,**
September 13, 2013: US Consulate Attack, Herat, Afghanistan.

HAVANA 1960

SAIGON 1975

DUBLIN 1987

WARSAW 1990

KINGSTON 2009

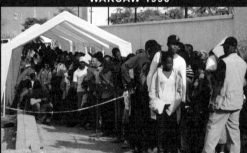

PORT-AU-PRINCE 2010

LIMA 2011

SHANGHAI 2011

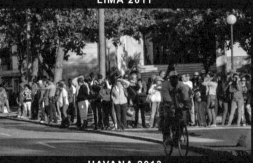

HAVANA 2013

GUANGZHOU 2013

In 2009 the AIA 21st Century embassy task force reminded its audiences that: "The location, appearance and convenience of, and the presence and maintenance of public spaces in and around the embassy often contribute to the first impression of the US

PORT-AU-PRINCE 1980

NEW DELHI 1985

CHENNAI 2008

SEOUL 2008

SAN SALVADOR 2010

BEIJING 2011

MOSCOW 2011

MANILA 2012

JAKARTA 2014

TEL AVIV 2014

bassy for all visitors. Even the extent of protection from the elements while waiting outdoors plays a role in how visitors perceive
experience in a US facility."

Little America: Enclaves of US Housing in Japan

Antonin Raymond & L.L. Rado

US Embassy Housing
Tokyo
1953

Source: David Leavitt Collection, The Architectural Archives,
University of Pennsylvania.

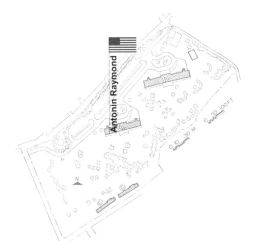

Source: Architectural Record.

Harry Weese Associates

US Embassy Housing
Tokyo
1980

Source: Google Earth.

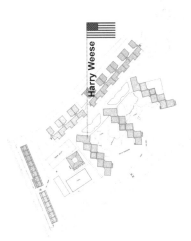

Drawn by Emily Chen.

Residential architecture in Japan prior to rapid postwar urbanization is principally a history of houses: timber structures with straw mat covered floors (tatami) partitioned by sliding screens (fusuma) with a low entry vestibule (genkan) and garden. In 1954, one such house was imported from Japan, a gift to the United States as a symbol of peace, and exhibited at the Museum of Modern Art in New York.

The history of Japanese multi-story housing finds a point of origin the year before, with the completion of Antonin Raymond's US Embassy Staff Housing in Tokyo. The first multi-story concrete structures in Japan, they were an export of expertise: a solution to a severe housing shortage, and a bulwark against the kind of massive urban fires that occurred as a result of WWII bombings of predominantly timber-built cities. They were also an enclave of American culture, with function-specif rooms filled with furniture for a nuclear family. In 1980, tl housing was replaced with a project designed by Harry Weese. Weese's units are on average four times the size of the units they replaced, reflecting the expectations of Americans migrating to ever-larger suburban homes.

A second pair of projects—Void Space/Hinged Space Housing by Steven Holl Architects and Slither Housing by Diller Scofidio + Renfro (DS+R)—share not site but a common ancestry. Both were selected by Arat Isozaki as part of an international group of architects for housing complexes he master-planned. Void Space

teven Holl Architects

id Space/Hinged Space
kuoka
91

rce: Steven Holl Architects.

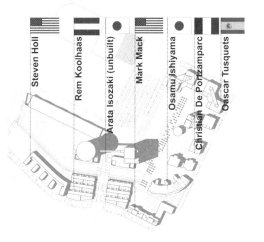

wn by Hao Wu.

Steven Holl
Rem Koolhaas
Arata Isozaki (unbuilt)
Mark Mack
Osamu Ishiyama
Christian De Portzamparc
Oscar Tusquets

Diller Scofidio + Renfro

Slither Housing
GIFU
2000

Source: Diller Scofidio + Renfro.

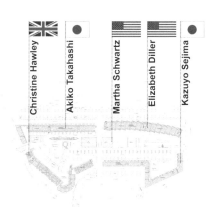

Source: Diller Scofidio + Renfro.

Christine Hawley
Akiko Takahashi
Martha Schwartz
Elizabeth Diller
Kazuyo Sejima

---

ged Space is part of Nexus World Housing, a commer-
 development in Fukuoka intended to create more
ign diversity in Japanese housing. Slither is part of the
agata public housing complex in Gifu meant to diversify
 only designs but designers, fore-fronting Elizabeth
er alongside an all-female cast. Both draw on Japanese
ition to combat the standardized planning of modern
sing practices.
Andrew Colopy

Sources

G.F. Helfrich and William Whitaker, ed., *Crafting a Modern World: Architecture and Design of Antonin and Noémi Raymond* ceton NJ: Princeton Architectural Press, 2006). sing for the United States Embassy Staff in Tokyo, Japan,"

Architectural Record 116 (Sep 1954).
Ann Waswo, *Housing in Postwar Japan: A Social History* (London: RoutledgeCurzon, 2002).
Ann Waswo, "Housing Culture," *Modern Japanese Culture*. Ed. Yoshio Sugimoto (Cambridge: Cambridge University Press, 2009).
Arata Isozaki, "Nexus World," *Japan Architect* (Oct 1991).
Arata Isozaki "Kitagata Apartment Reconstruction Project, Gifu," *Dialogue* (Sep 2000).
Jane C. Loeffler, *The Architecture of Diplomacy* (Princeton NJ: Princeton Architectural Press, 1998).
Toshihiko Kimura, "On the Structure of the United States Embassy Housing Development in Tokyo," *Japan Architect* 58 (Sep 1983).
Harry Weese, "Image Recollected," *Japan Architect* 58 (Sep 1983).

2000

Raymond

Average unit area: 635 ft² (59 m²)

Two-level duplex apartments are single-loaded, permitting cross ventilation, with floor-to-ceiling glazing, balconies, and a secondary servant access . *Source: Architectural Record.*

An American Suburb In Tokyo

Raymond's Embassy Housing consists of two seven-story apartment blocks oriented with southern views and units arranged hierarchically: efficiencies at the base, duplexes on top. The embassy staff who lived there criticized the apartments as too small and too public; they resented that their belongings didn't fit and were particularly unhappy with the small beds designed to Japanese standards. Weese answered the call for more and larger units, creating two types of connected townhouses at the site's perimeter and three apartment towers within. The townhomes, many with interior courtyards, were more private. Their larger size allowed for additional differentiated rooms, including a breakfast room, study, and garage. Within the towers, units span two levels with entries on alternating floors arranged along a diagonal corridor—strategies to increase privacy among residents, effectively suburbanizing the towers.

Weese

Average unit area: 2,715 ft² (252 m²)

Fourth Floor

Third Floor

Second Floor

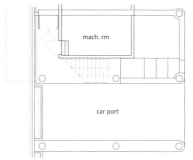

First Floor

Mitsui Townhouse. *Drawn by Yao Xia & Yu Xin.*

verage unit area: 1,235 ft^2 (115 m^2)

Average unit area: 570 ft^2 (53 m^2)

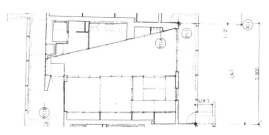

n of unit I2 West. *Source: Steven Holl Architects.*

Plan of typical unit. *Source: Diller Scofidio + Renfro.*

Units slip in both plan and section, providing a frontal entry and each at a different elevation relative to the next. *Source: Diller Scofidio + Renfro.*

ume of units shift in both plan and section.
rce: Steven Holl Architects.

kan Dwellings

aymond and Weese exported familiar US housing
idards and adapted them to a Japanese context, Holl
DS+R instead imported diversity into Japan through
identity of US architects. Both projects were attempts
he part of Isozaki to generate new urban spatial
ditions and architectural variation in contrast to the
ntless repetition of typical Japanese postwar apart-
t blocks.

Void Space/Hinged Space Housing is a five-story
meter block with a series of large voids facing south,
rior meditative spaces flooded with water at the second
r that connect to a corresponding set of play areas
hildren on grade to the north. The remaining volume is
ed into twenty-eight dwellings, each shifting vertically
laterally to define a variable set of interior spaces within.

Slither Housing is comprised of fifteen stacks of
s, seven high, each rotated 1.5 degrees from the next to
uce a subtle curvature over the building's length.

Each stack slips laterally one meter against the next
to produce a frontally approached entry while also
slipping vertically one step, so that each unit occu-
pies a unique position within the overall elevation
and the building gradually tilts up along its length.

Both projects are a departure from Raymond
and Weese's Embassy Housing, abandoning the free
plan in favor of a differentiated floor plate. For Holl,
this strategy occurs at the scale of the domestic interior; for Diller, at the scale of the unit. One produces a
terraced series of rooms; the other, of dwellings. Not
unlike the genkan, space is first defined vertically in
relation to ground.

Source: David Leavitt Collection, The Architectural Archives,
University of Pennsylvania.

							pcs	
1	SOFA					¥ 38,000 00	26	
	SOFA BED					54,000 00	32	54,000 00 24
	SOFA					48,000 00	1	48,000 00 1
	SEAT					37,500 00	1	37,500 00 1
2	TEA TABLE	8,500 00	60	8,500 00	26			
	COFFEE TABLE	9,700 00	1	9,700 00	1			
3	ARM CHAIR	18,100 00	135	18,100 00	117			
	ARM CHAIR					28,000 00	4	28,000 00 4
4	FOOT STOOL	7,300 00	16	7,300 00	22			
5	DINING CHAIR WITH ARM					8,500 00	322	

Interior with custom furniture, project furniture schedule.
Source: Raymond Collection, The Architectural Archives,
University of Pennsylvania.

Interiors with FBO-provided standard American furniture.
Source: Shinkenchiku-sha.

Fixing Function

Japan maintained a floor-sitting culture into the twentieth century with flexible multi-purpose spaces defined by tatami and fusuma so that one might eat and sleep in the same room. Space was, however, differentiated by family structure with the most prominent room reserved for the patriarch. Foreign (and especially US) influence contributed to the rapid transition to a chair-sitting culture and more egalitarian family structure.

The introduction of tables and chairs for dining and raised beds for sleeping, along with the new demands of privacy imposed by the model of a nuclear family, contributed to the increasingly fixed and functionalized division of the interior while exerting pressure on the overall dwelling size. The division became most explicit as the Japan Housing Corporation began building urban apartments, or danchi, just two years after the Raymond Embassy

Housing opened, using a model known as "nLDK." The government standard, implemented in 1955, mandated a fixed number of sleeping rooms, a western style kitchen and dinning area, and eventually a space for living. Yet, even in Raymond's Embassy Housing, a space for American Raymond maintains some spatial flexibility with sliding plywood partitions, and he personally designed the furnishings, along with his wife and partner Noémi, using traditional Japanese proportions and craftsmanship. Weese's interiors, by contrast, are expansive volumes filled with thick furnishings that were imported by the US Office of Foreign Building Operations. Swinging doors, modest apertures, and interior courts all give the sense of a more inward-oriented and private interior.

ged Space" interior variability: closed, open.
rce: Steven Holl Architects.

Interior variability: closed, open
Source: Diller Scofidio + Renfro.

uma Lofts

the Holl and DS+R projects space is first defined
-ically, not unlike the genkan, that space is made
-rally variable through the reconstitution of the flexible
-anese interior defined not by walls but by sliding
-ens or fusuma.

Holl's "hinged space" is fashioned from a series
-rticulated and multi-colored wood panels that swing,
-, and slide to capture an ever-changing variety of activ-
-s and lighting conditions. Quite literally these panels
-onstruct the walls of fixed rooms that engendered the
-K standards and create, if not an entirely open inte-
a series of variable interior rooms, `while maintaining
-now-familiar triangulation of kitchen, dining, and
-g spaces.

At Slither, a central cone of space expanding
-u entry to balcony is bracketed by sliding panels of

wood and metal-framed plastic. The former conceal a
wedge of fixed service spaces (kitchen, bath, and storage)
while the latter define a set of tatami-proportioned volumes
that can be configured as a series of multi-purpose rooms
or expanded to a number of larger configurations. Of all
the projects, Slither perhaps most closely recalls the traditional Japanese interior and represents the greatest departure from the mid-century minimal housing standards.

Despite the use, whether literal or interpretive, of
tatami and fusuma (required by the governing authority
for public housing) the interiors of both projects are more
often compared with the open, flexible spaces of New York
lofts (and therefore with the culture of the project architects) than with the traditional Japanese housing models
that they reinterpret.

Source: Architectural Record.

Stucco facade with large black neoprene joints to prevent damage from earthquakes. *Source: Architecture magazine.*

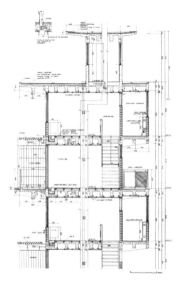

Detail building section. *Source: David Leavitt Collection, The Architectural Archives, University of Pennsylvania.*

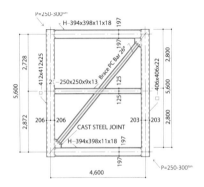

Structural detail. *Drawn by Wassef Dabbousii.*

Concrete Inside & Out

Raymond synthesized modern and vernacular building practices in Japan, introducing concrete innovation to a culture where wood structures had predominated. As the country's first multi-story reinforced concrete building, his Embassy Housing marks an important development in the postwar urbanization made possible by structures resistant to fire, earthquakes, and typhoons that today help make Tokyo the world's largest metropolis.

Raymond's Embassy Housing is a box-frame structure of shear party walls that act as vertical cantilevers to resist seismic events, with floors and transverse ribs that form a stiffening membrane. Raymond's attention to the tectonic language and exposed concrete finish, with formwork crafted using traditional Japanese carpentry, preserves a legacy of wood construction. Unlike the closed street wall common in urban Japanese residences of the time, the facade is free and open, with expansive views to the surrounding landscape and city beyond.

The Weese project too was innovative, using a adapted form of the box frame concrete structure at the perimeter townhomes. The steel towers are novel in the use of higher-strength concrete reinforcing steel bars as diagonal bracing. Despite their different structural syste the facade expression of Weese's two buildings are iden cal. Weese himself has attributed the aesthetic to his d observations of Japanese architecture and the half-timbe and plaster houses of Europe. He suppressed an exter reading of the buildings' heavy structure, using stucco separated by oversized black neoprene joints that limi cracking but also recall the linear wood tracery of Euro pean half-timber facades. The visually striking compositi with modest fenestration contributes to a sense of inwardly-focused and private dwellings.

posing facades facing into raised water garden.
...urce: Steven Holl Architects.

Personal effects expressive of the building inhabitants.
Source: Michael Moran.

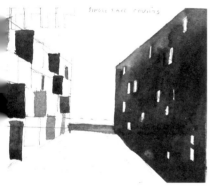

...ercolor rendering of the two opposing water garden facades.
...rce: Steven Holl.

Slightly concaved, Slither hugs the garden designed by
Martha Schwartz. *Source: Michael Moran.*

...lic Intimacy

...h Holl and DS+R sustain the legacy of concrete
...ctures. In contrast, however, to the uniform expres-
... of Weese and Raymond's exteriors, Holl and DS+R
...sent more nuanced and layered facades.

For Holl, each orientation receives a different
...tment. The street edge is the most private, with a
...-stained concrete finish and small openings only at
...corners. Within the void spaces, one side contains
...er window openings, with an irregular composition of thin
... that eliminate reference to any individual dwelling
...right). The facing side has more generous fenes-
...on, surrounded with bright aluminum scribed to an
...osed and undulating floorplate, which clearly demar-
...s the dwelling within (top left). Most units are
...nted inwardly, away from the street, facing onto a
...er garden and its shimmering reflection upon the
...e solid facade beyond, while also peeking back to a
...nd garden and the more open neighboring units.

DS+R's project has a similar structural box
frame organization to that of the original Embassy Housing,
though terraced along the building's length. But where
Raymond lays bare the interior, Slither slinks from its perforated metallic skin. A more private dwelling is laminated
with a semi-public space, with balconies to the street and
the main circulation along the interior courtyard of the
larger complex. Activities at the balconies and the interior
are delicately screened by the perforated skin, while
the same surface is used to dry laundry along the corridor,
displaying personal effects to those in the garden below.

In both Void Space/Hinged Space and Slither, the
most expressive facade doesn't terminate the building
but extends into the garden beyond. Neither is an object
in a landscape, but a mediation between a constructed
exterior environment, the garden, and an expressive space
of dwelling.

THE U.S. TECHNICAL COOPERATION PROGRAM*

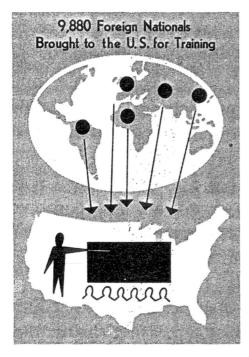

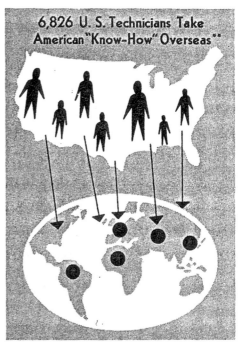

1053	EUROPE	99
610	AFRICA	656
2703	NEAR EAST AND SO. ASIA	1827
3385	FAR EAST	2527
2129	LATIN AMERICA	1061

*Data cover participants financed under fiscal year 1959 program and technicians estimated as of June 30, 1959.

**Includes 227 field complement and 395 domestic program staff not assigned by region and 34 in the worldwide malaria program.

The imagined reach of the US Technical Program. From The Dramatic Story of Helping Others to Help Themselves (United States Technical Cooperation, 1959). *Source: UN Archives, New York.*

IJLAL MUZAFFAR

"The World on Sale"[1]: Architectural Exports and Construction of Access

The Immigration and Nationality Act of 1965 signed by President Lyndon Johnson opened the doors to professionals as well as higher education students across the global South.[2] Driven in large part by the Cold War urgency to spread American influence in the decolonizing world, the new act paid dividends, boosting US economic growth with money and talent. This trajectory, which has come to be known as the "brain drain," continues to set a new apex every year. In 2013, a record number of international students, nearly 820,000, up 20 percent from 2012, arrived in the US, pumping upwards of $24 billion into the economy.[3]

What is surprising is that the tide of brain drain has continued to rise despite the increasing costs of US education and requirements for immigration.[4] From the great number of variables — changing Cold War political dynamics, global economic recalibrations, emerging pockets of wealth, and global mobility among them — that could explain this complex global equation, one stands in striking correlation with this surprising trend: the rising costs of partaking in the American "dream" is tied to the cheapening of "reality" elsewhere. As the requirements for participating in the American socio-economic setup become harder to fulfill, the requirements for intervening in comparable capacities elsewhere become simpler.[5] If at first it was the United Nations (UN), United States Agency for International Development (USAID), and World Bank consultants parachuting into different countries on month-long stints, today, thousands of American college students participate in week-long "development" projects in Third World contexts, from villages to urban slums.[6] It's a chance to see the world, experience "diversity," and pad the resume.[7] If the East was a career, the Third World is now an internship.[8]

These two trajectories are not commonly connected, nor is the possibility entertained that one produces the conditions for the other. Development projects driven by a comparative world vision, ensuring the expert's ease, hide the historical constraints specific to each context, perpetuating Third World conditions that stimulate human and capital flight to the First World.

Architecture has been central to this flattening of the world and the access and drain cycle it sustains. Since the inauguration of Harry Truman's 1949 Point IV program that extended American "technical assistance" to the decolonizing world in light of the emerging Cold War,

(1)
"The World on Sale" is a slogan used by *Condé Nast Traveler* magazine. It's a variation on "The World is on Sale" used earlier by British Airways for its limited time promotions.

(2)
The new act shifted the immigration criteria to professional and educational categories, ending the immigration quota system that had favored Northern and Western European countries based on race and nationality. Johnson and his advisors, however, were not just looking past racial prejudice. They were also focusing on the "skilled labor reserves" in the decolonizing world, a potential work force which the Soviet Union had as much an eye as the US. For a concurrent evaluation, see "Effects of the Immigration Act of 1965 on Selected Population Characteristics of Immigrants to the United States" by Dr. Charles Keely in *Demography* vol. 8 no. 2, 1971.

(3)
See "Record Number of Foreign Students Flocking to US," in *The Wall Street Journal*, Nov 11, 2013; and "Record Number Of International Students Attend US Colleges" on NPR, Nov 11, 2013. Similar trends were previously reported in "Foreign students flock to the US," by the *Boston Globe* on July 5, 2008.

1949

2014

architecture and design have served as critical alibis to make the strange familiar. Modern architecture and urban planning—in all their forms, from built projects to feasibility reports—produced such categories as the "community," the "poor," the "migrant," the "neighborhood," the "city," or the "village" that made complex conditions accessible to the expert's mode of operation, while hiding the differences that challenged its legitimacy. Architecture has been a specific export that renders the ground on which it is imported neutral, as if waiting outside of modern power structures for modernization to arrive.

This role was performed once again at the Museum of Modern Art (MoMA) in New York, where *Small Scale, Big Change*—on view from October 3, 2010, through January 3, 2011—featured architectural projects from around the world that were carried out with a critical eye for "sustainable local resources" and "participatory" engagement.[9] Words like "community" and "the poor" appear innumerous times in the exhibition catalog in relationship to different projects. Yet their meaning remains the same: community everywhere represents a willing group in "need," waiting for an opportunity to come together and improve its collective condition. The architects provide this chance and the community flourishes. There are no ghosts of past political conflicts or injustices, historical social hierarchies, or existing contesting interests, only shared "needs." A community in Burkina Faso appears to possess the same characteristics as a community in Bangladesh.

But this apparent simplification is itself not so simple. Once dehistoricized, a sub-Saharan African community haunted by the divisive legacy of Indirect Rule during the colonial period[10] appears similar to the one marked by de facto exclusion of tribal populations from colonial and national politics in South Asia. And that is not all; there is also a certain common future projected onto them. The communities also appear comparable because they have been endorsed with a shared potential: a universal, creative, entrepreneurial spirit possessed by their members that equates involvement with empowerment.

As Barry Bergdoll states in the introduction to the *Small Scale, Big Change* catalog, "[these projects] have a new model of *empowerment* of local communities that goes beyond the consultative models developed a generation ago. Their conception of design extends beyond undertaking a building or a site plan to devising procedures in place, and to creating new models of *involvement* for local populations."[11] (emphasis added)

The site of these new projects is the inhabitant, not the building. The primary project goal is in fact capturing the inhabitant's potential by setting these procedures in place. For Andres Lepik, the show's curator, "The building of the school [designed by Diébédo Francis Kéré at Gando, Burkina Faso was truly a community endeavor with villagers supplying most of the labor. Some of the workers who trained in the production of clay bricks and the construction of the school have since found work as skilled laborers at other building sites."[12] The project turns community members from "unskilled" to "skilled" labor, opening doors to opportunities elsewhere. This coupling of training and empowerment, with the

④
For an expansive account of Cold War contestations and its effects on Third World political makeup, see Mike Mason's seminal book, *Development and Disorder: A History of the Third World Since 1945* (Hanover, NH University Press of New England, 1997).

⑤
This asymmetry has been shaped under the umbrella of what Arturo Escobar has famously termed the "development discourse," a discursive arrangement marking a "new era of understanding and managing the world affairs" that is enacted through international institutions such as the UN, the World Bank, the IMF, the Ford Foundation, and their various national and NGO collaborators. This framework, Escobar argues, broke the complex reality of decolonization into a manageable knowledge structure of "client categories," such as the poor, Third World women, peasants, and migrants, each with a unique set of deficiencies that could be fulfilled with particular scientific prescriptions and measured against particular project goals and national plans. Equally shared by the various Third World governments, global NGOs, First and Second World powers, and international institutions, this framework has constituted, Escobar asserts, "a regime of representation" that has held reality hostage in its shifting yet congruent categories for over half a century. See Arturo Escobar, *Encountering Development: The Making and Unmaking of the Third World* (Princeton, NJ: Princeton University Press, 1997).

⑥
This trend is augmented further still by the countless

"Community participation" at the school designed by Diébédo Francis Kéré at Gando, Burkina Faso. From Small Scale, Big Change, Moma (2010). *Source: Diébédo Francis Kéré.*

At the "METI-Handmade School" designed by Ana Heringer and Eike Roswaq in Rudrapur, Bangladesh. From Small Scale, Big Change, Moma (2010). *Source: Kurt Hoerbst.*

two poles connected by the subject's creative agency, underpins the very idea of the "community" before the project even begins. The project provides the missing link of an assumed, untapped potential. A similar potential was assumed for the Bangladeshi community members who helped build the "handmade" school designed by Austrian architect Ana Heringer in the remote village of Rudrapur,. "Aside from two craftsmen from Germany and several students from Linz," Lepik reminds us, "all the work was done by unskilled laborers from Rudrapur, with the idea that they would gain useful experience in cob construction."[13]

A presumed dormant creativity forms the common dominator between groups across different contexts that allows them to be compared to each other in a single sentence and called by the same appellation: "community."

Now, I might be accused of not recognizing the creative spirit of poor Third World communities, of taking an elitist and patronizing stance by reasserting the expertise of the expert from above, of being blind to the initiatives from below. That is not what I am arguing. What I am arguing is quite different: The projection of a certain kind of creativity onto the inhabitants allows us to ignore, erase from view and under-standing, the structural and historical limitations that bind them, no matter how creative they are. These limitations are different in each context and unevenly mark the community members we would like to celebrate. If we do not pay attention to this uneven historical ground, then we become complicit in maintaining the exclusions, the hierarchies, and the power structures that exist in each context.

Let's take the example of Burkina Faso. The rural areas in the country form a fraught arena with a long history of strong French neo-imperialist involvement, favoring a minority rule after independence in 1945, that gave rise to a highly contested center-driven state power structure, complicated further by periods of militia infiltration from Côte d'Ivoire. Held as a forced-labor reserve before decolonization, the countryside is marked by ethinicization and religious divisions that were historically shaped through restrictions on the movement of different

studio classes taken by most of the 154 NAAB and 322 NASAD accredited architecture, art, and design, programs in conjunction with global NGOs to different parts of the Third World.

⑦ A fraternity of young college students/development experts in Africa looking for "fun" and "experience" form the background of Lionel Shriver's short story "Kilifi Creek" in The New Yorker, Nov. 25, 2013, 110–17.

⑧ The phrase, "the East is a career," was famously uttered by Benjamin Disraeli, the hawkish British prime minister (in office from 1874–80); it was equally famously evaluated and situated in the discursive context of the culture of imperialism by Edward Said in Orientalism (Vintage Books, 1978).

⑨ See the exhibition catalogue by the show's curator, Andres Lepik, Small Scale, Big Change: New Architectures of Social Engagement, with an introduction by Barry Bergdoll (New York: Museum of Modern Art, 2010).

Core house in Ghana,
finished by self-help

Hassan Fathy's New Gourna project near
Luxor, Egypt (1945 to 1948), shown in UN
publications as an example of modernization
without the shock of change. From the United
Nations' Manual on Self-Help Housing (1964).
Source: the UN Archives, NY.

Core housing without a "core" in the Gold Coast (Ghana), proposed by
Charles Abrams and Otto Koenigsberger. From the United Nations' Manual on
Self-Help Housing (1964). *Source: the UN Archives, NY.*

groups during indirect colonial rule.[14] Though mediated by linguistic overlaps, the countryside still constitutes a strata of highly uneven access to resources, elevated particularly by, as political scientists James Fearon and David Laitin put it, a "time-bomb in the agricultural colonization of the west and southwest by Mossi migrants that began in the drought years of the 1970s."[15] Why are these cursory details, this slightest texture of political divisions and hierarchies, excluded from the project descriptions, subsumed under the flattening and compartitive developmentalist language of "skilled" and "unskilled labor," "community," and the "poor"?

These historical dimensions of tradition and community are absent in the exhibition not because they are buried deep in archives. They do not surface in the discussion because they would contradict the particular profile of the community presented here. The history invoked in the projects is a phenomenal history that dwells on questions of materiality, sensuality, and the "balance" between the inhabitant's cultural body (incidentally, always male but never declared as such) and the environment. On this phenomenal plane, differential hierarchies of gender and race, of class and tribe, can be subsumed under leveling assertions of "basic needs" and innate desires, including the desire to improve one's shelter. It avoids framing the inhabitant as a "noble savage," locked in a permanent, primitive, static embrace with nature, yet still forecloses the possibility of raising questions of politics, agency, and access to imagination. She is bound to history through the logic of her body and sensuality. All discussions of culture and tradition, of the suitability of materials and techniques invoke this sensual and habitual dimension. This is, in the main, the moral undergirding of most discussions on sustainability: a phenomenal understanding of the

(10)
For a history of the British, and to a lesser extent French, ideology of Indirect Rule through an oppressive structure of Native Authorities and laws, ironically constructed in the name of preserving "local culture," see Mahmood Mamdani's famous study *Citizen and Subject: Contemporary Africa and the Legacy of Late Colonialism* (Princeton, NJ: Princeton University Press, 1996).

(11)
Small Scale, Big Change, 2010, *op. cit.,* 10. Bergdoll goes on to argue these projects provide a model of learning from below. "One important lesson to draw from these architects as they work against both the forces and assumptions of globalization, is that the flow of knowledge can move in multiple directions, that the new perceptions about the needs of a severely challenged developed world can be found in practices developed in the underdeveloped world,

inhabitant's body and her dynamic connection with the environment. Here, architecture is a restorative apparatus, brought in to restore the balance that modernity promised but never delivered.

The sheen of this phenomenal history obscures the fiction of a traditional community at work. Lepik delves at length into Hassan Fathy's well-known New Gourna Village (1945–48) near West Luxor, Egypt, as a precedent for a community-driven architectural innovation based on traditional aesthetics and building techniques.[16] But New Gourna was also a project where community and tradition were invoked to displace rural populations from tourism sites and to carry out the modernizing agenda of an oppressive state apparatus and its international sponsors. Its images regularly appeared in development publications as an example of a carrot-and-stick approach to modernization. Lepik's introduction carefully elides these details. The majority of the villagers abandoned the project despite repeated forced relocation to the site.[17] The project's shortcomings didn't result from Fathy's failure to articulate some true "local traditions." It was a failure because the "local" and the "traditional" were themselves misnomers, projecting unity on a diverse and contested sphere that resisted such unification.[18]

If tradition empowers, liberates, and enables, it also kills, oppresses, and excludes. And these processes happen simultaneously. We have to account for the trajectories that shape a particular situation every time we celebrate traditional practices and community empowerment.

The comparative mode of celebrating community, grounded in an innate and phenomenal entrepreneurial creativity of its Third World subject, has a particular history in the postwar era. It is helpful to chart this trajectory to see how this subject was carefully assembled, piece by piece, to support a new model of expertise and intervention.

Thin Air

In the postwar era, architecture was employed to capture this strange yet commonly invoked protomodern subject to resolve a particular question: How should Third World developmental modernization be inaugurated in the absence of capital? Everyone has an innate capacity to construct a shelter, the premise went. Provide the right framework and the inhabitant would do the rest. Architecture would be the origin of development. The desire to construct one's own shelter would summon modern values as well modernization and profits out of thin air.

And thin air is what we see at the center of Charles Abrams and Otto Koenigsberger's "core" self-help houses proposed in Africa and Asia. Abrams, the chairman of the Urban Planning Program at Columbia University and the sometime rent commissioner for the State of New York, was instrumental in passing major anti-segregation housing laws in the US and consulted regularly for the UN and USAID in the 1950s and 1960s.[19] He was joined on many missions by Otto Koenigsberger who, before becoming the director of the Tropical Architecture Department at the Architectural Association (AA) in London in the1950s, had spent considerable time in India as the chief architect and planner of the

particularly as the issue of appropriate technology becomes the mantra for architectural practice everywhere, from the villages of Burkina Faso to the five boroughs of New York City." Ibid., 10–11. One might then be entitled to ask, why does the discussion keep locating such initiatives within the history of European and American "avant-garde" architecture, from the nineteenth-century's Saint-Simonians to Henri Labrouste? The knowledge from the "undeveloped" world remains unnamed, or acquires a name through developmental categories of the poor, partners in development, members of the community, etc. These different forms of address speak to the different status of the knowledge being compared: conscious and conceptual on one side, behavioral and communal on the other side. This exchange could have been described through different nomenclature, identifying the political divisions and the activists that mark poverty as complex and contested a sphere of existence as avant-garde musings. The only named voice from the underdeveloped world in Bergdoll's essay is Sheela Patel, the chair of the board of Shack/Slum Dwellers International, quickly lifted from the group's website to support the claim of knowledge exchange with the presence of a native informant. Couldn't the history of these projects be told from a different perspective in which the architects and their work represented here appear as contested figures, being deployed in multiple directions by the political undercurrents and interests on the ground?

⑫
Ibid., 34.

state of Mysore before the country gained its independence in 1947.[20] Koenigsberger, together with others at the AA, coauthored the famous *Manual of Tropical Housing and Building* that remains a central feature of curriculums in Third World architecture schools.[21]

If the ingenuity of the inhabitant is invoked through mud and brick walls in the recent MoMA exhibition, Abrams and Koenigsberger invoked it in the roof. For them, standardized housing approaches held onto a preconceived notion that a house be finished before occupation. In their proposed core house model,[22] however, the sponsoring agency developed lots with only a plinth and a roof — together with elemental services such as water, sewage, and electricity — so that the sites were inhabitable before the houses' completion.[23] The inhabitants lived on site during the remaining construction process, erecting walls and other enclosures as resources permitted.

Even though the house had no physical core, for Abrams and Koenigsberger, it was still appropriate to call it a core house because it spoke to the fundamental moment when architecture brought the inhabitant into the discourse of individuation and family. The moment was not written in the language of form but in the language of formalization, the realm of legislation and law. The house with only a roof defined the inhabitant as an individual in legal terms, binding him into circuits of modern finance, before the house. As the house was built, the argument went, the inhabitant became further embedded in it, generating the basis of a modern economy. Architecture was the vehicle of the inhabitant's formalization into law.

For Abrams and Koenigsberger, the process of legal formalization was very different from the one carried out by selling a completed house to an individual. The latter model required the presence of not only a fully functioning building industry but also a financial and legal setup supporting it; the individual, as a legal entity, needed to precede the house. In the development context, however, the presence of a working financial system and a regulatory state and civil society could not be taken for granted. Development was a problem of construction of these economic and institutional apparatuses. The core house was a kind of short-circuiting. It allowed what was to be the effect of economic and civil society, the individual, to emerge as its cause. The civil society and its economic structures emerged after the inhabitant entered the house as an effect of inhabitation itself.

There is, however, a sleight of hand in this brilliant reformulation. The house without a core defined not only what the inhabitant would become after he entered the house, an individual defined in terms of law and civil society, but also what he was before he had entered this house. He, and very soon she, was defined as a peculiar traditional being; not a premodern, primitive one, but a protomodern one, a prototype of his later self, very much in the manner of the members of the community in the recent MoMA exhibition. He himself possessed a core quality: the ability to turn scarcity into productivity. The house with only a roof was a site of scarcity. When faced with a wall-less house, this protomodern traditional

(13)
Ibid., 12.

(14)
Deep divisions persisted at independence. The precolonial ruling regime, the Mossi, were marginalized by cosmopolitan Dylas Muslim traders who, in the colonial period, were allowed by the French to travel across the territory. Political divisions also abound: the western tribes favored a larger federation of West Africa including alliances with *Rassemblement Démocratique Africain* (RDA) in the Côte d'Ivoire. These aspirations later shifted to forming a federation with Mali, but the pressure from the residing French high commissioner quelled both. See James Fearon and David Laitin's "Ethnicity, Insurgency, and Civil War," in *The American Political Science Review*, February 2003 (Issue 01), 75–90. Also see their "random narrative" draft paper (July 5, 2006) on Burkina Faso that constitutes a larger project of "statistical findings in regard to civil war onsets" at Stanford University: http://www.stanford.edu/group/ethnic/Random%20Narratives/BurkinaRN2.4.pdf (accessed January 15, 2014).

(15)
Ibid., 5–6. For an analysis of gendered asymmetries of access to land, see Ambreena Manji, *The Politics of Land Reform in Africa*. (London and New York: Zed Books, 2006).

(16)
Andres Lepik, "Building on Society," in *Small Scale, Big Change* (2010), *op. cit.*, 13–14.

(17)
For this other history, see Panayiota Pyla, "Hassan Fathy Revisited: Postwar Discourses on Science, Development, and Vernacular Architecture,

subject was provoked by an innate need to finish the structure and give birth to his modern self.

Seeing scarcity as a sign of resourcefulness, rather than just scarcity, emerged as a response to a fundamental conundrum that haunted all initial theories of inaugurating economic and social development. Unlike the famous Marshall Plan, which had subsidized Europe's postwar economic rehabilitation with some $16 billion, development theorists imagined that Third World economies would industrialize with only technical advice. On the one hand, the Third World subject was presumed outside of modernity, to justify the need for development; on the other hand, he was defined as already possessing sufficient capitalist rationality to become a self-mobilizing engine of development in the absence of capital investment. How could the development subject be explained as being both inside and outside of modernity? How could it appear as both its effect and its cause at the same time?

This conundrum, this aporia, was resolved by schemes such as core housing that framed precapitalist scarcity as itself a source of productive resourcefulness. The subject was seen as an entrepreneur. The root of this entrepreneurship was scarcity itself. Bad housing, terrible living conditions, and slums created an incentive and drive to improve one's conditions. This Third World subject needed mere amounts of capital to lift the restrictions placed on his inherent individual capacity to enter capitalist production. The core house was the stage for this entrepreneurship. It did not place any restrictions of plan or form on the entrepreneur. In fact, it provided an incentive for him to take loans, find time, build himself and with others' help, and generate demand for a building and financial industry. The core house was both similar and different from Marc Antoine Laugier's "primitive hut." Well loved by architects, his primitive hut marked an emergence from nature into culture. The core house was also a marker of emergence into culture, modern culture, but the nature that it emerged from already possessed cyborg qualities. It was a nature with a keen eye for profit.

Thick Sense

This entrepreneur would soon become the imagined unit of the community. If Abrams and Koenigsberger saw placing the roof above the inhabitant's head as a way to capture him as a subject of development, Bernard Rudofsky, the Austrian architect and émigré to New York, was busy formulating the floor beneath his feet as a starting point of modernization. As Felicity Scott has argued, Rudofsky, in his obsessive focus on the feet and footwear in history in the MoMA exhibition *Are Clothes Modern?* (November 1944 to March 1945), sought to present the feet as an alternate form of "untransposable" fetishism that resisted hosting displaced Freudian desires or entering the circuits of commodity fetishism through which they pulsed.[24] The feet stood *for* themselves; desirable, not because they represented something else, but because of the immediacy of sensual and tactile contact they afforded with the ground. The feet constituted a fetishized object that formed a self-sufficient whole even in its partiality.

Journal of Architectural Education, 2007 Feb., v. 60, n. 3, 28–39. Many of these criteria are evident in Fathy's own writings. See Hassan Fathy's *Report on Egyptian Village Housing, Building Materials, and Methods of Construction to Administrator, Technical Cooperation Administration, Department of State* (Cambridge, MA: Arthur Little, 1952); and *Architecture for the Poor* (Chicago: The University of Chicago Press, 1973).

(18)
The local inhabitants preferred diverse styles representing upward mobility and modernization, from aluminum roofs to concrete walls, and shunned mud construction, no matter how sustainable it was deemed by the architect and the national and international institutions involved. See Hana Taragan, "Architecture in Fact and Fiction: The Case of New Gourna Village in Upper Egypt," in *Muqarnas: An Annual on the Visual Culture of the Islamic World*, XVI, 169–78.

(19)
Abrams' US career is described in detail by Scott Henderson in *Housing and the Democratic Ideal: The Life and Thought of Charles Abrams* (New York: Columbia University Press, 2000).

(20)
Abrams and Koenigsberger went on joint missions to the Gold Coast (Ghana), Pakistan, Philippines, Singapore, and Nigeria. The reports for these missions were published by the UN: *Report on Housing in the Gold Coast*, prepared for the government of the Gold Coast by Charles Abrams, Vladimir Bodiansky, Otto H.G. Koenigsberger (New York: United Nations Technical Assistance Administration, 1956); *A Housing Program for Pakistan with Special*

Cherrapunji, India (above), and "moving day in Guinea" (below, left). Reed roofs along Tigris and Euphrates, Iraq, (below, middle) and the "air-conditioners of Hyderabad Sind," Pakistan (below, right). From Bernard Rudofsky, Architecture Without Architects (1964). *Source: India and Guinea images, Dr. Palis collection de Musee l'Homme. Source: Gavin Maxwell. Source: Hyderabad image, Martin Hurliman.*

Even though Rudofsky would end up rehearsing the Freudian fetish he so detested, he would tacitly secure the Third World as a site of the possibility of that desired unmediated, sensual contact with the environment. In his next MoMA exhibition, *Architecture without Architects*, in 1964, a series of photographs from Cherrapunji, India, and rural Guinea, Africa, depicted roofs traveling to their future sites on the inhabitants' heads. The body literally stands in for the architecture that is to follow, forming a site of the origin of a sensually driven exchange with the environment celebrated in the exhibition. The sensual contact that could only be realized as a fetishized moment in the First World, swells to include the entire body as a continuum fused with its surroundings. Turning walls into roofs (Iraq), air into interiors (Pakistan), architecture only attempted to fill the space of this body and the sensual immediacy it embodied.

In seeing in the Third World body itself an embedded architecture of untransposable fetishism, Rudofsky identifies in it another history and another future, a combination that could not only redeem the history of First World capitalism, but also change its trajectory in the Third. The Third World is imagined at the threshold of capitalism, erasing the long history of how it had already been thoroughly embedded within structures of globalization.

Reference to Refugee Rehabilitation, prepared for the Government of Pakistan by Charles Abrams and Otto Koenigsberger, September 14, 1957 (New York: United Nations Technical Assistance Administration, 1957); *A Housing Program for the Philippine Islands*, by Charles Abrams and Otto Koenigsberger (New York: United Nations Technical Assistance Administration, 1959).

[21]
Otto H. Koenigsberger, *Manual of Tropical Housing and Building* (London: Longman, 1974–73).

[22]
The term "core" was devised by Abrams in his *Man's Struggle for Shelter in an Urbanizing World* (Cambridge, MA: The MIT Press, 1964).

Rudofsky was not alone in imagining this threshold. From John Turner to Abrams and Koenigsberger and to Fathy, modern architects and planners differentiated between Third World "needs" and "wants." On a mission to the Philippines, Abrams and Koenigsberger argued that the biggest threat to Third World development came from within, from the attraction of unnecessary "wants" toward which the populace being newly initiated into modernity felt itself helplessly pulled. If only it could maintain its focus on its bodily needs, rather than on mental wants, spending could be channeled into investment rather than wasteful expenditure.[25] In positing the Third World body as a site of conflict between bodily needs and mental wants, Abrams, Koenigsberger, and Rudofsky summoned it as an alibi against its own beholder. Not yet fully digested into the workings of global capitalism, the sensually driven entrepreneurship embedded within this body's depths kept alive the promise of another capitalism for the world. This body also props up the promise of "sustainability" in MoMA's *Small Scale, Big Change*. [26]

Rarefied Ethics

Defining the Third World subject of development as a protomodern being could also seem commendable. What could be wrong with seeing in poor populations the potential of new and "sustainable" ways of living? The story in these images, from Abrams and Koenisberger, Rudofsky, and *Small Scale, Big Change* at MoMA, however, comes at the cost of erasing historical constraints. They present architecture as an alibi, creating a framework in which different historical conditions can be compared (India and Guinea, Burkina Faso, and Bangladesh) and seen as signs of the same creativity. This comparative framework allowed Abrams and Koenigsberger to imagine core houses taking any and all forms once the roof was up — from modular one-room houses expanding to multiple room configurations, to round mud houses multiplying to form chains of multiple units — yet being part of the same mix.[27] It is possible to argue that this duality, this comparable, universalizing framework built on and under what I will call sensual architecture, can serve as a medium to build solidarity. Indeed, many liberal critiques have been too quick to dismiss universals and universalization as signs of homogenization. As Anna Tsing has famously shown in her book *Friction*, universals are necessary to build solidarity across difference.[28] After all, if we do not appeal to any universal, if we do not homogenize to a certain extent, how can we have ethical discourse? Assuming a commonality is the basic condition, the necessary founding violence, of an ethical, empathetic relationship that strives to see in the other an image of the self. Without this universalizing impulse, we only have exaggeration of difference and fetishization of the local. [29]

The celebration of creativity, of entrepreneurship, in sensual architecture, however, is not a universal that struggles to maintain sameness in difference and difference in solidarity. It is a universal that leaves no room to raise the question of difference. As such, it only works to create space for the expert to intervene, quickly and easily, rather than stressing

[23] See, Charles Abrams, *Man's Struggle for Shelter in an Urbanizing World* (1964), *op. cit.*, 171.

[24] Felicity Scott, "Underneath Aesthetics and Utility: The Untransposable Fetish of Bernard Rudofsky" in *Assemblage*, April 1999, n. 38, 58–89. The exhibition material was published in the book by Bernard Rudofsky, *Are Clothes Modern? An Essay on Contemporary Apparel* (Chicago: Paul Theobald, 1947).

[25] See Abrams and Koenigsberger, *A Housing Program for the Philippine Islands, by Charles Abrams and Otto Koenigsberger* (New York: United Nations Technical Assistance Administration, 1959).

[26] More recently, this argument has been made by Rem Koolhaas, who when flying over Lagos discovered, not surprisingly, under the tin roof sea, invisible entrepreneurial networks extracting value from recycling everything from garbage to used TV sets from Dubai and Moscow. In this framing too, the roof is not only a sign of shared scarcity, but also an image of untapped, brooding productivity. See Rem Koolhaas, et al, "Lagos: Harvard Project on the City," in *Mutations* (Barcelona: Actar, 2000), 651–719. A similar argument was also made by Koolhaas in "Fragments of a Lecture on Lagos" in *Undersiege: Four African Cities: Freetown, Johannesburg, Kinshasa, Lagos*, edited by O. Enwezor, C. Basualdo, U.M. Bauer, S. Ghez, S. Maharaj, M. Nash and O. Zaya. *Documenta 11: Platform 4* (Hatje, Cantz: Ostfildern-Ruit, 2004).

the need for recognizing the historical specificity and the constraints it poses in those contexts as we built solidarity.

To clarify this point, let me return to another example in the *Small Scale, Big Change* exhibition catalog, the "METI-Handmade School" in Rudrapur, Bangladesh, designed by the architects Anna Heringer and Eike Roswag.[30] The mud and bamboo school constructed with "local traditional building practices," presented as an example of sustainable design, won the coveted Aga Khan Award in 2007. The catalog heavily cites the World Bank's statistics on Bangladesh to produce a picture of local poverty and how efforts such as the school, with limited means, provide opportunities for participation and self-improvement. But one World Bank statistic that might challenge the project's claim is not quoted: fifty-two percent of Bangladesh's rural population is landless or works less than one-half acre of land.[31] World Bank privatization agenda underpinning these numbers notwithstanding, we might be able to see in these distinctions the unlikelihood of more than half the village population participating in the project.

It is easy to call these divisions, and subdivisions, a problem of Bengali tradition. Yet, there is nothing "traditional," i.e. premodern (that's the sense the term is mostly used in the catalogue), about these divisions. Tradition is a result of careful manipulation and legislation over centuries by colonial, national, and international institutions. It was the Land Settlement Act of 1871 that divided the land in Bangladesh into a hierarchical system of *zamindars* and *patnidars* for expedient tax collection, erasing the existing codes of overlapping land rights and usages.[32] The new system continued after national independence, first under the East Pakistani government and, after 1971, under the independent Bangladeshi government. For many in the fifty-two percent of that landless population, independence was not a new beginning, but a displacement, a continuation of previous oppression now on new registers.[33] An invitation to participate in the project does not eradicate these historical and systematic discriminations, only renders them more opaque. In the MoMA exhibition narrative, this complexity and its historical construction and continuation have no place. The village community is presented as a homogeneous and creative mass collectively benefiting from the school's presence, and the school serves as a model for community improvement across the country, and by extension, across the Third World.

Surprisingly, the exhibition catalogue defends this erasure of historical complexity. It defends architecture's limitations in the face of larger systemic inequalities, especially those inequalities whose legacy reaches back to colonialism. The architect and curator in this example argue that projects like the school are "architectural acupuncture," relieving pain and providing some relief while we diagnose a larger ailment. Projects of this scale, we are told, never claimed to solve the land distribution problem. They simply claim that we should do something now, tap into people's creativity to improve their condition, instead of waiting for those larger inequalities to be addressed. Yet this view does not take into account that the way these stopgap solutions

(27)
Constantin Doxiadis also employed this strategy designing low-income housing in Pakistan (at both Karachi and Islamabad) and Iraq. There, too, the roof and floor were summoned as armatures to guide the naturally driven, sensually grounded entrepreneurial qualities of the Third World subject. The infinite grid of the floor was the translation of Rudofsky's tactile floor into a new sensually driven economic calculus. For Doxiadis' projects in Karachi, see my "Boundary Games: Ecochard, Doxiadis, and the Refugee Housing Projects under Military Rule in Pakistan, 1953–1959," in *Aggregate: Governing by Design*, A. Dutta, T. Hyde, and D. Abramson, eds. (Pittsburgh: University of Pittsburgh Press, 2012). For an acute analysis of Doxiadis' projects in Iraq, see Panayiota Pyla's detailed account in "Rebuilding Iraq 1955–58: Modernist Housing, National Aspirations, and Global Ambitions," in *Journal / International Working-Party for Documentation & Conservation of Buildings, Sites & Neighborhoods of the Modern Movement* (2006) Sept., n. 35, 71–77.

(28)
Anna Tsing, *Friction: An Ethnography of Global Connection* (Princeton: Princeton University Press, 2005).

(29)
The very possibility of ethical relationship with the other is premised on a certain violence. Ethics requires, at the very least, to empathize with the other, to turn her experience into one's own. This founding violence that enables a dialogue across difference. See Gayatri Chakravorty Spivak's well-known essay dealing with the question of ethics in translation, "The Politics

frame the idea of the community and creativity ensures the perpetuation of long-term systemic inequalities; that the idea of an entrepreneurial creative subject obscures the actual historical constraints people face, thereby ensuring that they continue onto new registers. As Mahmood Mamdani has argued, "[it] is one thing to argue that nothing short of death can extinguish human initiative and creativity, but quite another to see in every gesture evidence of historical initiative." Here one is also reminded of Talal Asad's famous remarks that "[e]ven the inmates of a concentration camp are able in this sense, to live by their own cultural logic...but one may be forgiven for doubting that they are therefore 'making their own history.'"[34]

The sensual architecture of participation and empowerment, by framing scarcity as an occasion for individual and collective creativity, turns historical constraints invisible. The predominance of inhabitants in the projects' images is a historiographic argument. The buildings, with their mud and brick walls and hand-welded steel and string-tied bamboo roofs, give the impression of cultural specificity. Yet this framing of difference is, to refer to Mamdani again, "history by analogy," where the understanding of historical processes specific to one spatial and temporal context is transferred to understand the circumstances of another. Here, it is an analogy to the history of private enterprise in the industrial metropoles. "What happens," Mamdani has asked, " if you take a historical process unfolding under the concrete conditions...as a vantage point from which to make sense of subsequent social development [elsewhere]? The outcome is a history by analogy rather than history as process. Analogy seeking turns into a substitute for theory formation. The [historian, or the expert] is akin to those learning a foreign language who must translate every new work back into their mother tongue, in the process missing precisely what is new in a new experience."[35]

Through this comparative framework, the world appears as an analogy to the historical experiences familiar to the expert. She thinks that she is listening to those she is helping by celebrating their creativity, yet she is only listening to her own voice, silencing the many for whom the very traditional and cultural uniqueness and creativity being celebrated in the projects has been the medium of their exploitation.

In Bangladesh as well as Burkina Faso, building is a task marked by caste and class, gender, race, and tribe. These categories are not ghosts of bygone eras, but define lives in the very contexts in which these school projects intervene. What would the bamboo roof of the Rudrapur school look like if its design acknowledged that it was to be built by tribal labor whose children will not attend the school? What would it look like if we acknowledged that all participants were not participating in the community project on the same terrain, that some were watched over, bore the title of "denotified" tribes, assumed to be thieves who would steal materials if not kept under a careful watch?[36] To acknowledge the existence of this hierarchy, why couldn't material meant to be stolen over time have been added to the roof in the project representations shown at

of Translation" in *Outside in the Teaching Machine* (New York: Routledge, 1993) 179–200. Also see Emily Apter's recent *Against World Literature: On the Politics of Untranslatability* (New York: Verso, 2013).

(30)
Small Scale, Big Change (2010), *op. cit.*, 23–32.

(31)
The World Bank has long insisted that the only recourse for these millions is through their incorporation into systems of individual rights and property, without acknowledging the historical restrictions and global structural exclusions that make such participation open doors to only new modes of credit-baiting. By citing the Bank's statistic on (mostly tribal) landless population, I am not endorsing that model of privatized "empowerment." For a historically informed discussion of the politics of tribal rights that gives the lie to both international and national developmental agendas, see Mahasweta Devi's meticulously researched short fiction, especially "Douloti the Bountiful," trans. Gayatri Chakravorty Spivak, in *Imaginary Maps: Three Stories* (New York: Routledge, 1994), and Kalpana Bardhan's "Women's Work, Welfare and Status: Forces of Tradition and Change in India," in *South Asia Bulletin*, 6:1 (1986): 3–16.

(32)
For a history and politics of the Land Settlement Act of 1871, see Ranajit Guha's seminal book, *A Rule of Property for Bengal: An Essay on the Idea of Permanent Settlement* (Durham: Duke University Press, 1996).

MoMA? What would the roof trusses of the Gando school look like if they acknowledged that those welding every steel joint couldn't transfer the skill they learned there without confronting the restrictions on movement and employment put in place by Indirect Rule? Could they have different welding joints for different tribal classifications? As these craftsmen (and they all appear to be men, already indicating a gender divide in the community) move, could their particular welds on different roofs betray a cartography of constraint?

Architecture has the power to acknowledge history and specificity as much as generality and universality. If architects are shy about including such differentiations in their buildings in the name of pragmatism couldn't such power structures at least be recognized in the representative realm of the museum? After all, haven't we learned from the history of modernism and modern media that architecture does not begin or end with the building? (One key organizer of the MoMA exhibition, upon hearing these suggestions, remarked to me: "But what would our sponsors say if we included extra materials to be stolen in the building?").

The mode of celebrating the entrepreneurial qualities of the poor analyzed in this essay is all too prevalent not only in architectural exhibitions but also in architectural education, in the countless studios where First World students venture on short stints in the Third World to experience globalization. If something is to be changed in architectural education, we must ask ourselves, why is the primary requirement to build a school in Bangladesh knowledge of mud construction and passive solar techniques? Why is the history of the political divisions complex intertwined divisions, which have excluded fifty-two percent of the population from any meaningful participation in colonial, national, and NGO-driven development, not a requirement for claiming to act in that context? Why is knowledge of history, especially political history, considered the purview of other disciplines?

If sustainability, or participatory development, in architecture is to be more than an instrument of rendering these systems of exploitation invisible, than architects, both historians and designers, have to raise the minimum requirements for intervention in decolonized contexts, for us and for our students. Right now, this requirement seems to be limited to buying a plane ticket and acquiring technical knowledge of locally available materials with some general and historically inaccurate impressions of local culture.

If we are going to help the underprivileged (and that patronizing model should be questioned in itself) than it is our responsibility to learn the complexity of the context, including the differences in dialects and languages, in which we are to operate. This would certainly be the requirement for someone coming from the decolonized world to the US or Europe with the intent of helping the disenfranchised, be they in inner cities or rural areas. If a studio would only travel to Bangladesh when all the students have taken advanced level language and history courses, so be it. Our modes of operation are not determined by the omnipresent specter of something called "globalization."[37] We shape the idea of

㉝ For contemporary effects of property relations and grain loan structures on tribal women's lives in Bangladesh, see the astonishing work of Bengali activist Farida Akhter with the organization, UBINIG, of which she is a founder: http://www.ubinig.org/ (accessed January 15, 2014).

㉞ Talal Asad, *Genealogies of Religion: Discipline and Reasons of Power in Christianity and Islam* (Baltimore: John Hopkins University Press, 1993), 4, quoted in Mamdani, *Citizen and Subject* (1996), *op. cit.*, 10.

㉟ Ibid., 12.

㊱ For an acute description of the colonial and national history of classification of Indian tribals, see Mahasweta Devi's short interview, Mahasweta Devi: Witness, *Advocate, Writer, a Der Documentary* at http://www.der.org/films/mahasweta-devi.html (accessed January 15, 2014). "Denotified tribes" was the title given to Indian tribals by the colonial government under the Criminal Tribes Act of 1871. Betraying the uncertainly of control over landless populations, the colonial administration declared that since the tribals didn't reside in a fixed location they were criminal by nature in search for a crime. The act of 1871 required the tribals to register themselves with the local magistrate wherever they went, placing on them the burden of proving their innocence even in the absence of a crime. After much political protest, the act was repealed in 1949 after Indian independence and the "criminal tribes were "denotified" in 1952. Yet even with this change, the burden globalization with specific qualities through our discursive, institutional, and material practices. If we are not willing to accept the challenge of imagining another globalization, then it does not matter what kind of buildings we produce. Architecture as an accessible image, without careful attention to the complexity of history, turns into a bludgeon, flattening the persistent inequalities of global capitalist exploitation into a simple caricature of the poor that fits neatly into project goals of global institutions, curatorial models of museum exhibitions, and travel schedules at architectural schools. As an image of unified creative communities, architecture once again has acquired the power to ensure that this exploitation is erased from view to continue on new registers for the benefit of new and few actors.

of proof still remained on the tribals. At "donitification," the Criminal Tribes Act was replaced with the Habitual Offenders Act of 1952. Against the rising tide of political resistance, however, individual states started releasing different tribes from the law, but to this day they are still commonly referred to "Vimukta jaatis" or the "ex-criminal tribes" in the legal language and policing culture of both West Bengal and Bangladesh.

(37)
When I presented an early version of this paper at the conference The Future of History, in 2011 at the Taubman College of Architecture and Urban Planning at the University of Michigan, I was told that in advocating stringent requirement, particularly linguistic, for travel courses, I was suggesting that we should not "do globalization" at all. This response presumes that globalization is some self-sufficient functioning system that determines its own speed autonomous of the actors that mobilize it. I subscribe more to the view professed by Anna Tsing in Friction (2005), op. cit., that "globalization" is (only) a universal that is mobilized by different actors in different concrete situations, giving it pace and quality that is demanded by the ends they want to achieve with it. From this perspective, we have the power to give the processes and procedures of "globalization" another meaning: not of hastily driven actions erasing differences and benefiting the few, but of slow and deep contemplative reflection that strives to learn to talk and design across difference.

INDUSTRIAL DESIGN

February 1957   *$1.50 per copy*

2

Design as a political force

Aids and sources for the designer: Modelmaking

Cars '57: review and questions

In February 1957 *Industrial Design* published a feature article on the role of design in international exhibitions. Cover is shown above.

Facing page: Guides in orange Brookhaven coveralls, at the 1955 New Delhi fair (top left); Afghan workers assembling the Buckminster Fuller pavilion, in 1956 in Kabul (top middle); workers assembling the Jungle Gym, at the 1959 exhibit in Moscow (bottom left); *Source: Lucia DeRespinis Voting booth on exhibit, in 1958 in Brussels; NARA National Archives and Records Administration Moon rock exhibit in 1970, in Osaka (right). Source: Jack Masey unless otherwise noted.*

Cold War Technological Encounters: The US Information Agency's International Exhibition Program

From 1955–70, in the midst of the accelerating arms and space race, a series of international events played out a new front for the Cold War. Organized and funded by the US government, the international World Fairs, Trade Fairs, and special exhibitions held during that time were crucial sites in the ideological confrontation between the West and the East, or between capitalism and communism. While they ranged in scope, mission and ambition, these exhibitions emphasized technological achievements as a central theme and sought to prove the United States' superiority in science, economy, lifestyle, and culture. Through the vehicle of technology, the exhibits celebrated national accomplishments while also making a public and visible case for America's strengths.

Jack Masey, who led the office of exhibits at the US Information Agency (USIA), was perhaps the single most influential figure behind the Cold War exhibition program. Masey understood that these international events were key opportunities for winning—and changing—the minds of the general audiences and saw architecture and design as tools of political and cultural value. Writing in 1956, he noted, "The bouncing ball bearing; the Lionel model trains; the talking cow and [chicken] and all very amusing gimmicks, but it is doubtful whether they are going to change men's minds about the United States." (1956 Evaluation letter) Masey pushed for substance over entertainment and for bold statements through both building and content.

In the exhibitions, technology took on multiple facets—from nuclear science to entertainment media and household appliances. Unlike the Soviet reliance on scale models, US exhibits sought to showcase real technologies—not simulations or mock-ups. In addition, as evidenced by the fairs in New Delhi, Kabul, and Moscow, Masey added human guides to explain the exhibits, a strategy which proved to be immensely successful. Versed in both the exhibit content and the local languages, the guides made a convincing case for the featured technologies as easily accessible and understandable.

If the exhibits showed actual technologies, the pavilions put technology into action. A combination of aesthetic and technical considerations, the pavilion designs aimed for innovation and expertise. Examples included: Buckminster Fuller's prefabricated geodesic dome in the 1956 Kabul fair, which took only two days to assemble; George Nelson's large-scale plastic umbrellas in Moscow in 1959; Fuller's three-quarter sphere in 1967, in Montreal; and the large-scale inflatable dome roof by Davis Brody in Osaka, in 1970 spanning the length of two football fields. In both their location and size, the pavilions were the sites of direct aesthetic confrontation with their Soviet counterparts.

In February 1957, *Industrial Design* magazine featured an article entitled, "Design as Political Force," and published Trade Fair pavilions on its cover. Author Jane Fiske Mitarachi praised the participation of designers in the exhibitions program and wrote that it was "undoubtedly one of the most serious responsibilities that the design profession had ever known." The examples that follow represent a unique—though short-lived—confluence of design and politics on the international stage and an invaluable opportunity for the design community to take position in the trenches of the Cold War.

Irina Verona

"Against the dark background of the
atomic bomb ... the coming months wi
be fraught with fateful decisions...
may they be the decisions which lead
this world out of fear into peace."

—

**President Eisenhower, Atoms for Peac
speech to UN, Dec 8, 1953**

Atoms for Peace: A New Frontier

Organizer: USIA (US Information Agency) & OITF (Office of
International Trade Fairs); Atomics exhibition design by Jack Masey;
US Pavilion—designed by John Vassos; Size: 100,000 sq. ft.;
Budget: $622,000 (for exhibit); Technology: traditional construction
(brick). Exhibit/main theme: "Industry Services Man" in Electronics,
in Technology and in Atomics; nuclear reactor; peaceful use of

Above: US Atoms pavilion, with model of atom on top.
Below: Construction of the pavilion relied on traditional materials ar
assembly methods. These included brick and bamboo scaffolding.
Source: Jack Masey.

astering the Atomic Age

ove, left: Mechanical Hands, in the Atomics Section of the exhibition.
s section of the US pavilion was designed to demonstrate "the
st developments in the harnessing of atomic energy for peaceful
poses. "Jack Masey suggested the use of sixty Indian guides to
lain the exhibits and to make "the complex topic of atomic energy
prehensible to a large number of visitors." The guides were fluent
nglish, Hindi and at least two other Indian languages.

Above, right: Jack Masey takes Soviet leaders Khrushchev and
Bulganin through the American exhibit. USIA, *Source: Jack Masey*.

Prefab Ingenuity: A New Cold War 'Object'

Organizer: USIA / Jack Masey; US Pavilion—designed by Buckminster Fuller; size: 100 ft. diam; 35 ft. high at center; 8,000 sf floor area; budget: $35,000; technology: geodesic dome; materials: aluminum tubes (3 in. diameter) for frame, 480 pieces; nylon skin; erected in 48 hours; [three months between commissioning and opening on entire exhibition]; Exhibits: agriculture, transportation, working TV studio; giant outdoor cinemascope film screen

Above: Asked to come up with a proposal for the Jeshyn Fair a mere six weeks before opening day, Jack Masey turned to Buckminster Fuller. Fuller's dome was designed in seven days; manufactured in thirty days; and built in two days. The dome frame was relatively small compared to its Soviet bloc counterparts—8,000 sq ft, as opposed to the Soviets' 35,000 sq ft or the Chinese' 25,000 sq ft. Nonetheless, according to Masey, it "highlighted the potential for a strong architectural statement as a way of distinguishing the American entry as original and exciting." *Source: Cudney Collection.*

> "In some ways, the Kabul dome was a
> quintessentially Cold War object, created
> for a specific confrontational purpose."
>
> —
>
> From Jack Masey, *Cold War Confrontations*

"No longer should we select exhibits solely on an inductive basis and fit themes around them. The bouncing ball bearing; the Lionel model trains; the talking cow and [chicken] are all very amusing gimmicks, but it is doubtful whether they are going to change men's minds about the United States. Entertain we must in Southeast Asia but I think we must have substance, too. Without it, I see little value in participating in Southern Asian fairs at all."

—

Jack Masey
in 1956 Jeshyn Evaluation letter

echnology For [Mass] Consumption

cing page, below: Photos of erection of frame and nylon fabric
n. Frame connections were color-coded to facilitate assembly by
skilled labor. *Source: Jack Masey.*
ove: Visitors at the Lionel model train set.
low: Dome at night, with exterior Cinemascope screen.
urce: Cudney Collection.

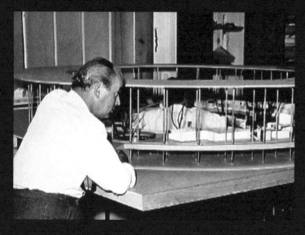

Monumental Harmony

Organizer: US State Department; US Pavilion—designed by
Edward Durell Stone; exhibit designers: Peter Harnden, Bernard
Rudofsky; Saul Steinberg; also Chermayeff & Geismar; budget: $14
million (for entire US exhibition); materials: roof made of plastic,
supported by steel tension cables; curtain wall; oculus at the center;
Exhibit/technology: IBM RAMAC; American street-scape; voting
booths; medical technology

Above: Night view of the US pavilion, designed by Edward Durell
Stone. Source: Jack Masey.
Below, left: Peter Harnden, seen with a model of the building, led the
design of the interior and exhibits.
Below, right: View of visitors arriving at the US pavilion. *Source: both
NARA National Archives and Records Administration.*

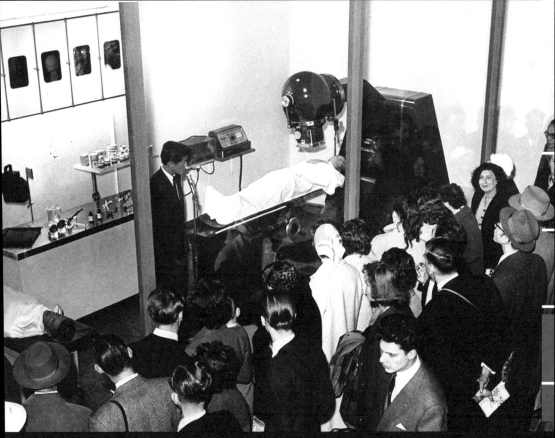

"Everybody knows that America is a giant. The planners of your exhibit have shown that, not withstanding his size, this giant is a warm human being... not constantly boasting about being bigger and stronger and richer than everybody else.... America has shown itself an essentially humane country."

Review of US exhibition in Belgian trade journal, as recounted in Jack Masey's *Cold War Confrontations*

New Humanism

ove: Radiation treatment demonstration. *Source: NARA National chives and Records Administration.*

low, left: Street scape exhibit showing American urban life. *Source: ermayeff & Geismar.*

low, right: The fashion show, organized by Lee Canfield, used atwalk that reached the center of the pavilion. *Source: NARA tional Archives and Records Administration.*

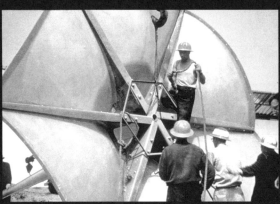

Information Machine

Organizer: USIA / Office of Exhibits / Jack Masey; US Pavilion—
Kaiser-Fuller (dome); George Nelson (plastic umbrellas); Welton
Beckett (glass pavilion); Budget: $3 million; Technology: plastic
umbrellas / fiberglass. Exhibit / main themes: the modern appliance;
the "Miracle Kitchen"; the products of industry; Individual companies
included: RCA for the color television studio; Singer for the sewing
machines; Whirlpool for the kitchen; and Grand Union for

Above: Plastic umbrellas by George Nelson, during installation.
Source: Jacqueline Nelson.
Below, left: Detail of umbrella assembly. USIA, *Source: Jack Masey.*
Below, right: Family of Man exhibit, one of the several exhibits
displayed under the umbrellas. © Robert C. Lautman Photography
Collection, National Building Museum.

he Consumer Experience

ove: Baking demonstration observed by onlooking visitors.
is installation was one of the many exhibitions of the American
perience and of household technologies in action. *Source:*
llection of Dr. Shelly Weinig.

"If it was not the show of actual machines and technical processes which the Russians expected and wanted, it was perhaps something better, for it went beyond the machine to suggest the kind of life that an advanced technological society provides for its citizens."

—

Irma Weinig, *Industrial Design*, September 1959

Operation "Skybreak" Bubble

Organizer: USIA/Office of Exhibits/Jack Masey; US Pavilion: architects: Buckminster Fuller & Shoji Sadao; Cambridge Seven Associates, Inc., Golden Metak Productions (exhibit design); Pavilion Size: 250 ft. diameter; 200 ft. tall; Budget: $9.3 million (for entire US effort); Technology: geodesic dome; Materials: steel and molded acrylic; retractable shading panels; Exhibition/main theme: "Man and His World"; US Pavilion theme: Creative America (overall theme); "Destination Moon" Apollo mission; also Pop Art; Technology: 125 ft. long escalator (longest free-span at the time). *Source: All images, Chermayeff & Geismar*

estination: Moon

cing page, above: View of workers on scaffolding, during the
nstruction of Fuller's dome. The pavilion had a steel frame and
rylic panels, with motorized shades.

cing page, below: View of air train, which connected the geodesic
me with the rest of the Fairgrounds.

Above: The pavilion's theme of "Creative America" played out between
the opposite poles of space program technology, on the one hand, and
American art and popular culture, on the other.

"The open, relaxed, sheltered environments created by a climate-controlling, light-transmitting dome might encourage the virtues of small lively towns, which they feel have so conspicuously ceased to exist. Not only towns, but civilizations."

—

Marguerite Villecco, writing in *Architectural Forum*, September 1970

Weightless

Organizer: USIA/Office of Exhibits/Jack Masey; US Pavilion: architects: Davis Brody & Associates; Exhibit designers: Chermayeff, Geismar and de Harak; Size: 265 ft. wide × 465 ft. long; Budget: $2.6–3.2 million for the pavilion; $10 million for the entire US effort; Technology: Air structure; Materials: translucent fiberglass roof; earth berm; cables; Exhibit main theme: Progress and Harmony for Mankind; astronauts; space capsule; moon rock. *Source: All images USIA, Jack Masey.*

Above: View of pavilion under construction, showing berm, concrete ring, blowers, and inflated fabric roof. Below, left: In this construction photo, workers stretch the roof fiberglass fabric over cables. Below: According to an article published in *Architectural Forum* in 1970, the pavilion roof was "the largest clear span, air-supported roof ever built."

Spaceship Earth

Above: The Space Exploration exhibit celebrated the Apollo 11 Lunar
Mission, which had landed on the Moon in July 1969. Exhibits included
an actual lunar module, moon rock, as well as the recreation of
the landing site on the Sea of Tranquility.

Hilton Hotels: The Politics of Pleasure

In 1963...12 New Hilton Hotels Around the World

Progress is the word for Hilton Hotels. This year the largest group of hotels to open in any single year will be welcomed into the Hilton family. They represent an investment of over $200,000,000 which will bring more than 8,000 new guest rooms to the world traveler and create 12,000 new jobs for people in the areas. In addition these hotels will serve as a stimulus to business and provide a center for community and international life in 12 important cities around the world. Individually, each embodies the traditions of its particular locale. Collectively they, together with the 49 other Hilton Hotels shown in the background, play a leading role in promoting peace through international trade and travel.

Little Americas Abroad

Between 1949 and 1966 Hilton International constructed seventeen luxury hotels outside of the US. In 1963 *TIME* magazine projected twelve million Americans would travel abroad that year alone. Conrad Hilton, the slender, permanently tanned Texas businessman who loved dancing, was not alone in providing these traveling Americans the "comforts of home" they desired abroad.

By 1963 Sheraton had opened seven and the Intercontinental Hotels Corp (Pan American World Airways Subsidiary) had built nineteen hotels outside of the US, many of which were similarly sited in the hot cities of the Cold War. Yet Hilton's frequent proclamation of his ideological motivations secured him the support of the US government and its Marshall Plan funds.

— Margaret Arbanas and Ana Miljački

1955

1962

Hilton Advertisements, Needham & Grohmann.
Source: Hospitality Industry Archives, Conrad N. Hilton College, University of Houston.

Key Sources:

Conrad Nicholson Hilton, *Be My Guest* (First published in 1957 by Simon and Shuster, New York, NY: Prentice Hall Press 1987).

Andy Kopkind: "Hotels: By Golly!" *Time Magazine*, July 19, 1963, 66–72.

Annabel Jane Wharton, *Building the Cold War: Hilton International Hotels and Modern Architecture* (Chicago, IL: University of Chicago Press, 2001).

Cathleen D. Baird, Director & Archivist Hospitality Industry Archives, "Conrad N. Hilton, Innkeeper Extraordinary, Statesman and Philanthropist, 1887–1979", 2004.

Michael Wise, "The Ideological Coding Behind Hilton Hotels: A Cold War weapon disguised as a place to spend the night," The New York Times, July 21, 2001.

http://www.hotelhabanalibre.com/en/history.html

http://hiltonglobalmediacenter.com

Star Power

Gary Cooper is offered a cup of Turkish coffee from the Istanbul Hilton hostess a year after the hotel opened. His family visit to this air-conditioned instant "modern classic" in the sizzling Turkish city included a "mandatory" press conference. He was one among many international celebrities who chose Hilton hotels as a stage for their public appearances and in return, placed Hilton hotels repeatedly in the news. The long list of these characters included the hot and the powerful members of the international jet set ranging from Elvis Presley to Mikhail Gorbachev, from Sophia Loren to Indira Gandhi.

Istanbul Hilton: Gordon Bunshaft, SOM with Turkish architect Sedad Eldem (opened in 1955).
Source: Istanbul Hilton Archive.

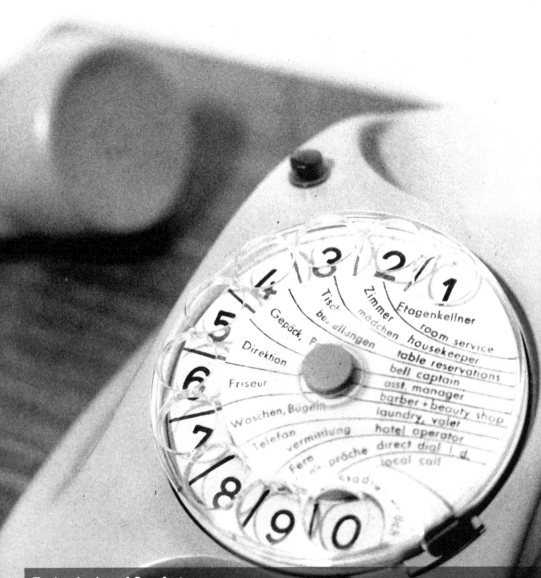

Technologies of Comfort

In the July 1963 issue of *Time* magazine, the second issue dedicated to Conrad Hilton and his empire, the journalist Andy Kopkind described Hilton's rise to prominence by characterizing the American tourist as the type that dares everything and risks nothing: "And nowhere do they risk less than at Hilton hotels. Whether he is in Tehran or Trinidad, the traveler can be sure that Hilton will offer him a clean bed, pleasant surroundings, plentiful ice-water, and food that he can also safely eat."

Hilton hotel was the first hotel chain to install televisions in all guest rooms (1951), air-conditioning in every hotel in the chain (1955) and direct-dial telephone service in every room (1957). By deploying the cutting-edge technology in service of comfort, Hilton spearheaded the idea of modern traveling whereby one doesn't need to forsake the conveniences of one's home when visiting the most exotic of places.

World According to Hilton

A 1957 Hilton Hotels advertisement states: "World Peace through International Trade and Travel. This is the credo of Conrad Hilton. Realizing the important role played by hotels in helping to achieve this desired goal, Hilton Hotels is undertaking the largest world-wide expansion in history." The Hilton expansion fueled in part by Marshall Plan funds, coincided with State Department's vigorous embassy building campaign. In contrast to the "hard power" represented by the embassies, Hilton hotels decidedly mixed politics with pleasure. On the occasion of the 1958 opening of the Hilton Berlin, West Berlin's

mayor Willy Brandt addressed the crowds, while Yugoslavia's President Tito attended the official Nile Hilton opening in Cairo side by side with Egypt's president Gemal Abdel Nasser.

Left and Right, Berlin Hilton: Pereira and Luckman with German architect Schwebes and Schoszberger (opened in 1958).
Source: Photos, F.C. Gundlach.

Political Theater

Providing comfort, legitimacy, and neutrality interchangeably, Hilton hotels often served as venues for important political events. The 1970 Arab League Summit took place at the Nile Hilton in Cairo and included all the key figures involved in shaping the subsequent three decades of Middle Eastern politics. Gemal Abdel Nasser died immediately after the Summit, presumably poisoned by a coffee made at the hotel. In 1971, Africa Meeting President Anwar El Sadat of Egypt held talks with African heads of state at the Nile Hilton in Cairo; in 1995 Yasser Arafat met Ariel Sharon. A few years later, in 2001, another round of

Palestine-Israel peace negotiations took place at Hilton Taba. More recently, President George Bush met Ecumenical Patriarch Bartholomew at the Hilton Istanbul in 2004. In 2012 US Secretary of State Hillary Clinton and Turkish Foreign Minister Ahmet Davutoğlu met at the Istanbul Hilton, still the most stunning of Istanbul's hotels.

Nile Hilton, Cairo: Welton Becket & Associates with an Egyptian Architect (opened in 1958).
Source: Corbis.

Takeover

The march of Fidel Castro's revolutionary army into Havana on January 8, 1959 terminated at Hilton hotel. For the first three months of his rule, Castro governed from the temporary headquarters on the top floor of the hotel, Suite 2324, which provided both supreme comfort and an appropriately commanding view of the city.

Despite the spectacular overtake extensively documented by international press, Hilton remained in charge of the hotel operation for the next two years after which the building was nationalized and renamed: Hotel Habana Libre. The resultant financial losses to Conrad Hilton were minimal. His usual arrangement

with the local capital involved financing the operating of the hotel and collecting one third of the profits, never securing the land or the building. His losses in Havana were then merely one third of the operating profits of the Hotel. But Conrad Hilton's dream: "to show the countries most exposed to Communism the other side of the coin—the fruits of the free world," retroactively hit the bull's-eye in Havana.

Havana Hilton: Welton Becket & Associates with the Cuban firm Arroyo-Menéndez (opened in 1958).
Source: Joseph Scherschel, Getty Images.

Bed-In

Drove from Paris to the Amsterdam Hilton
Talking in our beds for a week
The newspapers said, "Say what you doing in bed?"
I said, "we're only trying to get us some peace."
The Ballad Of John And Yoko

In 1969, at the height of the Vietnam War, John Lennon and Yoko Ono staged a two-week nonviolent antiwar protest in their bed in Hilton Amsterdam. Having just gotten married, the couple harnessed the media attention around their wedding for promoting world peace. Their part-art performance, part peace-protest was intended to have a second iteration in New York, but John was banned from entering the United States because of his 1968 cannabis conviction. The couple decided to stage their second protest at the Sheraton Oceanus Hotel in Bahamas, but after spending a sweltering night there decided to move the event north, to Montreal. At the end of their seven day stay at the properly air-conditioned Queen Elizabeth hotel (also operated by Hilton) they recorded the 1970s peace anthem, "Give Peace a Chance," on June 1, 1969.

Hilton Amsterdam: Dutch architect Hugh Aart Maaskant (opened in 1962).
Source: Getty Images.

Office*US*: Diagram

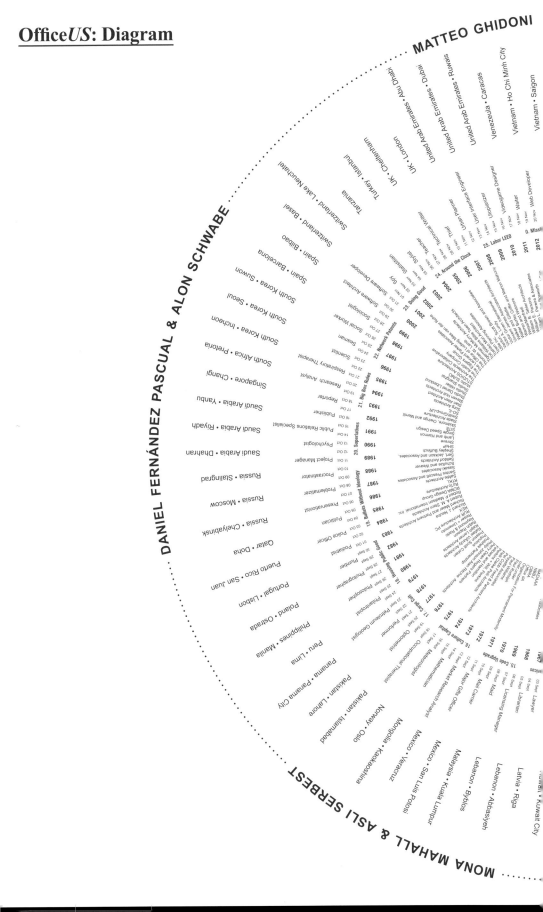

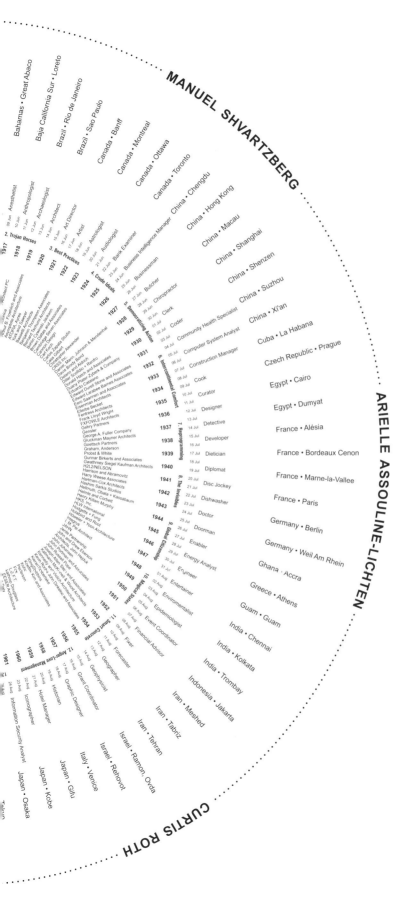

MANUEL SHVARTZBERG

ARIELLE ASSOULINE-LICHTEN

CURTIS ROTH

Bahamas • Great Abaco
Baja California Sur • Loreto
Brazil • Rio de Janeiro
Brazil • Sao Paulo
Canada • Montreal
Canada • Banff
Canada • Ottawa
Canada • Toronto
China • Chengdu
China • Hong Kong
China • Macau
China • Shanghai
China • Shenzen
China • Suzhou
China • Xi'an
Cuba • La Habana
Czech Republic • Prague
Egypt • Cairo
Egypt • Dumyat
France • Alésia
France • Bordeaux Cenon
France • Marne-la-Vallee
France • Paris
Germany • Berlin
Germany • Weil Am Rhein
Ghana • Accra
Greece • Athens
Guam • Guam
India • Chennai
India • Kolkata
India • Trombay
Indonesia • Jakarta
Iran • Meshed
Iran • Tabriz
Iran • Tehran
Israel • Ramon, Ovda
Israel • Rehovot
Italy • Venice
Japan • Gifu
Japan • Kobe
Japan • Osaka

09 Jun Anesthetist
10 Jun Anthropologist
12 Jun Archaeologist
14 Jun Architect
15 Jun Art Director
16 Jun Artist
19 Jun Astrologist
20 Jun Audiologist
21 Jun Bank Examiner
23 Jun Business Intelligence Manager
24 Jun Businessman
25 Jun Butcher
28 Jun Chiropractor
29 Jun Clerk
30 Jun Coder
01 Jul Community Health Specialist
02 Jul Computer System Analyst
04 Jul Construction Manager
05 Jul Cook
07 Jul Curator
08 Jul Designer
09 Jul Detective
11 Jul Developer
12 Jul Dietician
13 Jul Diplomat
14 Jul Disc Jockey
15 Jul Dishwasher
16 Jul Doctor
17 Jul Doorman
18 Jul Enabler
19 Jul Energy Analyst
20 Jul Engineer
21 Jul Entertainer
22 Jul Enviromentalist
23 Jul Epidemiologist
24 Jul Event Coordinator
25 Jul Financial Advisor
26 Jul Fixer
27 Jul Forecaster
28 Jul Geographer
29 Jul Geophysicist
30 Jul Graphic Designer
31 Jul Historian
01 Aug Hotel Manager
02 Aug Iconographer
03 Aug Information Security Analyst
04 Aug
05 Aug
07 Aug
09 Aug
11 Aug
12 Aug
13 Aug
14 Aug
15 Aug
17 Aug
19 Aug
20 Aug
21 Aug
23 Aug
24 Aug

1917
1918
1919
1920
1921
1922
1923
1924
1925
1926
1927
1928
1929
1930
1931
1932
1933
1934
1935
1936
1937
1938
1939
1940
1941
1942
1943
1944
1945
1946
1947
1948
1949
1950
1951
1952
1953
1954
1955
1956
1957
1958
1959
1960
1961

2. Trojan Horses
3. Best Practices
4. Crude Ideals
5. Democratizing Action
6. Intercontinental Comfort
7. Reprogramming
8. The Invisibles
9. Global Citizenship
10. Magical States
11. Smart Concrete
12. Anger-Drive Management

Altorelli B. Froelich and Associates
Architext PC
A'Dora Anyer
A'Dora Architecture
Balmori Architects
Barton Thompson Associates
Bohlin Cywinski Jackson
Bohlin Powell and Associates
Callison Design
Callison Design Studio
Carol Ross Barney
Caria Zabala Studio
CASS Inc.
CASS Christopher Alexander
Diane Brody Bond
Delani and Aldrich
Diller Scofidio + Renfro
Duany Plater-Zyberk & Company
Donald Hatch and Associates
Edward Durell Stone and Associates
Eduardo Catalano
Eero Saarinen and Associates
Edward Larabee Barnes and Associates
Eisenman Architects
Ellerbe Becket
Fentress Becket
Frank Lloyd Wright
FXFOWLE Architects
Gehry Partners
Gensler
George A. Fuller Company
Gluckman Mayner Architects
Goettsch Partners
Graham, Anderson
Probst & White
Gunnar Birkerts and Associates
Gwathmey Siegel Kaufman Architects
H2L2/NELSON
Harrison and Abramovitz
Harry Weese Associates
Hartman-Cox Architects
Hashim Sarkis Studios
Hellmuth, Obata + Kassabaum
Helmle and Corbett
Henry Killam Murphy
HKS, Inc.
HLW International
Hodgetts + Fung
Howard and Root
Ingenus
I. M. Pei Architect
J-Max Partnership
James e Drew Eisenman
Architects John Hejduk
John Portman and Associates
John Portman Associates
Kallmann, McKinnell & Wood Architects
Kohn Pedersen Fox and Associates
Kohn Pedersen Fox and Associates
Kohn Pedersen Fox Associates
Kohn Pedersen Fox Architects
Kohn Pedersen Fox Associates
Kohn Pedersen Fox and Associates
L&M F.T.
Leo A. Daly
Leopold Eidlitz
Lescaze Architecture
EES Inc.

AUTHOR BIOGRAPHIES

DANIEL A. BARBER

Daniel A. Barber is Assistant Professor of Architecture at the University of Pennsylvania, where he teaches the history of modern architecture. His research explores the relationship between design fields and the emergence of global environmental culture across the 20th century. Articles have recently been published in *Grey Room* and *Technology and Culture*. His book, *A House in the Sun: Modern Architecture and Solar Energy in the Cold War* will be published by Oxford University Press in early 2015. Daniel received a PhD from Columbia University, and was recently a fellow at the Harvard University Center for the Environment.

BEATRIZ COLOMINA

Beatriz Colomina is Professor of Architecture and Founding Director of the Program in Media and Modernity at Princeton University. She is the author of *Manifesto Architecture: The Ghost of Mies* (Sternberg Press, 2014), *Clip/Stamp/ Fold: The Radical Architecture of Little Magazines 196X-197X* (2010), *Domesticity at War* (2007), *Privacy and Publicity: Modern Architecture as Mass Media* (1994) and *Sexuality and Space* (1992), and curator of the exhibitions Clip/Stamp/Fold: The Radical Architecture of Little Magazines 196X-197X (Storefront for Art and Architecture, 2006) , Playboy Architecture, 1953-79 (NAi Maastricht, 2012), and Radical Pedagogies: Architectural Education in a Time of Disciplinary Instability (Lisbon Triennale, 2013).

PEGGY DEAMER

Peggy Deamer is Assistant Dean and Professor of Architecture at Yale University. She is a principal in the firm of Deamer, Architects. She received a B.Arch. from The Cooper Union and a Ph.D. from Princeton University. She is the editor of *Architecture and Capitalism: 1845 to the Present* (Routledge), *The Millennium House* (Monacelli Press), and co-editor of *Building in the Future: Recasting Architectural Labor* (MIT Press) and *BIM in Academia* (Yale School of Architecture) with Phil Bernstein. Her research examines the nature of architectural work/labor. She is the organizing member of the advocacy group, The Architecture Lobby.

KELLER EASTERLING

Keller Easterling is an architect, writer and professor at Yale University. Her books include *Enduring Innocence: Global Architecture and its Political Masquerades* (MIT, 2005) and *Organization Space: Landscapes, Highways and Houses in America* (MIT 1999). Easterling's most recent book, *Subtraction* (Sternberg Press, 2014), considers building removal or how to put the development machine into reverse. A forthcoming book, *Extrastatecraft: the Power of Infrastructure Space* (Verso, 2014), examines global infrastructure networks as a medium of polity. An ebook essay, *The Action is the Form* (Strelka Press, 2012), previews some of the arguments in *Extrastatecraft*.

BRANDEN HOOKWAY

Branden Hookway is author of *Pandemonium: The Rise of Predatory Locales in the Postwar World*. His recently released book from MIT Press, *Interface*, discusses issues of subject formation, agency, power, and control, within contexts that include technology, politics, and the social role of games. He teaches in the Department of Architecture and the Department of Design and Environmental Analysis at Cornell University, and is currently working on a theoretical treatment of the cockpit as a prototypical twentieth century space.

TIMOTHY HYDE

Timothy Hyde is an architectural historian and theorist at the Harvard Graduate School of Design, where he is Associate Professor of Architecture. He is the author of the book *Constitutional Modernism: Architecture and Civil Society in the Cuban Republic* (University of Minnesota Press, 2012) and articles published in *Perspecta, Log, Thresholds,* and *Praxis*.

MICHAEL KUBO

Michael Kubo is a Ph.D. Candidate in the History, Theory, and Criticism of Architecture at MIT, where his work focuses on The Architects Collaborative and the emergence of corporate architectural practice in the United States after the Second World War. With Chris Grimley and Mark Pasnik he is director of pinkcomma gallery and co-editor of *HEROIC,* a forthcoming book on the history of concrete modernism in Boston. With Jon Lott and William O'Brien Jr. he is a founding partner of Collective–LOK, which is currently designing the new street-level headquarters of Van Alen Institute in New York.

IJLAL MUZAFFAR

Ijlal Muzaffar is assistant professor of architectural history at the Rhode Island School of Design. He is willing to bet the house on the claim that modern architecture and planning have shaped not only the dominant forms of bio-politics in the 20th century global arena but also the contours of its geo-politics. He is as much attracted by the sexiness of the built projects as by the lure of World Bank feasibility reports, United Nation master plans, and Ford Foundation statistical analyses that have employed different architectural notions of space, scale, and materiality to design new modes of expertise and intervention across the world. He is member of the architectural history collaborative, Aggregate, which is also committed to claiming a bigger piece of the pie for architecture.

JORGE OTERO-PAILOS

New York–based architect, artist, and theorist Jorge Otero-Pailos is associate professor of historic preservation at Columbia University's Graduate School of Architecture, founder and editor of the journal *Future Anterior*, and author of *Architecture's Historical Turn: Phenomenology and the Rise of the Postmodern* (University of Minnesota Press, 2010). His writings on experimental forms of preservation have been published in *Artforum, Art in America, Architectural Record, Abitare, Volume* and others. He collaborates with leading architects on projects that rethink world heritage. His artworks have been exhibited internationally, including in the 53rd Venice Art Biennale in 2009.

IVAN RUPNIK

Ivan Rupnik is Assistant Professor at Northeastern University. His research, on the relationship of architectural design and crisis, had been disseminated through lectures, exhibits, and publications, including *A Peripheral Moment* (2010) and *Project Zagreb* (2007) with Eve Blau. He has applied his research to his design work, including the strategic planning of an academic campus with Bojan Baletic, and a multi-sensory urban landscape, with Helena Njiric, both in Zagreb. He is currently studying how to better leverage tourism development to generate more resilient coastal communities and is completing his dissertation at Harvard University on the impact of American industrial engineering on European modernist settlement design.

HILARY SAMPLE

Hilary Sample is Associate Professor at Columbia University, GSAPP. As an architect and principal of MOS, she has received the Architecture Award (2010) from the American Academy of Arts and Letters, was named one of North America's "Emerging Voices" (2008) by the Architectural League of New York City. The firm has been featured in exhibitions at the Museum of Modern Art, the Venice Biennale, the Shenzhen Biennale, The Creator's Project with Vice/Intel, and the Art Institute in Chicago. The firm's first monograph, *Everything All at Once: The Software, Video, and Architecture of MOS (2012),* is published by Princeton Architectural Press.

CLAIRE ZIMMERMAN

Claire Zimmerman, Associate Professor at the University of Michigan, is the author of *Photographic Architecture in the Twentieth Century* (University of Minnesota Press, 2014) and a co-edited essay collection, *Neo-avant-garde and Postmodern: Postwar Architecture in Britain and Beyond* (with Mark Crinson) that appeared as Volume 21 in Yale Studies in British Art (Yale University Press, 2010). She is co-curator of *New Brutalist Image, 1949–1955: Hunstanton School and the Photography of Life and Art,* opening at Tate Britain in October 2014.

OFFICE_US_

US Pavilion, 14th International Architecture Exhibition –
la Biennale di Venezia

Commissioner
Storefront for Art and Architecture

Curators
Eva Franch i Gilabert, Ana Miljački, Ashley Schafer

Associate Curator
Michael Kubo

Co-Organizer
PRAXIS

Assistant Curators
Carlos Mínguez Carrasco, Jacob Reidel

Exhibition Design
LEONG LEONG: Dominic Leong, Chris Leong,
Gabriel Burkett; Jackie Woon Bae, Clare Johnston,
Yu-Hsiang Lin, Jane Jonghyun Yi

Graphic Design
Pentagram: Natasha Jen,
Jeffrey Waldman; Justin Chen, Oeun Kwon

Technology Architecture
CASE

Global Network Strategy
Therrien-Barley

Media Producer
Andrew Fierberg

Web Design
M-A-U-S-E-R; Partner & Partners

Publishing Partner
Lars Müller Publishers

Media Partner
Architizer

Project Coordinator
Irina Chernyakova

Research Coordinator
Juan Jofre

Development, External Relations and Special Events
Kara L. Meyer

Technology and Production Coordinator
Piotr Chizinski

Outreach and Communications Manager
Zeynep Göksel

Project Assistant
Natalie Snyder

Editorial Team
PRAXIS: Amanda Reeser Lawrence,
Margaret Arbanas, Andrew Colopy, Megan Miller,
Fred Tang, Irina Verona

MIT Department of Architecture
Kyle Barker, Christianna Bonin, Kyle Coburn,
Nathan Friedman, Sam Ghantous, Anastasia Hiller,
Jessica Jorge, Karen Kitayama, Gabriel Kozlowski,

Jasmine Kwak, Patrick Evan Little, Ann Lok Lui, Moojin
Park, Austin Smith, Tyler Stevermer, Evelyn Ting,
Michael Waldrep, Sarah Weir, Natthida Wiwatwicha, Rixt
Woudstra, Wenfei Xu *Support:* Daniel Chang, Kristina
Eldrenkamp, Nicolo Guida, Lee Moreau, David Oliver,
Chiranit Prateepasen, Claire Shafer, Trygve Wastvedt

Austin E. Knowlton School at The Ohio State University
Laila Ammar, Levi Bedall, Tyler Brozovich, Joe Carifa,
Nicholas Castillo, Luke Dougal, Clay Ellerbrook,
Abdelrahman Elzamly, Talia Friedman, Chris Mannella,
Nicholas Miller, Dustin Page, Darren Spensiero,
Alexander Stagge, Jacqueline Stern, Jianning Zhong,
Michael Zumpano

Project Support
Silvia Callegari, Tyrene Calvesbert, Diandra Cohen,
Ian Costello, Ashely Kuto, Francesca Lantieri,
Itzel Lavanderos, Anu Lill, Yuma Shinohara, Michael
Signorile, Zaina Soueid, Melody Stein, Elise Stella,
Mario Torres

Project Advisors
Laurie Beckleman, Aaron Betsky, Holly Block,
Beatriz Colomina, Keller Easterling, Campbell Hyers,
Cathy Lang Ho, James von Klemperer, Marc Kushner,
Lars Müller, Douglass Rice, Bob Rubin, Sylvia J. Smith,
Lisa Phillips, Artur Walther, Sarah Whiting, Karen Wong

Special Thanks
Peter Aaron, Zahra Ali Baba, Dana Aljoud`er, Jordan
Anderson, Alan I. Appel, Iwan Baan, Chiara Barbieri,
Cecil Barnes, Roberta Bartalone, Cameron Blaylock,
Barry Beagan, Brett Beyer, Gary Boyd, Roy Brand,
Beth Broome, Bryan Cave LLP: Alan Appel, Greg Galvin,
Nicole Gates, Robert Lancaster, Margery Perlmutter,
Stefan Skulesch; Michael Cadwell, Rebecca Chamberlain,
Alan Cross, Nicholas de Moncheaux, Giacomo DiThiene,
Patricia Driscoll, Ignacio Peydro Duclos, Ellen Finnie
Duranceau, Nazareth Ekmakijan, Igor Ekštajn, Rami
el Samahy, Britt Eversole, Alia Farid, Enrico Fontanari,
Christine Foushee, Frener & Reifer: Thomas Geissler,
Michael Purzer; Miles Fujiki, Curt Gambetta, Emil
Rodriguez Garabot, Roland Halbe, Jim Harrington,
Sarah Herda, Dessen Hillman, Adam Himes, Margaret
Ho, Yasmina Khan, Duncan Kincaid, Ryan John King,
Arianne Kouri, Naho Kubota, Ricardo Leon, Neil Levine,
Nicolò Lewanski, Rungu Lin, Rob Livesey, Hannah
Loomis, George Louras, Elizabeth Gill Lui, Sebastian Lux,
Richard Mandelkorn, Mark Jarzombek, Sandro Marpillero,
Melissa Marsh, Jack Masey, Lorrie A. McAllister, Brendan
McGetrick, Cathleen McGuigan, John McLaughlin,
Franco Micucci, Antoni Muntadas, Hansrobyn van Oosten,
Saverio Panata & Silvia Zini, Janet Parks, Partner &
Partners: Greg Mihalko, Zach Mihalko, David Liss;
Beverly Payeff-Masey, Ivan Rašković, Bika Rebek, Karl
Roarty, Julian Rose, Marco Ariso Rota, Ryan Rothman,
Joel Sanders, Adèle Naudé Santos, Kelly Schein, Ori
Scialom, Neslihan Sen, Karin Šerman, Douglas Sershen,
Sarah Sherman, Tarek Shuaib, Amber Sinicrope, Monica
Socorro, Erica Stoller, Hicks Stone, Sam Sweezy, Nader
Tehrani, Wayne Thom, Dicle Uzunyayla, Gary Van Zante,
Ana Cristina Vargas, Davi Weber, Ann Whiteside, Mark
Wigley, Jaren Wilcoxson, Mark Young, Ines Zalduendo

Office*US* Sponsors
Austin E. Knowlton School of Architecture
    at the Ohio State University
Autodesk *Creative Partner*
Bureau of Educational and Cultural Affairs,
    US Department of State
Herman Miller *Creative Partner*
Peggy Guggenheim Collection, Venice
    (Solomon R. Guggenheim Foundation, New York)
The Massachusetts Institute of Technology,
    Department of Architecture

Office*US* Supporter
AECOM
Arup
Esto
Graham Foundation for Advanced Studies
    in the Fine Arts
Hewlett Packard | AMD
Kohn Pedersen Fox Associates (KPF)

Office*US* Benefactor
Elise Jaffe and Jeffrey Brown
Frederick Iseman
FXFOWLE Architects
Oldcastle BuildingEnvelope
Robert Melvin Rubin and Stéphane Samuel
Skidmore, Owings & Merrill LLP
Walther Family Foundation

Office*US* Leader
Arthur H. Schein Memorial Fund
JAHN

Office*US* Contributor
Lanny and Sharon Martin
RTKL

Office*US* Patron
Charles Renfro
Control Group
Iwan Baan
Michael A. Manfredi and Marion Weiss
OTTO Archive
RD RICE Construction Inc.
The American Institute of Architects

Office*US* Circle
Barbara Jakobson
David and Jane Walentas
Elizabeth Gill Lui
Eva Ching and Jeff Small
Frederieke Taylor
Knowlton School Alumni Society
Lauren Kogod and David Smiley
Peter Aaron
Richard Mishaan Design
Roland Halbe
Todd DeGarmo

Office*US* Friends
American Printing Company
Belmont Freeman
Carlos Brillembourg and Karin Waisman
Claudia Gould
C & M Shade Corporation
Glenn Horowitz
Holly Block
Jinhee Park + John Hong, SsD
Karen Wong
Linda and Harry Macklowe
Mabel Wilson
Margery Perlmutter
NRI (National Reprographics Inc.)
Sara P. Meltzer
Soho Art Materials
Steven T. Incontro and David Joselit
The Henry Ford
Vram Malek

This project is commissioned by Storefront for Art and
Architecture, on behalf of the U.S. Department of State's
Bureau of Educational and Cultural Affairs

Storefront for Art and Architecture

Founded in 1982, Storefront for Art and Architecture is a nonprofit organization committed to the advancement of innovative positions in architecture, art and design. Our program of exhibitions, artists talks, film screenings, conferences and publications is intended to generate dialogue and collaboration across geographic, ideological and disciplinary boundaries. As a public forum for emerging voices, Storefront explores vital issues in art and architecture with the intent of increasing awareness of and interest in contemporary design.
www.storefrontnews.org

PRAXIS

Founded in 1999, by Ashley Schafer and Amanda Reeser Lawrence, *PRAXIS: a journal of writing + building* has established itself as a distinctive voice in international architectural culture. Emphasizing the interdependence of technology, design, theory, and history, the journal addresses contemporary design issues in both depth and breadth, promoting connections between diverse fields of architectural production. It has engendered an architectural discourse uniquely rooted in practice.
www.praxisjournal.net